D0801896

For Laurel
     Nicholas
     Nathaniel René

WRPW

ROBERT
PENN
WARREN

WRPWRPWRPWRPWRPWRPWRPWRPWRPWRPWRPWRPWRPWRPWRPWRPWRPWRPWRPWRPWRPWRPWRPWRPWRPWRPWRPWRPWRPWRPWRPWRPWRPWRPWRPW

CRITICAL PERSPECTIVES

WRPWRPWRPWRPWRPWRPWRPWRPWRPWRPWRPWRPWRPWRPWRPWRPWRPWRPWRPWRPWRPWRPWRPWRPWRPWRPWRPWRPWRPWRPWRPWRPWRPWRPWRPW

Edited by Neil Nakadate

THE UNIVERSITY PRESS OF KENTUCKY

WRPWRPWRPWRPWRPWRPWRPWRPWRPWRPWRPWRPWRPWRPWRPWRPWRPWRPWRPWRPWRPWRPWRPWRPWRPWRPWRPWRPWRPWRPWRPWRPWRPWRPWRPW

Publication of this book has been assisted
by a grant from the Andrew W. Mellon Foundation.

Library of Congress Cataloging in Publication Data

Main entry under title:

Robert Penn Warren, critical perspectives.

   "The works of Robert Penn Warren, 1929-1980": p.
 . Bibliography: p.
    1. Warren, Robert Penn, 1905-   — Criticism
and interpretation — Addresses, essays, lectures.
I. Nakadate, Neil.
PS3545.A748Z863   813'.52   79-57569
ISBN 0-8131-1425-X   AACR2

Scholarly publisher for the Commonwealth
serving Berea College, Centre College of Kentucky,
Eastern Kentucky University, The Filson Club,
Georgetown College, Kentucky Historical Society,
Kentucky State University, Morehead State University,
Murray State University, Northern Kentucky University,
Transylvania University, University of Kentucky,
University of Louisville, and Western Kentucky University.

Editorial and Sales Offices: Lexington, Kentucky 40506

Acknowledgments

   "*All the King's Men:* The Matrix of Experience," by Robert Penn
Warren, reprinted from *Yale Review,* Vol. 53, No. 2 (Winter 1964), 161-
67, by permission of the author.   "The Art to Transfigure" (original
title, "The Poetry of Robert Penn Warren: The Art to Transfigure"), by
William Tjenos, reprinted from *Southern Literary Journal,* Vol. 9, No.
1 (Fall 1976), 3-12, by permission of The University of North Carolina
Press.   "The Case of the Vanishing Narratee: An Inquiry into *All the
King's Men,*" by Simone Vauthier, reprinted from *Southern Literary
Journal,* Vol. 6, No. 2 (Spring 1974), 42-69, by permission of The University of North Carolina Press.   "The Deep, Twisting Strain of Life:
The Novels of Robert Penn Warren," by H. P. Heseltine, reprinted from
the *Melbourne Critical Review,* No. 5 (1962), pp. 76-89, by permission
of the author.   "The Function of Colloquy in *Brother to Dragons*"
(original title, "Voices of Community: The Function of Colloquy in

Brother to Dragons"), by Neil Nakadate, reprinted from *Tennessee Studies in Literature*, 21 (1976), 114-24. © 1976 by The University of Tennessee Press and reprinted by permission of the Press. "The Historical Novelist and the Existential Peril: *Band of Angels*" (original subtitle, "Robert Penn Warren's *Band of Angels*"), by Walter Sullivan, reprinted from *Southern Literary Journal*, Vol. 2, No. 2 (Spring 1970), 104-16, by permission of The University of North Carolina Press. "The Inklings of 'Original Sin,'" by John Crowe Ransom, reprinted from *Saturday Review of Literature*, 27 (20 May 1944), 10-11. © Saturday Review, 1944. All rights reserved. "Robert Penn Warren: The Conservative Quest for Identity," reprinted from *Fiction of the Forties*, by Chester E. Eisinger, by permission of The University of Chicago Press. © 1963 by Chester E. Eisinger. "Robert Penn Warren's Promised Land," by Sister M. Bernetta Quinn, reprinted from *Southern Review*, NS 8, No. 2 (Spring 1972), 329-58, by permission of the author. "Sacramental Vision" (original title, "Sacramental Vision: The Poetry of Robert Penn Warren"), by A. L. Clements, reprinted from the *South Atlantic Bulletin*, Vol. 43, No. 4 (November 1978), 47-65, by permission of the *South Atlantic Bulletin*. "The Stiff Smile of Mr. Warren," by James Wright, reprinted from *Kenyon Review*, Vol. 20, No. 4 (Autumn 1958), 645-55. Copyright 1958 by Kenyon College. Reprinted by permission of the author and *The Kenyon Review*. "Tangled Web," by Robert B. Heilman, reprinted from *Sewanee Review*, Vol. 59, No. 1 (Winter 1951), 107-19, by permission of the editor of the *Sewanee Review*. Copyright © 1951 by the University of the South. "The Uses of Gesture in *The Cave*" (original title, "The Uses of Gesture in Warren's *The Cave*"), by James H. Justus, reprinted from *Modern Language Quarterly*, Vol. 26, No. 3 (September 1965), 448-61, by permission of *Modern Language Quarterly*. "Warren's Osmosis," by Victor Strandberg, reprinted from *Criticism*, Vol. 10, No. 1 (Winter 1968), 23-40, by permission of the author and the Wayne State University Press. Copyright © 1968 by the Wayne State University Press. "Irony and Orthodoxy: Robert Penn Warren," reprinted from *American Poets*, by Hyatt Waggoner. Copyright © 1968 by Hyatt H. Waggoner. Reprinted by permission of Houghton Mifflin Company. "The Mariner and Robert Penn Warren," by James H. Justus, reprinted from *Texas Studies in Literature and Language*, Vol. 8, No. 1 (Spring 1966), 117-28, by permission of the author. "The Narrator's Mind as Symbol: An Analysis of *All the King's Men*," by Norton R. Girault, reprinted from *Accent*, Vol. 7, No. 4 (Summer 1947), 220-34, by permission of the author and the University of Illinois Foundation. "*Night Rider* and the Issue of Naturalism: The 'Nightmare' of Our Age" (original title, "Warren's *Night Rider* and the Issue of Naturalism: The 'Nightmare' of Our Age"), by Richard Law, reprinted from *Southern Literary Journal*, Vol. 8, No. 2 (Spring 1976), 41-61, by permission of The University of North Carolina Press. "Psychology and Theme in *Brother to Dragons*," by Frederick P. W. McDowell, reprinted by permission of the Modern Language Association of America from *PMLA*, Vol. 70, No. 4 (September 1955), 565-86. "The Way *Brother to Dragons* Was Written" (original title, "The Way It Was Written"), by Robert Penn Warren, reprinted from the *New York Times Book Review*, 23 August 1953, pp. 6, 25. © 1953 by The New York Times Company. Reprinted by permission. "Willie Stark and Huey Long: Atmosphere, Myth, or Suggestion?" by Ladell Payne, reprinted from *American Quarterly*, Vol. 20, No. 3 (Fall 1968), 580-95, by permission of the author, *American Quarterly,* and the University of Pennsylvania. © 1968, Trustees of the University of Pennsylvania.

The editor is particularly grateful to the Iowa State University Research Foundation and its executive director, Daniel L. Griffen, Jr., for support which has made possible the publication of this book in its present form.

Contents

Introduction

In recent years it has been said more than once that Robert Penn Warren is America's foremost man of letters. But while such pronouncements are meant to honor the man and his work, it is not always clear what burden of meaning is sustained in the title. Perhaps it is useful, in talking about Warren, to have a practical sense of what a man of letters is.

In 1952, six years after the publication of *All the King's Men* and five years before the publication of *Promises,* Allen Tate ventured a definition which seems right. The man of letters, he wrote,

> must recreate for his age the image of man, and he must propagate standards by which other men may test that image, and distinguish the false from the true. But at our own critical moment, when all languages are being debased by the techniques of mass control, the man of letters might do well to conceive his responsibility more narrowly. He has an immediate responsibility, to other men no less than to himself, for the vitality of language. He must distinguish the difference between mere communication...and the rediscovery of the human condition in the living arts. He must discriminate and defend the difference between mass communication, for the control of men, and the knowledge of man which literature offers us for human participation.[1]

It should not surprise us that Tate, a novelist, poet, and critic in his own right, should venture such a definition; nor should it come as a revelation that Warren, a longtime friend and colleague of Tate's, can be seen (especially in hindsight) to fit the definition. What is worth noting is the level of relevance on which Tate's words prevail. Tate was concerned with the relationship — the rhetorical, moral, and aesthetic relationship — set up between the man of letters and the world. The man of letters takes upon himself some responsibility for "the vitality of language" and "the rediscovery of the human condition." The man of letters must know and discriminate, he must be alive to the promises of his craft and the needs

of his time — and show it. And it is in terms of vitality and
rediscovery and constant "participation" that Tate's formulation fits Robert Penn Warren.

It has not always been easy to see this, much less say it,
especially of the author of *All the King's Men*. For the unfortunate effect of the success of Warren's third novel was a
simplistic response to him as a writer, an unearned sense of
familiarity and understanding: Warren is obviously, triumph-
phantly, a novelist; he is possessively, provincially, a
southerner; his place is somewhere in the wake of Naturalism,
modernism, or Faulkner. Even the many inspired, attentive
readings of *All the King's Men* and Warren's other fiction cannot obscure the fact that such limitations do injustice to the
writing he has done.

To begin with, in only a limited sense is Warren of another time and a specific place, the time and place of his
beginnings as an artist: Vanderbilt University, Nashville,
Tennessee, in the 1920s — or more specifically, the freshman
English class taught by John Crowe Ransom. For while the aura
of Vanderbilt might have been southern and the time an unusu-
ally productive one for American letters, such facts carry
more truth than information. To be sure, it is important to
remember that Warren became, by virtue of talent, initiative,
and simple good fortune, one of the "Fugitives," literary and
ideological, a gifted and energetic gathering which included
Tate, Ransom, and Donald Davidson, among others. But it is
also important to recall that by 1928 Warren was a Rhodes
Scholar in England and had left narrow regionalism, Agrarianism, and even some of the Fugitives behind. It is perhaps
even more important to recognize that Warren's most permanently influential early book, *Understanding Poetry* (1938), was at
once teacherly and collaborative, the beginning of a long colloquy on language and art, not only with Cleanth Brooks, but
with the literary professions and their audience at large. In
other words, almost immediately after his apprenticeship years
Warren became a Fugitive engaged in argument and exploration,
a southerner addressing the great issues of our time, a teacher (Memphis, Baton Rouge, Minneapolis, New Haven), always
attentive to the challenges of the larger, the "impure" world.
For Warren the analytical question was never criticism per se,
but the teaching and reading of poetry and fiction; the social
question was not, "simply," segregation versus integration,
but people. The record of Warren's engagement and growth is
there, in *Understanding Poetry*, *Understanding Fiction* (1943),
and *Modern Rhetoric* (1949); it is there in *Band of Angels*
(1955), *Segregation* (1956), and *Who Speaks for the Negro?*
(1965).

In the same way, a survey of the fiction shows that while
Warren's career began during the later years of Naturalism and
was permanently influenced by the great modern writers (including Conrad and Faulkner, to cite the most prominent), it

is consistently a career in motion beyond Naturalism, beyond
modernism, beyond categories and comfortable affiliations.
This is evident in *Night Rider* (1939), Warren's first novel,
which in effect questions the naturalistic premises on which
its development depends. It is clear at the end of *All the
King's Men* (1946), when journalist-cum-researcher Jack Burden
goes "out of history into history and the awful responsibility
of Time" — a paradigm of the artist who knows the matrix of
experience and is consciously, precariously, engaged in action
that is costly but ultimately creative. This motion is clear
in Warren's fiction generally, which has drawn from and expanded the traditions of the political novel and roman á clef,
the historical and romantic novels, the novel of ideas. And
this sense of motion, of growth and extension, is clear in the
poetry too.

Warren's poetry was inspired by Donne and the English metaphysicals and encouraged by the appearance of T. S. Eliot.
It developed in a poetic era dominated by the wry and beautiful presence of Robert Frost and the lavish imagination of
Wallace Stevens. The sense of motion and extension is evident
in Warren's ability to accommodate such influences and forces
and to develop a unique poetic voice. In the poetry, as much
as in books such as *All the King's Men* and *World Enough and
Time* (1950), Warren has given transcendent meaning to native
sources by drawing expanded patterns out of traditional forms.
Again the record is clear, as early as *Thirty-six Poems* (1935)
and *Eleven Poems on the Same Theme* (1942), with their combination of vernacular reference, shadowed metaphysics, and studied shape. It is clear in the language and form of "The
Ballad of Billie Potts" (1944), and in the subdued lyricism
and emblematic vision of *Promises* (1957). It is manifest,
perhaps most impressively, in the blend of the lyric, meditative, and dramatic in Warren's poetic sequences, gatherings of
finely crafted elements which end up as long poems. It is not
even necessary to claim *Eleven Poems* as the early model for
these sequences or to say that Warren's work is consistently
on the same theme (original sin, self-knowledge, love) to see
that the creation of *Audubon: A Vision* (1969) and *Or Else:
Poem/Poems* (1974) has significantly enlarged our sense of poetry as both detail and statement, our sense of the precision
and cumulative power of the poet's craft.

The risks of this exploration have been great, of course,
and there have been casualties — failed poems to accompany
the failed novels (though even here the critics do not always
agree), occasional lines which falter or lunge. But more important, such brave and serious literary venturing has given
us a Warren renewed and rediscovered from time to time, never
duplicated. It has given us, with regularity, a communicant's
newly perfected offerings of love and knowledge — "Reading
Late at Night, Thermometer Falling," for example, and "The Red
Mullet." It has given us *Brother to Dragons: A Tale in Verse*

and Voices (A New Version) (1979). Warren's career, then,
follows what we might call the shaping impulse, the belief
that however unanticipated, tentative, or vulnerable, a *new*
poem, a *new* order is, even for our world, possible. And this
belief, manifested in the disciplined expansion over the years
of his *Selected Poems,* has brought Warren into the company of
Eliot, Frost, and Stevens as a major American poet of this
century.

The claims of greatness on behalf of Warren are many, of
course; they include membership in the American Academy of
Arts and Letters (1959), the Bollingen Prize (1967), the National Medal for Literature (1970), and the Pulitzer prizes
for *All the King's Men, Promises,* and *Now and Then* (1946,
1957, 1979). But the foundation of the claim is the great
body of critical prose that Warren's work has inspired, from
reviews to full-length studies. There have been flurries of
critical energy from time to time — after the publication of
All the King's Men, in the early and mid-sixties (when emphasis was still on Warren's fiction), and in the late seventies
(in recognition of the poetry) — and not all of this criticism
has been affirmative. But overall production of Warren criticism has kept up with the pace of Warren's own work, and the
best of that criticism, positive and negative, establishes
firm points of reference for the measure of his writing.
This volume includes both overviews of significant por-
tions of Warren's career and readings of individual works, and
it contains a range of critical approaches, including the historical, formalist, psychological, and rhetorical. The explicit emphasis among the pieces is on the fiction and poetry,
but several essays also discuss the complementary relationship
between Warren's critical writing and his creative imagination.
There are some early, and in certain respects seminal, pieces
and a number of recent ones, including several that contribute
to the recognition of Warren's poetry. The pieces by foreign
critics represent only insufficiently Warren's large audience
of international readers — readers who, after all, may be in
the best position to appreciate his contribution not only to
American letters but also to literature in the English language.
At this writing, Warren's papers continue to grow and ac-
cumulate in the Beinecke Library at Yale. His contribution to
the world of letters is almost a volume a year for half a century — poetry, prose, criticism, texts, editions, and collections. Those readers and listeners who have attended closely
to the shaping of this work have felt his vigorous commitment
to language as a form of communion and knowledge — knowledge
of the author, of the human condition, of the audience as individual and collective self. Since this knowledge, conveyed
to us in his writing, emerges from a long-standing commitment
to the risky but unqualified creative gesture, it is instruc-

tive to remember how (in Allen Tate's recollection) the gesture was first made, by a sixteen-year-old Vanderbilt sopho-
more from Guthrie, Kentucky, "'Red,' Robert Penn Warren, the
most gifted person I have ever known": "He was tall and thin,
and when he walked across the room he made a sliding shuffle,
as if his bones didn't belong to one another. He had a long
quivering nose, large brown eyes, and a long chin — all topped
by curly red hair. He spoke in a soft whisper, asking to see
my poem; then he showed me one of his own."[2] This is the vital, living gesture which, in the end, fulfills itself as art.

---

1. Allen Tate, "The Man of Letters in the Modern World," in *Essays of Four Decades* (Chicago, 1968), p. 3.
2. Allen Tate, "The Fugitive, 1922-1925: A Personal Recollection Twenty Years After," in *Memoirs and Opinions: 1926-1974* (Chicago, 1975), p. 31.

The Works of Robert Penn Warren, 1929-1980

John Brown: The Making of a Martyr. New York: Payson and Clarke, 1929.

Thirty-six Poems. New York: Alcestis Press, 1935.

An Approach to Literature: A Collection of Prose and Verse, with Cleanth Brooks, Jr., and John Thibaut Purser. Baton Rouge: Louisiana State Univ. Press, 1936.

(Ed.) *A Southern Harvest: Short Stories by Southern Writers*. Boston: Houghton Mifflin, 1937.

Understanding Poetry: An Anthology for College Students, with Cleanth Brooks, Jr. New York: Henry Holt and Co., 1938.

Night Rider. Boston: Houghton Mifflin, 1939.

Eleven Poems on the Same Theme. Norfolk, Conn.: New Directions, 1942.

At Heaven's Gate. New York: Harcourt, Brace and Co., 1943.

Understanding Fiction, with Cleanth Brooks, Jr. New York: F. S. Crofts & Co., 1943.

Selected Poems, 1923-1943. New York: Harcourt, Brace and Co., 1944.

All the King's Men. New York: Harcourt, Brace and Co., 1946.

Blackberry Winter. Cummington, Mass.: Cummington Press, 1946.

The Circus in the Attic and Other Stories. New York: Harcourt, Brace, 1947.

Modern Rhetoric, with Cleanth Brooks. New York: Harcourt, Brace, 1949.

World Enough and Time: A Romantic Novel. New York: Random House, 1950.

Brother to Dragons: A Tale in Verse and Voices. New York: Random House, 1953.

(Ed.) *An Anthology of Stories from the Southern Review,* with Cleanth Brooks. Baton Rouge: Louisiana State Univ. Press, 1953.

(Ed.) *Short Story Masterpieces,* with Albert Erskine. New York: Dell Books, 1954.

Band of Angels. New York: Random House, 1955.

(Ed.) *Six Centuries of Great Poetry,* with Albert Erskine. New York: Dell Publishing Co., 1955.

Segregation: The Inner Conflict in the South. New York: Random House, 1956.

Promises: Poems 1954-1956. New York: Random House, 1957.

(Ed.) *A New Southern Harvest: An Anthology,* with Albert Erskine. New York: Bantam Books, 1957.

Selected Essays. New York: Random House, 1958.

Remember the Alamo! New York: Random House, 1958.

The Cave. New York: Random House, 1959.

The Gods of Mount Olympus. New York: Random House, 1959.

All the King's Men: A Play. New York: Random House, 1960.

You, Emperors, and Others: Poems 1957-1960. New York: Random House, 1960.

The Legacy of the Civil War: Meditations on the Centennial. New York: Random House, 1961.

Wilderness: A Tale of the Civil War. New York: Random House, 1961.

Flood: A Romance of Our Time. New York: Random House, 1964.

Who Speaks for the Negro? New York: Random House, 1965.

Selected Poems: New and Old, 1923-1966. New York: Random House, 1966.

(Ed.) *Faulkner: A Collection of Critical Essays.* Englewood Cliffs, N.J.: Prentice-Hall, 1966.

A Plea in Mitigation: Modern Poetry and the End of an Era. Macon, Ga.: Wesleyan College, 1966.

(Ed.) *Randall Jarrell, 1914-1965,* with Robert Lowell and Peter Taylor. New York: Farrar, Straus & Giroux, 1967.

Audubon: A Vision. New York: Random House, 1969.

(Ed.) *Selected Poems of Herman Melville: A Reader's Edition.* New York: Random House, 1970.

Homage to Theodore Dreiser, On the Centennial of His Birth. New York: Random House, 1971.

John Greenleaf Whittier's Poetry: An Appraisal and a Selection. Minneapolis: Univ. of Minnesota Press, 1971.

Meet Me in the Green Glen. New York: Random House, 1971.

American Literature: The Makers and the Making, 2 vols., with Cleanth Brooks and R. W. B. Lewis. New York: St. Martin's Press, 1973.

Or Else — Poem/Poems 1968-1974. New York: Random House, 1974.

Democracy and Poetry. Cambridge, Mass.: Harvard University Press, 1975.

Selected Poems: 1923-1975. New York: Random House, 1976.

A Place to Come To. New York: Random House, 1977.

Now and Then: Poems 1976-1978. New York: Random House, 1978.

(Ed.) *Katherine Anne Porter: A Collection of Critical Essays.* Englewood Cliffs, N.J.: Prentice-Hall, 1979.

Brother to Dragons: A Tale in Verse and Voices (A New Version). New York: Random House, 1979.

Being Here: Poetry 1977-1980. New York: Random House, 1980.

Jefferson Davis Gets His Citizenship Back. Lexington: Univ. Press of Kentucky, 1980.

WRPW

FICTION

WRPWRPWRPWRPWRPWRPWRPWRPWRPWRPWRPWRPWRPWRPWRPWRPWRPWRPWRPWRPWRPWRPWRPWRPWRPWRPWRPWRPWRPWRPWRPWRPWRPWRPWRPWRPW

FICTION

Chester E. Eisinger

Robert Penn Warren: The Conservative Quest for Identity

The conservative southern imagination may be best summed up, for the 1940's, in the work of Robert Penn Warren. He belongs to this period, as Faulkner does not. But, like Faulkner, he is a writer of such considerable achievement that he cannot be totally contained within a formula. Or perhaps it would be better to say that Warren reveals, better than any other writer except Faulkner, the potentials for a universal interpretation of experience that lie in southern conservatism.

The particularities of Warren's revisionist and conservative position may be framed in a dialectic of affirmations and repudiations. Such a formulation may ignore the spontaneity of Warren's mind, but it will have the advantage of setting before us the naked girders in the structure of his thought. To begin, then, he rejects the heritage of eighteenth-century Enlightenment. He finds its optimistic view of human nature shallow and its faith in reason and abstract principle misplaced; most of all he fears its untrammeled individualism, which leads to the autonomy and thus to the heresy of the self, by which he means a destructive overconfidence in the capacities of the self-isolating individual, cut off from society and God. He accepts a more complicated and darker view of man, whose good is always susceptible to corruption. He is suspicious of reason and impatient with abstractions, since he brings to bear on life an ironic and sceptical vision which abhors dogmatic decisions and makes a virtue of provisional resolutions. While he regards the realization of the self or of human identity as the highest, final goal of man, he believes this realization can be achieved only by reference to authority beyond the self. He rejects the heritage of nineteenth-century science, which is responsible for our God-abandoned world of today and which has bred the variety and multiplicity

that contribute so heavily to the disintegration of society
and of individual consciousness. He accepts an unorthodox
orthodoxy which rests on the validity of religious myth and
religious metaphor; out of the Christian conception of the
communion of men will come unity to replace the present fragmentation. He rejects the industrialism and the metropolitan-
ism of the twentieth century because they too stifle the human
personality. And they cut man off from the fructifying past.
He affirms the enduring value of the past, of its tradition
and its myth, in establishing the continuity of human identity
in the present and for the future. He rejects the romantic,
"democratic" conception of the West as the land of golden opportunity, settled by Frederick Jackson Turner's individualis-
tic and independent frontiersmen. This myth of America he in-
verts, and he sees the West as a region of license and as an
escape from responsibility. The West is the world of nature.
While man is in and of nature, as Warren recognizes, man must
nevertheless separate himself from nature if he is to achieve
the discipline commensurate with his humanity. For Warren, in
short, Jeffersonian liberalism, Darwinian science, and American industry comprise an unholy trinity that has spread its
infection throughout the modern world, fragmenting our universe, inducing a chaos of beliefs, destroying the possibility
for stable society, and threatening the existence of the human
personality itself. He is at war with all these forces.

The Background and Sources of Warren's Fiction

He did not suddenly declare war in 1939, when he published
his first novel. He had committed himself to this war when,
under the influence of the Fugitive group, he was writing his
life of John Brown in 1928, as Louise Cowan tells us.[1] He had
carried on the unremitting struggle later as one of the Southern Agrarians — as a contributor to their manifesto, *I'll Take
My Stand,* and as an editor of the *Southern Review*. The Agrarians had looked to Edmund Burke for direction, a thinker who
was one of the ancestors of Warren's mind. The group was
convinced, like T. S. Eliot, that Western man had suffered a
cultural breakdown. It aimed, consequently, at cultural integration, trying to embody in traditional modes of thought and
action a concrete way of life. The southern way the Agrarians
sought to establish, or really to re-establish, included a
class society as an instrument of stability, religion as an
instrument of order, the rejection of abstract rights, a sense
of mutual obligation on the part of all members of society.
Warren shared many of these ideas.

Warren's religious attitudes were early shaped by John
Crowe Ransom's *God Without Thunder*. An unorthodox defense of
orthodoxy, that book expresses its religious convictions in
mythic and poetic terms, avoiding commitment to established
religion or formulated dogma. The religious spirit, Ransom

says, is always the tragic spirit. Now Warren's novels are
lit by a rich play of religious metaphor and extensive use of
Christian conceptions like redemption; and the tragic sense
that hovers over his work and the ready acceptance of evil in
it — cosmic, human, and natural evil — indicate firm agreement
with Ransom's dedication to the myth of religion. At a later
period Warren seems to have been influenced by the "hard"
spirit in the Christian realism of Paul Tillich and Reinhold
Niebuhr. Indeed, the latter's book, *The Children of Light and
the Children of Darkness,* seems of immediate relevance to Warren's work. The children of darkness says Niebuhr, are those
moral cynics who know no law beyond their own will and interest. The children of light are those who believe that self-
interest should be brought under the discipline of a higher
law, a more universal law. Niebuhr refers, I take it, to the
law of God, and this Warren has not accepted. But the description of the children of light applies with uncanny accuracy to
those characters in Warren's fiction who find their sanctions
somewhere outside themselves. And likewise the children of
darkness describes those who are the victims of what Warren
calls the heresy of the self. Warren's position is thus analogous to that of the young postwar writers in England as G. S.
Fraser reveals it. They yearn toward religious orthodoxy, but
they cannot bring themselves to make an outward act of faith
and acceptance.[2]

It was Warren's southern orientation that brought him as a
novelist to historical revisionism before the historians themselves had fully embarked on this course. What the historians
came to through research, he came to through vision. All,
historians and novelist alike, sought the meaning of the past
in order to establish a conception of identity. Warren's goal
in all his fiction is to know man, to free him from whatever
forces would crush and distort him. In the spirit of revisionism, Warren rejected the frontier myth and repudiated the West
as the home of hope because he wished to give man back his
past so that man might claim his self. In Warren the man on
the frontier, rootless, motherless, fatherless, without a past,
is a lost soul. Man must return to the mother, the father,
and the home place — this is the archetypal pattern of return
— if he is to claim his identity.

Warren also regards industrial capitalism as a threat to
the realization of the self. Just as the Industrial Revolution brought home to Marx the realization that now only a cash
nexus existed among men, that capitalism had imposed a new,
impersonal character on human relationships, so Warren, viewing American economic life from the opposite pole, paradoxically comes to the same conclusion. He knows that industrialism
and mechanization threaten the agrarian and patrician identities that have traditionally been at home in America, indeed
threaten all identities.

If the conditions for ego identity in Warren are reactions

against modern industrial society and against the American
myth of the West, if the conditions are patterns of return to
parental sources of security and life and acceptance of tradition, what then is the process of individuation, to use a
Jungian term, in Warren's fiction? The process is dialectical
for Warren, as it is for Jung, whose description of the emer-
gence of the individual personality tallies to a remarkable
degree with the struggles for the self that dominate Warren's
novels.[3] In fact, Warren's fictional characters aim at precisely what all men, Jung says, must aim at: "...everyone's
ultimate aim and strongest desire lie in developing the fullness of human existence that is called personality," and "*one
must learn to know oneself in order to know who one is.*"[4] For
Jung, the psychological process of individuation consists in
the play, the conflict, of the consciousness and the unconscious, of the reason of the former and the chaotic life of
the latter; there is collaboration between them as well as
conflict, and out of both comes the individual. Individuation
is a centralizing process, during which a new center for the
personality develops. That center is the self. As one reads
Warren, it is this sense of process and the insistent quest
for self-discovery that one perceives at the heart of his novels. His great conflicts are carried on within the individual
souls of his people, who darkly struggle with the disparate
elements of their characters to find and make their ultimate
identities, to shuck off mask after mask and come to the quintessential self. It is their deepest need, as it is, I suspect, Warren's and Jung's, to fall back on a realized self in
a world that seems engaged in a gigantic conspiracy to eliminate the self.

Warren as His Own Critic

The terms that Jung uses to describe the nature of the
self are consciousness and the unconscious. Warren's term is
self-division or sometimes, in a somewhat larger sense, the
doubleness of life. For Jung, writing on "The Spiritual Problem of Modern Man" in the thirties, man faces alone, without
the help of traditional creeds, the problem of his subjective
processes. Warren, writing in the following decades, turns
man in upon himself in order to find fulfillment beyond the
self. These two differences — in terms and in the nature of
self-independence — can be easily illustrated. In his little
book on *Segregation,* significantly subtitled *The Inner Conflict in the South,* Warren concludes by saying that the segregation problem in the South is the problem of irremediable
self-division, which angers men because they cannot find identity. In his poem, *Brother to Dragons,* he says that fulfillment of the self is possible only in the recognition of the
common lot of mankind, "And the death of the self is the beginning of selfhood." Man must find himself outside himself

in the community of men, which is, I take it, a conception of
secularized brotherhood.

Both Warren's criticism — and he is a critic of high seriousness and brilliant perceptions — and his poetry reveal from
first to last an abiding preoccupation with the problem of
identity; his explicit treatment of that problem, especially
in the criticism, lays bare many of the assumptions of his
fiction and provides a guide to the intelligent reading of his
novels. Indeed, the whole range of ideas, attitudes, and method in his novels is so accurately reflected in his criticism
that he is his own best critic. With respect to the problem
of identity, he says that good fiction must give us "the stimulation of a powerful image of human nature trying to fulfill
itself." The method of finding the personality, as in Jung,
is in a process of living whereby mutually competing versions
of life and being confront each other, and the personality is
created out of the antinomy. Warren has expressed these ideas
about Katherine Anne Porter's Miranda in describing the terms
of her "dialectic of living."[5] But his most complete nonfictional statement on identity is in an essay called "Knowledge and the Image of Man." Here he argues that man's right
to knowledge is indispensable to his right to define himself.
This view of personality is a heritage of the emphasis of
Christianity upon the value of every soul in the sight of God.
When man has an image of himself, he discovers separateness.
That discovery leads him to knowledge of the pain of isolation
and self-criticism. With this recognition of the tragedy of
life, man can return to a communion with other men and nature,
having accepted love and law, that is, having achieved moral
awareness which now makes his redemption possible.[6]

Communion and redemption are Christian terms always present to Warren's mind. Although he is not an orthodox believer,
redemption is nevertheless necessary and appropriate to Warren's world view. In *Brother to Dragons,* Lucy Jefferson tells
her brother that his was a noble dream, but there is a nobler:

> It will be nobler because more difficult and cold
> In the face of the old cost of the human redemption,
> And knowledge of that cost is, in itself, a kind of
>   redemption.

Earlier in his career, Warren was able to use in a purely secular sense an argument for community of interest between owner
and sharecropper which assumes, I believe, that the integrity
of the human communion is a good. The two conceptions come
together in his discussion of Conrad's *Nostromo.*[7] Warren
admires the sense of human community in Conrad, whose characteristic story, he says, is the relation of man to the human
communion. The story of awakening and redemption engages
Conrad most deeply: the story of those who sin against human
solidarity and then save themselves. That redemption must be
earned, and continually re-earned, through a man's identifica-

tion with the general human condition. But since contamination is implicit in the human condition, as Warren says in an
essay on Faulkner, it is through love that man must cleanse
himself if he is to achieve redemption.[8] As a critic, Warren,
clearly, is very close to the orthodox Christian view. His
fiction, from the beginning, is concerned with Christian
themes, especially love and redemption, which are the avenues
to the self.

From the beginning, like Conrad and like the "hard" theologians, Warren has feared reason, because it can deny life;
and he has cherished illusions, because they may provide man
with the truth. In the twentieth century we have lived in a
world dominated by reason, as he sees it, and hostile, consequently, to Christian ideas. Warren's writing is a work of
reconstruction, as I have said, because he strives to impose
order and stability upon a world which is suffering from moral
confusion induced by unmitigated rationalism. The chief cause
of our present disorder is nineteenth-century science, the
most destructive offspring of reason, which poses for Warren
now the same difficulty that it posed for Matthew Arnold in
the last century: the ethical and epistemological implications
of science are at war with the religious and/or humanistic impulses in man and seek to destroy those impulses. Warren's
most succinct statement of our general plight is made in his
discussion of Faulkner. The modern world, he writes, "does
suffer from a lack of discipline, of sanctions, of community
of values, of a sense of a mission. It is a world in which
self-interest, workableness, success, provide the standards.
It is a world which is the victim of abstraction and of mechanism...."

It is a world that has pushed Warren into the past where
he seeks answers that will sustain him as he lives in the
present. Since the central task of the writer is always self-
definition, the past exists for Warren as a storehouse from
which he can draw some sense of who he is. As southerner, especially, he lives in a present that has been exposed in a particular way to shock, to a clash of values brought on by rapid
industrialization and by the growing self-consciousness of the
Negro. The consequent dislocations have forced him as a southerner to seek a redefinition of life. Warren tells us this in
a *Paris Review* interview. In the introduction to *A Southern
Harvest* he reveals that any effort at such redefinition would
involve, for him, a consideration of American history and
myth.[9] Since men also define themselves in time, the past is
valuable in providing the line of continuity to us and through
us. In these ways Warren constructs the traditionalist's
rationale for reverence toward history and at the same time
explains the need for a past and for an interpretation of the
past that will support a life-giving myth. The uses of the
past in Warren's fiction, it may be concluded, go beyond an
attraction to historical setting and historical event; Warren

is searching for a meaning for life which he feels can be
found only by placing man in time and history.

As Warren's fiction is dependent upon the ordering of the
past, so it is dependent upon the ordering of nature. And, as
always, his criticism mirrors his fictional practice, and his
analyses of other writers' work reveal the preoccupations and
predilections of his own creative life as a novelist. When he
says that Hemingway's characters sink into nature, he is describing what happens to some of his own. In Hemingway the
famous code is the discipline that helps to impose order on
nature. Only when man thus exerts his will can he assert his
selfhood. In Warren's fiction, idea takes the place of code.
Idea is the formulation of a conception which transcends the
naturalistic level of human experience; it is therefore different from nature. Man's hope for realizing his humanity rests
on maintaining a resolved tension between idea and nature.

The clearest nonfictional exposition of this complex relationship is found in Warren's commentary on Stein's remark in
Lord Jim: "In the destructive element immerse." Conrad means,
Warren asserts, that man must justify himself by an idea; he
must find moral significance and order. For man is, in one
sense, a creature of nature, "an animal of black egotism and
savage impulses." So man might live only on the naturalistic
level. But there is a "supernatural" level, the world of idea
or dream. Man is not born to swim in the dream, but he can
try. Man's fate and his triumph, if his humanity is not to be
frustrated, are to recognize the necessity of the idea. What
Warren sees in Conrad (and in Eudora Welty, too, as he shows
in another essay) is that wisdom lies in recognizing and resolving the constant oppositions imposed by the human condition: idea to nature, justice to material interests, innocence
to experience, individuality to communion.[10] The dialectical
process he so acutely observes in these writers is precisely
what underlies the themes and structure of his own fiction.

The Fiction

Night Rider (1939), Warren's first novel, is a book in
which his mind outspeeds his imagination and he knows better
than he does. The major problems of the novel are two: how a
man may become the victim of events, contingencies, when he
does not know who he is, and how the quest for social justice
can lead to injustice. These two problems pose a series of relationships between the private and the public world, between
politics and identity, between the community and the self. In
the history of the novel in America during the twentieth century, this book must occupy a pivotal position, precisely because it does combine the examination of social problems with
concern for the nature of selfhood. It represents a turning
away from social realism and proletarian fiction, as Warren
himself has recognized. In the *Paris Review* interview Warren

has said that he was aware of the shadow that the events and
the fiction of the thirties cast on his own book; in one sense,
then, *Night Rider* is a novel about "social justice." But,
Warren continued, he was trying to find a different and deeper
point than those his contemporaries in fiction were looking
for.[11] This modification of social realism by introducing a
treatment of the tensions between private and public realms of
being is not only the beginning of a characteristic novelistic
method for Warren, but it marks, virtually at the opening of a
new decade, the introduction of a distinguishing feature in
the fiction of that decade.

The central social irony of the book emerges from the im-
peratives of a situation in which independent tobacco-growers
seek a just price for their crop from the tobacco companies.
The action, based upon the tobacco war of 1905 to 1908 in Kentucky, begins with the establishment of the Association of
Growers of Dark Fired Tobacco, organized by men of probity for
the purpose of wrenching justice from those companies. Pursuing this end, the leaders discover the necessity for a growing
intensity in the coercive methods they use; they discover they
cannot control their membership; they discover that inevitably
the fight for justice leads to a degradation of the goal — to
destruction of property, to usurpation of civil law and order,
to murder. Later in the book, the Free Farmers' Brotherhood
of Protection and Control is organized as a terroristic group
which Warren endows with strongly fascistic characteristics
like militarism and blind obedience. The irony involved in
this unleashed social momentum is double: the necessity to win
the struggle with the companies overshadows the ideals of justice that originally motivated the farmers; and the resort
to violence and civil disorder, which means the sacrifice of
those ideals, does not lead to victory but to defeat, a defeat
in which nothing, not even honor, is salvaged.

The tobacco war, then, is the public scene against which
the private destiny of the characters is worked out. It is
Warren's practice to give the reader a firmly conceived sense
of the exciting historical events and movements that swirl
about his characters. These are not merely *mise en scène;*
they are formative in the life of the characters; and Warren
wishes us to feel a vital connection between characters and
society. Warren in this respect is comparable to Stendhal,
who involved his characters in political intrigue for the
throne of France or in the massive confusions of the Battle
of Waterloo, insisting upon the impact of these public events
upon them, but viewing the public event primarily as it contributed to the meaning of the self. Balzac, on the other
hand, was at least as interested in an analysis of society for
its own sake as he was in his characters, and saw them as more
definitely the product of their society than Warren does.
Warren, of course, understands that social forces may mold
character and dictate human action, but he establishes a ten-

sion between the individual and society in a relationship that
permits character to jerk free and transcend events in the
search for its own meaning.

In the contrasting fates of Percy Munn, the protagonist in
Night Rider, and Captain Todd we can see these tensions worked
out. At the beginning of the novel, Munn is caught up in the
movement of a crowd on a train, as people come into Bardsville
for an organizational meeting of tobacco-growers. Munn feels
this pressure, both human and inhuman (because in the mass no
one person is responsible), and resents it. We see Munn at
once, then, as a character who has chosen and yet not chosen
his fate. He has chosen to come to the meeting, but he is
subjected to pressure outside himself and pushed further in
participating than he might have anticipated. He yields up
a kind of reluctant but free commitment, and at the same time
his action is determined by the pressure of the crowd and of
friends. The play between free will and determinism in Munn
is an early example of Warren's characteristic dialectic. And
the failure of Munn's will signalizes his failure to achieve
full identity. Captain Todd, involved also in the growers'
association, enjoys a sense of his own identity that is drawn
from an inner certitude that Munn does not possess. Todd's
scepticism and relative solipsism — he has no confidence in
things and events — help him to understand who he is. At a
critical point he withdraws from the association, because it
is taking a course he cannot approve. He knows his own mind
because he knows his self. Munn, not knowing who he is, remains in the group and is destroyed.

Munn, wishing to be free and to be himself, constantly
turns to others and to the organization for some definition.
When he is told that he has been made a member of the board of
the association, he involuntarily says no. Later, even when
the association had claimed "the inner substance of his being
which was peculiarly himself," he reflects on his initial refusal, but he does not understand it. Warren's tactic is to
depict Munn often as an uncomprehending man, unable to analyze
the experience he undergoes because he has not established essential criteria with reference to the self. In this instance,
I believe that Warren is simply asserting that Munn will fail
in self-knowledge if he is dependent upon the association for
it, since that organization, and any other, will sap a man's
powers of individuation.

Munn cannot find himself in other people, either. He goes
hopefully to his wife for an explanation of who he is, but she
cannot help him. When he makes his first speech for the association he is filled with despair, because he recognizes that
his words have not come from a man who has found himself or
from a man who fully understands the common tie of humanity.
In Warren's scheme of things, the activated sense of communion
is possible only as a final transcendence made on the basis of
a realized self. In still another abortive attempt to define

himself, Munn has an affair with a young woman. He sees her
at one point standing "as though she could sink at will into
the deep and complete satisfaction of her own being." But
possessing her does not give him the sense of identity that
she has. Munn's last desperate effort to find himself through
others comes in his design to kill Senator Tolliver, the man
who has betrayed the association and in so doing violated the
human community. He thinks that if he could kill Tolliver he
would not be nothing. But when he reaches the senator he can
do nothing. He is immobilized. At this point soldiers track
him down and kill him. He dies because he never knew who he
was.

He had tried to learn about himself throughout the novel,
as he had been aware of others' identities. But he had been
overpowered by failures of his own judgment and by the tide of
event. His relations with Buck Trevelyan capsulize his fate.
He has successfully and altruistically defended Buck against a
murder charge, but he comes to feel that Buck is guilty. Later, when Buck tries to blackmail a member of the Free Farmers'
Brotherhood of Protection and Control, the fascistlike organization that grows out of the association, the brotherhood decides to kill Buck. It falls to Munn to fire the shot. Here
Warren has made the now obvious point about human fallibility,
and about how evil comes out of good, as blackmail and now murder come out of Munn's disinterested defense of Buck. We are
made to see the danger inherent in good intentions. Before
Munn shoots Buck, he tears off the mask he is wearing so that
Buck will know who kills him. Munn has been brought to murder,
but, pathetically, he wishes to commit the murder in his own
person, so to speak, to identify himself. He takes off the
mask as if he wishes to find himself in the open air, a free
man committing an act of his own will. The measure of his
failure comes toward the end of the book when he knows that
the "seed of the future in himself, the live germ," had gone
out of him. Man, he realizes, is what he is in the act, and
not what he says he is or conceives himself to be. And Munn's
act was murder willed by a group.

Near the end, Warren brings Willie Proudfit into the novel
and permits Willie to tell Munn the story of his life. Willie's excursion into the past is designed to reveal the past
as a deposit containing the secret of identity. For the past
defines a man, and we come to know Willie as he knows himself.
Furthermore, Willie, who had gone West and lived among Indians,
had now come back to the homeland: he is the native returned,
acting in obedience to one of the archetypal patterns that
Maud Bodkin remarks.[12] Aesthetically, Willie is in the novel
to reveal how identity is realized in contrast to Munn's descent to nothingness. But since there are no parallels between Willie and Munn as there are between Captain Todd and
Munn, the introduction of Willie seems to me merely Warren's
device to assert certain of his conservative convictions — and

to assert, perhaps too insistently, his interest in the process of definition of the self.

As Irene Hendry has said, Munn is the divided man who turns to the objective world of action and organization and there loses his subjective existence.[13] Warren tells his story relentlessly and at times mechanically, pursuing Munn's disintegration as thoroughly as Dreiser did Hurstwood's. The melodramatic, the consistently underplayed scenes that are never fully convincing, the abrupt introduction about halfway through the novel of Munn's two dark angels, Professor Ball and his son-in-law, are the faults of a beginning novelist whose imaginative and technical resources are not equal to his themes. These are the themes, however, of Warren's mature work, running from Burke's admonition that reformers forget man's nature to Jung's process of individuation, and here they are all opened for exploratory investigation.

At Heaven's Gate (1943) is not altogether successful either, although it is not a falling off, as so many second novels seem to be. Warren deals with the disintegration of character in both novels, and feels it necessary, for this reason, to maintain considerable distance from his people in order not to become auctorially involved. The consequence in both novels is a certain remoteness in the *reader's* relation to the characters as well. The reader is aware of a chilled air in these books, which is the proper if inhospitable atmosphere for the author's brisk, almost clinical efficiency in the matter of destruction. Subsequent novels do not suffer from this inadequacy; they are saved by a hard-won redemption or by a philosophical density which engages the characters and the readers.

This is not to claim that Warren fails to achieve a certain measure of philosophical complexity in *At Heaven's Gate*. He has said that he was deep in Dante when he wrote the novel and that the Seventh Circle of Hell, with some liberty of interpretation, provided "the basic scheme and metaphor for the whole novel. All of the main characters are violators of nature."[14] In Canto XI of the "Inferno" we are told that this violence may have three objects: God, oneself, one's neighbor. In the succeeding cantos devoted to this circle, specific kinds of violators are named: the usurer, the suicide, the spendthrift, the sexual aberrant. In Warren's novel, Bogan Murdock is the usurer; Slim Sarrett the homosexual; Sue Murdock, with self-destructive tendencies, the potential suicide; Jerry Calhoun the violator of family bonds and the spirit of familial piety; Ashby Wynham, in the beginning, is violent against God; Private Porsum, through most of the book, does violence to his neighbors. The book may be seen, then, as variations on this Dantean theme.

Or it may be seen as a series of misadventures with the self in which the characters try to find themselves in each other, as Percy Munn tries to find himself in his wife and in

other people; and in which they put on, figuratively, one or
another mask to hide or distort their identity. Sue Murdock,
perhaps the most desperate character in the book, plays the
part of the respectable debutante as Jerry's betrothed; she
wears the mask of bohemianism, as Slim's creature; she wears
the mask of lover with Jerry and with Jason Sweetwater. Jerry,
the farm-boy who became an All-American back, wears with gnaw-
ing discomfort the mask of college man; with equal discomfort,
he wears the mask of Sue's lover; with equal inappropriateness,
he wears the mask of banker and broker. Slim, the homosexual,
is the most sophisticated mask-wearer. He is the virile boxer;
he is the poet in a garret whose mother, touchingly, was a
whore; he is the perceptive critic of Shakespeare. Bogan Murdock wears the mask of quiet power and omniscience. Underneath, he is nothing. These characters, then, appear to be
one thing, but turn out to be something quite different, like
Slim. Or they are people who have lost the notion of who they
are and later find it with tragic consequences, like Private
Porsum. Or they never find it, and in the end must die, like
Sue, or face bewilderment and impotence, like Jerry.

Perhaps the chief irony in this novel is that a character
like Slim should give us in positive terms the theme of the
novel, that the bone-deep truth should be in a man who is a
liar, a poseur, a murderer. It is he who knows the mystery of
personality — that people must discover themselves. It is he
who claims such discovery for himself because he is a poet:
"Poetry is a [superior] technique for achieving self-knowledge." Warren's dialectic is obviously at work when out of
Slim's factitious and melodramatic story of his own life comes
his valid statement of the need for the tragic sense and the
knowledge of isolation and discipline. Out of this same manu-
factured story comes his sound view that, "The man who has not
fulfilled his nature is the man who needs sympathy." When
Slim writes his paper on Shakespeare for a graduate course, he
says that the theme of all tragedy is the necessity for self-
knowledge. The tragic flaw in Shakespeare's heroes is a defect in self-knowledge. Again the dialectic is at work, and
the irony too, when Slim confronts Bogan in the struggle for
ascendance over Sue. Slim has been feeding his obsession with
power by manipulating Sue. Yet he says Bogan is guilty of
"the special disease of our time, the abstract passion for
power, a vanity springing from an awareness of the emptiness
and unreality of the self which can only attempt to become
real and human by the oppression of people who manage to retain some shreds of reality and humanity." In the "Introduction" to the Modern Library edition of *All the King's Men,*
Warren, comparing Bogan to Willie Stark, says quite explicitly
that Bogan was supposed to embody the desiccating abstraction
of power and "to try to fulfill vicariously his natural emptiness by exercising power over those around him...."[15]

Warren arranges the fate of his characters in such a way

as to illuminate and embroider his ideas. The lineaments of
power apparent in Bogan are actually a façade; he is revealed
as an empty coward. Sue, driven by perversity and desperation,
comes to live as if she were out of time. For Warren, life is
meaningless when men are removed from the stream of time that
bears their personal histories. Because men are defined by
the past, they must maintain in the present a sense of continuity with the past, for this continuity makes the future possible. Jerry's fate is related to this general proposition.
His sin has been a terrible failure of piety, for he denies
his family and his history. He faces the truth about himself
late in the book: men are the sum of their heredity and experience in the past, and they must fashion their lives to accommodate that totality.

Jason Sweetwater seems to have discarded piety altogether;
he embodies, not the neglect of ancestors we see in Jerry, but
the positive rejection. In the pursuit of the self, Jason
casts off his lying, sentimental father. He goes into his
father's church on weekdays, as a boy, as a "kind of avowal of
self, a compensation for, a repudiation of, the not-self which
he was when he sat there on Sunday...." Jason learns some
hard lessons in his quest. He knows for instance that "A man
could not believe in himself unless he believed in something
else." For Jason, apparently, this "something else" was not
his father's religion but the cause of labor. It seems to me
that Warren is not clear about how Jason's beliefs enable him
to fix so securely his image of himself, but Warren is clear
in the formulation of the proposition that man can know himself only by transcending himself. Jason knows that a man
must pay for what he gets, and so he will have to pay for being in love with Sue: always, "you paid...with a chunk right
out of your soul...." He is no "God-damned Liberal" to feel
you can get something for nothing. The payment demanded of
him is marriage to Sue, who will bear his child. He will not
violate his own conception of what he is in order to pay,
since Sue sees in him a father-image and a father-substitute
which she both wants and repudiates. He will not assume this
role.

The comment about the liberal that I have quoted above
is Warren's most succinct and provocative statement on the
political-social scene of the thirties. With it, he separates
Jason at once from the proletarian heroes of social realism
and he repudiates the easy hope of liberal reform. With it,
he shows both the connection his novel has with the fiction
and the times that immediately precede it and the difference
between his work and that of others who wrote about labor or-
ganizers. And with it, he reveals again how attractive the
world of affairs is to him, how, indeed, he wishes to bring
his conceptions of self and society into the open and not to
trust in cloistered virtues. Behind this novel lies the world
of labor unrest and strike-breaking, the world of high finance

and political maneuver. The prototype for Bogan Murdock is
supposed to be Luke Lea, onetime United States senator from
Tennessee who served a term in jail for his part in the
$17,000,000 failure of the Asheville Central Bank and Trust
Co. The prototype for Private Porsum seems, in some ways, to
have been Sergeant York, a hero of the first World War.

I feel that in this novel Warren fails to resolve all the
problems that he raises, just as he fails to dispose satisfactorily of all the characters. A cryptic quality pervades the
book, qualifying and sometimes even crippling Warren's commitments and his conclusions. But the novel clearly points to
his major work, and the conceptions which are here rehearsed
are being readied for a grander performance.

In *All the King's Men* (1946), Warren emerges from apprenticeship and brings his many characteristic themes together in
one of the most distinguished novels of the period. Politics
is the framework for his story, and amid the thrust and surge
of the public scene where a great, virtually omnipotent political boss takes and wields his power Warren weaves his complex
of beliefs. The end of man is to know, he demonstrates. What
man seeks is the knowledge of good and evil, and the knowledge
of truth, and out of these, self-knowledge. But man's way is
hard, not simply because truth is elusive, but because it has
different shapes for different men, who are all the victims of
the modern world and of their own self-division. Man's way is
hard because he must come to the painful recognition of what
he is as man, which takes him apart from and enables him to
transcend nature. Since man exists in time, however, he has
history, and history may help him to find the truth and to
understand the world. The past may reclaim for a man the
present and give him a world he can understand and live in.
The past may give a man his father and his mother, and giving
them, it may release him to live in the world and understand
himself.

If these are the themes to be discovered in the novel, we
are prepared to consider sympathetically Warren's contention
that Huey Long did nothing more than suggest Willie Stark.[16]
Yet I suspect that Warren's comment was prompted by tactical
considerations: he wished to give the authority of his own
voice to the repudiation of a purely political reading of his
novel. A sound enough purpose. But the social scene, Warren
and his *Sewanee Review* champions notwithstanding, has the largest kind of meaning for this novel. I do not speak of the
class tensions that are present and exploited by Willie in the
conflicts between aristocracy and rednecks. Nor even of Jack
Burden's treason to his own class at Burden's Landing when
he allies himself with Willie, the cocklebur candidate whose
economic policies are a threat and an affront to the well-born
and the well-to-do. (Although Jack's dilemma, the conflict
in social and political loyalties, is instructive, because the
resolution of such a dilemma is a step on the road toward self-

knowledge....) What I am saying is that the social-political
scene, aside from its intrinsic value for movement and interest in the novel, is the indispensable background for working
out the view of man's character and destiny that Warren wishes
to set before us. All the ideas in the novel, then, are in a
sense socially oriented, for they have their reality, not as
abstractions which emerge as valid for Warren or Jack, but as
strands in the fabric of social interaction. The obvious
should not be overlooked: men in life are political creatures,
living in society among other men and by institutions created
by men and according to moral standards conceived by men
and preserved for their use as a social heritage; and it is
equally obvious that the actions and beliefs of such men are
the raw materials of fiction. *All the King's Men,* to be
sure, is not the story of a dictator. But that story, like
the story of Jack's social dilemma, takes its place in the
novel to say something about the nature of man, about man
and human history, about man's morality, so that what Warren
finally achieves is an integrated view of man *and* the world
he lives in.

The totality of that view can be formulated in terms of
the Hegelian dialectic. Men are good, like Adam Stanton, Hugh
Miller, the Scholarly Attorney, or Lucy Stark; these characters may stand for thesis. And men are totally bad (depraved
would not be an inaccurate term here), like Tiny Duffy and
Byram White; these characters are the antithesis. And men are
mixed, like Willie Stark and Judge Irwin, and finally Jack
Burden himself; they are the synthesis. Everyone in the first
two groups, with one possible exception, is incomplete. In
the last group Willie, with the potentials of indivisibility
within his grasp, gives way to a fatal yearning for absolute
good, in violation of his intrinsic character and beliefs.
Judge Irwin dies to preserve the successful synthesis as he
had lived by it. Jack, alone of the last group, survives to
embody the final understanding and acceptance of this position,
this acceptance of good and evil, this burden of an optimum
condition of life which is at best only a set of provisional
resolutions.

Adam Stanton makes the fullest statement of the thesis.
He is a brilliant surgeon and the son of a former governor.
He wants to do good. But he is appalled by the world when it
does not conform to his picture of what it ought to be. Since
for him all politics is dirty, he holds aloof out of a spirit
of moral fastidiousness that is absolute. The structure of
his moral ideas, while it is simple, is nonetheless appropriate to the rational and scientific mind. Morality, for him,
is as orderly, straightforward, and predictable as physical
laws. Because he cannot stay aloof and because he cannot, in
his simple-minded morality, cope with the evil in the world,
he consummates his life in violence, which is usually the end
of uncompromising principle and undeviating rationalism (a

lesson Warren might have learned from the French Revolution as
Burke did). Faced with the charge that he was made director
of Willie's hospital because Willie is sleeping with his sister, Adam's only possible response is murder. He kills Willie
in the capital and is in turn shot down. They were doomed to
destroy each other, Warren says, because they were two halves
of each other: Adam the man of idea and Willie the man of fact.

Hugh Miller, Willie's attorney general, also takes a
straight-line view of morality. He believes that if a man is
guilty of malfeasance in public office, such a man should be
prosecuted and condemned. When Willie saves Byram White, who
is certainly guilty, Hugh resigns. Willie saves Byram because
he has to use the Byrams of this world and because he cannot
permit the opposition to use Byram, i.e., to bring his administration into bad odor by revealing Byram's corruption. Willie has to stay in power in order to bring his conception of
good to his people and his state. He is acting in accordance
with a moral idea, but it has not the rigidity of Hugh's abso-
lutism. Hugh has the satisfaction of intact principles, but
he surrenders the public arena in which he might display them.
Willie is still in power fighting to bring into effect his
vision of good despite the evil that surrounds it.

The Scholarly Attorney, Ellis Burden, is another good man
who, unable to cope with the evil of the world, withdraws from
it. When he discovers that he is not Jack's father, he leaves
his wife. He becomes a religious fanatic and undergoes a perpetual debasement of the self, losing his individuality in the
lives of others. His position is ultimately life-denying and
cowardly, resting as it does on the failure of the world to
conform to his subjective notion of reality.

Lucy Stark disturbs a little the schematization here established, for if she is incomplete in her attachment to the simple verities, she is nevertheless close to irreproachability.
She and Miller represent two varieties of simplistic morality;
hers is a naïve, stubborn, biblical, folk honesty which has
all the strength, and some of the limitations, of Hebraism.
She tells Willie that if he protects Byram White she will
leave him, and she is as good as her word. When her son
promiscuously fathers a child, she takes it unquestioningly,
exchanging her love for its innocence. When her son is seriously injured, she rejoins her husband, understanding that
the great crises of parenthood, the crises of life and death,
supersede differences in moral evaluations. Before her adherence to a given code, an adherence where the cost in pain and
responsibility is always hers and no one else's, loyalty to
Willie's realistic, ambiguous morality must blush.

The characters who are evil are nothing, as Percy Munn was
nothing. Willie says of Byram White that he is a thing, less
than a man. He has no inner essence, but is, in his being,
what Willie tells him to be. The same is true of Tiny Duffy,
who, as Willie's campaign manager during the first gubernator-

ial campaign, was a part of the double-cross that victimized
Willie. After Willie breaks the Harrison organization to
which Tiny had belonged, he permits Tiny to join him. He
makes Tiny his creature so that Tiny's success is a measure of
Willie's. Tiny is the complete politician, the very stereotype of the pig in the trough; as Willie's other self, Tiny
provides an outlet for Willie's self-contempt. It is Tiny who,
frustrated in the pursuit of that graft which is natural to
his species, sets Adam on Willie. The irony is that a man who
is nothing should kill the man who gives him substance and ani-
mates him. But I must say, parenthetically, that Tiny is not
alone in this, for like the death of the Swede in "The Blue
Hotel," many people must share that responsibility.

Among them, Willie himself. Warren is not altogether fair
to Willie when he describes him, in the "Introduction" to *All
the King's Men,* as "the politician [who] rises to power because of the faculty of fulfilling vicariously the secret
needs of others, and in the process...discovers his own emptiness."[17] What Willie so fatally discovers is the lure of the
absolute. All through the novel, from the time of his great
drunk during his first campaign to the moment when he decides
to build his hospital, Willie lives with the stern knowledge
that good must come out of evil, and the evil it comes out of
is man, who is conceived in sin and born in corruption and
passes from the stink of the didie to the stench of the shroud
(for Willie, it must never be forgotten, went to a Presbyter-
ian Sunday school). Willie knows that men cannot go into the
world without getting the dirt of the world upon them or the
poison of it under their skin. He knows that the government
of his state is made up half of slaves and half of sons of
bitches. But he tells the mobs, who listen raptly, your will
is my strength, your need is my justice, and he is not at all
sure that this is demagoguery. Warren gives us in Willie a
brooding, thoughtful man of destiny with a sense of the mystery of life. He is a man who, as he sat studying law, felt
growing inside himself, painfully and imperceptibly, his own
world. Out of his reflection comes a conception of good and
an understanding of how at least limited good can be imposed
on people. And of how means, even evil means, must be adapted
to good ends. Knowing all these things, Willie inexplicably
sets them aside. He decides to build a hospital that shall be
a memorial to purity and a justification for his political chicanery. It is his expiation. It is the sacrifice he offers
to placate the stern Hebraic God whom he cannot, after all,
escape. This inconsistency — the knowledge that good comes
out of evil but the refusal to let Duffy (who is certainly
evil) negotiate the usual crooked deal in the construction of
the hospital — leads to Willie's death. Warren has said that
Willie was corrupted by power, even power exercised against
corruption. The statement is true enough. But it seems to me
also to be the case that Willie could not live with the truth

he had discerned. He could not accept finally the mixed nature of man and things.

Judge Irwin, in many ways Willie's most formidable political opponent, is the living demonstration of Willie's theories
about the nature of man and ethics. His aristocratic appearance of unimpeachable probity does not deter Willie from ordering Jack to get something on the judge, because there is
always something. Jack finds it. Irwin had once taken a
bribe when he was broke. When Jack tries to use this knowledge to force the judge to call off a political offensive
against Willie, the judge commits suicide. He does not swerve
from his principles when confronted with an impossible situation. He does not use the fact that he is Jack's father to
persuade Jack to call off the attack. He had been a good
judge and he had done good. But he knew, like a Russian that
Warren may have had in mind, that you have to break eggs to
make an omelette. He had been a strong man and he had broken
plenty. He had cuckolded his friend and betrayed his own wife.
He had taken a bribe and driven a man to suicide. Warren's
point is that good and evil are intertwined, but it must be
pointed out that there is no necessary connection in the
judge's case between the good he does and the evil. Irwin is
simply an illustration of the proposition that, in the nature
of things, man achieves good despite himself.

The only completely successful synthesis is achieved by
Jack Burden. It is not simply that he survives, but that he
is reborn, as Norton Girault has so cogently argued. Or that,
to use Joseph Frank's formulation, Jack transcends the good
and evil of reality to reach a dualism which caps his moral
evolution.[18] Jack succeeds in reconciling good and evil because his synthesis is on a grand scale: he brings together
history and time, knowledge and self-knowledge, apparent truth
and real truth. His synthesis is his maturation as it is Warren's resolution of the problems raised by the novel.

Jack is the narrator of the novel, and very close to the
beginning he gets at its ironic center. "The end of man is
knowledge," he observes, "but there is one thing he can't know.
He can't know whether knowledge will save him or kill him.
He will be killed, all right, but he can't know whether he is
killed because of the knowledge which he has got or because
of the knowledge which he hasn't got and which if he had it,
would save him...the end of man is to know." Jack's struggle
is to know himself, but in order to do this he must work out
a means of knowing and he must understand the past. In college he believes in Idealism, which holds that if you did not
know a thing or recognize it, it did not exist. He persists
in this epistemological subjectivism well into the novel. If
you think you are sorry, then you are, he tells Anne Stanton,
and that's an end to it. He will discover that objective
truth exists, and when it is uncovered, he will know with
finality whether he is sorry or not. When he discovers the

truth about his father, that makes a real difference in how he thinks and feels. Warren is concerned to show that part of the maturation of Jack is the shucking off of this Idealism, which is the heresy of the self and which cripples the human capacity to deal with reality.

As a student of history, Jack makes two extensive excursions into the past. The first, a failure, is a doctoral dissertation which convinces Jack that if the human race never remembered anything it would be happy. He will revise this judgment when he comes to understand the meaning of his materials. These are the adultery and expiation of Cass Mastern during the Civil War. And the meaning is that the world is one, and to be in the world is to be evil, for evil is a function of living. What is seen in the story of Cass is seen and reinforced in Jack's story.

The second investigation into the past is the one that reveals Judge Irwin as a bribe-taker and Governor Stanton, the judge's friend, as an accessory to the crime. It is successful in the sense that Jack finds what Willie has asked him to find. It is successful because it yields Jack a father and a mother. When the judge kills himself, Jack's mother, a woman he has despised, tells him that Irwin was his real father. Jack has, then, in one blow, found his father and killed him. These are the fruits of the pursuit of truth. Later, his mother summons Jack to Burden's Landing. This much-married lady tells him she is leaving her present husband because she knows now that she always loved the judge. When she does this, she gives Jack back the past, "...which I had before felt was tainted and horrible. I could accept the past now because I could accept her and be at peace with her and with myself." In killing his father, accepting and loving his mother, Jack is liberated. He is freed for love and marriage to Anne; together they may go forth into the convulsion of the world, shed of their innocence, like Adam and Eve walking hand in hand out of Milton's paradise.

For the past and the future are forever tied together, and "we can keep the past only by having a future." Self-trust gives us the confidence to live in the future; having such confidence, we need not live in the past. Warren wants his characters to take account of the past but not to be bound to it. This attitude toward the past, linked to Jack's growth toward self-knowledge, is illustrated in the episode at Burden's Landing when Jack undresses Anne in his room but fails to sleep with her. He fears to destroy the meaning of the idyllic summer that they have had; in fact, he is afraid for their total past as companions. Such a need for the past exists for the immature man who does not understand himself and does not know where he is going. The sentimental view of the past paralyzes action. And not knowing who he is, he does not know how to act. The deepest meaning of this episode lies in the paralysis it reveals. But another meaning may be discerned as Jack

rationalizes his behavior, hiding from his own identity. With
Anne lying on his bed, he suddenly says, we can't, it isn't
right. His explanation for his failure is that he was noble.
But if he had slept with Anne, they would probably have been
married, and then she would not have become Willie's mistress
later on. My nobility, he says, had as dire a consequence as
Cass Mastern's sin. I suspect that Warren wants us to see the
irony here as a valid manifestation of the ambiguous relationship of good and evil and at the same time to see Jack's ra-
tionalization for what it is.

The maturation process in Jack consists in large part in
his learning to accept and absorb such ironies in which apparent evil comes out of apparent good, to accept the notion that
the discovery of the truth is more often than not calamitous.
Early in the novel, in a conversation with Anne, he is confi-
dent about grasping the plain truth, as he talks about why
Ellis Burden, his putative father, left his mother. In the
event, it turns out that Jack did not know the reason or have
the truth at all. The truth about Jack's father, when it is
discovered, leads to the death of his father, as I have already said. Pursuing the truth about Judge Irwin, Jack reveals to Adam and Anne that their father had helped Irwin to
take the bribe. Later, when Jack asks Anne why she is sleeping with Willie, she says because she loves him and because
there was no reason not to once she had heard about her father.
The truth has destroyed an image of moral integrity by which
Anne had lived. Jack thinks, I only told her the truth, and
from this truth has come this sin, this adultery.

Hard-boiled Jack Burden, armed with a mucker-pose, finds
it excruciatingly painful to deal with the complexities he has
uncovered. He throws up a series of defenses, all of them escapes from the self-knowledge that will ultimately be forced
upon him, or obstacles to it. These are the ways, Girault
says, in which he resists being reborn. These are the Great
Sleep, the Great Twitch, and the flight to the West. Jack's
response to crisis is withdrawal — when, for instance, he
loses his job; or flight — when he learns that Anne is sleeping with Willie. But he always returns, to consciousness or
to home. The Great Sleep is an induced and deliberate failure
of consciousness which makes it impossible to continue pursuit
of the truth; it may be a withdrawal to the womb out of an inability to face life. When he runs away to California, he discovers the Great Twitch, which is, I take it, a philosophy of
nihilism, a belief in a purely mechanistic view of man and nature. He thinks for a while that he has uncovered knowledge
which will give him power, but he soon surrenders this empty
belief as he had surrendered Idealism. In the West responsibility is meaningless and life is an illusion. Jack is momentarily soothed and believes he can return home with a defense
adequate to his need. He is to learn that he must return home,

there to find the truth that will release him to a life of responsible action.

The maturation process in Jack includes also his rejection of a role as alter ego. The masks that hide the self in *At Heaven's Gate* are transmuted into a technique of alter egos in this novel, whereby a personality is complemented or completed by another personality. As in the earlier novels, so too here, Warren makes the point that self-definition cannot be achieved through another person. Cass Mastern knows this. It is part of Willie's failure that both Tiny and Adam represent elements in his personality — irreconcilable elements. Near the end of the novel, Jack finds himself in a position to be like Duffy in order to kill Duffy. Such action would be the perfect revenge for Duffy's having unleashed Adam against Willie. By this time, however, Jack is strong enough to resist this kind of complement to his selfhood.

The synthesis Jack makes is reflected in the structure of the novel. If all things are in time, and time is a continuum, then it is necessary to peel back layer after layer of experience in any individual life to reveal how an event came to pass and why it had precisely the impact it had. It is necessary to move deeper and deeper into the past, exploring contingent lives, if time makes all things one. If one theme of the novel is that man must possess and believe in his history in order to live in the present and look forward to the future, then there must be constant movement in time in the novel. There is such movement, and the manipulation of time levels becomes an informing device both structurally and thematically. The scheme of the book therefore reinforces the theme; the structure is carefully adapted to the end. Despite the time shifts, the first chapter begins at what is essentially the beginning — Burden's Landing where Jack comes from and Mason City where Willie comes from — and in neat circularity it suggests and contains the ending, which is the death of the Boss and Adam and Judge Irwin, and the consequent freeing of Jack. Furthermore, abandoning straight chronology permits Warren to show the irregular and abrupt stages of self-revelation in Jack Burden, as any given episode leads him into the past.

This novel is Warren's finest work to date. No writer in our time except Faulkner has given us a book that speaks so eloquently with a conservative voice; no writer has so well anatomized the modern world, showing it to be the product of history expressed in those social terms we call politics.

In 1947 Warren collected his short stories in a volume called *The Circus in the Attic and Other Stories*. My feeling is that the stories do not, on the whole, succeed. When they are not discursive and loose in structure, like the title story, they are too neatly packaged, like "The Patented Gate and the Mean Hamburger." The humor and the irony are sometimes so obvious that it is difficult to understand why Warren

should have wanted to preserve such work; I have in mind especially "A Christian Education" and "Confession of Brother
Grimes."

The most authentic note Warren strikes in this volume is
that of reminiscence, because looking backward gives scope to
his piety and opportunity to assess the growing-up process.
These characteristics make meaningful such stories as "When
the Light Gets Green" and "Blackberry Winter." The second
story treats the maturation theme as a series of disorienta-
tions from the lovely green world of nature and the secure,
isolated world of the farm. "When you are a boy...you want
to stand there in the green twilight until you feel your very
feet sinking into and clutching the earth like roots and your
body breathing slow through its pores like the leaves...."
But one cannot retain the innocence of boyhood. The stranger,
who does not grow into the ground, brings the meaningless vi-
ciousness of the urban world to the boy. The dead cow in the
river and the old veteran of Forrest's cavalry bring home the
horror of nature and life to the boy. Even the familiar and
gentle Dellie, now irascible and mean in her illness, shows
the unhappy reality that lies under the surface of human life;
and her usually spotless yard, now littered with filth brought
out by the flooding creek, signalizes the destructiveness of
nature. Not everyone can survive the knowledge of good and
evil and the wrenching away from nature. The boy in this
story does. But the men in stories like "Goodwood Comes Back"
and "The Patented Gate" cannot do it; they thus reveal themselves as only half-men.

"The Circus in the Attic," the title story, is another approach to the dualism of life, an examination of the relation
between the world of illusion and the world of reality as it
bears on the discovery of truth. Warren seems to be showing
that what is important is what men choose to live by. In so
doing they make an enduring truth, and it makes no difference
whether or not it is a verifiable truth. The counsels of imperfection and tentativeness contained in this story, like the
use of time as a continuity which helps to create a truth that
never was, are typical of the Warren syndrome, even as the in-
decisive conduct of the story is an aberration from the disciplined form he so often provides.

World Enough and Time (1950), the novel which followed *All
the King's Men,* is a considerable falling off from the level
of excellence achieved by that latter book. Warren has become
here a victim of his own manner. The New Critic in him has
throttled the novelist. The New Critic knows that the novelist must not moralize. He knows the novelist must give aesthetic form and imaginative meaning to moral ideas. Warren
has learned the lesson so well that, one feels, he has over-
burdened *World Enough and Time* with ironic complexities; he
has pressed too hard with his characteristic dialectic. He is
so intent upon the doubleness of life that the reader cannot

always tell when he must laugh, for this part is farce, or
when he must weep, for this part is tragedy.

Perhaps these judgments are too harsh. For the novel does
give us at least Warren's most protracted effort simultaneously to separate and unite conceptions of the world or reality
and of idea or idealism. It does give us his fullest account
of the world of non-human nature as the quagmire of the spirit.

In dealing with the reality-idea dichotomy, Warren creates
a protagonist whose idea of reality is private. Even though
this man's idea encompasses justice and honor, the man fails.
The external world intrudes upon his reality to frustrate him,
but his ultimate failure is in the realization that private,
subjective judgment must always be false. The assertion of
that judgment, without reference to any scheme of transcendent
value, is the heresy of the self. The dichotomy thus posed
lends itself in the novel to the theme which Warren calls the
doubleness of life. The complexity of this work may be judged
by suggesting that the following three meanings, at a minimum,
may be attached to that phrase: obviously, to begin with, the
world and idea as antithesis; the dualism of man, which includes both the good and evil in man and his life-urge and his
death-urge; the confusion between appearance and reality,
whereby friend is really foe and the seemingly guilty are
really innocent.

This same dichotomy is the basis of "To His Coy Mistress,"
the poem by Andrew Marvell that provides Warren with his title.
In the poem, reality or the world is more highly regarded than
an impossible ideal — of courtly love, in this instance. Warren's predilection for the dialectic complicates his resolution of these opposites. While he is no champion of the ex-
pediency and opportunism of the world, neither is he ready to
accept the ideal as subjectively conceived. Warren believes
that the validity of the ideal is conditioned by the adjustment of the ideal to the terms imposed upon it by the world.
Poor, deluded Jeremiah Beaumont, the protagonist in this novel,
is the victim of the painful farce enacted here precisely because he does not understand the necessary interplay of idea
and reality. He tries to live only by the idea.

But since the world is present always to man, we must now
ask what its meanings are in the novel. First, the world is
palpable in the novel as history and social force. The story
is based on a famous murder trial which took place in Kentucky
in the 1820's when the parties of Relief and anti-Relief were
in conflict. Warren's principal source is the "Confessions of
Jereboam O. Beauchamp." The world is also embodied in Wilkie
Barron, Jeremiah's friend, who betrays him. "For what was
Wilkie's face but the mask of all the world?" Wilkie is the
essence of the world, utterly at home in it in his malignancy
and diabolism, in his skill at manipulation and duplicity, in
his unbroken series of successes. Yet Wilkie kills himself
finally because he realizes that man must be something in him-

self; man cannot live by the world alone. And the world is at war with the idea. Jeremiah thinks he must live by an idea of honor. To reclaim honor he must kill Cassius, who had seduced Rachel Jordan before her marriage to Jeremiah. But Jeremiah is lulled by the comfort of the world and bemused by the contradictions in it between private and public justice.

Jeremiah cannot live in the world. He cannot reconcile his own ideals and impulses to the demands of the world. It is necessary for him, then, to create both his own world and a self that will fit into it. The tragic quality of the novel is in the picture of a man who is unfulfilled and incomplete because he perversely cuts himself off from other men, from society. Jeremiah's failure is in dedication to the pure idea in a world which cannot tolerate the pure idea, only diluted and compromised ideas with which men must learn to live. Jeremiah is thus like Adam Stanton and must fail like Adam, as all men fail who do not achieve the synthesis which is the consequence of the logic and movement of Warren's dialectic.

Responding to the need for self-definition, Jeremiah must search out the situation that excludes worldly interest. By finding and performing the completely gratuitous and disinterested act, he will discover the self. In pursuit of this purity he marries Rachel, a wronged woman, and kills Fort, her seducer and his benefactor. It must be added here that he performs these acts in obedience to another need beside the one to reject or flaunt the world. He is the victim of compulsive self-immolation; he is the victim of victims. Against reason and principle, he rushes to the aid of the helpless and the wronged. This irrational and sentimental streak in him, first apparent in his childhood reaction to the picture of the burning martyr, prevents him from ever achieving selfhood. In these aspects of his character, as in his preoccupation with the idea, Jeremiah is a fool, and Warren, for this reason, must deny him maturation.

Yet Warren forces Jeremiah constantly to seek selfhood. Jeremiah wants to know and live by the truth within him. At one point, about to confess the murder to the lawyers who defend him, he is poised "on the brink of myself...for the moment when a man falls into himself, into the past which is himself...," but he cannot confess. Not until it comes home to him that he has acted for honor, but all has come to a bitter end in degradation, is he ready to confess. Not until the end, when he realizes that his crime was in trying to isolate the idea from the world and to live by it, when he recognizes that he has isolated himself, is he ready to confess. Even then he knows he cannot seek redemption. All that remains for him is to suffer.

Nature, as we have seen, is as gross as the world. Jeremiah's response to nature is represented to us in a childhood experience, as his self-sacrificial tendency is explained by the martyred maid in the fire. Swimming in the Kentucky River,

he watches a keelboat approach and pass and listens to the
music coming from it. Later, on the river himself, escaping
from prison, he remembers this event. The two times merge for
him. He is sucked into the river and the darkness, and he
feels at peace. It is the same peace that he felt when he
lived at his ease with Rachel on his estate — an animal peace
that does not know the voice of moral duty. Warren is here
suggesting Jeremiah's desire to bury himself in the world of
non-human nature and to identify with it, as an alternative
to the more difficult human course of separating oneself from
nature. The peace Jeremiah experiences on the river he feels
again when he flees west to the incredible domain of La Grand'
Bosse. It arises from a surrender of the moral will — the
essential and human quality which distinguishes us as human
beings — to sloth and filth, to the degradation of the appeti-
tive life. Clearly, Warren does not accept the myth of the
West as innocence. The West is raw, non-human nature that
pulls man down to its own bestial level.

In addition to his treatment of the world and nature,
Warren plays persistently in this novel with an idea of drama.
He makes Jeremiah conceive of his life as a drama, and he has
Rachel also see parts of her experience as drama. By using
this device, he succeeds again in setting off action and idea
from the world. At the beginning of the book Jeremiah says he
has prepared an "ambiguous drama which seemed both to affirm
and to deny life, to affirm and to deny humanity." Such a
drama is necessary if one is to live "against the ruck of the
world." Jeremiah's was to be a tragedy of blood, but the actors sometimes turned it into bloody farce. For the characters, the idea of drama is refuge; for Warren it is a technique for gaining aesthetic distance. Twice-removed from his
characters — who are in the drama within the story — Warren
can manage the detachment necessary for irony. Rachel can say
that she is acting in a charade which becomes the essence of
truth and her only reality, and Warren, divorced so to speak
from any responsibility for her position, can speak about her
plight from the reference point of a more solid-seeming world.
But when the drama ends in a pratfall, when the suicide pact
of Rachel and Jeremiah ends only in miserable vomiting, one
wonders if we have Jeremiah's ambiguities or Warren's — if
Warren did not, after all, get too close to his material?

Which brings me back to the point at which I began talking
of this novel. It seems often to be a literary exercise for
Warren, who stands outside calculating the number of devices
he can work into it and the way to apply them. Sometimes he
miscalculates. It occurs to me to ask, is this a great joke
Warren has perpetrated on us giving us this apparently serious inquiry into the mixed nature of man and the dark nature
of reality in a contrived vehicle that he himself does not
believe in? Maybe not. But my final judgment is that Warren
did not master his materials. Its people and its plot cannot

carry the weight of speculation imposed upon them. Here the
intricate play of moral nuance is dull and confusing, not il-
luminating. It is, finally, a pretentious book.

Band of Angels (1955) is beyond the limits of the present
study. But a word about it will serve, perhaps, to suggest
some of the problems that Warren must face as a novelist.
The book reveals a further development of Warren's penchant
for the melodramatic and the bizarre. Melodrama does not yet
threaten to become an end in itself in his novels, but it may
come to overwhelm or obscure for the reader the more serious
aspects of Warren's work. The style of this novel is resource-
ful and elaborate; the danger is that a further elaboration of
this style will make the writing fancy and bookish, as some
critics think it is now.[19] *Band of Angels* deals again with
the question of identity. The series of masks for his characters that Warren has worked out in treating the quest for the
self is more labored and more deliberately schematized than
anything he has done before. Such treatment raises the possibility that Warren may be substituting ingenuity for original-
ity. It suggests that he has reached the intellectual limits
of this question of identity. Once again his characters try
to feed on each other to find themselves; once again they are
alienated from the father or from the past. One feels that
the repetitions in Warren's work derive from intellectual
commitments that have imposed a bondage upon his imagination.

The final question raised by Warren's work concerns the
lure of orthodox religion. Critics may and do read his novels
as religious statement and find in them religious conceptions
like paradise and innocence, communion and guilt. In *Band of
Angels* religion is not rejected; it is simply not accepted.
One wonders, given Warren's over-all allegiance to conservatism, if he will resist that religious conversion which seems
to be the logical end dictated by the convictions that now
guide his writing. What restrains him, I suppose, is the importance he attaches to the tensions inherent in a sceptical
and provisional attitude. This conflict within the conservative mind between orthodoxy and scepticism makes for the most
fascinating kind of speculation Warren affords us.

---

1. Cowan, *The Fugitive Group* (Baton Rouge: Louisiana State University Press, 1959), p. 247.
2. See Fraser, *The Modern Writer and His World* (London: Derek Ver-
schoyle, 1953), especially p. 117.
3. Carl Jung, *The Integration of the Personality,* trans. Stanley
Dell (New York: Farrar and Rinehart, 1939), p. 281.
4. Ibid., p. 70. Jung's "The Spiritual Problem of Modern Man"
appears in his *Modern Man in Search of a Soul* (London: Kegan Paul,
Trench, Trubner and Co., 1933).
5. Warren comments on the problem of identity in his essay "Hem-

ingway," *Kenyon Review,* 9 (Winter 1947), 27. See also his "Katherine Anne Porter," *Kenyon Review,* 4 (Winter 1942), 29-42.

6. Warren, "Knowledge and the Image of Man," *Sewanee Review,* 63 (Spring 1955), 189-92.

7. Warren, "Nostromo," *Sewanee Review,* 59 (Summer 1951), 363-91.

8. Warren, "Cowley's Faulkner," *New Republic,* Aug. 12, 1946, p. 177.

9. Warren in Malcolm Cowley, ed., *Writers at Work: The "Paris Review" Interviews* (New York: Viking Press, 1958), p. 193; Warren, ed., *A Southern Harvest* (Boston: Houghton Mifflin Co., 1937), xiv-xv.

10. Warren, "Nostromo," p. 376. See Warren, "The Love and Separateness in Miss Welty," *Kenyon Review,* 6 (Spring 1944), 246-59.

11. Warren in *Writers at Work,* p. 190.

12. See Bodkin, *Archetypal Patterns in Poetry* (London: Oxford University Press, 1951).

13. Hendry, "The Regional Novel: The Example of Robert Penn Warren," *Sewanee Review,* 53 (Jan.-Mar. 1945), 84-102.

14. Warren, "Introduction," *All the King's Men* (New York: Random House, 1953), iii n.

15. Ibid., iii.

16. See ibid., v-vi, where Warren mentions Long.

17. Ibid., iii.

18. Girault, "The Narrator's Mind as Symbol: An Analysis of *All the King's Men*," *Accent,* 7 (Summer 1947), 220-34; and Frank, "Romanticism and Reality in Robert Penn Warren," *Hudson Review,* 4 (Summer 1951), 248-58.

19. An unfavorable view of Warren's style is taken by Wallace W. Douglas, "Drug Store Gothic: The Style of Robert Penn Warren," *College English,* 15 (Feb. 1954), 265-72.

Richard Law

Night Rider and the
Issue of Naturalism:
The 'Nightmare' of Our Age

A year prior to the publication of *Night Rider* (1939),
Warren was working on the materials which eventually became
All the King's Men. Among the many elements which shaped the
early versions of those materials were a series of related
issues which he later characterized as "...the theme of the
relation of science (or pseudo-science) and political power,
the theme of the relation of the science-society and the power
state, the problem of naturalistic determinism and responsibility...."[1] The links suggested here between a "pseudo-scientif-
ic" world view and the huge dilemmas of the modern world not
only inform Warren's famous Pulitzer Prize-winning work, but
provide the major themes for his ambitious first novel as well.

The core of these issues which Warren was pondering was
the crude determinism popularly derived from scientific assumptions; empiricism, narrowly understood, had, he felt, become the ruling premise of the modern world, the mythology of
the "science society." In his views of the consequences of
that mythology, Warren is clearly the student of John Crowe
Ransom. Both mistrusted this mythology they called "scientism," and both traced a good many of the ills of the modern
world to its destructive underlying assumptions. In 1930, Ransom had devoted an entire book, *God Without Thunder,* to the
problems posed by the acceptance of this deterministic or "naturalistic" world view. "Naturalism," he asserted, is based on
the "belief that the universe is largely known, and theoretically knowable...."[2] It means accepting what William James
called a "block universe" in which everything is finished and
predictable and where effects flow inalterably from definable
causes. The determinism inherent in such a world view must
lead, Ransom felt, to an alarmingly truncated view of experience and of the nature of man. No system of values or ethics

can be founded upon such a narrow empiricism; no reason for
being or motive for action is implicit in it. It not only
leaves out the chief part of man's subjective experience, it
reduces the whole cosmos to meaninglessness. The consequence
for the individual life, he implied, must ultimately be nihilism.

While Warren agreed substantially with Ransom's assessment
of the problem, his use of these assumptions in his fiction
has been surprisingly tentative and skeptical. *Night Rider* is
characteristic of Warren's best work in that such ideas — his
own or opposing ones — are treated as hypotheses to be tested
rather than as conclusions to be demonstrated. In his first
novel, Warren explores a world view he hates but cannot entirely repudiate, and which he disbelieves but cannot satisfactorily disprove. *Night Rider* is thus a philosophical novel in
the best sense of the term: it does not argue a position; the
action dramatizes, intelligently and comprehensively, the major facets of a philosophical problem — one which Warren was
later to call the "nightmare" of our age.[3]

I

The novel opens with a description of the crowded train
that brings the protagonist to Bardsville for a rally of tobacco growers who are protesting against the monopolistic buyers. The scene is emblematic of the uncertain relationship
between human will and the impersonal forces of history. In
a sense, it presages the action of the entire novel. The protagonist, Perse Munn, packed in a coach with a crowd of pass-
engers bound for the same rally, is hurled against the man in
front of him by an unexpected change in the velocity of the
train. He is caught up by a "pressure that was human because
it was made by human beings, but was inhuman too, because you
could not isolate and blame any one of those human beings who
made it."[4] Munn strikes the man in front of him because he
"was not braced right," and the other man blames the anonymous
and invisible engineer — a figure who stands perhaps for all
explanations of how things come about. The whole passage is
a complex emblem which parodies both the problem of knowledge
and the venerable issue of free will.

As we have seen, Warren associated the acceptance of scientific determinism as a philosophy with the rise of totalitari-
anism — partly, one supposes, because that philosophy appears
to be merely an expansion of the idea of cause and effect into
a universal principle as applicable to human affairs as to the
motion of billiard balls. Such a view *seems* scientific and
therefore carries with it the implicit authority of science —
an awesome authority, since the laboratory has become in our
time the only "sanctioned" mode of intercourse with the world
and our only criterion of truth. If, in an historical context,
determinism tended to bolster non-ethical forms of authoritar-

ianism, on the level of the individual life, Warren felt, with
Ransom and Allen Tate, that such a view of the world took man
dangerously near the abyss. Warren's strategy in exploring
that issue in *Night Rider* is to take a single catastrophic
action (such as is imaged in the first scene in the novel) and
to examine it in as many of its facets and implications as possible. The underlying question throughout is whether naturalism, as a frame of reference, is adequate to the "data" thus
discovered: Does it encompass and account for all that we see?
To borrow a phrase from William James, what is its "cash value"
as an explanation of the action either to the reader or to
Perse Munn, who himself comes to adopt a naturalistic view?

The issue of determinism is raised at several levels in
the novel, most obviously in the political elements of the
plot. Warren sets the action in a time of acute crisis analogous to the period in which he wrote, and the urgent and practical questions raised there translate very readily into more
modern terms: is it possible to resist "outside" forces which
threaten to plunge one's community into catastrophe? And if
the community fights for certain idealistic values it holds
dear, is it possible to preserve those values successfully on
the battlefield? Significantly, once the tobacco growers' association in this rural, turn-of-the-century Kentucky community turns to terrorism, to "night riding" in the phrase of the
countryside, the large moral issues of the conflict are immediately submerged in the confusion and fury of civil war. The
conflict proves to have a logic of its own and rules of development and extension independent of the aims which brought it
about. Under the pressure of the war's logic, the antagonists
commit acts inimical to their own aims and ideals of justice
expressly in order to obtain justice. Furthermore, the violence initiated by the night riders intensifies and spreads
in unpredictable ways, returning with fitting irony to plague
its inventors. Munn's own house is burned to the ground by
a group of poor whites who, infected by the fever of violent
reprisal, demonstrate their resentment of Munn's Negro farm
hands in the manner they had learned from their "betters." In
short, once the terror is unleashed, all the issues in the conflict are submerged in a single overwhelming imperative, the
necessity to win.

The bearing of these political events on the issue of naturalism seems clear: the antagonists seem unable to match the
consequences of their actions with their intentions; they cannot control or predict the results of what they do, and they
cannot act in the cause of "good" without committing "evil."
There appear to be two worlds of experience which intersect
only imperfectly in the action. The one, the external world,
is deterministic, or largely so, and the other is subjective
and internal. Human "will" in the latter does not translate
simply or easily into action in the other. There is, in fact,
as Warren has noted elsewhere, an "irony of success," some-

thing "inherent in the necessities of successful action which
...[carries] with it the moral degradation of the idea."[5]

At the political level, in fact, the evidence of the plot
seems to point toward naturalism. Taken at face value, Munn's
private fortunes also seem to confirm and illustrate the operation of deterministic forces. Initially, Munn's aims are
partly idealistic. He shares with most of the other farmers
in the association an ideal of economic justice. But as he is
drawn deeper into the conflict, those ideals are among the
first casualties of the war. Indeed, under the impact of what
he feels forced to do, his very sense of identity becomes a
casualty of the war. Munn's disintegration in turn calls into
question the traditional, simplistic notion of will, for that
conception presupposes a holistic entity or agent capable of
volition. Warren's depiction of Munn's decline is a careful
testing of our popular and largely unexamined mythology of
self, especially as it relates to the larger issues of will
and determinism. The calculated ironies between what Munn in-
tends to do and what he achieves are illustrative of the problem. Munn becomes preoccupied with discovering or defining
his own "real" nature, "a more than intermittent self."[6] But
in his search for self-identification, he kills a former client whom he had saved from hanging, rapes his own wife, helps
lead a raid on tobacco warehouses, and betrays his best friend
by committing adultery with his daughter. At the end, in an
ironic inversion of "poetic justice," Munn is sought for a
murder he did not commit, is betrayed because of an imagined
offense he had not given, and — immediately after his first
redeeming act — is ambushed and shot by soldiers sent to restore order to the community.

Like all the other events in his career, Munn's death is
ambiguous, its actual nature an impenetrable mystery. It is
impossible to determine whether it is a suicide "willed" by
Munn himself or is rather the inevitable conclusion of a chain
of events outside himself. His raised pistol and unaimed shot
the moment he is killed describe, as it were, a large question
mark in the evening sky. There is a strong suggestion that
his death may be an unconscious fulfillment of a longing for
oblivion which much of his previous behavior had implied.
But it may, on the contrary, represent a sudden revulsion on
Munn's part against the shedding of more blood and may be,
therefore, a conscious gesture of compassion and a reaffirma-
tion of his ties with mankind. Or like Melville's whale, the
gesture *may* be devoid of any significance.

The ambiguity of Munn's death-scene merely focuses the
larger ambiguities which pervade the novel. If the outer
world is a meaningless flux of forces as impersonal and amoral
as the law of gravity, what of the human antagonists? There
is the fact of their consciousness (the importance of which is
continually emphasized through Warren's control of narrative
perspective). But are the human actors in the drama neverthe-

less helpless atoms hurled this way and that in spite of their
awareness? Warren raises several possibilities, ironically
posing them for us in the consciousness of his baffled protagonist. In one of his periods of introspection, Munn explores
the possibility that his entire existence may well be the product of random forces:

> ...looking across the big, pleasant room with its soft
> carpet and fine furnishings and at the leaping firelight
> and the known faces, he was aware how strong accident was
> — how here he was, warmed and fed and surrounded by these
> people who, if he spoke a single word, would turn pleasant-
> ly to him, and how cold it was snowing outside, all the
> countryside filling up with snow that would blind all fa-
> miliar contours, and how but for the accidents which were
> his history he might be out there, or elsewhere, miserable,
> lost, unbefriended. How anyone might be. That made the
> room, and all in it seem insubstantial, like a dream. The
> bottom might drop out; it was dropping out even while you
> looked, maybe. (p. 103)

The significance of this reverie emerges gradually as Munn's
subsequent fortunes prove its accuracy. What he sees in the
friendly, well-lighted room *is* insubstantial; the bottom is
dropping out even as he stares.

Character and fate, however, are as symmetrically aligned
in the novel as in Greek tragedy, and Warren seems to imply
by that alignment yet another, and contrary, line of causation
adequate to explain the action. What happens to most of the
characters in the novel represents what they are at the deepest level. Their actions are a progressive and involuntary
revelation of their inner natures, and death comes as a final
epiphany of character. "Did you ever notice," Dr. MacDonald
asks Munn, "how what happens to people seems sort of made to
order for them?" "One way or another, that's what a man does.
What's in him. A man goes along, and the time comes, even if
he's looking the other way not noticing, and the thing in him
comes out. It wasn't something happening to him made him do
something, the thing was in him all the time. He just didn't
know" (355-6). Professor Ball's often repeated platitude,
"You never know what's in you," becomes an almost choral reiteration of this theme.

Moreover, as if this opposing line of causation were not
irony and complication enough, "what's in a man" turns out to
be another mysterious quantity not easily susceptible to analysis or definition. Munn frequently feels himself driven by
impulses which are in him, but not, in a sense, *of* him. Even
though they help to destroy him, Munn does not seem reducible
to the mean of his unconscious drives. He is partly aware of
his own darker impulses, and he often feels strangely entan-
gled in a pattern of behavior not of his will; or, if of his
will, it lies at a level inaccessible to his comprehension.

His decision to join the night riders, though it surprises
him, seems "inevitable, like a thing done long before and
remembered, like a part of the old accustomed furniture of
memory and being" (148).   Later, while riding out to warn Trevelyan of his danger, Munn experiences a feeling of *déjà vu*
and senses again that he is fulfilling a pattern which is outside his comprehension and which, if it does not contradict
his will, encompasses and drowns it (191).

The starkest image of character unconsciously "fulfilling"
itself in the novel is Munn's aunt, Ianthe Sprague.   In her
method of coping with the world by isolating herself from it,
she bears a significant resemblance to her nephew.   Her mode
of living is an implicit denial of all coherence and purpose-
fulness.   It is as if she deliberately chooses what is forced
upon Munn.   Her nephew recognizes in her an image of fate as
the fulfillment of one's deepest wishes (213), for when he
tries to picture her as a young and lively woman — that is, as
a different woman — he cannot: "She had really always been as
she was now.... Her present being was a sort of goal toward
which, confidently, she had always been moving.   This present
being had always been, he was sure, her real being, and now
she was merely achieving it in its perfection of negativity
and rejection" (210).   But whether one may speak of such "fulfillment" as actually willed or simply as a consequence of the
given qualities of one's nature (like the behavior of a toy
soldier constructed to march only in straight lines) is never
made clear.   For the problem is complicated by yet another
factor: Munn's deepest desires are often at war with one another and hence, with what he "is."   His most fundamental concept of what he is also changes radically in the course of the
novel, so as a result, there seems to be neither a center nor
continuity to Munn's being.   "The things you remembered," he
concludes at one point, "they were what you were.   But every
time you remembered them you were different" (352).

The inner, unconscious drives which help to destroy Munn
propel him as impersonally as any of the forces outside himself; they are as alien to him as the anonymous powers behind
Senator Tolliver.   Munn, who is aware of his self-division,
seeks constantly to impose or discover some coherence in himself.   But the difficulty of discovering that elusive "center"
of his being is inextricably bound up with the difficulty of
getting the outside world into focus.   Munn poses this problem
to himself with some insight:

If I couldn't know myself, how could I know any of the
rest of them?   Or anything?   Certainly he had not known
himself...; if indeed the self of that time could claim
any continuator in the self that was to look backward and
speculate, and torture the question.   Then, thinking that
the self he remembered, and perhaps remembered but imperfectly, and the later self were nothing more than super-

imposed exposures on the same film of a camera, he felt
that all of his actions had been as unaimed and meaningless as the blows of a blind man who strikes out at the
undefined sounds which penetrate his private darkness.
(113-14)

But if the self does not exist continuously over time, it can
scarcely "fulfill" itself in action. Munn, as the image of
the camera film indicates, comes to accept a naturalistic version of his own experience which virtually denies his own selfhood. But the reader, who watches Munn consciously arrive at
this self-negation, cannot so easily dismiss that selfhood.
The thread of the argument thus seems to ravel out into irreconcilable strands. Warren's technique here is to construct
a tangled dialectic of possible positions, the terms of which
are continually called into question. Alongside the hard logic of the case for determinism and beside the vexing haziness
of our conceptions of self and self-realization, he constructs
a tentative case for freedom of the will. Ironically, that
case rests largely upon the fact — absurd and anomalous as it
may seem — of Munn's painful awareness of his predicament.
Munn *knows* he is "selfless," knows he is a divided, alienated
creature helplessly in the grip of forces beyond his understanding or control. There remains to be accounted for, however, the paradoxical "knower" of these things, the existential consciousness which, as it is hurried to annihilation,
has power at least to recoil in disgust and nausea from what
it cannot control. And that knower is, of course, left unaccounted for in the naturalistic hypothesis. Admittedly,
none of Munn's attempts to direct his destiny is sufficient to
break or reverse the pattern of his decline. But on the other
hand — if we may paraphrase Dr. MacDonald — while a man may do
merely "what he must," what is in him, the simple fact of his
consciousness may, as a contributing factor in the situation,
alter the nature of what one "must" do.

   During the scene of the Bardsville rally, the possibility
of such a radical alteration of reality through a simple alteration of consciousness, the grasping of an idea, occurs to
Munn as he swelters on the platform:

Behind all the names he was hearing without attention
were other men, scattered over the section, in other
countries [sic], perfectly real men, all different from
each other in their own ways, but drawn together by the
fact that their names were on the pieces of paper which
Mr. Sills held. From that paper invisible threads, as it
were, stretched off to Hunter County and Caldwell County
and into Tennessee to those men. They were all webbed together by those strands, parts of their beings, which were
their own, different each from each, coming together here
and becoming one thing. An idea...seized parts of their
individual beings and held them together and made them

coalesce. And something was made that had not existed
before. (16)

An idea in the collective consciousness and will of these
various men constitutes a new "thing" in the world; reality
has been altered.

Warren suggests yet another way in which consciousness
may be consequential in a remark Professor Ball makes to Munn
while attempting to persuade him to join the night riders:
"You won't be making the trouble.... You won't be making it,
but you'll be making it mean something. You can't stop the
mountain torrent, but you can make it feed the fruitful plain
and not waste itself" (142). In this simple dichotomy between
what must be and the definition or creation of its significance lies a traditional resolution of the problem of free
will. It is roughly the same distinction which Milton implies
in *Samson Agonistes*: events may be predetermined (either by
God or by History), but the meaning of those events depends
upon the will with which the acts are performed. Even, presumably, if that will is mysterious and complex and divided
against itself. The will may then, in turn, operate as a
cause out of which other consequences grow.

We are dealing here with the most elusive of arguments,
but one which Warren poses repeatedly throughout his career,
paralleling rather than imitating the stubborn and contorted
positions of the European existentialists. Warren's intention
in his first novel, however, is to pose these issues rather
than resolve them. The most that one may properly claim is
that, in spite of the artist's careful objectivity, there is
some pressure exerted upon this "dialectical configuration"
of "truths" to cohere in Truth. And the Truth which is being
asserted is a definition of freedom of the will which transcends rather than denies the logic of naturalism.

Such a notion of truth, however, is so relative that it
becomes nearly synonymous with "myth," as Warren has consistently used the word, and presages his later large affinities
with the philosophy of William James. A myth is simply a version of reality, a construct by which the confusing welter of
experience is reduced to order and significance. Warren, like
James, seems to posit a "pluralistic" universe where no construct, however complex, is ever adequate to contain *all* of
experience. Therefore, knowledge, in the sense of a self-
orienting and meaning-giving myth, is difficult to obtain and
precarious once found. Munn, for instance, "finds himself,"
in the popular meaning of the phrase, as a bold leader of guer-
rilla raiders. But his certainty about what their struggle
against the tobacco companies has meant disintegrates in collision with other people's certainties concerning the same
events:

The truths of the others, they were not his own, which
was, if any one thing seizable and namable, that reeling

moment of certainty and fulfillment when the air had
swollen ripely with the blast. But that had gone. Like
the blink of an eye; and would not come back. Even that
self he had been had slipped from him, and could only be
glimpsed now, paling and reproachful, in fits as when the
breeze worries a rising mist.

The truths of these people [who testified at Doctor
MacDonald's trial] were not the truth that had been his
that night; but that truth was his no longer. The truth:
it devoured and blotted out each particular truth, each
individual man's truth, it crushed truths as under a blun-
dering tread, it was blind. (365)

One of the largest obstacles, then, to a straight naturalistic interpretation of the novel is the implied relativism
and tentativeness of truth which is apparent throughout. No
simple or single version of events seems adequate to account
for them. Scientific determinism, the very notion of cause
and effect, is (as Ransom had argued in *God Without Thunder*)
no more founded upon demonstrable premises than Christianity
is. Hence (in the words of William James), "...why in the
name of common sense need we assume that only one such system
of ideas can be true? The obvious outcome of our total experience is that the world can be handled according to many
systems of ideas...."[7] The nature of things appears to be
inherently mysterious and elusive, and man's fate is therefore
to act in the darkness of uncertainty.

II

In *Night Rider,* the issue of naturalism obviously flows
into the problem of defining the self, of discovering some
entity capable of willing or of being acted upon by mechanistic forces. Controversy over the novel has centered from the
first on Warren's characterization of Munn, but usually on
other grounds. Most critics have judged Munn inadequate as
a center of consciousness for the novel.[8] It seems clear, however, that the obvious and severe limitations of Munn's awareness, rather than being the result of a defect in Warren's
skill, are the point of the novel.[9] One may as well condemn
Melville for the moral obtuseness of Amasa Delano as charge
Warren with Munn's insufficiencies. The characterization of
Perse Munn is a brilliant device which involves the reader in
a direct perception of that incongruity between intention and
act, intellect and feeling, self and world, which so bewilders
Munn. The reader's close-up view of Munn's disintegration is
further calculated to dispel any predisposition toward a simplistic determinism or facile assignment of causes or motives
in his decline, and should dissuade most readers from the view
that the world is unitary and knowable.

Munn is indisputably an enigma, but he is an enigma to
himself as well as to the reader, so the sources of his puzzle-

ment are thematically significant. The narrative voice is
limited, except in three or four instances, to a perspective
approximately identical with Munn's, and those limitations
seem expressly intended to convey the boundaries of Munn's
vision. Munn, for instance, does not see very far into his
own motives, and in nearly every case where he engages in baffled introspection, the narrative forces the reader to confront the same invisible barriers which encompass the protagonist. Through such means, the gradual crumbling of Munn's
sense of identity is perceived directly by the reader, who is
allowed, as it were, to participate in the very process of his
disintegration.

In the first few scenes of *Night Rider,* Munn is established as a seemingly trustworthy center of consciousness and
a ready object for the reader's sympathy. Warren then proceeds to undermine that too readily granted confidence until,
by the end of the novel, the reader is largely alienated from
what Munn has become.[10] Precisely as alienated, in fact, as
Munn is from himself. It is interesting to note that from the
perspectives of most of the other characters in the novel —
from the crowds at Bardsville to intimate acquaintances such
as Benton Todd, Willie Proudfit, and Lucille Christian — Munn
seems an admirable, self-assured man. During the crisis in
his community, he is selected as a leader almost as a matter
of course. And it must be said in his behalf that he acts his
part credibly.

The point is, however, that Munn's public behavior is a
part which he acts, an unconscious role which both his community and he take for granted. Munn is the very figure of the
Southern gentleman, and Warren manages to convey Munn's sense
of his role very adroitly. He displays a dignified reserve in
speech and carriage, pays chivalrous court to the ladies, and
is deferential to all. He takes with commendable seriousness
the obligations which his talent and social position confer
upon him; he saves a poor man from the gallows out of his own
conviction of the man's innocence, and he refuses payment for
his services. Outwardly, Munn represents his culture's version of the decent, enlightened gentleman.

Perse Munn is not the kind of man to engage frequently in
deep soul-searching or introspection, but that, too, is part
of his self-image as Southern gentleman. Munn's unexamined
assumptions about his social identity unconsciously modify his
every gesture and attitude. The furniture of his life, and
even his wife May, seem selected according to the exacting
specifications of that identity. In his public appearances,
such as the raid on Bardsville, one can almost sense the way
Munn sits a horse and hear his easy tone of command. The narrative voice also reminds us of his ideal of himself through
its insistent reasonableness and gentility. Both the imper-
turbable reserve of that narrative voice and the consistent
use of the appellation "Mr." before masculine proper names are

echoes of Munn's own habits of address, and they suggest further how far he is imprisoned in a superficial public identity. Because he has no language — and no concepts, apparently
— adequate to his inner life, Munn seems intolerably passive
and emotionless. It is not that Munn lacks passions, but that
he lacks a way to acknowledge and deal with them.

Where he differs dramatically from Mr. Hardin of Warren's
earlier "Prime Leaf," whose self-image somewhat resembles
Munn's, is in his lack of that solid "moral certainty of self"
that Henry Adams attributed to the Southerner of his own day.
Why Munn's image of himself and his traditional role fail
to provide him with a comprehensive mode of feeling and with
values for dealing effectively with the world is left for the
reader to infer. While he seems to embody important agrarian
virtues and is the product of an agrarian culture, Munn is
not immune to nihilistic doubt; he succumbs as easily as the
Buchan family in Tate's *The Fathers* to the forces of cultural
change and upheaval. His social role and myth of himself become, under stress, a suffocating mask which distorts his
vision and disguises him from himself.

The depth of Munn's uncertainty is usually concealed by
his habitual reticence and manifests itself only indirectly.
He is not one to agonize or indulge in displays of emotion.
But his actions speak eloquently of his problems. He is continually drawn, for instance, to figures like Captain Todd and
Senator Tolliver and Lucille Christian, to whom he attributes
a strength and self-assurance he lacks. Ironically, the inner
certainty of each of these characters proves to be as fragile
as his own. Late in his life — too late for the knowledge to
be of benefit — Munn learns that Lucille Christian had sought
in him that same elusive assurance which he had supposed existed in her. All the characters in the novel, with the possible exception of Willie Proudfit, seem to suffer the same
insecurities.

Munn's desperate desire for certainty is also manifested
in his compulsion to explain himself. The frequent need which
Munn feels to discover the exact equivalent in language for
some event in his experience is analogous to Warren's notion
of the artist's task of rendering the world. To discover a
language adequate to convey one's experience is to discover
the meaning of that experience and to reduce it to coherence.
But Munn finds in the constant disparity between word and
event that same mysterious gap between conception and act
which confronts him elsewhere. The "definition" of things
on a page, he finds, is inevitably different from the things
themselves (173). And that difference produces in him a despairing lack of conviction in any construct or definition of
reality. The significance of what he does escapes him because
the world eludes the categories he imposes upon it. There is
no "word," he discovers, for any of it (312). "It did not
matter what name a man gave it" (149), his constructs do not

stick. As a result, his power to order or mythicize his experience fails, until he can "connect nothing with nothing."

The seriousness of Munn's disorientation is at first disguised by the apparent normality of the doubts that plague
him. His commitment to his work in the association seems
phony to him; he discovers he does not really know his wife.
But his reactions are always in excess of their proximate
causes, and the ordinary actions he performs begin to grow detached from his sense of the actual. He inflicts small cruel-
ties upon his wife in order, it would seem, to exhort from her
some glimpse of what she really is and therefore what *he* really is. Unconsciously, he is thrashing about for some solid
and tangible contact with a world which is becoming ever more
chimerical to him: "He tried to imagine her lying there, her
posture, the expression on her face, remote and rapt, but
could not. The image would not stick in his mind. It would
flicker and be gone. But the almost inaudible breathing, that
was steady, was real, was everything. Anonymous, nameless in
the dark, it was the focus of the dark. There was nothing
else" (109). In spite of his efforts, she seems progressively
to withdraw from him, "fading, almost imperceptibly but surely,
into an impersonal and ambiguous distance" (124). Later, the
newspaper accounts which he reads of the acts of terrorism he
himself has committed seem to possess the "same unreality, the
same lack of conviction," as if they described "something in
which he had had no part,...something that had happened a very
long time before" (173). In trying to reduce his affair with
Lucille Christian to some comprehensible category by asking
her to marry him, Munn is described as being "like the man who
tries to find in the flux and confusion of data some point of
reference, no matter how arbitrary, some hypothesis, on which
he can base his calculations" (251).

As Munn becomes detached from his own emotions, the language of the narrative becomes progressively detached and impersonal. There are provoking silences at crucial occasions
in which both the reader and Munn are puzzled at Munn's inability to feel anything. The continuing uncertainties which nag
Munn, his odd tendency to perform acts he has just decided not
to perform, and his moments of inexplicable elation or depression, all signal a deepening malaise.

The increasing separation of Munn's knowledge of facts
from his emotional response to those facts culminates appropriately in his midnight execution of Bunk Trevelyan, the man
whom Munn had previously saved from hanging. Munn's complete
emotional dissociation from the act is rendered by the insidious calm of the narrative: "he felt removed, even now, from
the present experience, as though it were a memory" (191).
But on his way home, he suddenly and unexpectedly vomits, as
if some submerged part of him had recoiled violently from the
deed. When he arrives home, Munn completes his repudiation
and desecration of everything he had previously felt himself

to be and to stand for. In a scene which is described with
a strange, dispassionate objectivity, Munn brutally rapes his
uncomprehending wife. It is but a short and inevitable step
from this psychological state to the nihilistic lethargy to
which he succumbs while hiding at Proudfit's farm. By then,
whatever threads of continuity had existed among the confused
and disparate elements of his being are irreparably snapped;
the "seed of the future" has died in him, and he is numb to
both the past and the future, able to exist imaginatively only
in the present moment (385). Toward the end Munn is startled
by the unrecognizable face that stares at him from the mirror.

Munn's difficulty in sustaining his conviction of his own
identity seems to imply the ultimate inadequacy of all such
"myths," whether of self or of the world. The novel is thus
not merely a depiction of the quest for "self-knowledge" that
it is usually taken to be, but a depiction of the illusory and
partial nature of all knowledge. The novel examines systemat-
ically the consequences of a loss of conviction in one's unconscious sense of self and all the unspoken, unexamined assumptions about the world which proceed from it. Toward the end,
Munn cannot maintain the simplest connection among things in
his mind: "the past..., which once seemed to have its meanings
and its patterns, began to fall apart, act by act, incident by
incident, thought by thought, each item into brutish separateness" (390). By the time he has his last interview with Lucille Christian, Munn can scarcely attend to the sense of what
is being said; the incoherent sound of insects buzzing nearby
rises instead to dominate his consciousness: "That dry rasping
sound from the insects in the dark trees yonder, that unpat-
terned, unrelenting sound, drew him, and enveloped him. It
was as though it was in him, finally, in his head, the essence
of his consciousness, reducing whatever word came to him to
that undifferentiated and unmeaning insistence" (431).

Perhaps the best image of Munn's experience lies in his
remembered glimpses in childhood of the world seen through the
lenses of a stereopticon (161). Removed from the viewing apparatus, the stereopticon card's dull, depthless confusion of
images closely resembles the world of Munn's perceptions. He
confronts everywhere the same blurred, unintelligible patterns
that refuse to focus. The stasis and clarity of the small
world within the stereopticon, however, provide (like the figures on Keats's Grecian Urn) a perfect image of the elusive
certainty which is denied Munn, and an emblem of his obsession
for permanance and meaning. It adumbrates also the half-
understood motives behind his every violent collision with the
world, all of which are attempts to clarify his experience.
Nearly the last act of his life, his abortive attempt to murder Senator Tolliver, is a final effort to make the meaningless pieces of his life fall together, to *force* them into
coherence with a single blow.

Munn's chief motive throughout the novel is the relatively

modest hope of understanding what his life is about; it is the mainspring even of his atrocities.[11] In this, and in his "restless appetite for definition," Munn is most typically human, most like ourselves, and like our conventional heroes. But everything Munn tries to grasp eludes him; for all his pain and effort, knowledge is not ultimately his. The naturalistic view of events at which he arrives late in the book clearly contributes to his problems rather than provides a solution. At best, naturalism can offer only an over-simplified model of Munn's actual experience; in fact, such a view leaves Munn himself and all his efforts to find moral vindication unaccounted for. Although he justifiably repudiates his early, unexamined sense of self, his subsequent behavior, his disintegration and death, all imply the impossibility of living "naturalistically" without some such self-concept. To take the straight look at Nothing, at the abyss undisguised by our myths of order, is fatal. There is thus, finally, a pragmatic inadequacy in naturalism; it offers Munn nothing he can use, nothing he can live by.

1. See Warren's "Introduction" to *All the King's Men* (New York: Modern Library, 1953), p. vi.

2. John Crowe Ransom, *God Without Thunder: An Unorthodox Defense of Orthodoxy* (1930; reprint Hamden, Conn.: Archon Books, 1965), p. 27. It is difficult to find an important early essay by John Crowe Ransom which is not visibly influenced by his hostility toward an overly narrow scientific world view. Both Warren and Tate frequently echoed his preoccupation with "scientism."

3. *All the King's Men*, p. 329.

4. *Night Rider* (1939; reprint New York: Random House, 1958), p. 1. I have used this recent and readily available edition of the novel throughout my discussion and shall refer to it hereafter by page numbers in the body of the text.

5. Warren's comments on a line from *Nostromo* in "'The Great Mirage': Conrad and *Nostromo*," *Selected Essays* (New York: Random House, 1958), p. 53.

6. Leonard Casper, *Robert Penn Warren: The Dark and Bloody Ground* (1960; reprint New York: Greenwood Press, 1969), p. 104.

7. William James, *The Varieties of Religious Experience: A Study in Human Nature,* intro. by Reinhold Niebuhr (New York: Collier Books, 1961), p. 110.

8. The following is a representative selection of comments critical of Munn's character. Taken collectively, they illustrate what is probably the "majority view" on the novel: "Perse Munn himself is at times too blurred as an individual, too cloudy as a reflector," Herbert J. Muller, "Violence upon the Roads," *Kenyon Review*, 1 (Summer 1939), 324; "...[Munn's motives are] not worked out with sufficient force or clarity; one observes Munn, as it were, under all sorts of tests of character without feeling one really knows him," unsigned review, *London Times Literary Supplement* (January 20, 1940), 29; "The man whom [Warren] has chosen for the role of Brutus is surely as unheroic a choice as could have been made. He is always presented under the colorless appelation of 'Mr. Munn,' and that vague phrase is al-

most our only impression of him, since it is a long time before we
are permitted to visualize him, and we never get into his mind," Basil
Davenport, "The Tobacco War," *Saturday Review,* 19 (March 18, 1939), 6;
"Mr. Warren has failed in his presentation of his chief character.
Perse Munn is conceived as a figure of tremendous significance: he is
the noble liberal gone astray in a world of power politics. Maneu-
vered by the logic of events from his democratic platform, he tries
to use Force, and Force uses him. Such a man must be very vividly and
subtly described by his creator — from the inside as well as from the
out. He must be an individual, not a mere type. Perse Munn, as I see
him, is the weakest character in this book," Christopher Isherwood,
"Tragic Liberal," *New Republic,* 99 (May 31, 1939), 108; "Mr. Munn
fails as a protagonist because of his essential emptiness. He moves
without direction; he is not guided by any deeply felt code. Old Man
Hardin's detachment provides a source of strength for him; Mr. Munn's
remoteness is a representation of his weakness. In *Night Rider* Warren
does not seem truly engaged by his protagonist, but for thematic reasons tries to remain at a distance and see him as the anonymous hollow
man of our time. Although we see individual actions with great clarity, there is an overall pervasive unreality to the novel. Munn is
the incomplete man who must draw his strength from others; yet we have
only the assumption, rather than a demonstration of why he is as he
is, spectral and divided," Allen Shepherd, "Robert Penn Warren's
'Prime Leaf' as Prototype of *Night Rider,"* *Studies in Short Fiction,*
7 (Summer 1970), 471; "In *Night Rider* there is a sense of blind hope-
lessness, of futile struggle. Although Perse's destruction stimulates
something of pity and terror, the novel falls short of being tragedy
because the nobility of the character and the 'human effort' is insufficiently realized," Roma A. King, Jr., "Time and Structure in the
Early Novels of Robert Penn Warren," *South Atlantic Quarterly,* 56
(Oct. 1957), 492. Leonard Casper's indictment is perhaps most revealing: "*Night Rider* can tell only half its story from the point of view
Mr. Warren has chosen.... Furthermore, because Mr. Munn's sensibility
is obscured, he can give the reader only an experience of evil; he
cannot direct one's insights into its innermost causes." *Robert Penn
Warren,* p. 106.

    9. My own views are an attempt to synthesize the insights of sev-
eral earlier commentators, including the following: "In a numb, awkward fashion...[Munn] attempts to arrest the loss of inner continuity.
He tries to fathom the ambiguous connections between things done and
things remembered, between the present self and the vanishing and
perhaps contrary selves of the past.... His sense of identity cannot
withstand the shock of his experience.... Despite this uncertainty,
Munn is wholly convincing...." Phillip Rahv, review of *Night Rider*
in *Partisan Review,* 6 (Spring 1939), 106-13; "Percy Munn remains empty
and unknowable even to himself, not because the writer is incompetent."
John Lewis Longley, Jr., "Robert Penn Warren: The Deeper Rub," *Southern Review,* n.s. 1 (Autumn 1965), 973; "Percy Munn is the divided man
turned outward, into the objective world of action and organization,
where he loses his subjective existence entirely in an effort to correct its flaws," Irene Hendry, "The Regional Novel: The Example of
Robert Penn Warren," *Sewanee Review,* 53 (Jan.-Mar. 1945), 97; "...War-
ren's detachment from his hero is clearly evident, notably in his
habit of referring to him throughout the novel as Mr. Munn. Because
Munn does defy central definition, his remoteness from the reader is
the significant thing about him. He is equally remote from himself
and from his world.... But since we can see the story from his point

of view, we must infer this hollowness from the complex of situations
and relationships which constitutes the structure of the novel,"
Charles H. Bohner, *Robert Penn Warren* (New Haven, Conn.: College and
University Press, 1964), p. 70.

10. Oscar Cargill, in his essay "Anatomist of Monsters," *College
English,* 9 (October 1947), 3, discusses the same point. Warren, he
asserts, "does an extraordinarily subtle and ingenious thing in turning the reasonable Mr. Munn into a zealot. So cunningly is the change
managed that it is a well-established fact before the reader is aware
it has taken place.... We spare Perse Munn because already our sympathies are enlisted on his side in the struggle to make the association
work.... It is only in retrospect, when we revert to Munn's murder at
a quarry edge of a man whom he had once saved from the gallows that we
exclaim that he who did this thing is mad or close to being mad. Even
here there are extenuating circumstances.... It is only later that we
see that all the extenuating things are the author's dodge to adum-
brate Mr. Munn's drift toward the kind of mania which possesses the
fanatic.... Never was character change more adroitly managed in a
novel." Immediately following this statement, however, Cargill apparently rejects his own insights, complains that the "story goes all to
pieces," and blames the failure upon the inadequacy of the characterization of Munn: "It is plain from the outset that Warren does not wish
to move us to compassion for Mr. Munn — he keeps him aloof by the constant use of 'Mr.' (Munn even thinks of himself as 'Mr. Munn'). Yet
his cause is presented to elicit reader sympathy" (pp. 3-4).

11. Warren, in a comment on Conrad's *Lord Jim,* has characterized
the apparently purposeless and savage massacre perpetrated by Brown in
that novel in terms applicable to the behavior of Perse Munn in *Night
Rider:* "Even in the act seemingly most brutal and gratuitous, Brown
has, somehow, in a last distortion, affirmed himself as human, not
brute, has affirmed, paradoxically, the human need for moral vindication." From a speech delivered at the conference on the Unity of
Knowledge during the bicentennial celebration of Columbia University
in 1954; first published in *Sewanee Review,* 63 (Apr.-June 1955), 182-
92; reprinted in John Lewis Longley, Jr., ed., *Robert Penn Warren: A
Collection of Critical Essays* (New York: New York Univ. Press, 1965),
p. 243.

Robert Penn Warren

All the King's Men:
The Matrix of Experience

When I am asked how much *All the King's Men* owes to the
actual politics of Louisiana in the '30's, I can only be sure
that if I had never gone to live in Louisiana and if Huey Long
had not existed, the novel would never have been written. But
this is far from saying that my "state" in *All the King's Men*
is Louisiana (or any of the other forty-nine stars in our
flag), or that my Willie Stark is the late Senator. What Louisiana and Senator Long gave me was a line of thinking and
feeling that did eventuate in the novel.

In the summer of 1934 I was offered a job — a much-needed
job — as Assistant Professor at the Louisiana State University,
in Baton Rouge. It was "Huey Long's University," and definitely on the make — with a sensational football team and with
money to spend even for assistant professors at a time when
assistant professors were being fired, not hired — as I knew
all too well. It was Huey's University, but he, I was assured,
would never mess with my classroom. That was to prove true;
he was far too adept in the arts of power to care what an assistant professor might have to say. The only time that his
presence was ever felt in my classroom was when, in my Shakespeare course, I gave my little annual lecture on the political background of *Julius Caesar;* and then, for the two weeks
we spent on the play, backs grew straighter, eyes grew bright-
er, notes were taken, and the girls stopped knitting in class,
or repairing their faces.

In September 1934 I left Tennessee, where I had been living on a farm near Nashville, drove down across Mississippi,
crossed the river by ferry (where I can't be sure — was it at
Greenville?) and was in North Louisiana. Along the way I
picked up a hitchhiker — a country man, the kind you call a
red-neck or a wool-hat, aging, aimless, nondescript, beat up
by life and hard times and bad luck, clearly tooth-broke and
probably gut-shot, standing beside the road in an attitude

that spoke of infinite patience and considerable fortitude, holding a parcel in his hand, wrapped in old newspaper and tied with binder twine, waiting for some car to come along. He was, though at the moment I did not sense it, a mythological figure.

He was the god on the battlement, dimly perceived above the darkling tumult and the steaming carnage of the political struggle. He was a voice, a portent, and a natural force like the Mississippi River getting set to bust a levee. Long before the Fascist March on Rome, Norman Douglas, meditating on Naples, had predicted that the fetid slums of Europe would make possible the "inspired idiot." His predictive diagnosis of the origins of fascism — and of communism — may be incomplete, but it is certain that the rutted back roads and slabside shacks that had spawned my nameless old hitchhiker, with the twine-tied paper parcel in his hand, had, by that fall of 1934, made possible the rise of "Huey." My nameless hitchhiker was, mythologically speaking, Long's *sine qua non.*

So it was appropriate that he should tell me the first episode of the many I had to hear of the myth that was "Huey." The roads, he said, was shore better now. A man could git to market, he said. A man could jist git up and git, if'n a notion come on him. Did'n have to pay no toll at no toll bridge neither. Fer Huey was a free-bridge man. So he went on and told me how, standing on the river bank by a toll bridge (by what river and what bridge was never clear), Huey had made the president of the company that owned the bridge a good, fair cash offer, and the man laughed at him. But, the old hitchhiker said, Huey did'n do nothing but lean over and pick him up a chunk of rock and throwed it off a-ways, and asked did that president-feller see whar the rock hit. The feller said yeah, he seen. Wal, Huey said, the next thing you see is gonna be a big new free bridge right whar that rock hit, and you, you son-of-a-bitch, are goen bankrupt a-ready and doan even know it.

There were a thousand tales, over the years, and some of them were, no doubt, literally and factually true. But they were all true in the world of "Huey" — that world of myth, folklore, poetry, deprivation, rancor, and dimly envisaged hopes. That world had a strange, shifting, often ironical and sometimes irrelevant relation to the factual world of Senator Huey P. Long and his cold manipulation of the calculus of power. The two worlds, we may hazard, merged only at the moment when in September 1935, in the corridor of the Capitol, the little .32 slug bit meanly into the senatorial vitals.

There was another world — this a factual world — made possible by the factual Long, though not inhabited by him. It was a world that I, as an assistant professor, was to catch fleeting glimpses of, and ponder. It was the world of the parasites of power, a world that Long was, apparently, contemptuous of, but knew how to use, as he knew how to use other

things of which he was, perhaps, contemptuous. This was a
world of a sick yearning for elegance and the sight of one's
name on the society page of a New Orleans paper; it was the
world of the electric moon devised, it was alleged, to cast
a romantic glow over the garden when the President of the University and his wife entertained their politicos and pseudo-
socialites; it was a world of pretentiousness, of bloodcur-
dling struggles for academic preferment, of drool-jawed grab
and arrogant criminality. It was a world all too suggestive,
in its small-bore, provincial way, of the airs and aspirations
that the newspapers attributed to that ex-champagne salesman
Von Ribbentrop and to the inner circle of Edda Ciano's friends.

For in Louisiana, in the 1930's, you felt somehow that you
were living in the great world, or at least in a microcosm
with all the forces and fatalities faithfully, if sometimes
comically, drawn to scale. And the little Baton Rouge world
of campus and Governor's Mansion and Capitol and the gold bathroom fixtures reported to be in the house of the University
contractor was, once the weight of Long's contempt and political savvy had been removed by the bullet of the young Brutus
in the Capitol, to plunge idiotically rampant to an end almost
as dramatic as the scenes in the last bunkers of Berlin or at
the filling station on the outskirts of Milan. The headlines
advertised the suicides, and the population of penitentiaries,
both Federal and state, received some distinguished additions.

But this is getting ahead of the story. Meanwhile, there
was, besides the lurid worlds, the world of ordinary life to
look at. There were the people who ran stores or sold insurance or had a farm and tried to survive and pay their debts.
There were — visible even from the new concrete speedway that
Huey had slashed through the cypress swamps toward New Orleans
— the palmetto-leaf and sheet-iron hovels of the moss pickers,
rising like some fungoid growth from a hummock under the great
cypress knees, surrounded by scum-green water that never felt
sunlight, back in that Freudianly contorted cypress gloom of
cottonmouth moccasins big as the biceps of a prize-fighter,
and owl calls, and the murderous metallic grind of insect life,
and the smudge fire at the hovel door, that door being nothing
but a hole in a hovel wall, with a piece of croker sack hung
over it. There were, a few miles off at the University, your
colleagues, some as torpid as a gorged alligator in the cold
mud of January and some avid to lick the spit of an indifferent or corrupt administration, but many able and gifted and
fired by a will to create, out of the seething stew and heav-
ing magma, a distinguished university.

And there were, of course, the students, like students anywhere in the country in the big state universities, except for
the extraordinary number of pretty girls and the preternatural
blankness of the gladiators who were housed beneath the sta-
dium to have their reflexes honed, their diet supervised, and
— through the efforts of tutors — their heads crammed with

just enough of whatever mash was required (I never found out)
to get them past their minimal examinations. Among the students there sometimes appeared, too, that awkward boy from
the depth of the 'Cajun country or from some scrabble-farm in
North Louisiana, with burning ambition and frightening energy
and a thirst for learning; and his presence there, you reminded yourself, with whatever complication of irony seemed
necessary at the moment, was due to Huey, and to Huey alone.
For the "better element" had done next to nothing in fifty
years to get that boy out of the grim despair of his ignorance.

Yes, there was the world of the "good families," most of
whom hated Huey Long — except, of course, for that percentage
who, for one reason or another, had reached an accommodation.
They hated him sometimes for good reasons and sometimes for
bad, and sometimes for no reason at all, as a mere revulsion
of taste; but they never seemed to reflect on what I took to
be the obvious fact that if the government of the state had
not previously been marked by various combinations of sloth,
complacency, incompetence, corruption, and a profound lack of
political imagination, there would never have been a Senator
Huey P. Long, and my old hitchhiker by the roadside would, in
September 1934, have had no tale to tell me.

Conversation in Louisiana always came back to the tales,
to the myth, to politics; and to talk politics is to talk
about power. So conversation turned, by implication at least,
on the question of power and ethics, of power and justification, of means and ends, of "historical costs." The big words
were not often used, certainly not by the tellers of tales,
but the concepts lurked even behind the most ungrammatical
folktale. The tales were shot through with philosophy.

The tales were shot through, too, with folk humor, and the
ethical ambiguity of folk humor. And the tales, like the political conversations, were shot through, too, with violence
— or rather, with hints of the possibility of violence. There
was a hint of revolutionary desperation — often synthetically
induced. In Louisiana, in '34 and '35, it took nothing to
start a rumor of violence. There had been, you might hear, a
"battle" at the airport of Baton Rouge. A young filling station operator would proudly display his sawed-off automatic
shotgun — I forget which "side" he was on, but I remember his
fingers caressing the polished walnut of the stock. Or you
might hear that there was going to be a "march" on the Capitol
— but not hear by whom or for what.

Melodrama was the breath of life. There had been melodrama in the life I had known in Tennessee, but with a difference: in Tennessee the melodrama seemed to be different from
the stuff of life, something superimposed upon life, but in
Louisiana people lived melodrama, seemed to live, in fact, for
it, for this strange combination of philosophy, humor, and violence. Life was a tale that you happened to be living — and
that "Huey" happened to be living before your eyes. And all

the while I was reading Elizabethan tragedy, Machiavelli, William James, and American history — and all that I was reading seemed to come alive, in shadowy distortions and sudden clarities, in what I saw around me.

How directly did I try to transpose into fiction Huey P. Long and the tone of that world? The question answers itself in a single fact. The first version of my story was a verse drama; and the actual writing began, in 1938, in the shade of an olive tree by a wheat field near Perugia. In other words, if you are sitting under an olive tree in Umbria and are writing a verse drama, the chances are that you are concerned more with the myth than with the fact, more with the symbolic than with the actual. And so it was. It could not, after all, have been otherwise, for in the strict, literal sense, I had no idea what the now deceased Huey P. Long had been. What I knew was the "Huey" of the myth, and that was what I had taken with me to Mussolini's Italy, where the bully boys wore black shirts and gave a funny salute.

I had no way of knowing what went on in the privacy of the heart of Senator Long. Now I could only hope, ambitiously, to know something of the heart of the Governor Talos of my play *Proud Flesh*. For Talos was the first avatar of my Willie Stark, and the fact that I drew that name from the "iron groom" who, in murderous blankness, serves Justice in Spenser's *Faerie Queen* should indicate something of the line of thought and feeling that led up to that version and persisted, with modulations, into the novel.

Talos was to become Stark, and *Proud Flesh* was to become *All the King's Men*. Many things, some merely technical, led to this transformation, but one may have some bearing on the question of the ratio of fact and fiction. In 1942 I left Louisiana for good, and then in 1943 I began the version that is more realistic, discursive, and documentary in method (though not in spirit) than the play, I was doing so after I had definitely left Louisiana and the world in which the story had its roots. By now the literal, factual world was only a memory, and therefore was ready to be absorbed freely into the act of imagination. Even the old man by the roadside — the hitchhiker I had picked up on the way down to take my job — was ready to enter the story: he became, it would seem, the old hitchhiker whom Jack Burden picks up returning from Long Beach, California, the old man with the twitch in the face that gives Jack the idea for the Great Twitch. But my old hitchhiker had had no twitch in his face. Nor had I been Jack Burden.

I had not been Jack Burden except in so far as you have to try to "be" whatever you are trying to create. And in that sense I was also Adam Stanton, and Willie Stark, and Sadie Burke, and Sugar Boy, and all the rest. And this brings me to my last notion. However important for my novel was the protracted dialectic between "Huey" on the one side, and me on the other, it was far less important, in the end, than that

deeper and darker dialectic for which the images and actions
of a novel are the only language. And however important was
my acquaintance with Louisiana, that was far less important
than my acquaintance with another country: for any novel, good
or bad, must report, willy-nilly, the history, sociology, and
politics of a country even more fantastic than was Louisiana
under the consulship of Huey.

Norton R. Girault

The Narrator's Mind as Symbol:
An Analysis of *All the King's Men*

If we are to judge from many of the reviews, *All the King's Men* is a very difficult novel to "explain" — difficult, it appears, mainly because of the oblique first-person narrator point of view. There have been many comments about the irrelevance of Jack Burden, as if he were a sort of displaced person who had found his way into the novel through the servants' entrance, or an exhibit guide with an annoying habit of stopping in the middle of his discourse upon the exhibit to digress on his domestic problems. Actually the novel is a dramatic monologue on a grand scale, and Jack Burden is as much the protagonist as he is the commentator. But it is apparent that the story has not been read as a product of Jack's mind. Attempts to explain Willie Stark, for example, have often dodged the problem of taking Jack's statements in character; apparently it has been assumed that the reader sees Willie Stark at first hand and not through Jack's sensibility, and that Willie can be understood and interpreted whether Jack is or not. Such an assumption is enough to cause serious misreading, because out of the first-person narrator point of view grows an important aspect of the novel's theme — that an understanding of the world depends upon an understanding of the self: Jack Burden cannot understand Willie Stark until Jack understands himself. (There is a question, of course, as to whether Jack ever fully understands either himself or Willie Stark.) We can get at an understanding of Robert Penn Warren's interpretation of the Boss only through a perception of the way in which the Boss's story was experienced by Warren's first-person narrator.

I

Jack's story is so intimately related to Willie's that, as the narrative develops, their stories are told simultaneously.

But phrases along the way like "at least that was the way I argued the case back then" remind the reader of the fact that Jack has lived through the actions he is describing and that he is trying to reorient himself in relation to them. It becomes more and more apparent as the story develops that Jack is telling it as a means of defining to himself what actually did happen to him: the manner in which he reconstructs the story gives the reader an insight into the nature of Jack's experience. For example, the fact that Jack withholds his father's identity until he learns that Judge Irwin has killed himself implies that he wants the discovery of the truth about his paternity to make the same shocking impact upon the reader that it made upon him; it is his way of dramatizing his reaction to the discovery. And when he attempts to describe subjective reactions to events that are past, the metaphors he uses provide the reader with an insight into why Jack Burden is an appropriate first-person narrator. A study of those metaphors indicates that they support a basic symbolism of rebirth that runs through the novel and unifies it, and after our participation in the total experience of *All the King's Men,* we realize that it is because Jack has been reborn, though not of woman (in a sense defined by the symbolism), that he is qualified to tell us what happened to Willie Stark.

The symbolic event that brings the rebirth symbolism into focus is Jack's being awakened in the middle of the night by his mother's screams. It is a "bright, beautiful, silvery soprano scream" that awakens him, and his mother, hysterical, accuses him of having killed his father. The accusation comes as the sudden revelation of the truth about his paternity: Judge Irwin, not the Scholarly Attorney, suddenly becomes his father. Jack has, as his mother charges, killed his father (his attempt to blackmail the judge for the Boss results in the judge's suicide); but he has also created a father, for it requires the violence of the suicide to wring from his mother, out of her love for Judge Irwin, the long suppressed information which gives Jack self-definition. The scream signalizes Jack's rebirth (symbolically, it is a scream of labor pain) in that it gives him a new mother and a new father, both of whom he can accept. It disintegrates his conception of his mother as a woman motivated by vanity and cupidity ("for years I had condemned her as a woman without heart"), because it reveals to him his mother's capacity for love; and it disintegrates his conception of his father as the weak, pious Scholarly Attorney, for in Judge Irwin Jack gains a father he can accept. The scream seems to release something in him, to allow him to see the world for the first time. It allows him to understand Willie Stark, but why it does Jack cannot say. He simply knows that his knowledge of the Boss and of himself grew, finally, out of the scream, that it marked the climax of his story.

Jack's story builds toward his mother's scream in terms of

his struggle to resist rebirth. At the beginning of the novel,
he sees the Boss's eyes bulge as he begins a political speech
and feels the "clammy, sad little foetus" which is himself,
huddled away up inside himself, cringing away from "the cold
hand in the cold rubber glove" reaching down to pull him out
into the cold. Jack feels that he is on the brink of a discovery about the Boss, but subconsciously he seeks the cozi-
ness of "not-knowing." His hesitation in his love affair with
Anne Stanton results, in part, from the same sort of recoil
from knowledge. And his dive and underwater embrace with her
are an attempt to submerge himself along with Anne in a cozy
womb-state of "not-knowing." (The medium will not retain them,
of course, and they burst forth into their separateness.) Finally, this subconscious shrinking from a particular kind of
knowledge becomes on Jack's part an attempt to repudiate his
sensibility, an attempt begun as a result of his frustration
in his love affair with Anne and of his dissatisfaction with
his past (as symbolized by his parents). On the verge of the
sexual act with Anne, he had sensed that to "know" Anne he
would have to violate his image of her; he hesitates long
enough to disrupt their love affair.

What Jack is searching for is a womb-state of innocence in
nature in which his image of Anne will be preserved. And this
search becomes a dominant motif leading up to his expulsion
from the womb when he unwittingly causes the death of his
father. Just before his discovery that Anne has become the
Boss's mistress, he sits in his office and envies the jaybird
perched in the tree outside his window: "I could look down and
think of myself inside that hollow chamber, in the aqueous
green light, inside the great globe of the tree, and not even
a jaybird there with me now, for he had gone, and no chance of
seeing anything beyond the green leaves, they were so thick,
and no sound except, way off, the faint mumble of traffic,
like the ocean chewing its gums" (p.281). The associations
with Jack's underwater dive with Anne are significant. Then,
when this reverie is interrupted by his discovery of Anne's
"infidelity" (of the Boss's violation of the image), Jack
flees to California in an attempt to "drown himself in West."
In all these struggles to lose himself in nature, there is a
paradoxical struggle toward rebirth: the greater the struggle
to resist rebirth, the greater the counter-struggle toward
rebirth, as if Jack's nature, unformed, were enveloped by the
womb of total nature, which reacts convulsively to reject him.
Through his attempts to lose himself in nature, Jack is actually struggling, without realizing it, toward a discovery of
his separateness in nature.

The significance of Jack's struggle to resist rebirth may
be stated in these terms: Jack shrinks from the discovery of
evil, of the taint in nature, of imperfection in the scheme of
things. He has seen ugliness and imperfection and, with a cynical smugness, acknowledges their presence in nature, but he

does not want to discover evil in himself. Subconsciously, he
shrinks from the terrible knowledge that he is capable of good
and evil, but until he is reborn through a revelation of the
guilt he shares with humanity, he is not fully man, but rather
embryonic and amoral. This aspect of the symbol's meaning is
pointed up by a conversation Jack has with Lucy Stark about
her son Tom's alleged fatherhood of an unborn child (it is significant in terms of the novel's structure that this conversation occurs just before Jack's rebirth):

> "It's just a baby," she almost whispered. "It's just a
> little baby. It's just a little baby in the dark. It's
> not even born yet, and it doesn't know what's happened.
> About money and politics and somebody wanting to be sena-
> tor. It doesn't know about anything — about how it came
> to be — about what that girl did — or why — or why the fa-
> ther — why he —" She stopped, and the large brown eyes
> kept looking at me with appeal and what might have been
> accusation. Then she said, "Oh, Jack, it's a little baby,
> and nothing's its fault."
>   I almost burst out that it wasn't my fault, either,
> but I didn't. (p.356)

The irony, once the symbolism is understood, is obvious. The
state of innocence Lucy has described is what Jack has been
trying to discover in his attempts to drown himself in nature.
He has been trying to hide in the dark where nothing will be
his fault.

Fourteen pages later (about a week has passed), Jack is
awakened by his mother's scream, and is shocked into the revelation that it has been his fault that his father has committed suicide. "At the moment," Jack says, "the finding out
simply numbed me." On a literal level, he is referring to his
discovery that Judge Irwin is his father. But, symbolically,
what numbs him is the disintegration of his whole conception
of himself. He has been sick with "the terrible division" of
his age. His sensibility dissociated by his repeated attempts
to escape into a womb-state of innocence, he has been living
in a world out of time and divorced from experience, a world
in which his actions have been neither good nor evil, but
meaningless. Then suddenly, in one shocking experience, this
illusory world is shattered, and he cannot define himself in
relation to the new world (in which Judge Irwin is his father
and a woman capable of love is his mother). When Jack's revelation of the truth about his paternity is taken along with
all the examples in the novel of attempts to change various
characters' conceptions of the world, it can be seen that his
revelation is a commentary upon these other attempts to cure
modern man of the sickness of his age. Jack himself, as the
Boss's private detective, has tried to change other men's pictures of the world. He has tried to change Adam's by giving
him "a history lesson"; and, ironically, he has caused his

father's death by trying to change Judge Irwin's convictions about Willie Stark. Finally, in Adam Stanton's operation on the brain of the man suffering from catatonic schizophrenia, we have the attempt through surgery to change the picture of the world man carries around in his head; after the operation, Jack tells Adam, "Well, you forgot to baptize him — for he is born again and not of woman," and, ironically, baptizes the patient in the name of the Great Twitch, symbol of one of Jack's attempts to submerge himself in nature. (Again, it is significant that this operation occurs before Jack's rebirth; Jack's wisecrack foreshadows the event and he does not realize the symbolic meaning it supports.) In one sense then, the whole novel depicts men "incomplete with the terrible division of their age," suffering from a schizophrenia they do not understand, men whose hope lies not in change from without (through surgery, "history lessons," and the like), but from rebirth from within. And because of the nature of Jack's malady, it is plausible that it should take some time for him to formulate a definition of what has happened to him.

The beginning of his reorientation is his discovery that he is, as his mother charges, guilty of his father's death. He realizes that by killing his father he has created him, and gradually he becomes aware of the fact that all of his detective work for the Boss has been a search for a father to replace the weak, pious fool he believed the Scholarly Attorney to be. The subconscious motive for his becoming the Boss's private detective is his attempt to find a father in Willie Stark, and his fidelity to the Boss is symbolic of his having substituted him for the alleged father with whom he is dissatisfied. But when, in Judge Irwin, Jack gains a father he can accept, he no longer requires the Willie Stark father-symbol; symbolically, the very detective work he has been hired by the Boss to do results in the end in the Boss's own death. In chapter nine, the day after the Judge's funeral, Jack walks into the Boss's office and refuses to do any more detective work for him. He wonders why, in fact, he does not quit the Boss's organization altogether. And, thinking of the Scholarly Attorney and Judge Irwin, he says, "True, since I had lost both fathers, I felt as though I could float effortlessly away like a balloon when the last cord is cut." But Jack has lost not two but three fathers — the Scholarly Attorney, the judge, and, though he does not realize it, the Boss — so, still numb from the disintegration of the conception of his father, he is unable to quit the Boss's machine.

Jack remains to discover, after the Boss's assassination, that it is he himself who has set the events in motion which culminate in the Boss's own death. After the Boss has died, Jack's independent detective work uncovers the complicity of Sadie Burke and Tiny Duffy (they are as responsible as Adam Stanton for the Boss's murder), but Jack discovers his own complicity too, for he sees that it is his earlier detective work

that has produced the facts which led to the involvement of
Anne and Adam Stanton in Willie Stark's enterprises and which
made Sadie's revenge and Duffy's opportunism possible. But,
ironically, the Boss has hired Jack to produce these facts.
The Boss has engineered his own assassination. Guilt for the
slaying seems to spread throughout the novel among all the
characters. What shocks Jack is the discovery that his crime
(as opposed to those of Sadie Burke, Tiny Duffy and Adam Stanton) is that his actions have been meaningless; the others
have intended to kill the Boss, whereas he has intended to be
the hired research man in search of objective fact, as fault-
less and amoral as Sibyl Frey's unborn baby. This perception
of his spiritual sterility occurs when Jack is unable to go
through with "the perfect duplication of what Duffy had done"
(that is, effect the murder of Duffy by putting the idea in
Sugar-Boy's head); Jack sees that he is as guilty as Duffy,
that his murder of Duffy would, ironically enough, be as
meaningless as Jack's unintended murder of the Boss. Jack is
appalled by this discovery that he has been "caught in a monstrous conspiracy": "I hated everything and everybody and myself and Tiny Duffy and Willie Stark and Adam Stanton... They
all looked alike to me then. And I looked like them" (p.442).

But what saves Jack from this loathing for himself and the
world is another discovery that grows out of his rebirth — the
discovery of his capacity for love. When he learns that his
mother is leaving the Young Executive, the scream is brought
back to him in such a way that he is able to formulate a partial definition of its meaning; it releases him from his disgust with the world: "The first hint was in the wild, silvery
scream which filled the house when the word of Judge Irwin's
death was received. That scream rang in my ears for many
months, but it had faded away, lost in the past and the corruption of the past, by the time she called me back to Burden's
Landing to tell me that she was going to go away. Then I knew
she was telling me the truth. And I felt at peace with her
and with myself" (p.458). His mother's leaving (in that it is
evidence of her love for Judge Irwin) makes him capable of loving her, and of loving the world (as his marriage to Anne indicates).

Jack Burden's reorientation grows out of a combination of
events that begin with Judge Irwin's death. And after he has
seen his friends die and his mother leave the Young Executive,
he can see a justice in the injustice of a nature that man can
never fully know. Like Cass Mastern, Jack has discovered that
man cannot escape guilt, and he has discovered too that it is
only through an acceptance of the evil in his nature that man
can achieve good. He can even say that in his "own way" he is
not certain that he does not believe the theological harangues
of the Scholarly Attorney (symbol, perhaps, of the Christian
tradition in the modern world). Through his rebirth, Jack has
caught sight of the limits, and likewise the potentialities,

of human knowledge. He had lived a long time in terms of a
false conception of his paternity, and, through killing his
father, had discovered his ignorance. He learns that man can
never be sure of his knowledge: one can never fully know one's
father. (There can be a pun in Warren's father-symbolism that
equates man's knowledge of his temporal father with his knowledge of the Heavenly Father.) The only knowledge that Jack
can be sure of is that tragic waste grows out of the limitations of human knowledge; therefore, man must strive constantly for that state *least* wasteful of human good. And so, as
the novel ends, Jack Burden speaks of going into the "convulsion of the world" (the everchanging nature wherein he may be
saved from the illusion of the absolute power of human knowledge) "and the awful responsibility of Time" (man's moral responsibility for the illusion of nature he creates).

II

Jack is qualified to tell Willie Stark's story because it,
too, is a story of rebirth, and, although Jack does not call
it that in so many words, the terms he uses to describe it are
significant. Huddled over his law books, Willie is "in a room,
a world, inside himself where something was swelling and growing painfully and dully and imperceptibly like a great potato
in a dark, damp cellar," and "inside him something would be
big and coiling and slow and clotting till he would hold his
breath and the blood would beat in his head with a hollow
sound as though his head were a cave as big as the dark outside. He wouldn't have any name for what was big inside him.
Maybe there wasn't any name." And, like the knowledge Jack
gains through rebirth, the Boss's knowledge comes to him with
the shock of revelation. When Willie realizes (before he has
become the Boss) that the Harrison machine is using his naive
political idealism to exploit the voters, it is — as Jack puts
it — as if Willie had been on the road to Damascus and had
seen a great light. When he says this of Willie at the time
of Willie's great disillusionment, Jack is not aware of how
apt his allusion is, and even after the years that separate
his telling of the story from the event, he is not certain
what name he should give Willie's "blind, inner compulsion"
("Maybe there wasn't any name."), but through his own rebirth,
Jack gains an insight into the meaning of the Boss's life.

The Boss's story starts with a revelation and ends with a
revelation. At the beginning of his story, it is revealed to
him (through his "luck") that man must run counter to amoral
nature and that man must create human good out of human bad.
(Willie learns this when the crooked politicians in the state
try to "run it over him like he was dirt.") But when Willie
tries to spread the light among his countrymen, when he tries
to awaken them to an awareness of their responsibility as human beings to separate themselves from exploitable nature, he

is frustrated by their failure to understand. They roar their
applause, but they do not see, actually, what is behind the
bulging eyes and the forelock of hair. They are as ready for
Willie to run it over them like they were dirt as they were to
be exploited by the Harrison outfit. Nevertheless, the Boss's
conviction, gained through a sort of revelation, impels him
to persist stubbornly throughout the novel in his attempt to
achieve a political state based on the assumption that men are
all, potentially at least, like himself — capable of seeing
the light. He becomes "the cold hand in the cold rubber glove"
trying to wrest men from their submergence in brute nature.
But in trying to enforce on them from without a knowledge he
gained from within himself, the Boss is trying to usurp the
work of the mysterious principle which brought him his knowledge. It is the same principle which operates through Jack
Burden to cause his rebirth and, finally, through the Boss to
kill him. But in the death of the Boss the knowledge he has
tried to live by is reaffirmed; Willie realizes that what has
killed him is his own failure to believe in the knowledge of
his earlier revelation. So the Boss's story ends with a revelation ("It could have all happened different, Jack"), and the
Boss is reborn in the sense that he regains, on his death-bed,
a conviction in the validity of the knowledge which has made
him the Boss.

　　Whereas Jack Burden's story starts out with his attempts
to submerge himself in nature, the Boss's story begins with
his attempt to separate himself from nature. It is as if he
were trying to prove, by exploiting it as it had never been
exploited before, that the human in nature will finally react
to resist exploitation and prove itself capable of self-realization, just as Willie had reacted when they tried to run it
over him like he was dirt. Throughout his career we have
Nature standing in animal-and-plant-dumb commentary upon the
Boss's actions: the stoic cows standing in the mist along the
highway staring dumbly at the soaring Cadillac, the 'possum
and the moccasin trying to cross the Boss's path only to be
run down and churned thumpingly to death against the underside
of the fender. And the domestic animals are absorbed into the
symbolism: the family dog Buck in the first chapter, whose un-
cooperative carcass is a latent hint of the recalcitrancy of
the unpredictable, uncontrollable, natural factor not only in
animal but in human nature as well (Buck is equated with Old
Man Stark in terms of the politically exploitable in Willie's
past). Also, in many of the images, there is an equating of
Willie's constituency with brute nature: "the gangs of people
who looked at me with the countryman's slow, full, curious
lack of shame, and didn't make room for me to pass until I was
charging them down, the way a cow won't get out of your way until your radiator damn near bats her in the underslung slats."
This is the nature in which Willie Stark seeks affirmation of
the knowledge that isolates him.

Willie's apparently brutal and vindictive treatment of Byram B. White, erring State Auditor, reflects the Boss's grind-
ing, probing attempt to prove to himself that man can detach
himself from brute nature. It is more than a simply graphic
metaphor that we get in Warren's description of Byram's bodily
reaction to the Boss's verbal abuse: Byram draws himself "into
a hunch as though he wanted to assume the prenatal position
and be little and warm and safe in the dark." The Boss is trying to force Byram's rebirth. And when Byram has left, the
Boss tells Jack:

> "I gave him every chance... Every chance. He didn't have
> to say what I told him to say. He didn't have to listen
> to me. He could have just walked out the door and kept
> on walking. He could have just put a date on that resig-
> nation and handed it to me. He could have done a dozen
> things. But did he? Hell, no. Not Byram, and he just
> stands there and his eyes blink right quick like a dog's
> do when he leans up against your leg before you hit him,
> and, by God, you have the feeling if you don't do it you
> won't be doing God's will." (p.142)

The same impulse that makes him vilify Byram in an attempt to
make the man separate himself from nature drives the Boss to
try to talk Adam Stanton into a realization that he can never
detach himself from nature in an absolute sense. Adam and
Byram represent opposite extremes of modern man's condition;
they symbolize attitudes the Boss's revelation has shown him
to be false.

Ironically, what makes the Boss's political success possible is the fact that his countrymen create in him a hero, an
alter ego, and the Boss is unable to get through that alter
ego to them. He wants to show them the light he has seen, to
prove his knowledge (to himself as well as to them) by changing the picture of the world they carry around in their heads.
But his downfall is a result, finally, of his inability to
break down the false conceptions of him held by the various
members of his machine and by his constituency, by his failure,
in other words, to make them understand the principle on which
his actions are based. One of the greatest ironies of the
book is that the Boss thinks that among all his men Jack Burden alone really understands him. When the others have left
them alone, the Boss confides in Jack as if Jack will understand where others have not. But in one sense Jack is simply
a more complicated and highly developed version of Byram B.
White and of the people who make up the Boss's constituency,
who want "the nice warm glow of complacency, the picture that
flattered him and his own fat or thin wife standing in front
of the henhouse."

Willie is a symbol of man's struggle toward integration in
terms of his whole nature. This integration is symbolized by
the successful control and cooperation he maintains in his po-

litical machine. All the Boss's men working in harmony symbolize an integration of a sort within the Boss. Separately,
each is a symbolic correlative for an aspect of the Boss's nature. When the Boss begins to try to operate independently of
any of them, the integration begins to crumble. When he tries
to build his hospital without the cooperation of Tiny Duffy,
he is trying to insist upon the idealistic aspect of his nature at the expense of the animal-gross and -predatory in his
nature. And Tiny Duffy, symbol of this aspect of the Boss's
make-up, and Sadie Burke, symbol of the indivisible bond between brute and human nature, participate with Adam Stanton,
symbol of the exclusively idealistic in the Boss's nature, to
kill him. By allowing these aspects of his nature to get out
of hand, to function as isolated impulses, the Boss kills himself. Yet in his death there is a form of salvation, for
through disintegration of his personality he is reborn to a
realization that man cannot violate the essential complexity
of his nature with impunity.

But what Sadie and Adam are trying to kill is an image of
the Boss each has created in terms of his own ego — the Boss's
integration has been doomed to fall because it has rested on
an unsound base. Although the Boss's own choices are responsible for his fall, his incapability of maintaining his integration in the world is a commentary on "the terrible division" of his age. After his death "all the king's men" cannot
put him together again; without the principle upon which the
Boss's control was based, they do not add up to the microcosm
maintained by the Boss's integration. An understanding of the
way in which the Boss's men stand as correlatives for aspects
of his nature is a key to his characterization.

Sadie and Sugar-Boy are symbols of adjustment to nature
in terms of an abstract code. When Sadie informs him of the
fraud perpetrated on him by the Harrison outfit, she "made him
what he is" (she is the mother of his rebirth), and it is significant that she has developed a sort of honor-among-thieves
code of retaliation based on her reaction to her pock-marked
face and her besotted father. And Sugar-Boy's relation to
nature has been the result of his limitations, too. His stuttering and his puniness at school made the big boys try to
"run it over him like dirt." So he has developed a code which
gives him mastery over his deformity and over other men.
Sugar-Boy stands for a kind of counter-predatoriness, which
is in harmony with the other elements of the Boss's nature as
long as it is held in check. After the Boss's death, Sugar-
Boy is set adrift, has no usefulness.

If there is an affinity between the Boss and Sugar-Boy,
there is no less an affinity between the Boss and another of
the men upon whom he heavily depends early in his career —
Hugh Miller of the "clean hands, pure heart, and no political
past." There is sincere regret in the scene of their parting:
"You're leaving me all alone," the Boss tells him, in semi-

comic woe, "with all the sons of bitches. Mine and the other
fellow's." Hugh Miller is a part of Willie's nature that he
never relinquishes, just as Tiny Duffy is a symbol of "that
other self of Willie Stark, and all the contempt and insult
which Willie Stark was to heap on Tiny Duffy was nothing but
what one self of Willie Stark did to another self of Willie
Stark because of a blind, inward necessity." Adam Stanton is
a symbol of the Hugh Miller aspect of Willie Stark's nature,
and Willie's visit to Adam is motivated by his desire to convince himself of the truth of his self-knowledge.

Ironically, Jack Burden stands for what finally frustrates
the Boss's attempt to achieve integration of his whole nature;
Jack stands for a malignant skepticism that the Boss puts to
work to disintegrate the other characters' conceptions of the
world, and which ends in disintegrating the Boss's own conception of himself and of the people around him.

The Boss's affair with Anne Stanton symbolizes Willie's
attempt to find in nature some means of achieving good through
triumph over the gross and brutal in nature (the Tiny Duffy aspect of his nature). Anne's sculptured, stylized beauty, as
opposed to Sadie's pock-marked, blemished face, points up the
symbolic contrast between the Boss's two mistresses. It is
significant that what brings the Boss and Anne together is her
plea to him for assistance in her welfare work, symbol on a
smaller scale of what Willie is attempting in his hospital
project. Anne's disillusionment about her father and Willie's
about his ability to control his son's destiny seem to determine the relationship between Anne and the Boss, as if their
affair were a natural outcome of their search for a satisfactory attitude toward nature.

Tom Stark, the Boss's son, is a symbol of human incorri-
gibility; he is a living rebuff to his father's necessity to
find proof in nature that somehow man is controllable. He is
continually making not only his father, but himself too, vulnerable to exploitation. To save Tom from marriage to Sibyl
Frey, Willie agrees to play ball with the opposition. In his
attempt to rectify his son's blunders, the Boss is indulging
a sort of parental pride that is in conflict with the code by
which he is trying to live. With his eye set on the abstract
political objective, the Boss is committed to give up certain
of his "necessities" as a human being. But something will not
allow him to relinquish his parental pride: this something is
the assertion of an essential part of his nature.

The hospital scene produced by Tom Stark's injury brings
Sadie, Anne and Lucy together and points up symbolic contrasts
already established. Sadie, Anne and the Boss have no defense
against the agony of raw grief, but Lucy, guided by her faith
in human goodness and love, is able to maintain control of
herself and assist her husband, unmanned by his suffering, to
leave the waiting room. This is not to say that Lucy becomes
the prim heroine of the novel. She does not regain her hus-

band in the end, and we last see her clinging to a faith which
makes her capable of adopting a child whose paternity is highly questionable on the long chance that it may be Tom Stark's
son, and, symbolically, on the longer chance that Willie may
be reborn through it. But Lucy does symbolize a faith which
pronounces commentary on the Boss's faith in himself, and on
Sadie's faith in her eye-for-an-eye code. Lucy's is a faith
in a power before which man is helpless; and it enables her to
endure the loss of her husband and of her son; ironically, it
affirms the same sort of belief in the potentiality of man as
that affirmed by the Boss's dying statement.

Sadie, on the other hand, has no defense against her loss
of the Boss. She cannot stay away from the hospital while Tom,
whom she has never liked, is suffering. Finally, when she realizes that the Boss is going to leave her permanently, she
cannot discipline her attitude toward the loss in terms of her
code. She kills the Boss, but, after the murder, she is unable to harden herself to the crime; Jack discovers her in
a sanitorium in a state of collapse: "So I continued to sit
there for quite a while, holding Sadie's hand in the silence
which she seemed to want and looking across her down toward
the bayou, which coiled under the moss depending from the
line of cypresses on the farther bank, the algae-mottled water
heavy with the hint and odor of swamp, jungle and darkness,
along the edge of the clipped lawn" (p.436). We have in the
landscape a juxtaposition of the brute natural and uncontrollable and the rational and man-controlled, the elements which
have gotten out of hand in Sadie's nature. But this is not to
say that Sadie Burke is the villainess of the novel any more
than that Lucy Stark is the heroine. Both Lucy and Sadie operate as dynamic symbols to qualify the central theme. Sadie
is frustrated because she tries to live in terms of a code
inappropriate to her nature. But she gains self-knowledge
through her collapse, and in her letter to Jack after her recovery there is the implication that she has achieved a sort
of mastery over herself in terms of this self-knowledge.

The Boss's downfall is a result of his losing sight of the
relationship between man and nature. Highway 58 is a symbol
of what Willie Stark achieves in terms of his knowledge that
good must be built out of the bad in man. Crooked politics result in Highway 58. Throughout the novel sections describing
the highway are repeated to develop a symbol of the precarious-
ness of this relationship between man's aspirations to idealism and the inescapable, irrational, gross aspect of man's nature, an aspect he shares with the dense, uncontrolled natural
world along the highway: the jungle at the edge of the clipped
lawn. As long as he realizes that he is cutting across nature
(Sugar-Boy realizes this with a vengeance when he swerves dex-
terously to run down the 'possum), he may maintain his separateness. But the "ectoplasmic fingers of the mist" reach out
of the swamp, "threading out from the blackness of the cy-

presses" to snag them — an eerie foreshadowing of the climactic catastrophe of the novel.

For Willie Stark loses sight of nature's resistance to complete control. When his son is killed, Willie's story comes to a climax. In the face of this blow, Willie loses sight of the inseparability of good and evil; he determines to fight back and force upon nature man's ability to achieve absolute good; so he sets out to build his hospital solely out of the "good" in man (Tiny Duffy and Gummy Larson are to have no hand in it). In spite of Lucy's insistence that the hospital — "those things" — does not matter in the face of their son's death, Willie sees it as a symbol of man's undaunted march toward triumph over disease and accident; through surgery, man will control accidents of the sort which killed his son. He begins by banishing Gummy Larson, the crooked contractor, and Tiny Duffy, whom he had promised an interest in the undertaking. But he is so hypnotized by his determination to impose his will upon the nature which has taken his son that he loses sight of the fact that he is running roughshod over Tiny and Gummy and Sadie Burke, as his Cadillac has run over 'possum and moccasin; he becomes hypnotized like the driver who, in an image in the opening page of the book, loses control of his car, crashes over the shoulder of the highway into the weeds, and is killed. Gummy, Sadie, and Tiny Duffy have all made him what he is, represent essential parts of his make-up. And, finally, Adam Stanton, symbol of idealism divorced from the brute natural, pulls the trigger. Willie has been struggling toward integration in terms of his whole nature, but the integration among his henchmen breaks down when he tries to divorce idealistic aspirations from their basis in his own pride and selfishness. His downfall is a symbol of the disintegration brought about by modern man's attempt to control the external world through will unguided by understanding. But the Boss's downfall is his "luck"; for through his own disintegration he gains faith in the potentiality of integration in man: he learns that something within man destroys him when he ceases to act as man.

III

Warren's point of view requires that all the imagery of the novel grow out of Jack Burden's mind, and, although it is beyond the scope of this paper to try to do more than suggest the psychological motivation for Jack's reveries, something should be said about the way in which the symbolism considered in this article is produced by Jack's state of mind.

At the time of the telling of the story, Jack is like a man recuperating, learning to walk again, or like a man whose mind has been liberated from the effects of a drug. He is feeling his way back over territory he had thought familiar, re-exploring it in an attempt to master the knowledge brought

to him through his rebirth.   Earlier, as a man sick with the
"terrible division" of his age, he had seen the world through
a diseased sensibility.   His feeling of betrayal after the disruption of his love affair with Anne had made him turn on his
sensibility as if it had betrayed him, for it had brought between them the image of Anne floating in the bay, had seemed
to make him incapable of going through with the sexual act.
Jack had tried, after this frustration, to develop a protection against further betrayals, had done so by seeking a "realistic" attitude toward the world.   Prior to his rebirth, his
speech and actions in the presence of others had shown him to
be a man subordinating sentiment to the requirements of the political world in which he worked (and in this respect he had
felt he was like the Boss), but in moments of inactivity, he
had lapsed into reveries that took the form of ambiguous overflows of sentiment: "You see a cow standing in the water up-
stream near the single leaning willow.   And all at once you
feel like crying."   After his rebirth, as he looks back on
those reveries and reconstructs them, Jack can see that they
were symptoms of a disease, but he cannot put a name to the
sickness; and, as he tells the story in retrospect, he seems
to reproduce those reveries with an almost loving and morbid
relish.   So what we get in the novel in Jack Burden's "style"
(which cannot be equated with Warren's style) is a marked
alternation between passages of straight, laconic reporting
(Jack Burden describing Jack Burden the ex-reporter) and passages lyrical, rhetorical and often sentimentally ironic (Jack
Burden trying to reproduce Jack Burden the ex-romanticist).
By more than simple juxtaposition this alternation involves a
mutual qualification; one Jack Burden qualifies the other and
gives us the whole character: a man whose incorrigibly active
sensibility is still resisting his attempts to subordinate it
to the requirements of his adopted cynical view.   In this alternation the conflict (the struggle toward and against rebirth) which is Jack's hope is dramatized.   But the tension
and conflict produced by this alternation do more than charac-
terize Jack Burden.   They bring to focus several meanings and
implications that sharpen our perception of the total intention of the novel; these meanings and implications are brought
to focus by the quality such passages possess of functioning
in a number of ways simultaneously.

For example, passages produced by his unchecked flow of
sensibility occur when Jack "relaxes."   Lolling in a hammock
while the Boss paces the yard pondering a political problem,
Jack sees the leaves above his head and reflects:

I lay there and watched the undersides of the oak leaves,
dry and grayish and dusty-green, and some of them I saw
had rusty-corroded-looking spots on them.   Those were the
ones which would turn loose their grip on the branch before long — not in any breeze, the fibers just relax, in

the middle of the day maybe with the sunshine bright and
the air so still it aches like the place where the tooth
was on the morning after you've been to the dentist or
aches like your heart when you stand on the street corner
waiting for the light to change and happen to recollect
how things once were and how they might have been yet if
what happened had not happened.   (p.37)

What starts out as an apparently casual, almost languid speculation about the leaves develops into a vague, aching nostalgia. By a process of association Jack arrives at a sardonic
carpe diem theme from which he is awakened by the crack of
Sugar-Boy's automatic from behind the barn where the gunman
is practicing fast draws.

   We have here a reverie framed by our awareness of the Boss
pacing the leaves and Sugar-Boy practicing his skill (both described in terms Jack Burden the self-styled hard-boiled hench-
man would use: "Well, it was his baby, and he could give it
suck" and "It was Sugar-Boy off down in the lot playing with
his .38 Special again"). The irony of the juxtaposition grows
out of the terms in which Jack describes the three activities.
He feels that he shares no responsibility for the Boss's problem: he is simply doing what he is paid to do. So he relaxes
in the hammock in a sort of luxury of irresponsibility, allowing his mind to drift in a vague lack of purpose like the
leaves he is contemplating; he is, in his withdrawal, trying
to submerge himself in the womb of total nature, but his reflections on the leaves lead him to a contemplation of the
inevitability of change. The leaves fall, the tooth deteri-
orates, the traffic light changes, and suddenly Sugar-Boy's
automatic cracks the silence. The critical problem is this:
How aware is Jack Burden, at the time of his telling of the
story, of the irony of this juxtaposition — Boss pacing, Jack
brooding, Sugar-Boy practicing? Certainly, at the time the
events took place, Jack was unaware of any irony in the fact
that while he mused on the futility of human action Sugar-Boy
was diligently practicing a highly developed technique of human action. The fact that Jack forgets the leaves, listens
for a while to Sugar-Boy's target practice, then dozes off in
the hammock is evidence that he missed the irony completely at
the time the events occurred. At the time, much later, of his
report of what happened, Jack reconstructs the events in a way
that suggests that he is still unable to define the irony of
the scene. But the reader, through his insight into Jack's
subconscious state of mind, can see how the whole sequence has
functioned to point up three conflicting attitudes toward nature which produce the basic conflict in the novel.

   Again, in his reverie just prior to his revealing the evidence of her father's participation in crooked politics to
Anne Stanton, Jack subconsciously struggles with the conflict
produced by his sensibility:

A month from now, in early April, at the time when far
away, outside the city, the water hyacinths would be covering every inch of bayou, lagoon, creek, and backwater
with a spiritual-mauve to obscene-purple, violent, vulgar,
fleshy, solid, throttling mass of bloom over the black
water, and the first heart-breaking, misty green, like
girlhood dreams, on the old cypresses would have settled
down to be leaf and not a damned thing else, and the arm-
thick, mud-colored, slime-slick moccasins would heave out
of the swamp and try to cross the highway and your front
tire hitting one would give a slight bump and make a sound
like *ker-whush* and a tinny thump when he slapped heavily
up against the underside of the fender, and the insects
would come boiling out of the swamps and day and night the
whole air would vibrate with them with a sound like an
electric fan, and if it was night the owls back in the
swamp would be *whoo*-ing and moaning like love and death
and damnation, or one would sail out of the pitch dark
into the rays of your headlights and plunge against the
radiator to explode like a ripped feather bolster, and the
fields would be deep in that rank, hairy or slick, juicy,
sticky grass which the cattle gorge on and never get flesh
over their ribs for that grass is in that black soil and
no matter how far down the roots could ever go, if the
roots were God knows how deep, there would never be anything but that black, grease-clotted soil and no stone
down there to put calcium into that grass — well, a month
from now, in early April, when all those things would be
happening beyond the suburbs, the husks of the old houses
in the street where Anne Stanton and I were walking would,
if it were evening, crack and spill out into the stoops
and into the street all that life which was not sealed up
within.   (p.257)

We have in such imagery a complex of references to the basic
symbolism. In the water hyacinth metaphor, for example, we
have the principle of natural change and rebirth which is
uncontrollable ("throttling mass"), miraculous ("spiritual-
mauve," the connotations of the ecclesiastical robe), gross
and irrational (the "obscene-purple" suggests the membrane in
which the foetus huddles; "violent, vulgar, fleshy, solid,"
the bestiality of lust), and in the face of which man seems
helpless. We have the "obscene-purple" played off against the
"spiritual-mauve" to produce a tension which reflects Jack's
conflicting impulse to worship and loathe nature, to find min-
gled hope and despair in natural fruition (the "misty green"
of the cypresses is a summons to idealism, to hope in an ultimately "good" end toward which natural process tends; but the
"misty green" turned "leaf and not a damned thing else" seems
to turn the hope to despair, like fragile girlhood optimism
frustrated in the adult experience of womanhood). The image

of the car running over the moccasin symbolizes man running
counter to brute natural process (the passage of the highway
through the dense, uncontrolled nature is antagonistic to the
passage of the moccasin impelled by the season to cross the
road): part of man's nature separates him from brute animal
nature. Yet his idealism is rooted in the mysterious, uncontrollable, gross and irrational process which determines his
environment. The undernourished cows are reminders that nature is, if not inimical to man, at least so organized that it
has no regard for his welfare: the lush fruition of the season
produces insects, snakes, owls, hyacinths, but it barely supports the domestic animal upon which man depends. One could
probe the passage further and discover new connotations which
function to point up the total meaning of the novel. It is
enough here to point out that the passage creates an atmosphere in which the reader's sensibility is focused on the mystery which furnishes the basis for the novel's theme.

It is to such passages as those just considered that critics must return for a proper evaluation of *All the King's Men*.
And those passages must be read as the product of Jack Burden's mind. Warren's choice of his particularly oblique point
of view is an index of his rigorous and thorough-going onto-
logical approach to the mystery of good and evil. We have in
All the King's Men the story of how Willie Stark was assassinated at the peak of his political career, but what we experience is that story happening inside Jack Burden's head. The
legend of political power is brought to us through a medium
which dramatizes the limits and validity of human knowledge.
In fact, one might say that the whole strategy of Warren's
technique thwarts any attempt to find the simplified, clear-
cut answer to the question of political power; the form of the
novel forces the reader to take the Willie Stark story as a
mystery — a mystery thoroughly explored in the psychological
terms of Jack Burden's experience.

Ladell Payne

Willie Stark and Huey Long: Atmosphere, Myth, or Suggestion?

*"And truth was what I sought, without fear
or favor, and let the chips fly." — Jack Burden*

In the twenty years since *All the King's Men* was published, Robert Penn Warren has repeatedly denied that Willie Stark is a fictional portrait of Huey Long. And by his own account, his denials have been "almost invariably greeted by something like a sardonic smile or a conspiratorial wink."[1] His two essays on the subject — an "Introduction" to *All the King's Men* (1953) and "*All the King's Men*: The Matrix of Experience" (1963)[2] — have certainly met with the written equivalents of a smile, a wink, and a nod. The most notable early disbeliever was Hamilton Basso, whose "The Huey Long Legend" seems to have prompted the 1953 disclaimer. After describing the protagonists of Warren's *All the King's Men*, Dos Passos' *Number One*, Langley's *A Lion is in the Streets* and his own *Sun in Capricorn*, Basso says: "He [Willie and the others collectively] may not be intended to represent Huey Long, but it is hard to see how he could represent anybody else," for "once a writer begins to write about these Hueys-who-aren't-Hueys, the real Huey jumps up and clings to his back like the old man of the sea."[3] Subsequently, Orville Prescott, in the course of attacking Warren's failure to see Stark as a step toward fascism, remarked that Willie is "obviously and closely modeled on Huey Long";[4] and such diverse writers as Louis D. Rubin, Jr., David H. Zinman, and William H. McDonald have echoed Basso and Prescott.[5]

Where, then, does the truth lie? In Mr. Warren's continued denials or in everyone else's continued suspicions? Of course, even Warren has readily admitted some relationship between Willie and Huey, acknowledging in 1953 that "it was the career of Long and the atmosphere of Louisana that suggested the play that was to become the novel" and in 1963 that if he "had never gone to Louisiana and if Huey Long had not existed, the novel would never have been written." Even so, Warren has stood by his earlier position that "suggestion does not mean identity," and that because he did not know "what Long was like, and what were the secret forces that drove him,... Long was but one of the figures that stood in the shadows of imagination behind Willie Stark." And, in 1963, he reinforced this emphasis on the generally suggested at the expense of the specifically copied by differentiating the "world of 'Huey' — that world of myth, folklore, poetry, deprivation, rancor, and dimly envisaged hopes" from a "factual world — made possible by the factual Long." Warren's point is that Long became a legend in his own lifetime, and that by the time the novel was started in 1943, the "factual world was only a memory, and therefore was ready to be absorbed freely into the act of imagination."

There seems to be a significant difference between Warren's 1953 and 1963 statements: the early statement implies that Long's career and Louisiana's atmosphere suggested the novel's general plot and perhaps some of Stark's characteristics; the later statement says that Long and Louisiana simply inspired Warren with a "line of thinking and feeling," implying that Warren was concerned less with Long than with questions of public and private morality prompted by a mythical "Huey" and a metaphysical Louisiana that were recollected in the tranquillity of Mussolini's Italy and written about in Minneapolis, Washington, and Connecticut.

While it is undoubtedly true that *All the King's Men* is not a literal biography of Huey Long, and equally true that much of the novel's literary value comes from the philosophical cogency of its subject matter — free will, determinism, human responsibility, the relationship between past and present — *All the King's Men* is much more directly based on the historical Huey Long than the words "suggested," "atmosphere," "line of thinking and feeling" and "world of myth" can possibly imply. Whether or not Warren tried "to transpose into fiction Huey P. Long and the tone of that world," the fact remains that he succeeded in doing so. For in the novel's sequence of events, in the subordinate characters and in the characterization of Willie himself, so much is drawn directly from the publicly-known career, cohorts, and character of Huey Pierce Long that Warren's statements, while not false, nonetheless have been misleading. Moreover, while Warren's claim not to know Long's secret motives is of course literally correct, many of those who wrote about the historical Kingfish attributed motives to him very much like those of Warren's fictional Boss.

The story of Huey P. Long, an obscure southern farm boy who became governor of his state, went on to the United States Senate after acquiring dictatorial powers, and was assassinated at the height of his political career for reasons never fully known, is also the story of Willie Stark.[6] Like Long, Willie is a "red-faced and red-necked farm boy" (*AKM*, p.7) from what had been the timber-producing part of a state that is obviously Louisiana. Taken together, the description of

the sharp break between the flat rich country of the lower
cotton delta and the low red hills of the poor upper-state region; the use of names such as Okaloosa for Opelousas, Marston
for Ruston, Harmonville for Hammond, and Mason City for Morgan
City; and the importance of oil in the state are things that
can only refer to Louisiana.

In Winn Parish (county) of this state, young Huey Long
supported himself by peddling shortening; young Willie ped-
dles his Fix-It Household Kit by day while studying at night.
Long's Baptist background and five months at the University of
Oklahoma parallel Stark's year at a nearby Baptist college and
his army time in Oklahoma. Long's fantastic achievement of
learning enough law in eight months at Tulane to pass the bar
examination becomes Willie's three-year period of rigorous
night study. (This capacity for intensive work over extended
periods later stands both Huey and Willie in good stead; both
governors were able to go without sleep indefinitely when the
occasion demanded.)

Willie Stark's early legal and political career also closely parallels Long's. Huey began with small-claims and workmen's compensation cases and became a well-to-do attacker of
corporations; Willie begins with small claims, wins his first
battle in a workmen's compensation case, and becomes financial-
ly independent attacking an oil company for some independent
leaseholders. Long was elected to the railroad commission as
the little man's champion and lost his power after he attacked
Standard Oil for some independent oil companies. When we
first see young Stark, he is a county treasurer fighting a corrupt administration and failing to win re-election because he
opposes those in power. In describing the campaign for county
treasurer, Warren gives Stark one of Long's political trade-
marks. As Huey did throughout his career, Willie distributes
handbills from house to house because the local newspaper refuses to print his side of the story.

Huey used the notice he attracted on the railroad commission to run for governor; Willie runs for governor because of
the attention he attracts as county treasurer. While Huey, unlike Willie, was certainly not tricked into entering the race,
it remains true that each man failed in his first attempt at
the governorship. Moreover, there is considerable evidence
that Warren's picture of the young, idealistic Stark is drawn
directly from some of young Long's characteristics. When Jack
Burden first sees the Boss, he is country Cousin Willie, who
refuses to drink beer, speaks politely, uses no profanity and
wears a "stiff high collar like a Sunday-school superintendent"
(*AKM*, pp.16-21). According to Hermann Deutsch, until Long
left Winnfield at sixteen, he was a devout church-goer who
used no profanity. Warren's description of Cousin Willie's
"seven-fifty seersucker suit which is too long in the pants so
the cuffs crumple down over the high black shoes, which could
do with a polishing, and a stiff high collar...and a blue-

striped tie" (*AKM*, p.16) reproduces almost exactly a widely-
published picture of Long as a traveling salesman in a rumpled
suit, baggy pants and high collar, holding a sample case in
one hand and an umbrella in the other. In 1963, Deutsch confirmed that young Long did indeed dress "like a misprint in a
tailored-by-mail catalogue."

Nor is the older Willie Stark at all unlike the mature
Huey Long. Willie is "five feet eleven inches tall and heavy-
ish in the chest and shortish in the leg" (*AKM*, p.16). His
eyes are "big and brown, and he'd look right at you"; he has
an "almost pudgy face," with "dark brown, thick hair...tousled
and crinkled down over his forehead, which wasn't very high in
the first place" (*AKM*, p.21), and with jowls which are "beginning to sag off" (*AKM*, p.8). According to Deutsch, Huey was
also five foot eleven with a "tendency toward incipient paun-
chiness," with "reddish-brown eyes" and a habit of "staring at
the person addressed as though seeking to hypnotize a subject."
Basso notes Long's "fleshy face" and his "tousled reddish
curls tumbled upon his forehead," and Hodding Carter remarks
that he was "heavy-jowled."[7] Even Stark's informality in the
governor's office — conducting official business in his shirt
sleeves and sock feet and settling "affairs of state through a
bathroom door" (*AKM*, p.32) — recalls Huey's habits of receiv-
ing dignitaries in shirt sleeves (at best) or green pajamas
(at worst) and of occasionally standing stark naked while lay-
ing down the law to lesser politicians.

Cousin Willie's dull, platitudinous speeches, made up of
"argument and language that was grand and bright" (*AKM*, p.74),
seem based on Long's early prose, that "florid and polysyllabic style he evidently admired most at that stage of his
career."[8] From polysyllabic grandiosity, both Huey and Willie
moved to the folksy, colorfully metaphorical language of their
days in power — language filled with invective, invocative
effects, and Biblical allusions and rhythms.[9] That Warren has
drawn on Long's speeches is evident from only a few examples:

> Huey: "We got the roads in Louisiana haven't we? In some
>   states they only have the graft."[10]
> Willie: "Sure, there's some graft, but there's just enough
>   to make the wheels turn without squeaking" (*AKM*, p.417).
> Huey: "They want these pie-eaters and trough-feeders put
>   out of control of the Democratic Party in Louisiana."[11]
> Willie: "It is just a question of who has got his front
>   feet in the trough when slopping time comes" (*AKM*, p.
>   417).
> Huey: "Those low-down, lascivious, lying, murderous, bunch
>   of skunks." "Dog-faced sons of wolves."[12]
> Willie: "Folks, there's going to be a leetle mite of trou-
>   ble back in town. Between me and that Legislature-ful
>   of hyena-headed feist-faced, belly-dragging sons of
>   slack-gutted she-wolves" (*AKM*, p.155).

Huey: "At birth the 'sugar-tit' of the state of Louisiana
    landed in L. E. Thomas's mouth."[13]
Willie: "Oh, I took the sugar tit and hushed my crying"
    (*AKM*, p.101).
Huey: "The people...and not Huey Long, rule the State."
    "Where are the schools that you have waited for your
    children to have, that have never come? Where are the
    roads and the highways that you send your money to
    build, that are no nearer now than ever before? Where
    are the institutions to care for the sick and dis-
    abled?"[14]
Willie: "You are the state. You know what you need. Look
    at your pants. Have they got holes in the knee? Lis-
    ten to your belly. Did it ever rumble for emptiness?
    Look at your crop. Did it ever rot in the field be-
    cause the road was so bad you couldn't get it to mar-
    ket? Look at your kids. Are they growing up ignorant
    as you and dirt because there isn't any school for
    them?" (*AKM*, p.97).
Huey: "I know the hearts of the people, because I have not
    colored my own."[15]
Willie: "My study is the heart of the people" (*AKM*, p.8).

The image of Willie making a speech — eyes bulging, face flush-
ing, sweat sluicing, arms flailing — has its source in Huey's
platform appearances, which consistently prompted the crowd,
like Warren's "rednecks," to respond as to a gospel preacher.

The patronizing contempt Tiny Duffy feels toward Cousin
Willie also is based on fact. The professional politicians
clearly considered Long something of a buffoon until it was
too late to stop him. And if Huey Long, unlike Willie Stark,
underwent no great moral or spiritual change during or after
his first campaign for governor, in their second campaigns
both Long and Stark relied much more on demagogic tactics and
folksy language to win the necessary rural votes.

Long's later political career falls into five phases: his
program of public works and social reforms, his fight against
impeachment, his attainment of absolute power, his rise to national prominence as a Senator and Share-Our-Wealth advocate,
and his assassination. With the exception of the Share-Our-
Wealth program, Willie Stark goes through all these phases.
Moreover, he goes through all of them in almost exactly the
same way as did Long.

In *Every Man A King,* Long said that the most important
parts of his first legislative program were highway construction; free school books; aid to the blind, deaf, and dumb; and
aid for the insane and charity hospitals. To finance these reforms, he proposed to increase the severance taxes on oil, gas,
timber and other natural resources. Stark, too, speaks proudly of his highway program, his public health bill, his extrac-
tion tax, and his increased royalties on state land.

Observers at the time recognized that the attempt to
impeach Long was not to prevent wrongdoing, but to eliminate
a political enemy. Warren makes it clear that the attempt
to impeach Stark is for the same purpose. The Articles of
Impeachment charged Long with, among other things, having
"bribed and attempted to bribe legislators," having used
"coercive measures," and with "high crimes and misdemeanors
in office, incompetence, corruption, favoritism or oppression
in office and gross misconduct."[16] Stark is charged with "attempting to corrupt, coerce, and blackmail the Legislature, in
addition to the other little charges of malfeasance and non-
feasance" (*AKM*, pp.154-55). Huey Long sped up and down Louisiana, making as many as seven speeches a day to gain support
and calling for his followers to fill Baton Rouge on April 3.
They crowded in for a massive night rally. Willie Stark roars
"across the state at eighty miles an hour," attends "five, or
six, or seven, or eight speakings in a day," and holds his
mass rally "the night of the fourth of April" (*AKM*, pp.155-59).
Opponents accused Long of trying to bribe and coerce members
of the Legislature to vote against impeachment; he is known to
have driven as far as two hundred and fifty miles in the middle of the night to secure the support of a wavering senator;
and by his own account, he simultaneously sent cars around to
fifteen senators to get their votes. Willie Stark does all
these things. And just as Governor Long escaped impeachment
when his fifteen Round Robiners (one more than the number
needed to block impeachment) announced "that by reason of the
unconstitutionality and invalidity of all impeachment charges
remaining against Huey P. Long, Governor, they [would] not
vote to convict thereon,"[17] so Governor Stark produces a list
of signatures stating that "the impeachment proceedings are
unjustified" and that the signers "will vote against them despite all pressure" (*AKM*, p.159).

Evidently Long never experienced any transformation comparable to that effected in Willie by Duffy and Sadie. Nevertheless, the impeachment attempt profoundly disturbed him — even
to the extent of weeping when the proceedings began. After-
ward, his attitude toward his political opponents was noticeably harsher, his methods noticeably more cynical. In 1930,
Long suggested this change: "I was governor one year before
I learned that I had to be governor or get out."[18] In August
1934, *Newsweek* quoted him as saying, "I was soft then...but
not now, Brother." And in an interview reported by Forrest
Davis, Long said: "When I got into politics I was just an
ignorant boy from the country. All the political tricks I
learned, I learned from them when they were trying to keep
Huey P. Long out."

Stark and Long acquired and used their power in almost
identical ways. Willie boasts of putting men on the Supreme
Court to rule as he wants. The Articles of Impeachment
charged Huey with using his appointive power to influence the

state judiciary and with boasting of controlling the courts.
Just as Willie announces to his followers that "there'll be a
little something coming to you now and then in the way of
sweetening" (*AKM*, p.140), so Huey's supporters became judges
and high-paid attorneys, and built homes with gold toilet fixtures. Willie forces his retainers to sign undated letters of
resignation; the Articles of Impeachment charged Long with the
same conduct. Jack Burden tells us that after Stark's elec-
tion "there wasn't any Democratic Party. There was just Willie" (*AKM*, p.103). Huey Long announced to the 1932 Democratic
National Convention, "I am the Democratic Party in Louisiana."[19] And, just as Willie confidently imposes his will upon
the state constitution to get the laws he wants, so Long announced once to a critic, "I'm the Constitution around here
now."[20] Indeed, when Willie says, "The law is always too
short and too tight for growing humankind. The best you can
do is do something and then make up some law to fit" (*AKM*, p.
145), he is directly paraphrasing Long's "Unconstitutional?
Hell, when I want something done I do it and tell my attorney
general to dig up a law to cover it."[21] Surely Willie's
explanation that the only way he can get things done is by
using corrupt methods, however distasteful to him, sounds like
Long's typical self-defense: "They say they don't like my methods. Well, I don't like them either. I'll be frank with you.
I really don't like to have to do things the way I do. I'd
much rather get up before the Legislature and say, 'Now this
is a good law; it's for the benefit of the people and I'd like
for you to vote for it in the interest of the public welfare.'
Only I know that laws ain't made that way. You've got to
fight fire with fire."[22]   True, Willie Stark does not become
a national political figure. Yet toward the end of the novel,
the Boss is planning to run for the Senate, and some of Willie's early, apparently facetious remarks at least suggest
presidential ambitions (*AKM*, p.43).

Stark's assassination, however, is obviously based upon
Long's. Dr. Carl Austin Weiss shot Long in the Capitol building as he was leaving a night Senate session. Dr. Adam Stanton shoots Stark in the Capitol after the "solons had broken
up shop for the evening and were milling about in the corri-
dors" (*AKM*, p.418). Long was walking between the Governor's
office and private elevator in the east corridor leading from
the Senate chamber; Stark is walking "along the east wall,
toward the inset where the elevators were" (*AKM*, p.420). According to Joe Bates, one of Long's bodyguards who testified
at the inquest, "a man in white walked up to Senator Long. I
thought he was going to shake hands. He shot him."[23] Other
eyewitness testimony had Weiss stepping from behind a pillar.
Jack Burden sees Stanton "leaning against the pedestal" of a
statue. As Stanton approaches Willie, Jack thinks: *"He's
shaking hands with him, he's all right now, he's all right."*
Then Stanton fires. Weiss was killed at once by a hail of

bullets — sixty-one wounds were counted in his head and body; Stanton was gunned down by a "positive staccato series of reports.... He was stitched across the chest" (*AKM*, pp.420-21). Public Service Commissioner O'Connor (who commandeered a car and took Long to the hospital) said that "On his way to the hospital, Senator Long sat silently, pressing his hand to the bullet wound in his right side. Only once did he say anything, and that was to ask: 'I wonder why he shot me?'"[24] He had been shot once in the stomach by a small caliber pistol. Although an emergency operation was performed, Long died some thirty hours after the assassination. Governor Stark sits, "both hands pressed to his body, low on the chest and toward the center" with "two little .25-caliber slugs in his body." Willie also is taken to the hospital for an operation; a few days later, shortly before he dies, he turns to Jack and asks, "Why did he do it to me?" (*AKM*, pp.421-24).

Even Willie's return to virtue shortly before his assassination seems directly based on Long's conduct. Just as Governor Stark drank heavily and chased "Nordic Nymphs," Governor Long "divided his time between government and dissipation," prompting Theodore Bilbo to speak of "Louisiana's pot likker governor's 'fondness for' liquor, women and green pajamas."[25] As he gained national prominence, Senator Long apparently tried to build a more favorable image of himself. George Sokolsky wrote that Huey gave up "a life-long habit of drinking heavily" a few months before his death. Hodding Carter observed the same change and noted that Long had toned down his rowdy conduct of the sort that Willie renounces when he returns to Lucy and tells Jack Burden "it might have been all different" (*AKM*, p.425).

Fact and fiction also reflect each other in the figures who surround the Boss and his historical counterpart. As his Tiny Duffy, Huey had O. K. Allen, an incompetent, notable only for invariably supporting Long. Allen, according to one, "would have made a good hay, grain, and feed merchant in Halitosis, Louisiana." When Long was first elected to the Railroad Commission in 1918, O. K. Allen was Tax Assessor of Winn Parish. When Cousin Willie is serving his first term as County Treasurer in 1922, Tiny Duffy is Tax Assessor of Mason County. During his term as governor (1928-32), Long made Allen chairman of the Highway Commission; Stark gives Duffy the same job. Allen succeeded Long as governor of Louisiana in 1932 and served as the Kingfish's puppet; Duffy is the Lieutenant Governor during Willie's last term and succeeds to the governorship after the assassination. As the man in Stark's organization most interested in graft, Duffy all too clearly resembles the Allen whose Highway Commission Long's enemies pointed to as the source of bribes and payoffs.[26] And though there is little physical similarity between the portly Allen and the obese Duffy, and no evidence to suggest that Allen had

a hand in Long's assassination, Huey treated O. K. much as
Willie Stark treats his principal sycophant. That is, Long
apparently bullied and despised Allen. The October 13, 1932,
issue of *Time* reported that "One day during the last legislative session, Senator Long called out roughly: 'Oscar, go get
me those goddam bills we was talking about.' Governor Allen,
embarrassed by the presence of others, pretended not to hear.
Huey Long howled: 'Goddam you, Oscar, don't you stall around
with me! I can break you as easy as I made you. Get those
goddam bills and get them on the jump.' Governor Allen got
them on the jump." At the 1932 Overton election-fraud hear-
ings, Huey's brother, Julius, testified: "He makes all candi-
dates sign undated resignations. I remember when he made
Governor O. K. Allen sign one. The Governor broke down and
cried." Julius added: "No man with the resentment of a bird
dog would take what Oscar took from Huey Long." And Earl Long
is the source of the story that when a leaf once blew in Allen's office window and fell on his desk, O. K. signed it.
     If Tiny Duffy is a reasonably accurate portrait of O. K.
Allen, then Sadie Burke, Willie's secretary, campaign assistant, and confidante, is clearly a modified picture of Alice
Lee Grosjean, Huey's twenty-five-year-old secretary, campaign
assistant, confidante, and eventually Secretary of State.
While Sadie is not blessed with Alice Lee's beauty, their careers are remarkably parallel. Jack Burden's description of
Sadie as "a very smart cooky" (*AKM,* p.79) echoes Forrest Davis'
characterization of Alice Lee as "the shrewdest 'man' of them
all"; and Beals' comment that Alice Lee is "a girl who talks
freely but reveals nothing, has been loyal to Huey, but stuck
out for her own rights," fits Sadie equally well.[27] Moreover,
the triangular relationship among Willie, Sadie, and Lucy
Stark seems noticeably similar to what was rumored to have
existed among Huey, Alice Lee, and Rose Long. When Governor
Long appointed Miss Grosjean Secretary of State in 1930,
Time's report (entitled "Long's Latest") was accompanied by a
picture of Alice Lee captioned "Her Governor was good to her."
"During this year's campaign Terrell [Miss Grosjean's divorced
husband] threatened to sue Governor Long for alienating his
wife's affections. Mrs. Rose McConnel Long...does not regularly reside with her husband in the executive mansion at Baton
Rouge or in his elaborate hotel suite in New Orleans. She remains at Shreveport where she says she prefers the schools for
the three Long youngsters."[28] Sam Irby, Alice Lee's disrepu-
table uncle by marriage, wrote that she "told me that she had
quarrelled with her mother, who had accused her of impropriety
in her relation with her employer, and had demanded that she
and her husband leave her home." Irby adds: "The next I heard
of them was when I learned that a divorce had been agreed upon
and arranged by Huey Long, who first asked Mr. Terrell to sign
a statement to the effect that Long was not responsible for

the separation." Irby also says pointedly that Huey's and
Alice Lee's "living quarters were on the same floor of the
Heidelberg Hotel."[29]

There is, of course, no indication that Alice Lee colluded
in the assassination. But Sadie's withdrawal to a sanatorium
at the novel's end and her confession — "Oh, God... Oh, God....
I killed Willie. I killed him." (*AKM*, p.435) — may have been
suggested by a widely believed false rumor. In 1936 Cleveland
Deer, the anti-Long candidate for governor, asserted that one
of Long's bodyguards, then in a mental institution, kept mut-
tering to himself: "I've killed my best friend! I've killed
my best friend!"[30]

While Mrs. Rose Long was perhaps not as saintly as Lucy
Stark, the two are similar in many ways. Lucy's retreat to
a poultry farm parallels Mrs. Long's separate residence in
Shreveport. Lucy's willingness, for appearance's sake, to
pose for photographs is analogous to Mrs. Long's brief stints
as hostess at the governor's mansion. And Mrs. Stark's qualities are the same as those one writer recognized in Mrs. Long:
"courteous and thoughtful, gentle in speech, and kind to all
associates."[31] Rose Long's Leibnitzean belief that "everything works out for the best" and that the "justification of
a life is in good works"[32] could well be attributed to Lucy
Stark. Even the close relationship between young Willie and
Lucy seems to reflect that between young Huey and Rose during
their Tulane days when, "for the first, last, and only time in
his life, Huey P. Long...lived withdrawn from the world. Absorbed in each other, he and his young wife embarked upon the
project of seeing how quickly a three-year law course could be
mastered."[33] Finally, Lucy's repeated affirmation that Willie
"was a great man" is remarkably like Mrs. Long's statement
that her husband "was the greatest man who ever lived."[34]

Sugar-Boy, Willie's stuttering, fast-driving, sharpshoot-
ing, dimwitted, absolutely devoted bodyguard appears to be a
composite of two of Long's protectors, Joe Messina and Murphy
Roden. Most of Sugar-Boy's personal traits come from Messina,
Long's chief bodyguard. While Messina did not drive for Long,
he had been a truck driver at one time, and as Long once put
it, could "shoot out a bird's eye at a hundred yards." Messina's stupidity was common knowledge. One person told me of
seeing him spend a day clutching campaign money in a paper bag
as a child would clutch a bag of candy. Davis reports meeting
him in an outer room spelling out the "balloons" in the comics,
much as Jack Burden meets Sugar-Boy looking at a picture magazine. Although Messina did not stutter, his simple-minded
attempt at the impeachment trial to explain why he was on the
state payroll without admitting he was a bodyguard seems a
kind of mental if not physiological stutter. Furthermore,
Sugar-Boy behaves very much like Messina during and after
Long's assassination. At the inquest, Messina was at first incoherent, then wept, and finally testified: "I ran up, pulled

my gun and emptied it at the man who shot Senator Long....
I killed him because he had killed Senator Long."[35]   At the
assassination, Sugar-Boy fires repeatedly at Dr. Stanton and
then leans over the fallen Willie "weeping and sputtering"
(*AKM*, p.421).

Murphy Roden, a crack shot who also fired at Weiss, was
Long's regular driver.   While there is no evidence that Long's
car ever wiped "the snot off a mule's nose" (*AKM*, p.5), it did
come "down Canal Street like a gulf squall...its rear end slewing to the gutters."[36]   Even Sugar-Boy's hostility toward the
"B-b-b-b-as-tuds" who fail to get out of the way as fast as he
wants, while perhaps not based specifically on either Messina
or Roden, reflects the general hostility of Long's bodyguard
corps toward those who did not make way for their charge.

Of all the characters who surround the Boss, Jack Burden
is by all accounts not only the most important to the novel
but the hardest to pin down to any prototype.   Hamilton Basso
says that "Long did have a sort of research man, a former jour-
nalist who printed his findings in Huey's personal newspaper,
Louisiana Progress.   It does not appear, though, that Mr.
Warren, in creating the character of Jack Burden, had him in
mind."   Basso is presumably referring to John D. Klorer, who
edited the *Progress* from its founding in 1930 until about nine
months after Long's assassination; but if research is the characteristic that identifies Burden with Klorer, a much stronger
case can be made for Warren's drawing this quality from Long
himself.   Certainly Jack Burden's habit of keeping "a little
black book" full of essential information was suggested by "a
little black book that all Louisiana knew and feared — Huey's
'sonofabitch book.'   Anybody who had ever done him a wrong...
was there."[37]   It is conceivable that Basso himself was the
model for Burden, since in 1935 Basso wrote of his experience
on a New Orleans opposition newspaper, of his pleasure in seeing Long win the governorship, of his belief in the sincerity
of the early Long, of the value of Long's many social reforms,
and of his conviction that "Huey is a possible good against a
positive evil.   It is a choice between Huey and the New Orleans' gang, and Huey is simply the better choice to make."[38]
Then, too, Earle J. Christenberry, Senator Long's private secretary (described by Deutsch in 1963 as one of Long's "two
closest friends") might have suggested Burden.   But there is
little substantial evidence for the contention that Warren had
Christenberry or Klorer or Basso or even Long specifically in
mind when he created Burden.   Instead, Burden seems the one
of Stark's close associates who was "suggested by" a knowledge
of Long and his cohorts rather than closely modeled on any
one of them.   And rightly so.   For by creating a wholly fictional narrator who not only chronicles and comments on the
factually-based Willie Stark story, but who himself has a past,
present, and future that constitutes a major portion of the
novel, Warren has legitimately and successfully accommodated

the world of fact within the world of fiction. For within the
context of Jack Burden's experience, historical matter takes
on the form of fiction.

Carl Weiss, while not one of Long's associates, is forever
linked to him as his assassin. And Warren's Dr. Adam Stanton
is recognizably like Dr. Carl Austin Weiss. Miss Louise Garig,
Weiss' former English teacher at Louisiana State University,
wrote and sent a moving eulogy to several newspapers after
the assassination.[39] She pictured the doctor as a thoughtful,
good, kind, cheerful, almost saintly man. Harris, too, described Weiss as "gentle, peace-loving, pious and filled with
hope and ambition for the future...a cultured and greatly be-
loved young doctor." Stanton has all these attributes. The
New Orleans *Item* reported on September 10, 1935, that "music
was [Dr. Weiss'] relaxation and he took it seriously, studying
in his spare time." Adam Stanton plays the piano both for relaxation and as a symbol of his frustrated desire for harmony
in a chaotic world. As the idealistic man who wants only "to
do good" (*AKM*, p.252), Stanton might well be the man described
by Weiss' mother in a widely published statement about her son:
"All we know is that he took living seriously. Right with him
was right. Right above everything." Indeed, even the deliberate contrast Warren draws between Stanton, the man of idea,
and Stark, the man of fact, may have been prompted by comments
at the time. One southern editorialist wrote: "Huey Long is
dead. He died by the hand of a man who was his direct opposite in every human trait."[40] Finally, while Stanton's
motives are clearly stated in the novel (as, of course, they
must be) and while we can only speculate about Dr. Weiss' (as
we have to in real life), both assassins seem to have been impelled by an insult to family or honor rather than by strong
political feelings.

If Weiss' motives remain conjectural, so too do Long's. A
number of people, however, believe that the forces which produced and motivated Willie Stark were also those which gave
rise to and moved Huey Long. Warren indicates that Willie is
the product of what happened in the South after the Civil War;
every responsible commentator who has tried to explain the
rise of Huey Long has discussed the condition of the post-
bellum South. Willie's personal indifference to money and his
moral and intellectual isolation from his retainers clearly
parallel Long's similar attitudes. Warren implies that Willie
Stark's irrational attitude toward his son is caused in part
by the deprivations of Stark's own youth (*AKM,* p.244); at
least one observer, Carleton Beals, thought that Long's attempt to make Louisiana State into the world's greatest university grew out of "a naive desire to experience a side of
university life denied him in his youth."[41] And just as Huey
publicly showed his concern for L.S.U. by his wild conduct at
football games, his willingness to give state jobs to football
players who made touchdowns, and his interference with the

coaching staff (his meddling caused Coach Biff Jones to re-
sign), so Willie shows his concern for Tom Stark by his manic
behavior at football games, his half-time promises not to
forget the players, and his willingness to override a coach's
disciplinary orders to win the championship. Even the fundamental question of Willie's sincerity, a problem central to
the novel, was raised repeatedly about Long. When Anne Stanton asks Jack Burden if Willie means what he says, Jack can
give her no answer because he wonders the same thing himself
(*AKM,* p.278). As Forrest Davis says, "The matter of Huey's
sincerity remains the great riddle of the Delta."[42]

At the beginning of this essay I cited Warren's 1953
statement that although "it was the career of Long and the
atmosphere of Louisiana that suggested the play that [became]
the novel," *All the King's Men* is not a "biography of or apologia for" Huey Long; I also cited his 1963 statement that a
mythical Long and metaphysical Louisiana gave him a line of
thinking that he wrote about after the "factual world was only
a memory, and therefore was ready to be absorbed freely into
the act of imagination." What Warren seems to have absorbed,
however, was most of Long's public career, including even
minor details. And such words as "atmosphere," "myth" and
"suggestion" do not seem adequate to describe the extent to
which Warren, consciously or not, reproduced recognizable
counterparts to people who actually associated with Long and
endowed his fictional Boss with almost every one of the Kingfish's factual characteristics.

Or in different terms, Warren's statements are comparable
to a claim that Shakespeare's Julius Caesar is neither a biography of nor an apologia for the historical Caesar but rather
the result of a line of thinking suggested by Caesar's career
and times. Such a claim would be true but would hardly reflect the degree to which Shakespeare relied on *The Lives of
the Noble Greeks and Romans* for his material, North for his
language, and Plutarch for his interpretations. Or, an explanation that Shakespeare's characterization of Henry V is based
on a legendary or mythical "Prince Hal" rather than on the
real Henry of Lancaster because Shakespeare did not know the
secret forces that motivated Henry would contain just as much
truth and be just as misleading as Warren's explanation. Both
writers have given us imaginative reworkings of historical materials. And if it be argued that Warren made obvious changes
in what he knew to be literally true, Shakespeare's example
should be a sufficient answer.

On the other hand, any suggestion that *All the King's Men*
is any less a work of art because it owes so much to Huey Long
is obviously as absurd as a similar charge would be against
Shakespeare. For, as most readers know, the value of *All the
King's Men* as a novel is not so much in the way people look
and talk, the events that happen, or the things said, as in
the meanings Jack Burden gives to all of these. It is one of

the marks of Warren's genius that he used the career of Huey
Long as the source of such a wealth of meanings without doing
violence either to what is known about Long or to the integrity with which the meanings are worked out: indeed, that he
was able to alter so little as he imposed the order of art on
the chaos of actuality.

----

1. "Introduction," *All the King's Men* (New York, 1953), pp. v-vi.
All future references to *AKM* will be cited parenthetically in the
text from this Modern Library edition.
2. "*All the King's Men*: The Matrix of Experience," *Yale Review,*
53 (1963), 161-67.
3. "The Huey Long Legend," *Life,* Dec. 9, 1946, pp. 108-10, 116.
4. "The Political Novel: Warren, Orwell, Koestler," *In My Opinion:
An Inquiry into the Contemporary Novel* (Indianapolis, Ind., 1952), p.
25. One of the ironies of *AKM*'s reception is that, while some thought
the novel too flattering to Huey Long, members of the Long family seem
to have resented the portrayal. Responding to Basso's "Legend," Mr.
(now Senator) Russell B. Long said: "I venture the assertion that no
man of our time has been more abused, vilified, and misrepresented by
the American press to its reading public than my father, Huey P. Long.
Most commonly he has been accused of being a ruthless dictator who
would have destroyed our system of democratic government as well with
the charge as a noisy low-grade rabble-rouser [*sic*]. A mass of fictional novels pictures him as possessed of an obsessive lust for sexual indecencies. All glory in the fact that at law there is no right
of suit by the decendants [*sic*] or relatives of a deceased man who
has been libeled.... As the son of the man, I must protest against
such enormous misrepresentation" (U.S. *Congressional Record — Senate,*
80th Cong., 1st Sess., 1947, 93, Pt. 1, p. 438).
5. Louis D. Rubin, Jr., "All the King's Meanings," *Georgia Review,*
8 (1954), 422-23; David H. Zinman, *The Day Huey Long Was Shot: September 8, 1935* (New York, 1963), pp. 257-58; William H. McDonald, "A Summer Rerun on Warren's Powerful Novel," *Montgomery* (Ala.) *Advertiser-
Journal,* July 24, 1966, p. 5A.
6. General information about Long's career comes from the major
studies published before Warren began his novel in 1943: Carleton
Beals, *The Story of Huey P. Long* (Philadelphia, 1935); Forrest Davis,
Huey Long: A Candid Biography (New York, 1935); Thomas O. Harris, *The
Kingfish: Huey P. Long, Dictator* (New York, 1938); Harnett T. Kane,
Louisiana Hayride: The American Rehearsal for Dictatorship (New York,
1941); Webster Smith, *The Kingfish: A Biography of Huey P. Long* (New
York, 1933); Huey P. Long, *Every Man a King* (Chicago, 1964). Many
specific details come from the first-hand studies of Hermann B.
Deutsch: "Hattie and Huey," *Saturday Evening Post,* Oct. 15, 1932, pp.
6-7, 88-92; "Huey Long of Louisiana," *New Republic,* Nov. 11, 1931, pp.
349-51; *The Huey Long Murder Case* (New York, 1963); "Huey Long — The
Last Phase," *Saturday Evening Post,* Oct. 12, 1935, pp. 27, 82-91;
"Paradox in Pajamas," *Saturday Evening Post,* Oct. 5, 1935, pp. 14-15,
34-40; "Prelude to a Heterocrat," *Saturday Evening Post,* Sept. 7,
1935, pp. 5-7, 84-88. I owe personal debts of thanks to Mr. Deutsch,
who generously gave me a morning from a busy day; to Robert H. Fossum,
who painstakingly criticized my manuscript; and to the librarians who
staff the Department of Archives and Manuscripts and the Louisiana

Room at Louisiana State University, the William B. Wisdom Collection at Tulane University, and the Louisiana Department at the Louisiana State Library.

7. Deutsch, "Paradox," p. 14; Hamilton Basso, "Huey Long and His Background," *Harper's,* 170 (May 1935), 664; Hodding Carter, "Louisiana Limelighter," *Review of Reviews,* 91 (Mar. 1935), 23.

8. *New Orleans Item,* "The Kingdom of the Kingfish," Aug. 2, 1939, p. 1; "Speech and Platform of Huey P. Long," Long Scrapbook I, Z-5 #1666 (Dec. 1923—Sept. 1925), p. 12, Department of Archives and Manuscripts, Louisiana State University.

9. Expressing the opinion of many observers, Carleton Beals in "Sharing Vice and Votes," *Nation,* Oct. 2, 1935, p. 377, called Long the "greatest 'Cain killed Abel...go thou and do likewise' Bible quoter in America."

10. George Sokolsky, "Huey Long," *Atlantic Monthly,* 156 (Nov. 1935), 526.

11. Harris, p. 36.

12. John K. Fineran, *Career of a Tinpot Napoleon* (New Orleans, 1932), p. 170; Kane, p. 73.

13. Beals, p. 67.

14. Louis Cochran, "The Louisiana Kingfish," *American Mercury,* 26 (July 1932), 283; Long, p. 99.

15. U.S. *Congressional Record — Senate,* 74th Cong., 1st Sess., 1935, 79, Pt. 3, p. 2953. This sentence and its context were widely quoted in Louisiana after the assassination.

16. Louisiana, "Calendar of the Senate Sitting as a Court of Impeachment," *Official Journal of the Proceedings of the Senate,* 5th Extra Sess., 1929, pp. 54-83.

17. Long, pp. 169-70.

18. Clipping identified as being from the *Shreveport Journal,* Sept. 18, 1930, "Administration of Honorable Huey P. Long." Scrapbook in 7 volumes prepared by the office of Eugene A. Conway, Supervisor of Public Accounts, III, 37, Louisiana Department, Louisiana State Library; also see Davis, p. 119.

19. Carter, p. 26.

20. Kane, p. 64.

21. U.P. Dispatch, Washington, Sept. 11, 1935, clipping identified as being from *Scranton* (Pa.) *Times,* Louisiana State University, Louisiana Room, Vertical Files.

22. F. Raymond Daniell, "The Gentleman from Louisiana," *Current History,* 41 (Nov. 1934), 172.

23. Quoted by Zinman, p. 216.

24. *New Orleans Times-Picayune,* Sept. 9, 1935.

25. Harris, pp. 92-93; *New Orleans Morning-Tribune,* Mar. 17, 1931.

26. Fineran, p. 3; Harris, p. 124; Sam Irby, *Kidnapped by the Kingfish* (New Orleans, 1932), p. 38. Shirley G. Wimberly, "Unmasking (Crawfish) Huey P. Long" (New Orleans, 1932), p. 6.

27. Davis, second page of an unnumbered "Postscript"; Beals, pp. 192-93.

28. *Time,* Oct. 20, 1930, p. 19.

29. Irby, pp. 22-23.

30. Quoted by Deutsch, *Murder Case,* p. 139.

31. H. O. Thompson, U.P. Correspondent, syndicated series of six articles published shortly after Long's death, Louisiana State University, Louisiana Room, Vertical Files.

32. F. Raymond Daniell, "Mrs. Huey Long Emerges, Modestly," *New York Times Magazine,* Feb. 9, 1936, p. 11.

33. Deutsch, "Heterocrat," p. 84.

34. *New York Times Magazine,* Feb. 9, 1936, p. 11.

35. *New Orleans Times-Picayune,* Sept. 16, 1935.

36. Walter Davenport, "How Huey Gets Away with It," *Collier's,* June 17, 1933, p. 10.

37. Kane, p. 62.

38. Basso, "Background," p. 671.

39. A typescript of this statement, along with correspondence between Miss Garig and Mrs. Carl Austin Weiss, is in the New Orleans Public Library, Louisiana Room, Vertical Files.

40. *Jackson* (Miss.) *Clarion Ledger,* Sept. 11, 1935.

41. Beals, p. 205. Long's concern for *his* L.S.U. is remarkably like Stark's obsession with *his* charity hospital. Even Huey's stated belief that a university should be kept "absolutely clean and pure" sounds like Willie's plan to keep his hospital free from corruption. See "My University," *Time,* Dec. 10, 1934, p. 43, and "Notes of the Seventeenth Annual Conference of the National Association of Deans and Advisors of Men, Feb. 28–Mar. 2, 1935," pp. 44–48.

42. Davis, p. 4.

Simone Vauthier

The Case of the Vanishing Narratee: An Inquiry into *All the King's Men*

While the narrator in *All the King's Men* has received much critical attention, his partner in the act of communication has been rather neglected. Yet not only are the two images of narrator and narratee[1] always dependent on each other but in Robert Penn Warren's novel the polarity is all the more marked because, contrary to common usage, the addressee is first to appear on the scene:

> To get there you follow highway 58, going northeast out of the city, and it is a good highway and new. Or was that day we went up it. You look up the highway and it is straight for miles coming at you, black and slick and tarry-shining against the white of the slab...and if you don't quit staring at that line and don't take a few deep breaths and slap yourself hard on the back of the neck you'll hypnotize yourself and you'll come to just at the moment when the right front wheel hooks over into the black dirt shoulder off the slab, and you'll try to jerk her back on but you can't because the slab is high like a curb,... But you won't make it, course.... Then a few days later the boys from the Highway Department will mark the spot with a little metal square painted white and on it in black a skull and crossbones....
> But if you wake up in time and don't hook your wheel off the slab, you'll go whipping on into the dazzle... Way off ahead of you, at the horizon where the cottonfields are blurred into the light, the slab will glitter and gleam like water, as though the road were flooded. You'll go whipping toward it, but it will always be ahead of you, that bright, flooded place, like a mirage.[2]

And on for two pages before the narrator-agent makes his appearance. Thus it is the narratee who is first made to take the trip to Mason City, to see the hypnotic road and the changing countryside, to face destruction or regeneration through baptismal waters that may be only part of a mirage. The narratee is shocked into awareness of a dangerous future in the extradiegetic world. But unwittingly he has been embarked on the perilous journey of the narration. And the man for whom God's mercy is implored at the end of the second paragraph, ("God have mercy on the mariner"), is not simply the man in the car, in "this age of the internal combustion engine," but the man on the road of the narration, the wedding guest suddenly turned mariner, whose precarious voyage through the text this paper proposes to retrace.

The trail of the narratee is not always easy to follow. In the first place the tracks which he leaves in the text are now very broad, now rather faint. Certainly, for long stretches, pronouns may clearly reveal his presence, either the recurrent "you" that proclaims the allocutor, as in the example just quoted, or the occasional "we" that includes the narrator and the receiver as in "we can be quite sure that Hubert had not named the behind guy..." (p.320) or that embraces the interlocutors and the generality of men:

> We get very few of the true images in our heads of the kind I am talking about, the kind which becomes more and more vivid for us if the passage of the years did not obscure their reality... (p.118).

Sometimes a change in tenses signals that the orientation of the utterance has changed and become more narrowly focused on the addressee:

> It *was* just the shade of question, of puzzlement.
>   But that *is* something. Not much, but something. It is not the left to the jaw and it does not rock them on their heels... Nothing lethal, just a moment's pause. But it *is* an advantage. *Push* it (p.237, italics added).

The passage from narrative to commentary marks the rise of the narratee who is confided in, enlightened, advised, and finally urged to act, with an imperative that introduces him directly in the text. Less obvious still is the network of rhetorical questions that riddles the narration. Sometimes they may be questions which the narrator asks of himself but which might also come from some interlocutor, like the following:

> Judge Irwin had killed Mortimer L. Littlepaugh. But Mortimer had killed Judge Irwin in the end. Or had it been Mortimer? Perhaps I had done it (p.353).

The narrator may also be challenging his audience: "A clam has to live, hasn't it?" (p.265) or taunting his self-pitying nar-

ratee: "You bloody fool, do you think you want to milk a cow?"
(p.76). Occasionally, however, the narratee puts his oar in:

> [Jack Burden] might come out and take a drink or take a
> hand of cards or do any of the other things they did, but
> what was real was back in that bedroom on the pine table.
>   What was back in the bedroom on the pine table?
>   A large packet of letters, eight tattered black bound
> account books tied together with faded red tape, a photo-
> graph... (p.160).

Needless to say, the narrator knows what is on the table; only
a narratee impatient to be told can ask the question from the
narrator, who simply relays it. This device is used repeatedly, often as a transition: *What had I read? I had read this.*
... Some of the narratee's interrogations are not formulated
but are revealed by a reiteration of some words or phrases:
"Then all at once something happened, and the yellow taste was
in the back of my mouth. This happened" (p.417). Indeed repetitions — a mannerism of the narrator's style — often convey
that an impression has to be made on an addressee:

> People still came here for picnics. Well, I had come
> here for picnics, too. I knew what picnics were like.
> I knew what a picnic was, all right (p.116).

Explanations also imply an allocutor who must be informed as
accurately as possible about what is going on in the diegesis[3]
(e.g. "the papers — the administration papers, that is") or in
the narration ("I am merely pointing that..."). Negations
that are in fact assertions suggest that he has to be set
right, or reassured: "The fabricator had, on this item, allowed himself the luxury of a little extra material. Not too
much. But enough" (p.104). Many sentences begin with an
assertive "no," or "yes," or "oh," and numerous phrases — all
right, no doubt, as I say, true, well — answer an implicit remark, objection or question of the addressee. In short, clues
to the narratee's presence are abundantly scattered throughout
the novel.
    Yet, pervasive as it is, this presence remains elusive and
after a first reading, one has only a blurred image of the narratee, who, on further investigation, turns out to be a many-
sided character. For the sake of brevity, only aspects of the
narratee as "you" will be examined here, although other elements of the narration — the questions and pseudo-questions,
the intimations and assertions, and the many analogies and
comparisons that convey something of the allocutor's habits,
attitudes and knowledgeability would also yield precious information. Obviously the addressee of the cited speeches (especially that of Willie's incantatory political speeches) would
deserve examination; such a study might throw light on the receiver of the narration but cannot be undertaken here.

The identities of the "you" are so many that some attempt at classification must be made. If we consider the relation of the "you" to the diegesis, we have, at one end of the spectrum, a narratee that is extradiegetic. Such is the case of the "you" that brings the addressee close to the reader. For instance after the narration has depicted at some length Sugar Boy driving the Governor's Cadillac, the narrator speculates upon the narratee's reaction: "No doubt, you thought Sugar Boy was a Negro. But he wasn't. He was Irish." Clearly, to entertain such a thought the person addressed must not have been given a sight of Sugar Boy; he is drawing an incorrect conclusion from his name and therefore he must stand in the position which the reader occupies. More obviously still, the person who is concerned by the remark, "Any act of pure perception is a feat, and if you don't believe it, try it sometime" (p.35), is challenged to accomplish an action in the extradiegetic world, and may be identified provisionally with the (mock) reader, as is the "you" earnestly advised to "burn his home movies" (p.272). At the other end of the spectrum, the "you" represents diegetic characters. Theodore and Adam are briefly addressed; Lois is saluted: "Goodbye, Lois, and I forgive you for everything I did to you" (p.308). A longer passage of the narration is donated to Lucy:

> Yes, Lucy, you have to believe that. You have to believe that to live. I know that you must believe that. And I would not have you believe otherwise. It must be that way, and I understand the fact. For you see, Lucy, I must believe that, too (p.427).

Sometimes the "you" refers to Willie Stark:

> One time I had wondered why the boss never had the house painted after he got his front feet in the trough and a dollar wasn't the reason you got up in the morning any more (p.22).

Sometimes, the "you" is a collective group of anonymous people, like those who send telegrams of condolence to the governor: "You couldn't tell that praying [i.e. getting off the telegram] would do any good, but it certainly never did anybody any harm" (p.384). A third position of the narratee as regards the diegesis must be briefly mentioned; in Chapter Four, Cass Mastern, being a metadiegetic narrator, can only have metadiegetic narratees.[4] These include an explicit "you," Gilbert, to whom Cass's letters are addressed, and implied narratees inasmuch as Cass's diary is oriented towards himself ("I write this down" that "if ever pride is in me, of flesh or spirit, I can peruse these pages and know with shame what evil has been in me" [p.161]), and also towards God, in the light of whom the young man tries to judge his life, and who is once directly addressed, "O God and my Redeemer!" (p.166).

The appearances of the purely diegetic and extradiegetic

narratees are few and far between in comparison with those of
yet another category to be studied next. But with the exception of the metadiegetic narratee, restricted to the confines
of Chapter Four, they are distributed fairly regularly throughout the novel. And significantly the appeal to a diegetic
"you" that is at once most developed in terms of the utterance
and most significant in terms of the theme, namely that to
Lucy, is placed towards the end. Worthy of notice, too, a
"you" is made to represent Willie only in the chapters describing his early career. Although *comparatively* little represented, these categories are important insofar as they project
a full range of positions and by setting up a number of secondary narratees, to whom the narration is only addressed occasionally, increase the complexity of the "implied dialogue"
which, as Wayne Booth has observed, goes on among author, narrator, the other characters, the reader, and it must be added,
the narratees.[5]

Furthermore, since, as narrator-participant the "I" has a
dual nature, so has the narratee; the duality is evidenced in
the report of Willie's rhetorical power over listening crowds:
"I would wait for the roar. You *can't help it*. I knew it
would come, but I would wait for it" (p.146, italics added).
In this case the "you" includes both a diegetic character —
the experiencing self — and an extradiegetic person — the narrating self[6] distancing himself from Jack Burden the participant — plus an undetermined someone, also extradiegetic — any
man in the same kind of situation. Or take the passage, too
long to be quoted here, when Jack muses on "the Friend of Your
Youth [who] is the only friend you will ever have, for he does
not see you" (p.234). The "you" designates again an undetermined man, who can bear any name, "Spike, Bud, Snip, Red,
Rusty, Jack, Dave,"[7] exemplifying a common human experience.
But the "you" addressed at the end of the meditation is so
close to the experiencing self that he is then called Jack:
The Friend of Your Youth "speaks your name...saying, 'Well,
Jack, damned glad you came, come on in, boy!'" (p.235). The
time flow of the narrative was interrupted, as Adam Stanton
came to the door to greet Jack, for a disquisition on "The
Friend of Your Youth"; we then are smoothly let back into the
narrative by the reduction of the "you" to one of its compo-
nents, the narrator, who now hears the words his friend has
been speaking. Moreover many occurrences of the second-person
belong to the level of the enunciation rather than to that of
the diegesis, introduced as they are in the images brought up
by the locutor (e.g. "[I could] let all the pictures of things
a man might want run through my head...and let them all slide
off, like a deck of cards slewing slowly off your hand. Maybe
the things you want are like cards" p.99).

Confronted therefore with a multiplicity of "you's" the
reader finds himself trying to assess the referential extension of specific instances, wondering how big or limited is

such and such a "you." In some cases, the second-person is,
so to say, all-inclusive:

> After a great blow, or crisis, after the first shock and
> then after the nerves have stopped screaming and twitch-
> ing, you settle down to the new condition of things...(p.
> 355).

This we may call, in parody of Jack Burden, The Aphoristic You.
(Of course, the Aphoristic You can only embody the wisdom of
mankind as filtered through the unconscious assumptions of the
narrator.) A more limited but still fairly extensive "you" is
the Mythical American:

> For that is where you come, after you have crossed oceans
> and eaten stale biscuits while prisoned forty days and
> nights in a storm-tossed rat-trap, after you have sweated
> in the greenery and heard the savage whoop, after you have
> built cabins and cities and bridged rivers, after you have
> lain with women and scattered children like millet seed in
> a high wind, after you have composed resonant documents,
> made noble speeches, and bathed your arms in blood to the
> elbows, after you have shaken with malaria in the marshes
> and in the icy wind across the high plains. That is where
> you come, to lie alone in a bed in a hotel room in Long
> Beach, California. Where I lay...(p.309).

We have here the Archetypical American Hero, already described
though less ambiguously, by Tocqueville,[8] and epitomizing American history. In another version, the historical archetype is
resolved into distinct roles — murderer, gold-rusher, Gree-
ley's young man, etc. — which reveal more clearly the American
nightmare along with the American dream.

> For West is where we all plan to go some day. It is where
> you go when the land gives out and the oldfield pines en-
> croach. It is where you go when you get the letter saying:
> *Flee, all is discovered*. It is where you go when you look
> down at the blade in your hand and see the blood on it.
> It is where you go when you are told that you are a bubble
> on the tide of empire. It is where you go when you hear
> that there's gold in them-thar hills. It is where you go
> to grow up with the country. It is where you go to spend
> your old age. Or it is just where you go (p.270).

The Mythical American is easily reduced into the Average American: "When you don't like it where you are, you always go west"
(p.309). Indeed the Average American and his experiences are
often invoked. On occasion he is even provided with a family:

> It was like a showing of a family movie, the kind the ad-
> vertisements tell you to keep so that you will have a rec-
> ord of the day Susie took her first little toddle and the
> day Johnny went off to kindergarten and the day you went

up Pike's Peak and the day of the picnic on the old home
farm and the day you were made chief sales manager and
bought your first Buick (p. 272).

Little Susie reappears at least twice as the average child of
the Average American, *you*. Occasionally, the Average American
turns Southerner: "You don't get rich being an Attorney General in a Southern State" (p.219). Clearly determined by the
narrative situation is the case of the Attentive Observer,
who has the opportunity to watch the characters in action, although sometimes the observer is only the Virtual Observer:
"the atmosphere would have reminded you of a morgue" (p.367).
Determined and yet indefinite is the Equivocal Participant,
the "you" that "represents" both a diegetic character and an
allocutor *persona,* singular or plural:

> The gentlemen from the city persuaded Willie that he was
> the savior of the state. I suppose that Willie had his
> natural quota of ordinary suspicion and cageyness, but
> those things tend to evaporate when what people tell you
> is what you want to hear (p.66).

A particular variety of the Equivocal Participant, the Disguised Narrator, is a recurrent figure: the above-mentioned
passage on the Friend of Your Youth furnishes a typical example. Hesitation as to the identity of the Disguised Narrator
is possible because somehow our expectancy is not answered.
For instance we naturally expect the "you" in the following
sentence to encompass the allocutor:

> For after the dream there is no reason why you should not
> go back and face the fact which you have fled from (even
> if the fact seems to be that you have, by digging the
> truth about the past, handed over Anne Stanton to Willie
> Stark), for any place to which you may flee will not be
> like the place from which you have fled, and you might as
> well go back, after all, to the place where you belong,
> for nothing was your fault or anybody's fault, for things
> are always as they are (p.311).

But although in the main sentence the second-person general-
izes and covers a multitude of experiences, on which the immediate context and the many allusions to the myth of the West
throw light, we realize with something of a jolt that the "you"
in the parenthesis can only refer to Jack Burden, since he
alone can have done the action mentioned. Then the other
"you's" of the passage are felt as representing the narrator.
 But such examples also provide us with a clue to the functioning of the second-person. Often it is made to stand for
the first-person in a figure that can be called *speaker/ad-
dressee (destinateur/destinataire) commutation.*[9] In *All the
King's Men* commutation of the interlocutors is a systematic
device which deserves closer scrutiny.

Destinateur/destinataire commutation is by far the most
frequent. Avowedly the story of Willie's rise from "Cousin
Willie" to Governor Stark, the narration is therefore apparently oriented towards outsiders who have some knowledge of
the Boss's career, without being in possession of all the
facts and, above all, of the meaning of them. But even before
the narrator discloses personal information about himself,
long before he owns that this "is [his] story, too," Jack
Burden betrays the autobiographic nature of his narrative when
he makes the "you" a reflection of his self, and the outside
allocutor an inner auditor. (Amusingly enough, this is symbolized in one minor detail: when Willie exerts his oratorical
spell on the Mason City crowd, "you could hear one insane and
irrelevant July fly sawing away up in one of the catalpa trees
..." (p.9). If here the "you" can represent the anonymous listeners, in the following repetition of the notation, the "you"
can no longer do so and the present tense underlines that the
sensation is one of the narrator's: "there was only the sound
of the July flies, which *seems* to be inside your head as
though it were the grind and whir of the springs and cogs
which are you..." (p.11).

But when the narrator declares "I have a story. It is the
story of a man who lived in the world and the world looked one
way for a long time..." and then goes on to summarize his evolution in third-person terms for three paragraphs (pp.435-6),
he uses a *terminal/non-terminal commutation* to put some distance between his past self and the regenerated self, which,
however, is grammatically and dramatically reborn at the end
of the last paragraph: "It looks as though Hugh will get back
into politics and when he does I'll be along to hold his coat."
And reborn, too, complete with a past still active in the present as indicated by the tense: "*I've had* some valuable experience in that line" (p.436, italics added). Seeing Willie for
the first time, Jack Burden is, unknowingly, meeting fate, so
this is how the narrator reports the occasion:

> Metaphysically it was the Boss, but how was I to know?
> Fate comes walking through the door and it is five feet
> eleven inches tall and heavyish in the chest and shortish
> in the leg and is wearing a seven-fifty seersucker suit...
> and a stiff high collar like a Sunday-school superinten-
> dent and a blue-striped tie which you know his wife gave
> him last Christmas and which he has kept in tissue paper
> with the holly card ("Merry Xmas to my Darling Willie
> from your Loving Wife") until he got ready to go to the
> city, and a gray felt hat with the sweat stains showing
> through the band. It comes in just like that and how are
> you to know? It comes in, trailing behind Alex Michel...
> (p.14).

In the whole paragraph, Willie is referred to by an a-personal
pronoun, except in the relative clause which deals with his

personal life, symbolized by the Christmas *tie* and represented
by a new correlation *my-your,* where, incidentally, one expects
his. However, when after the introduction of Willie as husband the narration returns to Willie as the embodiment of Fate,
not only is the a-personal "it" resumed, for an effect which
is now more marked than in the first occurrence from being
pointedly repeated; but with the repetition of the transformed
question and the use of "you," (how are you to know?), both
narrator and narratee are made responsible for the *person/non-
person commutation,* which betrays their common unawareness of
Willie's potentialities and of the mysterious ways of fate.
Definite/indefinite commutations are also to be found (e.g.
"*They* called that Idealism in *my* book I had when I was in college" p.30, italics added). But since such turns are common
enough in everyday speech they need not be emphasized. An
arresting sentence may be mentioned here:

> In a hanging you do not change a man's personality. You
> just change the length of his neck and give him a quiz-
> zical expression, and in an electrocution you just cook
> some bouncing meat in a wholesale lot (p.317).

One would rather expect something like: a man's personality is
not changed, and only the length of his neck is changed,
clauses that would leave the responsibility for these drastic
measures unassigned, whereas the "you" involves the allocutor
in the executioner's role or in society's meting out of punishment.

   Apart from commutations — the substitution of one person
(or non-person) for another on the paradigmatic axis of the
narration — permutations — a substitution on the syntagmatic
axis — also play a prominent part in *All the King's Men.* In
Chapter Four, the narrating self assumes toward a period of
his own life, with a measure of self-parody, the detached
stance which the acting self took as history graduate toward
Cass Mastern, the object of his research.[10] The first-person
narrator then turns into a third-person character, "Jack Burden" and "he," while Cass, a third-person in the diegetic narration, now becomes a speaking "I," whose letters and journal
are abundantly cited. As a consequence of this permutation,
the "you" of the overall narrative situation can become a "we."

> [The journal] did not report what book it was that Gil-
> bert's riding crop tapped. It is not important what book
> it was. Or perhaps it is important, for something in *our*
> mind, in *our* imagination wants to know that fact. *We see*
> the red, square, strong hand ("my brother is strong made
> and florid") protruding from the white cuff, grasping the
> crop which in that grasp looks fragile like a twig. *We
> see* the flick of the little leather loop on the page, a
> flick brisk, not quite contemptuous, but *we cannot* make
> out the page (p.164, italics added).

Here the first-person plural, while it excludes the first person singular subject of the embedded utterance, includes four kinds of participants in the act of communication — the implied author whose fairly discrete presence in the sequence is here made manifest, "Jack Burden," the narratee(s), and the reader; all four stand on almost equal footing in respect to the fact under scrutiny since to all of them (or us) it is something out of the past, fictive or real, which has to be deciphered. Obviously the "I" of the diegetic story can never say "we," meaning himself and his narratee and/or reader, when he tells or ponders about acts of his own life, but only when he speculates or moralizes on the human condition. (And as a matter of fact there are a few such cases of a universal "we.") He could, of course, write: "We wonder what books Cousin Willie read in the lonely, cold upstairs room." But this would shape a different relation between narrator and narratee from that which is firmly established from the opening sentence of the novel and the narrator never uses the first-person plural to puzzle out the enigma that is Willie Stark.

Commutations and permutations, as might be expected, often interact, creating complex moves across the narrational chessboard.

(1) At night you pass through a little town where you once lived, and you expect to see yourself wearing knee pants, standing all alone on the street corner under the hanging bulbs.... (2) You expect to see that boy standing there under the street lamp, out too late, and you feel like telling him to go to bed or there will be hell to pay. (3) But maybe you are at home in bed and sound asleep and not dreaming and nothing has ever happened that seems to have happened. (4) But, then, who the hell is this in the back seat of the big black Cadillac that comes ghosting through the town? (5) Why, this is Jack Burden. Don't you remember little Jack Burden? He used to go out in his boat in the afternoon on the bay to fish, and come home and eat his supper and kiss his beautiful mother goodnight and say his prayers and go to bed at nine-thirty. (6) Oh, you mean old Ellis Burden's boy? (7) Yeah, and that woman he married out of Texas — or was it Arkansas? — that big-eyed, thin-faced woman who lives up there in that old Burden place now with that man she got herself. Whatever happened to Ellis Burden? Hell, I don't know, nobody around here had any word going on years. He was a queer 'un. Damn if he wasn't queer, going off and leaving a real looker like that woman out of Arkansas. Maybe he couldn't give her what she craved. Well, he gave her that boy, that Jack Burden. Yeah.

You come into the town at night and there are the voices (pp.40-41).

In the first sentence, we may take the "you" to be the narratee (n) and a projection of the narrator (N) who has just been
telling about such a ride to Burden's Landing; "yourself wearing knee pants" is a reduction in time of N + n, a past self
of both narrator and narratee. But this past self takes on
an independent life and becomes a third person, *that boy, he,*
in sentence (2). The "you" of sentence (3) seems to be N + n
again, with the difference, however, that n seems to have
dwindled in size: the first narratee could be almost any reader of the male sex with a smalltown background; whereas now
the possibility that the narratee could also be the reader is
more radically excluded since n is perhaps asleep — which the
reader of *All the King's Men* cannot be, of course. With the
question of sentence (4) a *voice* is heard, which, as the answer makes clear, implies a speaking "I." However, this "I"
cannot be the first-person narrator since *he* is now ensconced
in the text as the referent of the query, the man in the back
seat of the Cadillac. The voice can only be the voice of n.
Nor is the transformation of N + n complete inasmuch as n further splits into two dialoguing characters, one who recognizes
"little Jack Burden" (n_1) and one (n_2) who has to be reminded
of the identity (through blood kin, a misleading index) of
Jack Burden. By now neither can be considered indefinite, extradiegetic addressees. Absorbed into the story, they also
become active participants in the narration as they take over
the narrating role, providing the reader with new information
on Jack Burden's background. The permutation is complete when
the knowledgeable n_1 uses the first person "Hell, *I* don't
know." Yet this is an empty "I," whose outlines will never
be filled and whose sole function is to displace the narrating
self, who could have given us this kind of information, and
thus modify the addressee, an effect which is enhanced by the
fact that the typography — the absence of commas, the juxtaposition of question and answer — makes it impossible at the
end of the dialogue to discriminate with certainty between the
two interlocutors.
   Another interesting transformation of the "you" can be observed in the following passage (pp.239-40):

(1) Which is nonsense, for whatever you live is Life.
(2) That is something to remember when you meet the old
classmate who says, "Well, now, on our last expedition up
the Congo —" or the one who says, "Gee, I got the sweetest
little wife and three of the swellest kids ever —" (3)
You must remember it when you sit in hotel lobbies, or
lean over bars to talk to the bartender, or stand in a
dark street at night, in early March, and stare into a
lighted window. (4) And remember little Susie in there
has adenoids and the bread is probably burned, and turn
up the street, for the time has come to hand me down that

walking cane, for I got to catch that midnight train, for
all my sin is taken away. For whatever you live is Life.

After comprehending N + n + n + n...in sentence (1), the extension of the "you" progressively diminishes until in the last
part of sentence (3) it coincides with N, the narrator who happened to be staring into a lighted window on an early March
night when he went into this philosophical mood. Yet with sentence (4) and the imperative *remember,* which modulates the earlier *it is something to remember,* followed by *you must remember,* the "you" designates a definite singular n; only, in this
case, the narratee is revealed as an alter ego of the narrator,
who then reappears as "me" and then "I." But, although defined through grammatical marks and through the situation
(Jack Burden is on his way to catch the night train to Memphis
and to uncover Judge Irwin's guilty secret), the "I" is in
fact more — therefore less — than Jack Burden's self: it is
the indefinite "I" of the popular song, the blues and the spiritual, as phrasing and rhythm connote, so that it can easily
become again the generalizing, aphoristic "you" at the end of
the paragraph: Whatever you/one/man live[s] is Life. In short,
the narratee is a Protean figure who alternately dilates and
contracts and keeps changing positions in the narration, with
the result that the distance separating it from the other figures increases or decreases accordingly, and the pattern of relationships between them shifts like a kaleidoscope.

Throughout all this, the characteristic feature of the
narratee is his dependence on the narrator. Even at the farthest distance — as fictive reader — the "you" is dependent
for his very existence on the "I" that projects him as an image of the Other. And this Other, notwithstanding his more
checquered career (as outlaw or family man, for instance) is
not very different from the experiencing self. The composite
narratee has participated in some of Jack's experiences, been
subjected to the fascination of Willie, seen Anne Stanton as a
young girl, taken the meaningful trip to the West, and has had,
in a word, an American education. Although he may be unaware
of certain aspects of the South, since things have to be described to him, he is still very familiar with Southern life
as many analogies show, and he knows for example what it feels
like to have "a sizable chunk of dry cornpone stuck in [his]
throat." A man of culture, he can pick up allusions to Prome-
theus (p.394) or echoes of Poe in the wind that "didn't chill
us or kill us in the kingdom by the sea" (p.103). More significantly, the narratee has Jack Burden's inquisitive mind —
witness all the passages developed through questions — and he
shares in his basic assumptions on life as evinced in the many
generalizations. Thus he reveals Jack's need to extract private meaning out of public events and to socialize personal
meaning in a dialectic process. (To this extent, the frequent
use and the nature of the adjunctive "you"[11] partly reflects

and shapes Jack's attempts to "re-establish his values within
a different social framework" from that of Burden's Landing.[12])
Even in his talents as a quick-change artist, the addressee
mirrors the narrator, a self-confessed *Svengali*.   Thus in his
choice of narratees, Jack Burden betrays both his anxiety at
being limited, defined, limited *because* defined, and his desire for self-definition.

For to turn to the Other is to meet the Self, but to face
the Self is to encounter the Other. *Je est un autre*. And in
All the King's Men, the "you" is an *alter* ego — not a past vanished self, however, to whom the narrator would talk across
the gap of years, in the typical autobiographical stance.
(Needless to say there is such a distance in time and identity
between the narrating and the acting selves, but it is marked
through a number of elements, temporal adverbs, tenses, whole
comments [*that was what I thought I had learned*] and an epi-
sodic use of the third-person, etc. — which cannot be studied
here.) On the contrary, the "you" would seem to speak for a
"not-dead" self since he relives in an intemporal, almost
dream-like present some of the experiences of Jack.

> But as the train pulls away, a woman comes to the back
> door of one of the houses — just the figure of a woman
> for you cannot make out the face.... She goes back into
> the house. To what is in the house...but you cannot see
> through the walls to the secret to which the woman has
> gone in.
>   The train pulls away, faster now, and the woman is
> back in the house where she is going to stay. She'll
> stay there. And all at once, you think that you are the
> one who is running away, and who had better run fast to
> wherever you are going for it will be dark soon....
>   But nothing happens, and you remember that the woman
> had not even looked up at the train. You forget her, and
> the train goes fast, and is going fast when it crosses a
> little trestle... [You] see the cow standing in the water
> upstream near the single leaning willow. And all at once
> you feel like crying. But the train is going fast, and
> almost immediately whatever you feel is taken away from
> you, too.
>   You bloody fool, do you think that you want to milk
> a cow?
>   You do not want to milk a cow.
>   Then you are at Upton (p.76).

Against the increasing speed of the train, (although it moves
through "cloying," "syrup"-like air), is balanced the stag-
nancy of the "you," the self becalmed in the treacly waters of
an eternal present, unable to detach himself from the images
and feelings which Jack believes have been taken away from him
but which "stay there" forever.[13] And surely, the woman ap-
pearing only to disappear, going back to her secret behind the

walls, and even the cow with her milk now forever unavailable
remain there in the narrator's *speech* because their verbal evo-
cation reanimates older images, older feelings — the longing
for a mother's love, the desire to know the secret behind the
parents' door. (This is, however, a privileged example, insofar as the metonymical chain of desire is short and the re-
pressed material can be perceived through the actual images.)
But it would be absurd to say that the disjunctive "you" is
Jack Burden's unconscious self. Rather when he addresses this
"you," the narrator projects a split state of consciousness.
Nor can this "you" be called Jack's "bad" self, for he is as
guilty as but no guiltier than the "I." In fact, he is a
double whose *raison d'être* seems to be his non-subjectivity.
Jack Burden suffers from a sense of unreality which makes him
see others as unreal too: "Oh, they are real, all right, and
it may be the reason they don't seem real to you is that you
aren't very real yourself" (p.58). Unable to see himself
clearly, he posits in the disjunctive "you" the double that
embodies him, that makes *him* visible because *he* can address it.
Percipi est esse, and to speak is to make oneself perceived.
     Therefore, if the polarity of "you" and "I" points to the
disassociation of Jack Burden's personality, what can hold
Jack-as-Humpty-Dumpty together is precisely the hyphen of the
interlocutory act. Furthermore the disjunctive "you" performs
its part in the act so satisfactorily that it is truly a "di-
dactic you." By in fact telling parts of his story — the trip
to Mason City, the trip to Burden's Landing, the trip to Upton,
in particular — through a second-person, the first-person narrator shows that he is not yet fully aware of all the aspects
of his own life or is at any rate reluctant to face them. The
"you" which conveniently separates and distances experience
also clarifies it, and assumes the function which Michel Butor
assigns to the second-person, marking "a progress in self-
consciousness, the very birth of language, or of *a* language."[14]
Indirect confirmation can be found in the Cass Mastern episode.
Cass, who is convinced of his personal guilt and can explain
his sinfulness in theological terms, simply records his testimony through a straight-forward first-person narration, although he is aware that his present "I" is different from his
past "I." So "you" is a form of address which, with but one
exception (p.175), he reserves for a "real" allocutor and whenever he wants to generalize he uses a-personal forms (such as
it is dishonorable to spy upon another) or the indefinite *man*
(*Man is never safe*) and "one" (*One can only know oneself in
God,* p.173). Direct confirmation is brought by the gradual
disappearance of the disjunctive "you" in Jack Burden's speech.
Already the last chapter contains noticeably fewer occurrences
and there are none after the visit to Lucy, which marks a high
point in Jack's acceptance of Willie Stark and of himself.
     From the beginning, in any case, balancing the egocentrism
and disintegration of a self refracted in a multiplicity of

"you's" there is the structure that both shapes and expresses
the relation of Jack to the world. Despite all temptations to
disengage himself, to retreat to the solitude of the anonymous
room in Long Beach or, more drastically, into the Great Sleep,
Jack also needs to establish relationships with an Other.
Thus, in his relation, discourse, "a statement presupposing a
locutor and an auditor, and in the first named an intention of
influencing the second in some way" predominates over "récit,"
a "narrative of past events."[15] Although passages from the
former type of utterance to the latter and back are frequent,
All the King's Men is overwhelmingly a discourse. Consequently, it is difficult to agree entirely with Franz Stanzel's
statement that

> the first-person narrator's eccentric position is the rea-
> son why long stretches of the novel contain no real first-
> person references.... From a given page of such a section
> it is often impossible to decide whether the work is a
> first-person novel or a third-person novel.[16]

Although the narrator may not be present, he is represented in
the text often through his faithful companion, the narratee.
See, for instance, the many signs of the latter in the description of Willie's early career, which the narrator reconstructs.
The permanence of the addressee, whether the disjunctive "you,"
the adjunctive "you," or the truly non-subjective person, tes-
tifies to the protagonist's deep need for relatedness. Besides, the narratee does not usually condescend to his allocutor, although he may be something of an authoritarian, enjoin-
ing behavior (*you ride*) or ideas (*you think*). On occasion too
he may give him a piece of advice: "If you ask something quick
and sharp out of a clear sky you may get an answer you never
would get otherwise" (p.207). But insofar as the narratee is
often made, through comments and analogies, to carry part of
the ideological burden of the novel, his experience is necessarily considered to be as valid as that of the narrator.

   This points to another of the many functions of the narratee. He does not simply contribute to the characterization of
the narrator but plays a part in the elaboration of the ideas
and themes of the novel. In the generalizations and similes,
the adjunctive "you" provides the clarifying parallel and
guarantees the general application of whatever Jack may feel
or think. Making the story more natural, the narratee also
makes its ideological message more acceptable, because apparently accepted within the textual dialogue. To him, indeed,
is delegated one of the functions which Robert Penn Warren assigned to his narrator, that of chorus,[17] for which it is better suited than Jack Burden, being collective, anonymous, and
already aware of the public aspects of the drama whose hidden
patterns Burden is seeking to trace out. Because it is change-
able and unobtrusive, this chorus does not harden temporary
half-truths into eternal verities, thus preserving the dialec-

tic complexity of the novel. Because it is undefined, it can enhance both the American dimension of the action and the "tragedy of incomplete personalities"—which, beyond the Southern or American affabulation, is the real theme of the work.[18]

The relation of narratee and theme is even more interesting. For one thing, if in *All the King's Men*, "a plurality of heroes is one symbol of a riven world,"[19] so is a multiplicity of narratees a further symbol of a riven self in a riven world, as the contrast between Jack Burden's narration and Cass Mastern's emphasizes. Yet regeneration, rebirth, in other words a newer integration, remains possible, partly because through language can be discovered anew the "complexity of relatedness." Moreover, although identity, contrary to what some of the characters may believe, is not fixed and unchanging, man is nonetheless responsible for his actions — a lesson for which Jack pays with "blood." While the Protean "you" becomes the mask of an uncertain, shifting self, the pronominal permanence of the "I" — despite a few eclipses — asserts the continuity of moral responsibility, notwithstanding. Conversely the persistence of the "you's" in the part of the narration concerned with the *discovery* of meaning affirms again that self-realization depends on the realization of the Other. Thus the autobiographical narration can be both the recognition and the acting-out of man's accountability.

If we go into the functioning of the text, the complex moves of the interlocutors, the permutations and commutations mirror the central metaphor of the novel, the image of the web. Just as "the world is all of one piece," so is speech: if you touch the "web of things" and the web of words — "however lightly, at any point," "the vibrations ripple to the remotest perimeter" (p.188). With every change of addressee, the narrator sends ripples that modify not only the arrangement of the verbal parts of his utterance but his relations to the allocutor, to the message and hence to the world. These substitutions also undercut the antimony of the "I" and the "you," the ego and the non-ego, the self and the world, which are then seen to be dialectically generating one another. "Direction is all."

In addition, the chess-like moves of the interlocutory figures may also serve to modalize the narrator's conscious attitudes. Alone in his car, Jack finds comfort in a sense of depersonalization:

> They say you are not you, except in terms of relation to other people. If there weren't any other people there wouldn't be any you because what you do, which is what you are, only has meaning in relation to other people. That is a very comforting thought when you are in the car in the rain at night alone, for then you aren't you, and not being you or anything, you can really lie back and get some rest. It is a vacation from being you...(p.128).

By the use of the introductory "*they* say," and of the condi-
tional tense, as well as by the flippancy of his tone in the
rest of the passage, Burden seems to discount the theory even
as he expounds it — a characteristic stance of Jack, who likes
to have his cake and eat it. But the text yet hints at a different story. The "I" installs an insistent "you" in place of
itself, thus suggesting inter-subjectivity and the inversibil-
ity of "I" and "you." This seemingly bears out the idea that
you are not you except in the presence of people. At the same
time, it suggests that the idea is acceptable only at a certain level. Even in solitude the "I" can posit a "you" to
relate to, in the socialized structure of language. Jack Burden, indeed, manipulates language so resourcefully that he convinces us that man, the speaking animal, can never be really
alone: language provides him with a built-in allocutor.

No wonder then that the relationship of narrator and narratee shapes the process of self-knowledge which is the protagonist's central experience. At the beginning of his narration
which not only tells about but mirrors his quest, Jack Burden,
who has little sense of identity, confronts himself with a
series of narratees, who, whether imaginary or "real," represent faces of the self he is looking for. He commits what
Cass Mastern, who lived in a world where men were more complete, less scattered and could relate more easily to a transcendence, considers a human error, the error of trying "to
know oneself by the self of another" instead of in "God's eye"
(p.173). In "the age of the internal combustion engine," however, it would seem to be less a defect than a normal pattern
of behavior. And the protagonist achieves maturity through
what Robert Penn Warren calls elsewhere an "osmosis of being
which in the end does not deny, but affirms his identity."[20]
With its use of narratees, its permutations and commutations,
its disjunctive and adjunctive "you's" that overlap and may
fade out into one another, the narration embodies the process
of interpenetration[21] and of readjustment of perspectives.
Through the shifting patterns of relations, "new perspectives"
and "new values" are being created and Jack comes to discover
his kinship with other men, i.e. his participation in human
guilt at the same time as he realizes his unavoidable isolation. Hence, as has been pointed out, the need for the disjunctive "you" reflecting the split self and for the adjunctive "you" mirroring the defining Other diminishes.

As Jack's quest for identity passes through tentative and
incomplete identifications with father figures that he in a
sense kills, for "the truth always kills the father," so does
his struggle for integration pass through incomplete cleavage
of the self, for "separateness is identity." And he can get
rid of the obsessive inner narratee when, having been reborn,
he is at last able to tell his version of the "family romance"
to Anne Stanton: "I had to tell it to somebody," he says to
Anne, "I had to say it out loud — to be sure it's true [that

he is changed]. But it is true.... It's my mother, you know" (p.435). Jack can now tell the significant encounter with his mother and the return to Anne without any mediation. Similarly, the next-to-last generalization of the novel is one that stresses no longer the interrelatedness of the subjective to the non-subjective but the relation between the one and the many, the individual and mankind. "For *each of us* is the son of a million fathers." No doubt as he goes out into "the convulsion of the world," Jack Burden will be involved in new patterns of relationships. No doubt the self-knowledge he has acquired is incomplete but he has achieved an awareness that enables him to stand alone and yet say "we," whether the "we" includes only his wife, or all of us, the children of a million fathers. Having told his story the narrator can make a *new* beginning and, turning historian, write the formerly abandoned life of Cass Mastern whom he "now may come to understand." And in the Life, *récit* ought to prevail over discourse, narrative over narration, in conformity with a scholarly code that Burden can now accept because he has found his true language.

In short, the narratee has become expendable. And his fate also concerns the reader. True, reader and narratee are not to be confused. But by the same polarity that creates the dependence of the narrative "you" and the narrative "I," the reversibility of "you" and "I" works not only within the story-telling situation but, to some degree, within the reading situation. I, the reader, cannot help feeling somehow implied in the "you" that is being addressed so insistently, even as I realize that this is a doubly fictive you with a fictive experience which may be quite remote from mine. The brilliant introduction that whizzes the narratee over the road to Mason City and the "great mirage" of the meaning of the novel may help set up the reader's partial identification with the narratee before he has had the opportunity to begin establishing the more usual identification with the protagonist and perhaps it brings him thus closer to the authorial *persona*. In any case, the reader is perforce implicated in the experience of the narratee, if only to the extent that he has to strip off his masks, and keep track of who and where he is. Thus the transformations of the narratee upset the reader's facile certainties and engage him in a quest of his own which parallels that of the narrator. Should he refuse to identify provisionally with the protagonist and to share in his burden of human guilt, he is jolted into awareness of his guilt as virtual narratee, whether the latter is cast in the role of conventional brigand or less conventional executioner. *L'hypocrite lecteur, mon semblable, mon frère* must acknowledge himself an accomplice of either the acting self, or the narrator, or the narratee — if not of all three of them. But he is thereby offered the chance — together with the advice — to "be baptized to be born again," too. Redemption is available to every reader

willing to change, to "burn his home movies," to accept his
commitment as reader and play the metonymic and metaphoric
game of the novel.

Yet woe to the unwary reader who has accepted in good
faith the role of next-of-kin to the narratee. When the regenerated "I" throws overboard the now useless "you," he may
feel like a castaway, may at least experience a sense of de-
pletion.[22] Having been allowed the freedom of many squares
across the board, he now discovers that his moves are severely
restricted, and few positions open to him from which to view
the narrator's "picture of the world." But he had had his
warning in the introduction with its recurrent images of car-
wrecks and the perils of water. So he too is, in a sense,
back at the beginning, as Jack Burden is back at his dissertation grappling with the task of understanding Cass Mastern and
relating his story. The task for the reader is to start asses-
sing anew the characters' half truths (Cass Mastern's and Willie Stark's and Jack Burden's) in the light of the whole truth.
But the whole truth, of course, can, in this case, only be
that embodied in the novel, a "myth" of "human nature's trying
to fulfill itself,"[23] Humpty-Dumpty poised back on his wall by
the grace of *All the King's Men*. To that extent too, it is a
form in which the reader collaborates in the dialectical process of reading, and for which he must therefore assume some
responsibility. God have mercy on all reading mariners.

---

1. I am indebted for this term to Gerald Prince whose two seminal
articles ("Notes Towards a Categorization of Fictional 'Narratees',"
Genre, 4, March 1971, pp. 100-5, and "Introduction à l'étude du narrataire," *Poétique,* 14, 1973, pp. 178-96) greatly helped me to cate-
gorize and define my interpretation of the allocutor in *All the King's
Men*.

2. Robert Penn Warren, *All the King's Men* (New York: Bantam Books,
1955), p. 1. Page references are to this edition.

3. These are in a somewhat simplified version the concepts established by Gérard Genette in *Figures II* (Paris, 1972), p. 202, and *Figures III* (Paris: Editions du Seuil, 1972), pp. 72, 238, 241 and passim.
Diegetic is what belongs or refers to the time-space world of the
story (the diegesis), metadiegetic what belongs or refers to the time-
space of a story within a story (the metadiegesis). Let us add that
for simplification's sake, we have said that the "I" *refers* to or *represents* Jack Burden, while the "I" can only refer to the individual
speech act in which it is uttered, designating the locutor. As "you"
only designates the allocutor.

4. Gérard Genette, one of the first critics to have paid any attention to the narratee, writes: "Comme le narrateur, le narrataire
est un des éléments de la situation narrative et il se place néces-
sairement au même niveau diégétizue" (*Figures III,* p. 265).

5. Wayne C. Booth, *The Rhetoric of Fiction* (Chicago: University
of Chicago Press, 1961), p. 155. Not only breadth but depth of communication is thus achieved, as a simple example will illustrate:

It was, in a sense, proper that Cass Mastern — in the gray jacket, sweat stiffened and prickly like a hair shirt, which it was for him at the same time that it was the insignia of a begrudged glory — should have gone back to Georgia to rot slowly to death. For he had been born in Georgia, he and Gilbert Mastern and Lavinia Mastern, in the red hills up towards Tennessee. "I was born," the first page of the first volume of the journal said, "in a log cabin in north Georgia, in circumstances of poverty...(p.161).

Here the implied narrator, who is a *persona* of the extradiegetic narrator, the "I," who has been telling the story so far, comments on the destiny of Cass (it was *proper*) for the benefit of a narratee. What with the anaphoric "he," the string of names, the redundancy of the Mastern surname, the phrasing (in *the* red hills *up toward* Tennessee) and the rhythm of the explanation, the illusion of a voice is created, thus emphasizing the encounter between locutor and allocutor. But when the narrator quotes Cass's journal, he does not simply substantiate his own statement. In the quotation, not only is a different locutor speaking but a different allocutor is addressed. So redundant as the information on Cass's birthplace really is, it is not received at the same level and the reader, who is, in a sense, the ultimate addressee, must himself assume different roles at different levels and shift positions.

6. Franz Stanzel has made use of these two concepts in his analysis of *All the King's Men*. *Narrative Situations in the Novel, Tom Jones, Moby-Dick, The Ambassadors, Ulysses* (Bloomington: Indiana University Press, 1971), pp. 63-4.

7. Since Robert Penn Warren is known to his friends as "Red," one may wonder if this is not a secret signature, a tiny image of the author hiding in the crowded canvas of the novel, like a medieval painter's self-portrait. More, it might suggest that one of Jack's names is RPW; but on the testimony of this same passage the RPW *persona* is to be sought behind the masks of the narratees as well as behind that of the narrator.

8. "Le peuple américain se voit marcher lui-même à travers ces déserts, desséchant les marais, redressant les fleuves, peuplant la solitude et domptant la nature. Cette image magnifique d'eux-mêmes ne s'offre pas seulement de loin en loin a l'imagination des Américains, etc." ("Sources de poésie," *De la démocratie en Amérique* [Paris: Gallimard, 1961], I, p. 79).

9. The following categorization of commutations is that of J. Dubois *et al.* in *Rhétorique Générale* (Paris: Larousse, 1970), pp. 159-70.

10. The reasons for the change of reference may be more complex than suggested above. But Franz Stanzel's explanation seems, in any case, inadequate: "the author was evidently faced with the problem of avoiding any confusion which might arise between the two first-person narrators while at the same time preserving the sense of immediacy in the content of the journal. His solution was to transform the original "I" of the main narrator into an objectified third-person novel figure and retain the first-person narrative situation of the journal" (p.63). The interpretation disregards in particular the resort by the first-person to a terminal/non-terminal, subjective/non-subjective commutation in scattered parts of the novel. See pp. 40, 103, 309, 311, 323, for instance.

11. We shall call disjunctive the "you" that represents a fragment of the self and adjunctive the "you" that subsumes a plural experience, in which the "I" can be included.

12. Louis D. Rubin, Jr., *Writers of the Modern South* (Seattle: University of Washington Press, 1970), p. 125.

13. Although time seems to freeze, this is not "a moment of frozen action," such as Robert Penn Warren observed in Faulkner's fiction ("The Art of Fiction XVIII: Robert Penn Warren," *The Paris Review,* reprinted in John L. Longley, Jr., ed., *Robert Penn Warren, A Collection of Critical Essays* [New York: New York University Press, 1965], p. 33). There is, in fact, continuous movement in the diegesis. And if the distance between narrative time and fictional time seems to decrease, it is not because, as happens in the last section of the novel, they have come to coincide. Narrating time dominates narrated temporality and almost conjures it away. Nor is the moment a suspended *memory of the narrator,* insofar as the experience is ascribed to a "you" which only exists in the present utterance of the "I." The "I" does not describe a recollection, he names — i.e. creates — the experience for the "you" as he goes on speaking: "you cannot make out," "you cannot see," "you think," "you remember," "you forget." Far from constituting a moment of frozen time, the passage exemplifies a "continuous creation."

14. "Si le personnage connaissait entièrement sa propre histoire, s'il n'avait pas d'objection à la raconter ou à se la raconter, la première personne s'imposerait... Ainsi, chaque fois que l'on voudra décrire un véritable progrès de la conscience, la naissance même du langage ou d'un langage, c'est la seconde personne qui sera la plus efficace." Michel Butor, "L'usage des pronoms personnels dans le roman," in *Essais sur le roman* (Paris: Gallimard, 1969), p. 81. Symbolical of this growth in self-awareness is the high recurrence of the "you" in the travel sequences which function as metaphors for Jack's Pilgrim's Progress.

15. "Il faut entendre par discours dans sa plus large extension: toute énonciation supposant un locuteur et un auditeur, et chez le premier l'intention d'influencer l'autre en quelque matière," Emile Benveniste, *Problèmes de Linguistique Générale* (Paris: Gallimard, 1966), pp. 241-42.

16. Stanzel, p. 63.

17. See Warren's introduction to the Random House edition of *All the King's Men* where he tells of his need for "a character to serve as a kind of commentator and *raisonneur* and chorus" (p.iv).

18. Robert Heilman, "Melpomene as Wallflower; or, the Reading of Tragedy," reprinted in Longley, p. 83.

19. *Ibid.,* p. 84.

20. Robert Penn Warren, "Knowledge and the Image of Man," reprinted in Longley, p. 241.

21. Interpenetration in *All the King's Men* does not concern only the animate world. Norton R. Girault has pointed out Jack's attempts to lose himself in nature ("The Narrator's Mind as Symbol, an Analysis of *All the King's Men,*" *Accent,* 7 [Summer, 1947], pp. 220-34). One amusing example, not mentioned by Girault and more directly related to our approach, is the passage when Jack sees himself from the point of view of a cow and then sees himself transformed into a cow: "The cow would stand there knee-deep in the mist and look at the black blur and the blaze and then, not turning its head, at the place where the black blur and blaze had been with the remote, massive unvindictive indifference of God-All-Mighty or Fate or *me,* if I were standing knee-deep in the mist and the blur and the blaze whizzed past and withered on off between the fields and the patches of woods. But I wasn't standing there in the field in the dark, with the mist turning slow around

my knees and the ticking no-noise of the night inside *my* head" (p.36, italics added).

22. Might not this account for the reaction of the critics who find the ending weak? Leonard Casper, for instance, has perceived something like "sheer fatigue or the weakness of insufficient reso- lution" in the conclusion. "It requires a faith equal to Jack's in Willie to believe that this is only the last effect of the purge that must precede the great appetite," Leonard Casper, *Robert Penn Warren: The Dark and Bloody Ground* (Seattle: University of Washington Press, 1960), p. 132. But the kind of self-knowledge which Jack achieves can only bring about a chastened, not an exultant mood. After all, in the words of *Brother to Dragons:* "The dream of the future is not/ Better than the fact of the past, no matter how terrible./ For without the fact of the past we cannot dream the future" (New York: Random House, 1953), p. 193. What faith the book requires is not to be applied to Jack's capacity for renewed life but to our readiness to integrate Jack's experience and language — and our capacity to keep that "speck of green" on our hope that, according to the epigraph, promises us re- demption.

23. This definition of "good fiction" is to be found in the essay on Ernest Hemingway in Robert Penn Warren, *Selected Essays* (New York: Random House, 1958), p. 116.

Robert B. Heilman

Tangled Web

In *World Enough and Time* Robert Penn Warren again tackles
the theme which was the core of *All the King's Men* — the failure of a private, subjective "ideal" realm to come to terms
with, to be integrated with, to be married to a realm of public life and activity, the realm of politics and society and
group action, of law and justice. Warren's fourth novel is
less neat than his third (not that neatness was a prime virtue
of it), in the sense that *Hamlet* is less neat than *Othello:* it
is longer, and its length springs from a mind that overflows
with its observings and recordings, and is relentless in its
questionings and questings; the seams are strained by a redun-
dance of plot; by the piercing, tireless images of outer and
inner life; by the figures that qualify and communicate so substantially as to belie the initial innocence, or justify the
initial shock, of the words; by the bursting intellectual action, the tracking down of motives, the search through the
labyrinth of personality, the formulation and reformulation of
meaning, the alternate embrace and rejection of theory which
are the co-ordinates of moral and philosophic growth. Here
is enfolded enough of the world and of time — enough for the
young protagonists to come to the borders of self-knowledge,
enough for the reader who would fix a little more clearly the
outlines of the world and of self, enough to make an adequate
definition of this work depend upon a great deal of studious
re-reading by many critical readers.

The immediate world is Kentucky and the time is the first
quarter of the Nineteenth Century: Warren sticks to the central method of his other three novels, digging up a pretty
well preserved skeleton of action from recent history, covering it with the flesh of imaginatively conceived story, and
giving it the life of human (supra-historical) meaning. Such
a literary anthropologist always runs the risk of a tap on the
head from some errandboy of science whose chief punch is: has
he tampered with the facts? Of course he has. And only by

A review of *World Enough and Time* — Ed.

doing so does he extend his anthropology beyond a museum operation and make it a proper study of man for mankind. Literary
anthropologists have for a number of years been very active in
Americana, and their recreation and transmutation of various
American pasts may be understood as an aspect of the development of an imaginative self-consciousness, of a feeling and
yet critical awareness, the achievement of which might well
let the artist reflect on his share in the forging of the un-
created conscience of his race. This throwing of a certain
coloring of the imagination over the ordinary — and extraordinary — things of the past, however, may minister to different
kinds of consciousness. The past itself may be used only as a
new veneer for stock literary sideshows ("entertainment literature"). The past may be used merely to create a sense of the
past (the standard "historical novel"). The past may be used
only to create a sense of the present (the historical allegory). Or the past may be used to create a sense of both past
and present, or of realities that are neither past nor present
because they are both. This is the field in which Warren
works brilliantly, though to the puzzlement and disappointment
of all those whose expectancies have been nourished in fields
one, two, or three. (Even among the professionals: read a
review by an established historical novelist, and see the anguish seeping through; or one by a semi-literary slickster,
and see what he sees — only an I-push-over-easy wink to Holly-
wood.) But if Warren's past is Everytime, there is no woozy
timelessness or lack of ubiety in the drama; documentation is
heavy. The dates are all there and can be checked in the record; the geography is meticulous, and can be checked on driving maps; many characters are given full biographies, and at
least some may be checked in *DAB*. But calendars, court tran-
scripts, diaries, maps, *DAB* and all that take us only to the
threshold of the work.

The narrative organization of the theme, despite the kinship between the two books, is quite different from that of
All the King's Men; the earlier book uses a narrator, Jack
Burden, who tells of tragically separated men of ideas and men
of action and of his involvement with both, who duplicates
within himself the split in society, and whose failure of understanding, until almost the end, is a major source of tension. In *World Enough and Time* the author tells directly the
story of the conflict between Jeremiah Beaumont and the world
in which he lives (his friend Wilkie Barron; his once mentor,
Cassius Fort, whom he murders; and all the private interests
and social and legal forces arrayed against him); then he uses
Jeremiah's journal as a means of comment on Jerry's intentions
and actions; and finally comments himself on both action and
journal. Thus we have not only a level of action, which itself is very complicated, but two levels of comment. Since
Jeremiah is made not only as articulate as Jack Burden but
also, if no more wise, at least a more conscious searcher of

motives and meanings, the element of reflection and inquiry
is larger in the present novel. Jerry's frantic philosophic
quest, which ranges from self-deception through various tentatively held views to new insight, rarely ceases. Yet at times
it covers pretty well worn ground so that, despite its intensity, it can let the story down into a stasis; and the tireless
repetition of questions can become actually nagging. But the
total effect is one of a manically exhaustive ripping apart of
excuses, justifications, defenses, ruses, consolations; of a
furious burrowing into ever deeper layers of self-understand-
ing until almost every clarity becomes a puzzle and every de-
pendability a delusion. Characters who end their search for
an author in Mr. Warren's fold come under a hardbitten task-
master, who has an indefatigable eye for subterfuge, for the
empty heroic, the phony benevolence, the slippery self-seeking,
the concealed or direct malignity, the impulse to wound or
sell or kill. Yet it is important to distinguish this deep-
lying suspicion, this embracing skepticism, from a mechanically, doctrinally hardboiled way of looking at things; it is the
difference between the maturely sensitive and the half-grown
sentimental. Wisdom has its affirmations and its negations;
here is the negative side of wisdom. The flaws and failures
of men are wonderfully dramatized, and they are in every sense
right; but the small acquisitions of joy or honor skim by thin-
ly. Let us by no means undervalue the awareness of Lilliput-
ian chicanery and Yahoo savagery; without them, narrative
can't get beyond polite reassurance and good clean fun. And
let us also keep in mind that, if affirmations are of the
threshold, tentative, acquiring somewhat less of dramatic conviction than the weaknesses, trickeries, malevolences so watch-
fully descried, in our day the wisdom of negation seems almost
the limit of the possible, at least for the man in the world
who will not live by cliché and slogan.

      Self-discovery is not an autonomous process, with the ma-
terials yielding up their own principles of definition; rather
it is the application to the self of the best available categories of meaning and value. The basic categories in *World
Enough and Time* are "world" and "idea," which, as we have
said, are clearly related to the governing concepts of *All the
King's Men* but which certainly aim at a larger inclusiveness
and are intended to put a finger on basic human motives.
Viewed neutrally, "the world" is simply the forum, the marketplace, the scene of public activity; viewed ideally, it is the
realm of the cooperative search for justice; viewed in terms
of the dominant facts, it is expedience, opportunism, flux-
worship, deriving principles from polls (private, unwritten,
but none the less taken), spotting the winner. This is the
inevitable degenerate form of the cooperative principle: cooperation unideally — without the "idea" — is getting on with,
and getting on with easily sinks into getting on, and getting
on into getting. Warren gives due play to all the potentiali-

ties of the world: at his trial for murder, Jerry is defended
by two attorneys of radically opposed political parties, em-
blems respectively of "worldly decency" and "unworldly truth";
and Cassius Fort, Jerry's victim, who like the lawyers lives
and acts in the world and who has a due share of "human weakness," is apparently actuated by political conviction. But
the chief figure in the world is Wilkie Barron (of whom we
have already seen something in Bogan Murdock of *At Heaven's
Gate*), Jerry's friend and his Iago, the Mr. Worldly Wiseman
of the tale, who never backs the wrong horse, fails to make
the proper gesture, or falls into an unprofitable passion
(like the too-successful sea captain in *Lord Jim,* he finally
commits suicide in mid-career). Among the men of the world,
he must be the principal actor for us of the Twentieth Century,
whose "every effort is to live in the world, to accept its
explanations, to do nothing gratuitously." Finally, beyond
clubman-competitor Wilkie in the range of worldlings are the
lesser and leaner fry of vote-sellers, perjurors, and cut-
throats — the success-boys with the make-up rubbed off.

Since for a novelist of Warren's stature the world is not
big enough game, the book naturally belongs to Jerry Beaumont
— to "idea." If one were a good positivist, he would scorn
the idea; if one were a sentimentalist, he might present it as
high nobility in itself; if a Platonist, he would define it as
reality. Instead of doing any of these things, Warren is writing a tragedy of the idea — to paraphrase Hardy, "a tragedy of
the unfulfilled idea." Jerry early discovered, he thought,
"the vanity of the world" and yearned to "live in the pure
idea." This was enough; he could renounce the world — retire
from a legal career and create a private idyl (by taking up
the cause of, and eventually falling in love with, a girl he
doesn't know, Rachel Jordan — so excellent a symbol of both
capacity for devotion and a fanciful separation from reality
that one is loathe to question the event and the way of its being brought about). But the idyl itself led back to the world,
and Jerry found his unworldly motives mixed with worldly; so
we find him trying to compel the world to "redeem" the idea
(murdering Rachel's seducer, Cassius Fort, whom he had made
into a symbol of the world; and by deceit striving to have the
world, through its courts, declare him "not guilty" and therefore acknowledge the innocence of his idea turned into act).
After the inevitable failure of this project, Jerry falls entirely into the world, accepting both a jailbreak appropriately engineered by Wilkie (for his own purposes) and a drunken
and lecherous sanctuary among Yahoos in a wretched junk-strewn
swamp controlled by an aged scoundrel whose last vocation in
treachery was piracy on the rivers ("the blank cup of nature,"
Jerry calls it. Murder, said the pirate, "c'est naturel" —
that happy phrase by which today we beatify so many cravings
and indolences. There is a reminiscence of Edmund's appeal to
"nature" in *Lear*. The episode is a biting parody of romantic

naturalism, of innocence secured in Arcadia). In Jerry's view
there has been a necessary evolution from the first of these
stages to the third.

The story has another representative of the "dialectic" of
the idea — Percival Skrogg, a tubercular father-hater who pursues "the Justice in my own mind" by various means from demagogic journalism to political trickery and inordinately successful dueling — a killer who is eventually assassinated.
But for years he had lived in fear, which in part superseded
the "idea" and allied him to the "world."

What, then, is the "idea"? If I read the novel aright,
Warren accords to the idea the same breadth of treatment which
he gives to the world. In one light it is aspiration, the
sought nobility, the good dreamed of, the felt ideal of justice, the uncontaminated and holy thing. Rachel and Jerry
read Plato, and Jerry once (from his accomplished murder)
rides home in the style of a knight of chivalry. But the idea
is held in the private mind, and it can become a purely private reality; yet it seems, in virtue of its withdrawn purity,
able to claim general fealty and public obeisance. The idea
becomes the *idée fixe,* the love of right the sense of rightness. Impulse and uncriticized motive creep into the idea.
It becomes will, drive, the compulsive personality, the doctrine without deviation or qualification, the end which claims
all means. It becomes mania. It tries to compel history.
Opposite, the Wilkie Barrons are only trying to ride history's
coat-tails. One gives too little (to time, to humanity, to
the world), the other too much.

If this sounds pretty simple, the narrative mass from
which it is extracted is not simple. There are all the inner
complications of Rachel and Jerry, in whom the author has
discovered an extraordinary range of impulses; there are the
fairly complete histories of various supporting characters
(Jerry's and Rachel's parents, various politicians, the
crooked lawyer Suggs Lancaster, Cadeau the pirate); there is
the incalculable interweaving of private life with the public
issue of Relief vs. Anti-Relief, New Court vs. Old Court; the
immense detail of plotting and executing murder, of a trial in
which state witnesses cross up each other and the prosecutor,
and the defendant tries by suborning perjury to outsmart both
the false witnesses and his devoted attorneys; of the slow un-
raveling of machinations and mixed motives and psychological
and political maneuverings (a mass of ingredients best held
together in the second half of the book, where the movement
is far more sure and the action yields less to the impedimenta
of explanation and discussion which have not fully surrendered
to, or been forced into, the narrative stream). But above all
this, the interrelationship of the parts is such as to yield
an immense suggestivity of meaning; there is a confluence of
diverse motifs and patterns; there are imaginative extensions,
constant examples of what Richards calls felt depth and re-

cession. The story can be read in the light of various ways
of organizing experience. Cut out enough, and the rest goes
neatly in psychoanalytic terms: the conditioning "trauma" in
the lives of Jerry, Rachel, and Skrogg (only in Wilkie the
worldling is adjustment hereditary, so to speak), the religion-
sex short circuit in Jerry's life, the father-murder pattern
in Jerry and Skrogg, the various scenes in Jerry's life where
the return-to-the-womb is hinted (a tip to the alphabetic ana-
lyst: look at the series of demonic and questing characters in
Warren's books — Jasper Beaumont, Jerry Beaumont, Jack Burden,
John Brown. Surely, by a brief flight at anagrams, that obsessive *JB* must be convertible into something or someone).
Cut out enough other parts, and the rest can go as a study of
the relationship between a man and a woman, especially of the
man's unwittingly forcing upon the woman a role which minis-
ters to needs of his not clearly understood; a kind of study
which makes possible the author's most complex and most generally successful portrayal of a woman. A more inclusive approach: through the traditional situations into which the
story falls. For instance, the tragic mechanism of the family
curse operates for both Jerry and Rachel, each of whom in some
way duplicates a parental bias or flaw and so increases his
burden of self-discovery. Again, Jerry plays Othello to Wilkie's Iago, in a variety of situations. More markedly, Jerry
is Hamlet, the student, the questioner, plotting a revenge (in
discoursing on which the author uses as his text "What's he to
Hecuba?"), using a literary mousetrap to secure the admission
of what he already knows to be a fact, thinking that "nothing
could repair the twisted time," refusing to kill Fort when the
act would seem morally incomplete (Claudius at prayer), abus-
ing his sweetheart and driving her mad, literally comparing a
hoodwinked plotter to Rosencrantz and Guildenstern, near the
end even listening to quips from a gravedigger. In Jerry is
focused the action-contamination theme so frequent in Shakespeare: how mediate between a fugitive and cloistered virtue
and the contamination inherent in the work that must be done
(a theme of interest to Warren since *Night Rider*)? The juxtaposition of sex and death, in both act and reflection, recalls
both a traditional association and the specific Elizabethan
ambiguity in the use of *die*. The idea that hardens into will
is a favorite George Eliot theme, and Jerry's attempted flight
and unforeseen involvement may be set against the roughly comparable experience of Heyst in *Victory*. It of course does
Warren no service if these comparisons are taken to imply that
his work somehow includes all these others; all the analogies
should suggest is the breadth of *World Enough and Time*. At
the same time there is a general Elizabethanness of cast — in
the combination of full and violent action (including a kind
of helter-skelter finishing-off of physical lives) with rich
rhetoric and overt philosophical investigation — that defines
an important influence on Warren's imagination.

Or the story can be read as a myth of America. *World
Enough and Time* is, like Warren's other novels, with their Kentucky, Tennessee, and Louisiana backgrounds, southern only in
the surface facts; yet it comprises more than the others of
the American story and temper. Half the characters are "self-
made" men, with the animus and drive generated on "the other
side of the tracks." Their stories are "success stories" seen
in tragic perspective. They have "dreams" — a word used just
often enough to comment lightly on the "American dream." In
the contest of Reliefers and Anti-Reliefers, both with clear-
cut twentieth-century analogues, we see the archetypal stand-
pat and reformist tendencies (since Warren contemplates neither side through rose-colored glasses, we may soon have a
communique from Northampton, Massachusetts, pointing out that
his treatment of Relief is not in accord with the most enlightened political thought of our day and is therefore deplor-
able aesthetically as well as morally). One characteristic
passage neatly debunks a modernist-positivist debunking of
dueling; any fight for an unseen, intangible, but felt value
— a war for instance — is a duel. Most of all we sense the
two "streams of American thought," the "idealist" and the
"practical," with their contradictions and overlappings and
ways of becoming corrupt. Jerry is obviously not written as
a national archetype, nor does he accidentally become one, but
in him there is much that we can see in ourselves: the turning
"from the victor to the victim," the conviction of inner rightness, the inconsistent dreams, the quickness to anger, the
sense of injury, the accidental involvement, the self-deception, the contradictory impulses to withdraw and to dictate to
others, the confusion about means, the desire to live by the
private view and yet to have public justification, the passion
and the calculation side by side.

There are other themes: the elusiveness of truth, however
fanatically pursued; the enigma of self; the "paradox and doubleness of life" (the enemy as friend, the coexistence of in-
compatible motives, all the lies against Jerry combining to
tell the truth); the seat of justice — in the heart or in the
law? (Jerry wavers between the two positions.) There are the
subtle comments of figure after figure: the pirate who betrayed the Cherokees had foreseen their end and "had cashed in
on his investment while the market was still good." The rich
dark-light imagery is a system of meaning in itself. Recur-
rency is structurally important, notably in the recollections
of scenes and sensations — the picture of the martyr, the
first sex experience, the enchanting music from the keelboat,
the sense of oneness with nature — which establish links among
different episodes in Jerry's life. There is a recurrence of
the lives of the fathers in the lives of the children; there
are a half dozen versions of the go-west-young-man dogma, most
of them commenting ironically on the dream. All these kinds
of communication will have to be taken into account in a final

assessment of this book; nor is it an abjuring of the critical
function to insist that the definition of a complex work of
art depends upon a continued collective experiencing of it.

The book is all these things, but it is one book, and the
author has indicated how he wants us to see its oneness. When
we first glimpse "A Romantic Novel" on the bang-bang jacket,
we automatically assume that Random House is bravely dreaming
of some deception in the drugstore. But "A Romantic Novel" is
also a subtitle, so that it is official as well as promotional.
It seems to me that there are three ways in which *romantic* may
be taken. At its simplest there is the "romance of adventure"
— the almost-perfect crime, the pursuit of the suspect, the de-
viousness of the trial, the jailbreak, the love story, the attempted suicide, the quick gunplay and fistplay, the bravado
and battles of wit. At this level it might all be out of
Scott, and from Scott might have come a workable title — "The
Tangled Web," which, despite the heavy moralism of the context,
would pretty well describe the complication of physical and
moral action. Yet all this apparatus of romantic melodrama,
when qualified by a central tragic awareness, yields something
more serious than a romantic-melodramatic effect. Again, *romantic* describes the kind of personality the book deals with:
Jerry as Byronic hero is intimated by his and Rachel's and
Fort's devotion to Byron. Indeed, *Childe Harold* is an arsenal
of mottoes and epithets for Jerry: "self-torturing sophist,"
"I have not loved the world, nor the world me," "I have
thought too long and darkly," "Wrung with the wounds which
kill not, but ne'er heal." Jerry is hardly so self-contained
as Byron-Harold imagined himself to be, but he is impulsive,
suspicious, bitter, melancholy, devoted to an ideal, in search
of the fine and noble, hoping for too much, disillusioned, at-
titudinizing, demonic, exacerbatedly sensitive, self-question-
ing, self-tormenting, self-deceiving, self-detecting, self-
pitying, with all the anguish and despair and nostalgia for a
happiness not accessible to the "dark" personality. (He even
employs "romantic irony" in commenting on his venereal sore.)
In "pure" romance he would be merely a suffering victim of the
world, and indeed Jerry has a neurotically active sense of betrayal by the world; but this romantic hero is seen in perspective. Compared with Wilkie's entire devotion to self-advance-
ment, Jerry's dedication to the gratuitous act is impressive;
but all his dedication does not dissolve the corruption which
encrusts the act itself. The second and final stage in the
tragic transformation of romance is Jerry's coming to understand and to reject his earlier self. At the end he does not
stand off and gesticulate. He judges himself.

At the third level, then, the book is a study of a basic
kind of impulse to action. Jerry calls himself guilty of "the
crime of self"; he speaks of having acted from "a black need
within me." We have already spoken of the tendency of the
"idea" to become "uncriticized motive" and "compulsive person-

ality." The kind of human motivation defined in Jerry is suggested by such terms as the self, the personality, the subjective; here we find the private sureness, the inner insistence,
the confidence in the rightness of the heart (as in Hitler),
the intransigence of the will, the flight from discipline, indeed the very summation of individualist pride. This "kind of
impulse" may lead to both scorn of the world (which may range
from simple retreat to challenge and defilement) and effort to
subjugate the world: Jerry ultimately comes to see what Rachel
had seen earlier, that he had "tortured" her into crying for
Fort's blood and thus providing a factitious moral imperative
as veneer for an almost instinctive drive.

The human pattern exhibited in Jerry, and with variations
in Rachel and Skrogg, is universal. If I am right in judging
the ultimate applicability of *romantic* to be to the "kind of
impulse" which moves Jerry, then the author is describing the
timeless by a time-word, using a term of specific historical
relevance as a means of concretizing the issue. Time and the
timeless meet when, in the failure of an ideal tension among
impulses, one or another enjoys a temporary historical domi-
nance, as did the Jerry-impulse — the basis, really, of the
cult of the individual — in the "Romantic" period and indeed
in most of subsequent American history. Whatever name one
might give to the antithetical and equally timeless impulse
— the Wilkie-impulse — it is clear that its period of domi-
nance was another one; Wilkie has affiliations both with Lord
Chesterfield and with the President of the Junior Chamber of
Commerce to whom the author refers in a double-voiced choral
comment near the end. The problem of these contending impulses, which provides the intellectual framework for the
drama of Jerry, really finds its analogy in Coleridge's epistemological doctrine of the subjective and the objective, which
in perception reciprocally modify each other. So in moral
life a "subjective" and an "objective" view of reality, of innocence, of justice — intention and deed — must interpenetrate,
lest the idea or the world run mad. This is not the "practical" principle of compromise — the doctrine that *the* truth is
the sum of many half-truths, or the political expedient of the
committee swollen into a metaphysic — but the insistence upon
a recognition of all the impulses and of the problem of finding a unity. (Extremes can compromise and even cooperate in
a remarkable way; mania and success can sleep together comfortably. Skrogg as idea and Wilkie as world always collabo-
rate politically. And Skrogg — the idea as gangsterism — has
a couple of thug body-guards, a fine concession to the way of
the world.)

The conception of the romantic here advanced in the name
of the author may grieve professional pedlars of romanticism,
at least those whose style is that of a stockholder with an
investment to protect. But in many ways it need not do so.
Warren has written a study, not a tract. Jerry always aspires;

he has the Ulyssean character — to strive, to seek, to find.
He is always played off against the positivists; his chief
error is to try to be positive — to guarantee the future. He
comes to grieve at, not to rejoice in, the "cold exile from
mankind" which results from an attempt at a purely private
ordering of life. The theme of alienation — that seclusion
which emerges from and punishes the crime of self — is always
present and is explicitly central in Jerry's final self-
analysis. Whether this be regarded as the summit of the dialectical progression of a romantic, or the saving modification
of a romantic credo, Jerry puts it this way: "There must be a
way whereby the word becomes flesh. There must be a way whereby the flesh becomes word. Whereby loneliness becomes communion without contamination. Whereby contamination becomes
purity without exile." In these words of longing for what is
impossible in life yet must always be sought if life is to
have order, Jerry speaks a religious, in part even a Biblical,
language. This way of speech, which is natural in the character that Jerry has been shown to be, serves not only to communicate the meaning of the moment but also to pull together
strands of suggestion that have run throughout the story.
Early in life Jerry had been under the influence of one of
those evangelists "who got their hot prides and cold lusts
short-circuited into obsessed hosannas and a ferocious striving for God's sake," and for years he was obsessed by a remembered picture of a female martyr in flames whom he could
imagine himself either rescuing or helping to destroy. He
declares himself an unbeliever but tends always toward a religious comprehension of experience. He thinks of his campaign against Fort as a "mission"; he thinks first that his
idea will "redeem" the world, later that the world must "redeem" the idea. Honest trial witnesses make him "as reborn."
He is passionate about his "innocence." He seeks "peace"
by confession. He is agonized by Munn Short's story of his
spiritual death and his recovery by faith. In fact, with his
early conversion establishing the pattern, Jerry has always
led a kind of pseudo-religious life: he needs an all-embracing,
peremptory spiritual command, but his way of finding it is to
universalize an unidentified cry from within. Nowhere is the
falseness of his devotion more apparent than when he finds
"peace" and "grace" in the ex-pirate's stinking sanctuary.
He is aware that it is a horrible parody of grace and innocence, but he clings to his raw Eden. He reads the New Testament in Greek and falls into drunkenness and debauchery. With
a dirty slut he finds "peace" and "communion."

But Jerry cannot rest in irony. Like Everyman, and like
the traditional tragic protagonist, he comes to knowledge, not
by magic illumination, but as the outcome of prolonged searching. Then he no longer seeks revenge, or pardon, or justification; he knows that "I may not have redemption." He must
"flee from innocence and toward my guilt"; he seeks suffering

and expiation. This is his ultimate renunciation of the doctrine of self, of the private determination of value; it is
the acknowledgment of spiritual reality, the bowing to cosmic
discipline.

     Jerry is killed before he can complete action in the light
of his new knowledge, but not before he can close his journal
with a question: "Oh, was I worth nothing, and my agony? Was
all for naught?" And the author closes the novel by repeating,
"Was all for naught?" At first glimpse this may seem a kind
of lady-or-tiger coyness, or an emcee's request for audience
participation, or even a romantic preference for the incomplete. Rather, I think, the rhetorical question does two
things: it is a kind of "de te, fabula," and it raises the
issue of whether such a tragic fable can be meaningful now.
The book does not raise a finger to make the answer easy: the
excellence of *World Enough and Time* is precisely its difficulty. The dramatic and intellectual texture is dense; nothing
is given away. Which is as it should be. The acknowledgment
of the crime of self and the acceptance of guilt are hardly
likely to seem pleasantly familiar to us unskilled in tragic
perception. Which is as it must be. Our bent is to look for
causes, and to find something, or someone, to blame.

James H. Justus

The Mariner and
Robert Penn Warren

Robert Penn Warren's virtuoso piece of criticism, his analysis of *The Rime of the Ancient Mariner,* is well known. That
poem, Warren says, posits as its primary theme man's necessity
for repentance and reconciliation after crime and punishment:

> The Mariner shoots the bird; suffers various pains, the
> greatest of which is loneliness and spiritual anguish;
> upon recognizing the beauty of the foul sea snakes, exper-
> iences a gush of love for them and is able to pray; is re-
> turned miraculously to his home port, where he discovers
> the joy of human communion in God,...[and the meaning of]
> the notion of a universal charity,...the sense of the "One
> Life" in which all creation participates.[1]

Warren further claims that the "unmotivated" killing of the
albatross is "exactly the significant thing about the Mariner's act" because it "reenacts the Fall..." (p.227). Warren
stresses the Mariner's willing perversity — his individual,
not inherited, responsibility for the act — and the crew's
willing complicity. Having then submitted himself to "the
great discipline of sympathy," the Mariner can walk again, in
Coleridge's words, "with a goodly company." In Warren's interpretation, the terms which the Mariner accepts for his reintro-
duction into human society are resonant of the traditional,
mythic punishment of Cain or the Wandering Jew and the dark
verbal gift of the *poète maudit* (pp.256–257).

Whether or not Coleridge's Mariner encompasses those typal
figures is probably academic, since the part of the story to
which most readers have always responded dramatically is the
Mariner's need to communicate his experience to as many wedding guests as he can find. In our own time we have come to
regard that need as a psychological — and even moral — commonplace. Warren's view of Coleridge's Mariner has been ques-
tioned, and it may or may not satisfy students of *The Rime of
the Ancient Mariner,* but there is no doubt that Warren's in-

terpretation of that famous figure in his critical essay is
anticipated and corroborated in his fiction.[2]

Warren's Mariner is characterized by a need, sometimes
compulsive, to recite his story. But Warren's Mariner is
not Coleridge's. In novel after novel, Warren rings his own
changes on Coleridge's pattern. In the episodes involving
this recurring character, who invariably proclaims his guilt
for the past acts, his storytelling itself is usually an attempt to justify the teller to others *and* to himself. In such
novels as *Night Rider* and *Band of Angels,* Warren's Mariner can
more often define his crime and punishment than he can his repentance and reconciliation. In some instances even part of
his punishment, the self-flagellating need to tell someone
about it, suffers from lack of focus; he is unable to see his
true role in his own act, and often the very recital of his
story is halting, convoluted, imprecise, even incorrect.

When minor characters act out the Mariner role, their stories become the interpolated tales which readers have come to
expect in many of Warren's novels. Sometimes the protagonist,
who impatiently or reluctantly listens to the story, becomes
in turn another Mariner, a wedding guest who comes to acknowledge the truth of what he has been told and acts upon it. The
recurrence of this figure and his checkered fortunes in the
Warren universe, in a variety of refinements and developments,
indicates two aspects of the author's concern in his fiction.

Morally, that concern is the burden of man's salvation and
the adequate verbalizing of it, which is to say, the resolution of guilt and responsibility requires confession (Coleridge's Mariner must explain, cajole, and persuade others of
both his sin and his salvation). Aesthetically, that concern
is providing statement with a necessary and appropriate vehicle (Coleridge's Mariner can begin his return journey after
he composes a poem of blessing). These two related interests
Warren writes of elsewhere in various ways —

Morally:

[Conrad's work] is about the cost of awareness and the
difficulty of virtue, and his characteristic story is the
story of struggle and, sometimes, of redemption.[3]

Man must make his life somehow in the dialectical process
..., and in so far as he is to achieve redemption he must
do so through an awareness of his condition that identifies him with the general human communion, not in abstraction, not in mere doctrine, but immediately. The victory
is never won, the redemption must be continually re-
earned.[4]

Aesthetically:

We must sometimes force ourselves to remember that the act
of creation is not simply a projection of temperament, but
a criticism and purging of temperament.[5]

[W]hat good fiction gives us is the stimulation of a powerful image of human nature trying to fulfill itself.[6]

The poet [creates]...a self as well as a poem — but neither except in so far as he creates a structure, a form.
... The poem is, then, a little myth of man's capacity for
making life meaningful. And in the end, the poem is not a
thing we see — it is, rather, a light by which we may see
— and what we see is life.[7]

In this respect certainly Warren's criticism and his fiction
are of a piece. Warren's Mariners morally relive the ceremony
of confession and aesthetically re-enact the process of the
artist. They do not always succeed in transforming themselves
into artifacts, examples of the "little myth of man's capacity
for making life meaningful." Some fall short of redemption,
but many reach at least a point in their spiritual development
where they can accept the high cost of knowledge. Since that
acceptance, however, demands a strenuous self-examination,
most of Warren's fictional Mariners pay dearly for their final
peace.

I

Warren's first Mariner is Willie Proudfit of *Night Rider*
(1939). Because we meet him after he has achieved regeneration, his story is told impersonally: "He would tell it, not
exactly for them [his listeners], it seemed, but for the telling, speaking slowly and tentatively." The act of speaking
about his experiences on the western plains becomes a personal
reminder of past complicity in crime — that he is still a human creature in constant need of grace. Proudfit verbalizes
in order to "name [that] passel of things" he is now ashamed
of, to identify them, to be certain that his past definition
of them still remains true. Proudfit recounts his buffalo-
skinning days in terms of a crime against nature; he emphasizes the hot rifle barrel, the crumpling of the shot animal,
the sympathetic gathering of the rest of the herd around the
fallen member, and finally, his own estimate of man's irrational impulse to kill the animals: "'A man lays thar, the sun a-
bearen down, and keeps on a-pullen on the trigger. He ain't
lak his-self. Naw, he ain't. Lak he wasn't no man, nor nuth-
en'."[8] By implication Proudfit also now accepts the shared
guilt of scalping an Indian, even though the act had been committed by a partner. Proudfit tells how he begins his expiation by living with the Indians, sharing their rituals and
accepting their remedies for fever. Only when he has a vision
of green grass, houses in a valley, a "white church with a
bell" hanging near a spring, does he end his exile of penance
to begin his journey to Kentucky. That homecoming, when he
falls "face down to the water" near his old home, becomes his
final gesture, and Warren sees it as a self-ennobling and
necessary act.

This story has only a subliminal effect on Perse Munn, the protagonist of *Night Rider,* whose vision is too limited to see that Proudfit's past parallels his own present. But when Munn finally decides to sacrifice the protection offered by Proudfit — to leave the sparse land for Monclair estate to kill Tolliver — the journey is an ironic reversal of Proudfit's journey from the plains to Kentucky. Munn the lawyer at last is a Mariner who has not yet learned what his crime was and who never fully understands the definition of his punishment. His first act, permitting an innocent old Negro to hang for a murder committed by a client, is an unconscious crime (he believes his client, Harris Trevelyan, to be innocent). But his belief is wholly intuitive, and according to all previous indications Munn should have known that his intuition was flawed. He vacillates between liberty and fraternity, between cherishing his definition in his own terms and in submitting his definition to the cause of the Free Farmers Association. Even after he has become a member of the Board he lives on through one fall and winter, alternately exultant and depressed, "as though poised on the brink of revelation." Whenever he is convinced that he can successfully define himself through others, he rides through the countryside persuading farmers to join the Association. After each success he experiences the sharp throb of exaltation; whenever he fails, he cultivates his isolation, seeking the "true and unmoved" center of his being.

His murky idea of self is reflected in his compulsion to explain himself to others. His feelings, because they are ambivalent and ambiguous, can never find adequate expression. He gropes for words that will give shape to his most precious experiences, but his speeches trail off until they have only a remote relevance to his desires. First to his wife, then to young Benton Todd, he tries to explain his motives. After he kills Trevelyan, the compounding of his guilt strikes him even more speechless and he more and more cherishes his isolation.

While hunting, he shoots a dove; the old spurt of exaltation revives, only to be quenched by revulsion. In contrast to Proudfit, who begins the process of regeneration after the buffalo hunts, Munn degenerates rapidly after the symbolic shooting of the dove. The difference lies in the quality of the impulse toward self-definition. Munn's is always contradictory and hazy, and, near the end, when he could make the most of Proudfit's successful impulse, he hardly hears the words.

A similar structuring of the Mariner theme is evident in Warren's second novel, *At Heaven's Gate* (1943). The Mariner here is Ashby Wyndham, whose handwritten "Statement" alternates with chapters dealing with Sue Murdock and Jerry Calhoun. Wyndham's Statement should serve as a kind of self-purgation, but it does not. It is merely another trial, part of a larger punishment. Unlike Proudfit, who finds peace, Wyndham finds only more pain. His theme is "the pore human man," whose di-

lemma is that he "wants to know, but it is his weakness."[9]
Wyndham's albatross is, literally, Marie's mule which he
drives into a gatepost and kills during one of his drunken
rampages, and, symbolically, his guilt for striking his brother Jacob in anger. This latter act causes Jacob to sell their
farm: he turns over the scanty proceeds to Ashby, and each
brother, permanently estranged from the other, sets out alone
in the world.

Leaving the farm of his ancestors takes Ashby into another
sin — to Massey Mountain, where he joins a timber crew strip-
ping the mountain of its trees. His tree-chopping parallels
the earlier mule-killing; both are crimes against nature. And
when he strikes Sweetwater, the unionist who heckles Private
Porsum as he pleads with the men to halt the strike, Ashby repeats his earlier crime against his brother. Ashby says, "I
ought never lifted up my hand agin him in no way. If I had
helt my hand, may be nuthin would happened" (p.193). Disas-
ters multiply: he is fired and his child dies. While waking
in anguish at night, he hears the voice of his dead child
admonishing him to "walk in the world" and tell of his sin
against his brother. This moment of illumination confirms
Ashby's Mariner role. From this moment on, his expiation is
"telling" the Word: "I stood in the street and I told folks
how it was. How the Lord had laid it on me to tell folks. I
told them my wickedness and how the wicked man will come down
low. I met folks in the big road and I told them" (p.233).

But even in this mission Ashby despairs as he gradually
sees himself being enveloped in spiritual pride: "A man can be
proud and high in the Lord lak he can in pore human pride and
it is a sin. It is a worse sin" (p.262). (Here the alterna-
ting chapters stop, the plots mesh, and Ashby sits in his cell,
convinced that God — in all justness — has turned away His
face.) Although Ashby never achieves his regeneration, his
adamant compulsion toward expiation has at least one positive
effect — his role stimulates the public confession of Private
Porsum, his cousin who is involved in Murdock's shady finan-
cial deals.

Like Munn of *Night Rider,* Jerry Calhoun is inflicted with
a Mariner impulse but is denied the concomitant gift for words
that can give release, and therefore meaning, to that impulse.
Unlike Murdock's other ex-hero, Porsum, Jerry does not have a
"silver tongue" to soothe the mobs; instead he becomes an echo
of Murdock in his assertive, confidential, cliché-studded rhetoric that persuades business associates of Murdock's honesty.
Porsum manages to repudiate his lackey role because he can
still define himself; Jerry crumbles passively, without the
will to resist or admit defeat, because he never successfully
defines himself.

At one time he is afraid of what Murdock will say to him,
and when his fears seem unjustified, he calls himself a fool,
"patronizing the self he had been and all guilts and fears and

confusions" (p.225). After his merely temporary sexual reunion with Sue, he thinks of himself as two people: "[T]he
Jerry Calhoun to whom it had happened kept trying scrupulously
to explain it all to the Jerry Calhoun to whom nothing had happened at all" (p.232). Only after being rescued by Duckfoot
Blake and returned to the care of his father is Jerry able to
begin the careful definition of self that has so long eluded
him.

II

In *Night Rider* and *At Heaven's Gate* a subordinate figure
plays the role of chief Mariner, and the protagonist becomes
the secondary, almost paradoxically speechless Mariner. In
All the King's Men (1946) the Mariner dominates both structure
and texture. Jack Burden's entire story is an I-narration, a
reliving and relieving of a burden — the protagonist's impulse
toward self-definition. His easy cynicism, his almost automatic rejection of family (and therefore tradition and the past),
his cautious but loyal acceptance of Willie Stark, his profession ("Student of History" and newspaperman), and a talent
which makes the maximum use of words — all these give him obvious advantages over Perse Munn and Jerry Calhoun. Whereas
those earlier protagonists had only the impulse to tell their
stories, Jack Burden has both the impulse and the talent.
His task, for all that, is no easier. His very gift involves him in a compulsion toward completeness, a need to in-
vestigate all motives, to speculate if not to conclude on actions. He is not haunted; he is merely nagged by his failure
to achieve a fuller self-definition. His mental and moral
bent encourages him to verbalize without fear of definitive-
ness; his philosophic stance, for example, moves from Idealism
to a scientistic Naturalism before coming even to a tentative
rest. After his trip West he can say, with a touch of dogmatism, that he had learned "two very great truths. First, that
you cannot lose what you have never had. Second, that you are
never guilty of a crime which you did not commit."[10] He finds,
however, in the thrust of events — the mutual destruction of
Adam Stanton and Willie Stark — that these "very great truths"
are not true, at least for him. And when the time comes to
change his mind, his words also change. The verbalizing of
his final position is less dogmatic and smug, but it is just
as thorough, just as freewheeling. In short, he is not paralyzed by an inability to "tell" at any stage in his development. This ambivalent gift of Jack Burden is an updating of
the central tactic used by the Mariner to release his burden
and to reclaim his place in nature: the "telling" is important
in itself.
The yardstick by which Jack Burden measures his growing
moral position is the diary of Cass Mastern, itself a "telling"
of guilt and punishment, which lies always in the background

waiting for Jack Burden's maturity. His first attempt to understand Cass Mastern (when he is a doctoral candidate) ends
in failure. The project is still waiting at the end of the
novel when Jack Burden, who has completed his own "telling,"
can now edit the document. And that which Cass Mastern
learned in the 1860's is finally what Jack Burden learns in
the 1930's, that "the world is all of one piece...like an enormous spider web and if you touch it, however lightly, at any
point, the vibration ripples to the remotest perimeter..." (p.
200).

In the end, he must accept his own involvement in sending
Anne Stanton to Stark's bed and in causing the death of his
two friends, Stanton and Stark, whose lives were perhaps
doomed but who themselves "lived in the agony of will." Responsibility for past events leads Jack Burden to find the
Scholarly Attorney ("for each of us is the son of a million
fathers"). Moreover, Jack Burden can see no easy reconciliation in his future: the magnanimous act may come, but "a long
time from now." Whatever victory he may achieve will be hard-
won, for it must exist in the "convulsion of the world" and
the "awful responsibility of Time."

As with Jack Burden's story, *World Enough and Time* (1950)
is the long, anguished "telling" of a Mariner figure. It is a
more ambitious presentation than Burden's because of Warren's
more complex manipulation of perspective. A nameless "effaced"
narrator (another Student of History) slips into the background, as Jack Burden does not do, to permit full play to *his*
Cass Mastern. His editing of Jeremiah Beaumont's journal and
the assembling of related objective reports about Beaumont are
sometimes accurate, sometimes not. But for all his flaws, the
narrator's energies are devoted not primarily to his own self-
knowledge, as was true of Jack Burden's concern with Cass Mastern, but to the unfolding of his subject's terrible progress
toward self-knowledge.

If it is true that Warren is exploring one modern version
of the old romance genre, then Jeremiah Beaumont becomes a
version of the most sophisticated hero of the romance — the
knight in search of the Grail. Despite the antireligious position of both Beaumont and Rachel and despite the substitution of the Ruined Maid for the Virgin, the intensity and
ardor of Beaumont's rather wormy courtly love are religious.
Throughout his life Beaumont's underlying motive — as well as
his determining pattern of action — is a personal search for
his own identity, not the disinterested search for justice,
which he affirms so loudly and so often that even his historian accepts it. Self, rather than Justice, is his Grail,
though its winning proves to be just as hard. Jeremiah Beaumont, the serious man of idea who pursues his dream of self
to its logical conclusion, upholds an idealism that is itself
flawed; he cannot bear the thought of corrupting compromise.

Beaumont is a more subtle and complex version of Ashby·Wyndham:
spiritual pride, because of its status in the hierarchy, carries with it a proportionate risk and punishment.

In the motionless stupor of a backwoods swamp (with sufficient time and enough of an independent world) the lovers reorient their relationship. It is appropriate that Rachel, who
throughout their fitful lives serves as her husband's excuse
for his acts, should be the agent who permits him his long
sought-for knowledge. Rachel both indicts and forgives Beaumont, charging him with doing all for himself, with using her
for his own dark needs, but, as she lies dying by her own hand,
she tells him that he could not have done otherwise. Only at
this moment does he come to the point where he can define his
sin (and therefore his elusive self): "It is unpardonable. It
is the crime of self, the crime of life. The crime is I."[11]
And in his last desperate days he seeks another act to restore
a balance that had been scarcely there anyway, the symbolic moment when he can "shake the hangman's hand and call him brother."

Beaumont writes his journal with a tenacious need to justify himself as if his definition lay in justification. Because
he is complex, and because his motives are buried beneath layers of surrogate motives, the explanations are involved and
tortuous. His style is courtly, learned, graceful. His rhetoric, which reflects his technique of doing, surrounds, sur-
mounts, and underpins the motive and the act so that the sheer
enveloping defines the motive and the act in their ideal existence, and, in that process, the self Beaumont hopefully seeks.

As Beaumont gradually sheds all tokens of his former self,
his civilizing symbols, he retains his manuscript. Even when
doing nothing more than wenching with a syphilitic or drinking
with louts, he is compelled to note these facts. Even when
his exposed rationalizations grow thinner, he must still scram-
ble for spare leaves of paper on which to record even them.
In short, his compulsion to "tell" falls short only of his primary compulsion to act. And when he undertakes to return to
Frankfort for his punishment, the well-wrapped parcel of manuscript is the most important item he carries. Even after his
unceremonious death, when he is cheated of the dignity of the
gallows, the confession remains important for Wilkie Barron,
who prefers to keep it in a locked case despite the fact that
its existence, if made public, would ruin him.

Beaumont suffers sin, punishment, expiation, and hovers
about the brink of reconciliation. And if the desire to shake
the hangman's hand is somehow equal to that act, perhaps the
last phase of the Mariner process is completed in Beaumont.
But for Beaumont, more than for any other of Warren's Mariners,
the "telling" itself becomes the major instrument for the final, successful definition, the purgation of self to locate
self.

III

In *Night Rider* and *At Heaven's Gate* Warren's adaptations
of this figure are Mariners who, though untutored, are highly
sensitive to the fact of their own guilt. One speaks out of
his recent "peace," the reconciliation after long punishment;
the other speaks out in the anguish of his perpetual punishment and his belief that reconciliation is impossible. Both
are "primitives," past middle age, who are repositories of
folk wisdom. In *All the King's Men* and *World Enough and Time,*
Warren turns to Mariners who are both learned and sensitive.
In the first the historical situation of a youthful figure
acts not only as an *exemplum* for the protagonist but also, because of his youth, as a relevant parallel to him. In *World
Enough and Time* the modification of the "ancient" Mariner is
projected out of a subordinate role into the role of the protagonist himself; the diary of one whose guilt and punishment
assert a paradigm of a severe, almost simple, conscience is expanded and elevated into a journal of one whose conscience is
complicated and involuted, and whose very confession reveals
a self-deception so radical that it constantly baffles and mis-
leads the shadowy historian who is trying to interpret it.

When Warren returns to a more conventional form in *Band of
Angels* (1955), the theme and technique of the Mariner device
are substantially modified. The Mariner figure, again with an
interpolated confession, for the first time bears a functional
relationship to the character who is the listener and to the
organic structure of the novel; and for the first time the anguished search of the protagonist, though lengthy, leads finally to a full reconciliation "in joy."

The Mariner figure in *Band of Angels* is Hamish Bond, the
man who buys Amantha. The statement which triggers the story
of Bond's life is his remark: "'You don't even know who I am'"
and, a moment later, "'Maybe I don't even know who I am'."[12]
The name is important for them both, because the formation of
the name or the shaping of the mask is accepted as a necessary
step in self-definition. Amantha at least holds passionately
to this view, for it is she who insists on knowing Bond's real
name, a curious request that gradually grows to desperation.
When he finally tells her, his story follows.

The pattern here is much the same as that of previous Mariners such as Willie Proudfit and Ashby Wyndham, whose crimes
have been obvious, explicit ones. Bond's crime as slave trader is, like those others, a crime against nature, but is more
heinously directed against other humans. Even the obscurely
motivated rescue of the African child, nominally an act of
conscience, is accompanied by killing the wounded, maternally
furious mother. But the child, who comes to be his *k'la,* Rau-
Ru, is Bond's one constant reminder of his crime. He serves a
special function — "like a brother or son or something" — and
finally comes to hate Bond with an intensified fury.

Unlike most of the other interpolated confessions, Bond's
comes at a point in the Mariner cycle when his punishment is
not yet over and his repentance only nebulously grasped. He
can still say, "I did wrong," but his governing position is
still the easy appeal to the "we're just what we are" argument.
Characteristically, Bond's story suggests little to Amantha except how she has been hurt by his ambiguous profession. She
confesses that she stops listening to him even in the process
of the telling and describes how she forges her self-pity into
a weapon: "[E]ven in that disorientation, some excitement of
power had suddenly grown in me" (p.201).

It is a familiar feeling with Amantha. As her relations
with Bond grow stronger, she perfects her technique for using
him, for assigning to herself the role of punisher of Bond —
not for Bond's own crimes, which certainly require punishment,
but because he had, without articulation and conscious art,
complicated Amantha's growing need to define correctly *freedom*
and *slavery*. It is Amantha's defining trait that she can use
her triviality of mind as an instrument of power over the male
at the same time she must depend on it as an instrument for
solving her more pressing problems.

As for her own story, the reader plays the role of unenthu-
siastic wedding guest not because her *story* is a mediocre one
(rather, it proclaims its historical, even philosophical magnitude at the same time its central concern is with an individual protagonist), but because *she* is mediocre. Unlike Jack
Burden's story, hers far outweighs her intellectual and foren-
sic equipment to tell it. Instead of holding us by a glittering eye, she fascinates us because she is so remarkably tire-
some when she plays the vain and hurt young lady, a type who
can barely discriminate between being snubbed at a ball and
being raped by a slave. Much as she communicates her anxieties, ambivalences, self-justifications, and confessions, rarely are there moments when the reader feels that Amantha knows
and understands what has happened to her even while she tells
all. She gives the impression of an inept raconteur, short
on art but long on ego, who expects the audience to share the
work. But if we are patient the irritations are mitigated.
Her story — every scrap and shred of it, every fragmented mus-
ing on it — falls into shape from the weight of its own pieces
almost in spite of her storytelling technique or the quality
of her mind. It is not accidental that what finally helps to
define and answer her primary question ("Oh, who am I?") is
not Amantha's overexercised sensibilities, or, as a wedding
guest, her ability to learn from Bond's story, but merely time
itself. Spiritually, she is an old woman when she achieves
her reconciliation.

Warren's concern in his fiction for the theme of self-
identity has been consistent and cumulative: for more than
twenty years of work in the novel form, the Warren protagonist
searches for self-definition despite the fact that the search

inevitably requires a difficult, thoroughgoing, and massive
outlay of energy and commitment. Those who achieve a viable
identity (Jack Burden, Amantha Starr) do so because they accept a personal responsibility for their public acts. Those
who fail (Jerry Calhoun, Jeremiah Beaumont) come to understand
that necessity too late, when the damage is too great for putting the pieces of self back together again. Moreover, in his
novels from *Night Rider* through *Band of Angels* Warren's technique for presenting the search in action is to use a figure
who duplicates the shape of experience which Warren sees embodied in and dramatized by Coleridge's Ancient Mariner.[13]

It would be less than just to insist that most of Warren's
memorable characters are merely variations on a single literary type; for all their similar patterns of behavior, each is
too complex to fit simply the outlines of a received convention. Certainly Coleridge's Mariner is a pertinent typal figure for most of us; so also is it for Warren, who sees him in
a special way — a view explicated at length in his essay on
The Rime of the Ancient Mariner and corroborated in the creation of his own fictional characters. They, like the Cole-
ridge-Warren figure, most commonly must survive the shock of
their perception of evil both in the world at large and in
themselves. From the older primitive folk types whose message
is heard impatiently or not at all, to the younger, more sophisticated sufferers whose tortured fluency sometimes obscures a desire to learn the secrets of self-knowledge, the
Mariner stalks the by-ways of Warren's world. As a figure,
the Mariner knits up favorite Warren themes in explicit patterns and supplies a consistent artistic strategy to give
those patterns tactical unity.

---

1. "A Poem of Pure Imagination: An Experiment in Reading," *Selected Essays* (New York, 1958), p. 222. Subsequent references to
this essay are incorporated in the text.

2. The essay appeared originally in 1946; when it was revised for
the *Selected Essays* in 1958, Warren recognized and replied to some of
the voices raised in objection to his interpretation. The most important demurrer that I have seen since 1958 is Edward E. Bostetter, "The
Nightmare World of *The Ancient Mariner*," *Studies in Romanticism*, 1
(Summer 1962), 241-54.

3. "'The Great Mirage': Conrad and *Nostromo*," *Selected Essays*,
p. 48.

4. *Ibid.*, p. 54.

5. *Ibid.*, p. 48.

6. "Ernest Hemingway," *Selected Essays*, p. 116.

7. "Formula for a Poem," *Saturday Review*, March 22, 1958, p. 23.

8. *Night Rider* (New York, 1939), p. 408.

9. *At Heaven's Gate* (New York, 1943), pp. 35-36.

10. *All the King's Men* (New York, 1946), p. 330.

11. *World Enough and Time* (New York, 1950), p. 505.

12. *Band of Angels* (New York, 1955), p. 176.

13. Even in his experimental verse novel, *Brother to Dragons: A Tale in Verse and Voices* (1953), Warren gives much of the same function of his Mariner figure to his own persona — "R.P.W." Beginning with *The Cave* (1959), Warren's narrative strategy for dramatizing his great theme alters radically. In that work and his two subsequent novels, *Wilderness* (1961) and *Flood* (1964), Warren drops the interpolated tale — often a vehicle for accentuating the speeches and actions of the Mariner figure — and, indeed, much of the solid circumstantiality of the actual world that has sometimes masked his penchant for melodrama. The later novels are marked by bold, if not always successful, manipulations of caricature and stereotype, artifice and rhetoric, of episodes that are more ceremonial and ritualistic than functional, and of the author's own voice as authority.

Walter Sullivan

The Historical Novelist
and the Existential Peril:
Band of Angels

I want to begin my consideration of Warren as historical novelist not with *Band of Angels,* which is the subject of this paper, but with the story of Cass Mastern, which is told in the fourth chapter of *All the King's Men.* It will be remembered that Mastern, the intended subject of Jack Burden's master's thesis, was a rich young man from ante-bellum Mississippi. He went to Lexington to attend college, there met Duncan Trice, seduced Trice's wife Annabelle, and survived long enough to observe the vast burgeoning of his sin and to expiate his guilt through suffering. He learned that "the world is all of one piece," that actions have consequences, having observed how a series of calamitous evils followed his "single act of...perfidy, as the boughs from the bole and the leaves from the bough." He sought painful death and at last found it, and at his end he thought himself more fortunate than those who remained alive.

The story occupies a secondary position in the novel, but taken alone, it seems to me to be an almost perfect piece of writing. Set seventy years before the main action of *All the King's Men,* told primarily through the device of Mastern's diary and therefore couched in the language of another era, it demonstrates a good many of the advantages that the historical perspective affords a work of fiction. The separation in time, the diction, the existence of the journal all help to create distance between the action and the reader. Because of the method, certain passages can be effectively summarized and the sweep of the story can be conveyed in great succinctness. It exists for us whole in stark terms of good and evil, sin and redemption and these values are made more readily available by the gap in time. Not only are we willing to believe of the past what we cannot believe of the present — the grand action,

the heroic character — but by employing attitudes and convictions of another age, Warren was able clearly to draw moral
and religious distinctions that are blurred or even obliter-
ated by our present stance.

But, of course, historical fiction, like all other kinds,
has to be written. Whatever grand theme it seeks ultimately
to exploit, it must begin — the writer must begin — with the
concrete, with a few specific characters set in motion by a
concatenation of individual acts. Then, as Conrad and others
have taught us, if the people are truly realized, if they come
to live and behave as we know human beings do and must behave,
and if the truth of their situations is told accurately and
fully and with sharp sensuous detail, the philosophy of the
writer, his world view, whatever larger truth is contained in
his concept of the human condition will emerge. And if he is
lucky and works exceedingly well, he will perhaps say more
than he knew he could say when he set out on his task of creation.

I rehearse this familiar set of principles only because
they seem to apply so aptly to the Cass Mastern story. Warren
found in Cass an image that was almost perfectly designed to
convey in microcosm the novel's theme of the unity of the moral fabric and the consequences of action. But we begin with
Cass, who reads the Latin poets, and Annabelle, whose deep
blue eyes sparkle above the candles. We see their gestures,
we hear their voices speaking the words that we know they
would have spoken. ("Yes, I am seven years older than you,
Mr. Mastern. Does that surprise you, Mr. Mastern?") Her tears
and the touch of the flesh are real, and the story is allowed
to make its own way to the suicide of Duncan Trice and the accompanying broadening of image, the evolution of the private
and individual guilt into the universal and public sin. Annabelle's sale of Phebe, Mastern's fight with ruffians in the
house of the slave trader, the war, and Cass' death agony in
an Atlanta hospital all support the final philosophical summation. "He learned that the world is like an enormous spider
web and if you touch it...the vibration ripples to the remotest perimeter and the drowsy spider feels the tingle and...
springs out to fling the gossamer coils about you who have
touched the web...." This is well put, but the humanity of
Cass and Annabelle had to precede it: the simple truth of
their lives sharply delineated had to come first. Such is
the nature of all fiction, historical or not.

But Warren knows this better than most other people, and
one suspects that when he came to write *Band of Angels* he must
have seen in his cast of characters images fully as promising
as those of Cass and Annabelle. By this time — nine years in-
tervened between the two books — he had progressed from his
original dialectic of fact and idea, the man of dreams against
the man of action, to an existential and activist orientation.

He had given up completely whatever notion he had previously
entertained of a created universe subject to a transcendent
order. Though he remained deeply interested in the dramatic
possibilities of the past, and in certain theoretical aspects
of the Civil War that seemed to him to bear on modern problems
of race, he had grown somewhat contemptuous of history in the
larger sense, for to the extent that life is absurd, it must
always have been that way. He had left the South and eschewed
what remained of the traditional society. All of which is to
say that he was properly alienated; his concern was with the
questions of individual identity and freedom, and he had come
to have the ordinary intellectual's ordinary interest in social justice.

So Amantha Starr must have seemed a splendid vehicle for
what he meant to do. She is deprived of identity by her mixed
blood, bound spiritually by her humanity and physically by the
circumstances that make her a slave, and her material condition symbolizes the anguish of her soul. Who am I? she asks
in the opening passage of the novel. How, she wonders, can
she be set free? Such is the overture, the introduction of
theme, and then Warren sets to work with his customary skill.
Initially, he allows Amantha her freedom; she looks at bondage
from the outside, regarding its victims with ineffectual and
pompous sympathy. The first climax of the novel comes when
Amantha stands beside her father's grave and discovers that
she is legally a slave, and that unless someone comes to her
aid, she must be delivered by the reluctant sheriff to her
new owner. That no one helps, that freedom will not come from
outside, foreshadows the book's conclusion. But there is a
good deal of action to be got through before this epiphany is
achieved.

The fact is that someone else does assist her. Hamish
Bond wanders into the New Orleans auction room, defends her
honor, bids her in and takes her to his home. Bond himself is
one of the lost people of the world: he is rich and self sufficient, but he knows no better than Amantha who or what he is,
and his fate, like hers, is bound up with race, although more
tenuously. His name is not Bond, but Alec Hinks, and the days
of his youth were filled with his mother's harangues, her lam-
entations for the slaves who used to serve her wants and the
gentility of the life she used to lead before she married and
came to Baltimore from South Carolina. It was partly to spite
his mother that Bond became a slave trader: with a sense of
irony, he immersed himself in Negroes and arrived at his love-
hate relationship with Rau-Ru, his dearest friend and his bit-
terest enemy, his alter ego, his *K'la*.

Since in spite of the ease of his worldly circumstances,
Bond is not free, he cannot offer freedom to Amantha. Or at
least, the freedom that he can give her, physical emancipation,
is not the freedom that she seeks. Early in their relationship after he has yielded to the temptation to make love to

her, he offers to send her north, but she remains with him until he discloses to her the story of his shameful past. Knowing at last what he has done and seen, regarding him in the
light of the vast evils he has perpetrated, she, like Rau-Ru,
discovers hate where she once felt affection. Now, with cotton burning on the wharfs and Farragut waiting to capture the
city, Bond turns to Amantha in bed, but these flames, this
smoke remind her of the conflagrations of African villages.
She feels that to be united with Bond sexually makes her a
party to his guilt, one with him in responsibility for the
trade he followed with all its accompanying bloodshed and
agony and degradation. He forces himself on her and thus she
is released — from Bond, but not yet into freedom.

This scene which occurs halfway through the book marks the
second distinct turn of the novel. At her father's funeral,
Amantha was enslaved; now she is forever physically free.
Bond has released her, but more than that, the North is winning the Civil War, the Emancipation Proclamation will soon be
issued. Tobias Sears arrives apparently ready to lead her into the white world and even into the most powerful segment
thereof, if only he can solve his own problems of loyalty.
Sears, a New Englander and captain in the Union Army, is
caught between his sense of reality, what he sees with his own
eyes about the war and reconstruction, and the narrow capital-
istic puritanism which is his heritage and which is exempli-
fied by his father. Sears is the quintessential white man:
Amantha insists on the paleness of his body at the moment of
their marriage's consummation. But in his despair over the
world and his argument with the self that he used to be, he
parodies Bond in a noble way and volunteers to lead Negro
troops and later works for the Freedmen's Bureau. He seeks
a new identity in the cause of the black man.

We are to believe, I think, that Sears' obsession with
the Negro's plight is the immediate reason, not the underlying
cause of Amantha's deserting him. She has searched for a definition of herself in his whiteness, and basic to Warren's philosophy is his conviction that self recognition comes from
within, not from without. Amantha's discovery of this principle is still far off, and she turns away from white to pursue
black in the company of Rau-Ru. This effort too fails, of
course, but identities do begin to be found within the framework of confrontation. Rau-Ru claims black; Bond claims white;
each proclaims the reality of self and chooses death in a final and absolute exercise of freedom. But Amantha is still
left, and she drifts away into the middle west with Sears,
growing older in boredom and disappointment and occasional
sharp grief until she and Tobias make their liberating discoveries.

Now it seems to me that the conclusion of this novel is unsatisfactory. Two Negro derelicts — one of whom remains nameless and both of whom appear only in the final pages — trigger

the action. Uncle Slop is a comic figure, I suppose, though
not a very original one, and he remains shadowy since we never
see him directly. There is a certain effective irony in the
reversal of roles: a somewhat seedy Tobias Sears is employed
by the rich and black Mr. Lounberry. And what Tobias discovers is the predictable existential enlightenment. He must be
himself. He must declare his own manhood. And he does so by
insulting Mr. Biggers and proving thereby that he does not
have to submit to the kind of persecution Mr. Lounberry has
just endured.

Amantha's epiphany is a result of her believing, errone-
ously and against her better judgment, that an old beggar with
scars on his back is Rau-Ru, escaped somehow from death in Louisiana. She gives him money she cannot afford to part with:
she goes to visit his grave when he dies. There, surrounded
by the sinking mounds and the parsimonious tombstones, she
hears the Kansas wind whisper the truth. No one can help you.
No one can set you free except yourself. Thus the questions
that are raised on the first page are answered. But the
conclusion does not seem to jibe with the main thrust of the
book's action: the solutions do not seem to be the inevitable
product of character and plot.

The failure of the ending is, in my judgement, indicative
of the general failure of the novel, which is largely unredeemed by the presence of many well conceived and fully realized scenes and some truly moving passages. Warren is a
splendid prose stylist, a competent craftsman, or more than
that: a thorough student of his genre, a master of technique.
I need not expand on his virtues, except to say that in at
least one way he is as well qualified as any living American
novelists to write about the past. He is a diligent research-
er and his eye for costume and equipment, his feel for manners,
his ear for archaic patterns of speech are unsurpassed. Open
Band of Angels anywhere, and you will find evidence of Warren's full grasp of the surface details of life as it used to
be lived. Such a talent is not to be minimized: it is exactly
with such minutiae that fiction begins its journey toward the
truth.

But accuracies of dress and gesture are not final, and
where critical argument with Warren often commences is with
the ideas that burden the dialogue and inform the scenes. Are
his people really believable in terms of the stern philosophical bases that start their yearnings and inform their impulses
and govern their fates? Such a question, let me hasten to say,
may be unfair and is certainly unchivalrous. It takes us immediately into a twilight area where the meanest sort of cav-
ils remain largely unanswered and where judgements that are
basically subjective are likely to be made. Whenever we debate the realism of characters, the verisimilitude of action,
we must keep reminding ourselves that all fiction is distortion: otherwise it would not be fiction but merely life unre-

fined and formless, a mundane record not yet vivified and made
revealing by the processes of art.

Still, fiction must convince us. Credibility is a *sine
qua non,* and I must confess that I find it very difficult to
believe that a teenaged girl on a plantation in ante-bellum
Kentucky ever really wondered who she was and what it would
take to make her free. Indeed, I doubt that very many people
in the eighteen fifties of whatever age or sex or place of
abode troubled themselves much about the problem of identity.
Existentialism as a popular philosophical stance is a manifestation of the modern age, and to hold otherwise in a piece of
fiction is to commit the most damaging sort of anachronism.
Whatever reappraisals and revisions the historians might make,
the novelist is obligated by the demands of his craft to keep
to the truth in its simplest form. That is, he must be faithful to the spirit of the time. His characters must share with
their now dead, but once actual counterparts a common view of
life and its sources, the way it should be lived, the ends it
should serve.

We know this to be true, because in the first place, if
the study of literature discloses anything, it teaches us that
social and cultural fragmentation are bad for art. Endowing
characters in an historical novel with attitudes that are not
indigenous to the age is one way of creating fragmentation or
exacerbating that which already exists. But this is a lateral
argument, and I shall not pursue it. More germane is the
combination of uniqueness and universality that every author
strives to achieve in the characters that he creates. Certain
writers such as Cervantes or Dickens may lean toward the idiosyncratic, but the final ambition of every serious novelist is
to create characters so firmly rooted in our shared humanity
that each becomes a kind of everyman, an example of human attributes that are and were and shall be recognizable to readers of whatever period. To succeed in this ambition is the
crowning achievement of the great novelist.

But again we must remind ourselves that we proceed from
the particular; or to speak more nearly in the context of the
present discussion, we must first apprehend the individual in
his specific time and place. Consider *War and Peace.* In the
opening scene of the novel, Pierre is almost completely indi-
vidualized. We are conscious of his hulking figure, his spec-
tacles, his uncertain manners; he is uncomfortable and at odds
with his fellow guests at Anna Scherer's party. His differences stand out on this most intensely Russian occasion.
Frequently in the future he will be in disagreement with both
friends and enemies over social and political matters. But he
exists always within the limits of historical actuality: in
the particulars of his life and thought, he never violates his
own age. Because he has first his roots in the realities of
the period, he can, under Tolstoy's genius, expand as image,
until, as Andrew Lytle has pointed out, he becomes during the

occupation of Moscow, the incarnation of his fatherland: he *is* the Russian bear. Nor is this all. At the very end of the novel, he along with some of the other major figures shows us the very sweep of life, the repeated patterns of human generations, so that the full implications of the book's title are made clear.

It may be argued here that my objections to Warren's characters are too procrustean. For certainly it is possible to take the position that all literature of all periods is to a greater or less degree existential, and as for the age under discussion, there is the example of Henry Fleming, who, if we can get around all the talk of Christian symbolism in *The Red Badge of Courage,* is in some ways as fine a figure of existential hero as we could demand. Men have always had to make commitments, endure crises, achieve accommodations with impending death. But self consciousness and the quality thereof count for a great deal. If the existential posture is to have any limits, then we must recognize the difference between those who postulate the absurdity of the world, the lack of identity, the loss of freedom, and others who take other views of the common human agony. Which is to say, existentialism is a way of looking at men and life, not a mere foreknowledge of mortality.

But it is a grim way of looking and it exacts its price. As Helmut Kuhn put it, in what seems to me a brilliant figure, the existentialist takes the road to Calvary, but when he gets there he finds only the crosses of the two thieves. A true belief in such a nothingness lacks both the dignity and the high sense of despair that accrued to our former postures of negation. It leads to a mock show — Faustus with no Satan to deal with, no God to betray. Small wonder it is then that only the very strong — Camus, for example, and the early Hemingway — can regard emptiness without flinching and write about it with such stringent fidelity that every small victory is effected totally from within. Others require a more promising context, a glimmer of hope that life may be made easier by means of social action or political reform. But this, I dare to say in spite of Sartre's vast reputation as writer and thinker, is a marriage of ideas that contradict and strive against each other. If the world is truly meaningless, then its nothingness is absolute and unalterable: if, on the other hand, the human condition and the frame which defines it are subject to melioration then the universal emptiness is not complete. Consequently, images that argue against each other tend to cancel each other and in *Band of Angels,* this damaging contention manifests itself in a weakening of motivation which grows more serious as the narrative proceeds.

After the second major climax, when Amantha turns in disgust from Hamish Bond who has just told her the story of his past, the emphasis shifts from the private suffering of Amantha to the public ordeal of the Civil War. This is a common

practice of the historical novelist. If his public and private actions are properly amalgamated, if his character is
truly drawn in terms of the historical context, then it is essential to the scope and success of the work that the smaller,
private images participate in and at best become one with the
larger configurations which have been constructed out of the
alarms and exigencies of the past. But once Amantha has left
Bond, escaped from slavery and married Sears, the credible
reasons for her anxiety are removed. She has as much identity
and as much freedom as are commonly thought to be necessary.
Yet out of some brooding sense of her unhappy past, some lin-
gering agony, she abandons Sears to follow Rau-Ru, now become
Lieutenant Oliver Cromwell Jones. We are to interpret this as
an effort which Amantha makes to discover her ultimate self in
terms of her vestigial black blood. The Freudian overtones,
her fascination with Jones' shape and color, her obsessive desire to see the scars on his back do not make her flight to
him more believable. She simply goes while the reader wonders
why, and all the while the story is held together, allowed to
happen by the historical situation which produces the chaos
that will partially mask the lack of motive and the violence
which keeps the novel moving along. Once Amantha has married
Sears, his conduct alone makes sense. At this juncture, he
comes close to knowing who he is, and his desire is to do good,
to improve the conditions of human existence through political
commitment and sacrificial devotion to programs of social
change. His actions fit the dimensions of history in the last
part of the novel even better, perhaps, than Amantha's predicament was symbolized by the larger milieu of the first. But
Amantha remains the principal character of the novel and she
no longer functions in terms of the book's main historical
thrust.

All this brings me to a fatally simple question: can existentialism as we commonly define and practice it ever furnish
the historical novelist with a proper thematic basis for his
work? I am aware as I ask this that our concept of the existential may be deeply flawed. For example, Jacques Maritain
warns us that anguish has no philosophical standing. It is
not a function of Cartesian analysis, nor is it the stuff of
a premise to be cast into an Hegelian figure. Rather, it is
an emotion which is essentially religious: it represents a
subjective cry unto the transcendent. When it is properly understood, according to Maritain, the existentialism of Kierke-
gaard, Kafka, Chekhov and others issues from the "nothingness
which is the nonbeing in the existent," which is to say in
the individual, rather than from any universal meaninglessness
which imposes the terms of the human condition from without.
I find Maritain's interpretation appealing, but I am conscious
that his is a minority report. In any event, whatever the
proper meaning of existentialism may be, Warren and virtually
all his contemporaries are certain that the nothingness re-

sides *outside* the existent and that there is no God to call
out to, and that the transcendent, in whatever form or dimension, does not exist.

And because life is change and nothing remains stable, our
posited nothingness, be it real or imagined, closes in. Our
possibilities, the choices that are available to us both in
life and in fiction, are diminished; because regardless of the
claims that have been made to the contrary, the death of God
has grievously reduced mankind. If there is nothing beyond
ourselves, and if, as we are told time and time again these
days, our first duty is the simple physical perpetuation of
our species, then soon there will not be anything to write
about or even to concern ourselves with except whether we live
or die. But I shall not dwell on this. I merely want to say
that existential philosophy imposes restrictions of theme and
vision on the novelist. And while it may be true that those
who write about their own time cannot avoid either the philosophy or the accompanying restrictions, the historical novelist
can and should.

I alluded earlier to the aesthetic or psychic distance the
historical image affords the novelist, but there is a moral or
philosophical distance to be achieved as well. The novelist
who writes of the past is freed of the prejudices and disagree-
ments and idiocies of the moment: he goes back into time and
thereby relieves himself and his readers of their predisposi-
tions. Only the characters have a stake in the action or the
outcome. The artistic vision is purified, so that, ideally
at least, man and his condition are more clearly seen. Warren
has given us an example of this, not only in the Cass Mastern
section of *All the King's Men,* but in his first novel, *Night
Rider,* which many critics consider one of his finest works.
It will be recalled that *Night Rider* is based on the often
violent struggle between the tobacco growers' association and
the organized tobacco buyers which took place in Tennessee and
Kentucky just prior to and around the time Warren was born.
By 1939, when the novel was published, this was a part of the
dead past: a solution had been found to the tobacco problem
and the old wounds had healed.

Curiously, Warren says in a note at the front of *Night
Rider* that although the story is based on actual events, the
book is not an historical novel, but I think it is easy to
guess what he means. I take it that he is disclaiming any interest in the surface attractions of history and emphasizing
his concern with human nature itself which is the novelist's
proper province. The main character in *Night Rider,* Percy
Munn, is a lawyer who allows himself, almost against his will,
to become involved in the tobacco growers' protest. In the
course of the novel we watch Munn's deterioration. As Munn
becomes more deeply involved with the association, he increasingly subordinates his individual responsibility to the will
of the group. He gives up both his right and his duty to make

his own moral choices, which is to say that he abdicates his
birthright as a man. For Munn, one act of evil leads to another; as his sins increase in severity and number, all aspects of his life disintegrate into disorder; thus the book
moves with inexorable power toward Munn's death at the end.
Night Rider is more than a sum of its parts: it transcends its
images in a way that *Band of Angels* never does. And yet, like
Band of Angels, it takes the question of human freedom for its
theme. The difference is that Munn begins free and as a result of his own weakness and poor judgment, he loses his freedom and therefore loses humanity and we in turn believe in and
are moved by his death. Amantha begins postulating a lack of
freedom, but except for her interlude of enslavement, this is
only something we are told about, and it is hard to see how
she is much freer on the last page than she was on the first.

I suppose what I am saying here is that truth for the historical novelist does not reside in the present, except as the
present is a part of the eternal. The truth of history is in
the past and always, but not in the restricted contemporary
view. Therefore, the historical novelist must trust the historical images and the historical context. He must be willing
to work with life as it was lived, knowing that history is indeed life and that human nature does not change. Above all,
he must avoid the temptation to impose the errors of the present upon the past. For the present is fraught with errors:
the one thing above all else that our secular, scientific culture should have taught us is that we are always wrong. Today's certainty is the instigation of tomorrow's superior
smile.

Which brings me again to a point I have been insisting
upon: the historical novel, like all other novels, must start
with the concrete: it must be built from the bottom, not from
the top. For whatever literature has to tell us about our continuing agony and glory, it must show us as individuals first,
single people in the here and now or the there and then of another era. Historical or otherwise, the novelist must start
with the scene, because the art of literature is not one of
definition or one of gathering proof for principles that are
already established in the mind of the author. It is rather
a search, an exploration begun and conducted in faith, a voyage toward a shore that is at best dimly seen. Whether we
look toward the past or to the present, we must take our
chances: we must submit to the risks of the craft, or we fail.

H. P. Heseltine

The Deep, Twisting Strain of Life: The Novels of Robert Penn Warren

Robert Penn Warren's is one of the most varied careers
in modern American letters. He has achieved distinction as
short story writer, poet, critic, sociologist: most of all,
perhaps, as novelist. Yet it is in fiction, the form in which
he has found his widest audience, that Warren's performance
can go most disturbingly awry. Only one of his novels, *All
the King's Men,* has been accorded universal praise; the rest
have sustained criticism which ranges from nagging doubt to
straight-out condemnation. Books like *World Enough and Time,
Band of Angels,* and *The Cave,* it is frequently felt, are irreparably damaged by Warren's predilection for melodrama and
bizarre action, by his sensational exploitation of sex for its
own sake or for the titillation of his readers.
  These weaknesses, when they occur in his fiction, are not
the manoeuvres of a writer lacking natural talent. Even Warren's failures can provide evidence of his mastery over prose
narrative. But in spite of his enormous aptitude for fiction,
when Warren fails it is because his method collapses under the
thematic burden laid upon it. Warren's failures are failures
of technique rather than of feeling. Such a judgment must
seem especially damning in the case of Warren, one of the most
articulate and sensitive of the American New Critics — critics
who have made themselves famous (in some quarters, notorious)
through their insistence on the identity of form and meaning.
As a novelist, that is, Warren offends most where his critical
acumen and theory should equip him to offend least. Such a
paradoxical state of affairs suggests that Warren's material,
remaining so resistant to his aesthetic strategies, must occupy an overwhelmingly important role in the play of his imagination. And it is this fact, I would suggest, that invests
the imperfect achievement of most of his novels with a signif-

icance not much less than that of *All the King's Men,* his one
complete success. Warren's very inability to produce thoroughly satisfactory novels embodies a characteristic dilemma
of the twentieth-century literary imagination. He has set out
to examine some of the key themes of contemporary thought, and
they have elicited from him a response so intense that only
rarely has he been able to shape it into the controlling forms
of literature. Warren's failures are the price he has paid
for his continuing attempt to keep the novel in touch with the
modern world.

Warren's fictional method is easy enough to detect. He
himself has described it as well as anyone, in his introduction to the Modern Library edition of Conrad's *Nostromo:*
"The philosophical novelist, or poet, is one for whom the
documentation of the world is constantly striving to rise to
the level of generalization about values, for whom the image
strives to rise to symbol, for whom images always fall into
dialectical configuration, for whom the urgency of experience,
no matter how vividly and strongly experience may enchant, is
the urgency to know the meaning of experience." It has often
been noted that these words apply quite as closely to the kind
of novelist that Warren tries to be as to Conrad. And the
principles that they lay down would seem to provide a perfectly workable formula for the philosophical novelist. Had Warren been able to follow it consistently — raising his images
of the natural world to the level of generalizations within
the organic framework of his fiction — he would have been a
consistently successful novelist. But the moments of perfect
fusion of the particular and the general have been unfortunately rare — not because of any inherent weakness in the formula
but because of the nature of Warren's abstractions about experience. His interpretation of the world has opened up a wider
and wider gap between the images and the generalizations.
Apart from *All the King's Men,* it is only in his very first
novel, *Night Rider* (1939) that they are held together in the
harmony of an achieved form.

Night Rider lays out all the themes of Warren's subsequent
novels. Set in Kentucky, in the early years of this century,
concerned with the tobacco price wars of the period, the book
is centred in the character of Percy Munn, a small farmer-
lawyer. Munn becomes involved in the conflict to the point of
violence: he joins the bands of tobacco growers who ride out
masked at night, seeking through a campaign of terror to enforce a fair price for their crops. At one level, *Night Rider*
is an exciting historical thriller, full of incident and racy
characters. Nevertheless, the development of the plot forces
problems, moral and metaphysical, on both protagonist and
reader. The novel, for instance, opens with the kind of scene
that Warren has re-created many times since, and that is perfectly calculated to display most of his leading concerns.
Percy Munn takes the train to Bardsville, where a mob has as-

sembled to discuss their feud with the tobacco buyers. By
chance, Munn finds himself on the official platform at a large,
excited outdoor meeting — even finds himself speaking, a task
which he accomplishes with considerable success and inner joy.
In controlling the mob, he feels a release into fulfillment
of some deep and vital part of himself. In stumbling on the
thrill of power he has come to know himself a little better
than before. And the desire to find complete self-realization
in the dark areas of his mind is, in part, responsible for
Percy Munn's whole career of violence, culminating in disaster
and death.

But the relaxation of civilized restraints is not the only
means by which Percy Munn seeks to know the true nature of his
self. Surrender to the mob means, to a degree, surrender of
personal integrity. From time to time, Munn restores and defines that integrity not through plumbing the resources of
irrational power but through contact with the physical world,
with things. He stands, for instance, in the kitchen of a
woman whose husband he is defending against a charge of murder.
"Because of the scrubbed pine top of the table, the small, dry,
cracked hands themselves became in their motionlessness eloquent and, as it were, beckoned him on to a fuller penetration
and knowledge." Later, while the night riders are planning to
dynamite the tobacco companies' warehouses, Munn resists the
impulse to surrender to the dark forces of human violence by
maintaining his contact with the phenomenal world. "He felt a
tightening of his muscles and a prickling of the skin against
his back and shoulders. Through the heavy cloth of his coat
he felt the roughness and solidity of the logs against which
he leaned. Gradually he relaxed, listening to the voices."

It can, I think, with justice be claimed that such moments
have affinities with the famous scene in Jean-Paul Sartre's *La
Nausée,* where Roquentin contemplates the root of a walnut tree
and finds in its merely sensible existence the key to all his
knowledge of the world. And not only in this particular does
Warren exhibit an existentialist cast of thought. It is implicit in nearly every aspect of his interpretation of experience.
For instance, the discovery that Percy Munn makes in *Night
Rider* — that the mere existence of the physical world can define his own being — is repeated in various guises by all of
Warren's later heroes. But a simple sense of his own existence is not enough for Percy Munn: he must know how he exists,
discover the means of making the truth of his being operation-
al in the world. One way of transforming existence into knowing is language. Percy Munn hopes that in the act of naming
the items of his experience he will find the knowledge he
craves. His response to the meetings of the night riders is
typical:

> When one of those men to whom he talked face to face at
> the small meetings around the section did sign, Mr. Munn

would regard the process with a cold avidity, his eyes
never leaving the red, strong-knuckled fingers that guided
the pen until he saw the last stroke completed. Each name,
it always seemed in retrospect, involved himself peculiarly, representing something of himself to himself; and
almost always, upon witnessing the act of signing, he experienced the grip of an absolute, throbless pleasure in
which he seemed poised out of himself and, as it were, out
of time. Then the man who had signed would slowly lay
down the pen, and look up.

In words, that is, Percy Munn sees both a way to knowledge and
a means of making that knowledge operative, by involving himself with others. And this, in effect, is the whole theme of
Night Rider — the problem of personal identity, the problem
of how to define one's self to oneself and in relation to the
rest of mankind. "If I couldn't know myself, how could I know
any of the rest of them? Or anything?" thinks Percy Munn.
And in that thought he verbalizes the burden of the entire
novel.
      Munn's experiments in understanding take three main forms
— the release of deep, sub-rational forces which place him in
violent *rapport* with the mob; direct contact with objective
phenomena, which establishes his identity in all its loneliness; the exploration of language, as a means of transforming
existence into knowledge and of rendering knowledge operation-
al in the world. In *Night Rider,* these philosophical strategies take on aesthetic validity for two ressons. First, they
emerge naturally from the interplay of events and character.
Percy Munn's adventures in epistemological and moral discovery
are at every point forced on him by the march of events. He
is caught up in the sweep of history more or less by accident,
but once involved in the tobacco price wars, his every response is adequately and specifically motivated, his entire
behaviour substantially documented. Second, the style of
Night Rider remains philosophically neutral. The plot itself
is a perfectly sufficient vehicle for the tenor of Warren's
thought; and in this first novel, he was wise enough to let
the plot speak unaided. The style is used to render the texture and tone of a Kentucky at war with itself. However,
even within the limits of this perfectly legitimate function,
Warren's characteristic sensibility impresses itself on the
writing. There is already in *Night Rider* a tendency towards
stylistic polarity. On the one hand, there is his flair for
salty dialogue, ironic reporting action, warm re-creation of
landscape. On the other, there is his marked predilection for
an abstracting vocabulary designed to move the quality of his
writing away from direct experience towards generalizing analysis. In *Night Rider* these stylistic extremes are held in harmony with each other and with the other parts of their novel
through the agency of some eloquent rhythms and their organic

relation to the plot. The style of *Night Rider* rises to one
or other of its twin peaks only when plot or character motivation demands it.

Percy Munn's search for self-definition, then, is conducted with sufficient formal skill to make of *Night Rider* at
least a satisfactory minor novel — minor, not because the issues are unimportant in themselves but because, technically,
they are subordinated to an interest in excited action *per se*.
It is equally important to note that within the total success
of the novel, Percy Munn suffers personal catastrophe. In the
course of the action he loses his wife, is betrayed by the men
he trusts, realizes that in his search for knowledge he has
merely come to know less. In the end, he is hunted down and
killed for a crime he did not commit. This tragic pattern,
discovered and worked out in the life of a single individual
in *Night Rider,* seems to have provided Warren with a view of
the world he has come to regard as necessary and inevitable.
In all his novels since *Night Rider,* he has done nothing but
rework its central theme, bringing it closer and closer to the
foreground of his writing, constantly intensifying its inherent difficulties. The interpretation of experience dramatically realized in *Night Rider* has been transformed into dogma.
The transformation has brought Warren to the point where it is
perhaps impossible for him to write aesthetically acceptable
novels.

"Oh, Who am I?" are the opening words of *Band of Angels*.
"Myself, oh, what am I?" thinks Jeremiah Beaumont at a crucial
moment in *World Enough and Time*. "I am me, I am me," insists
old, dying Jack Harrick in *The Cave*. The question which Percy
Munn came to by accident becomes for Warren's later protagonists a very condition of their existence. And their attempts
to answer it become more and more ferocious as Warren becomes
more and more aware of the enormity of their existential
dilemma. He has explored each of the three means of self-
definition adumbrated in *Night Rider,* only to find each leading to a metaphysical dead end. Thus, he has repeatedly come
back to the possibility of commitment to the deepest forces
within one's personality. On the face of it, this might be
a hopeful doctrine. A man might find himself in converting
psychological potentiality into actuality; might find freedom
in rejecting the speculative intellect. "Every man has to go
his own gait," says Captain Todd in *Night Rider*. But the comfort of such a belief has worn thin for Warren in the realization that a man's gait is not of his own choosing, that it is
a pre-determined function of all he has been and done. Some
men, like Isaac Sumpter in *The Cave,* may surrender to the
blind forces of their own being, may choose "to tread the joyful measure of necessity." But such a solution is an admission of defeat for those who seek freedom in the knowledge of
their own identity — and for Warren those are all who count.
The seductive possibilities of freedom opened up by a Freudian

view of personality end for Warren only in a tightening of
the bonds of necessity.

   Similarly, the phenomenal world, which from time to time
yielded such comfort to Percy Munn, has proved another false
hope to Warren. He speaks in *World Enough and Time* of the
doubleness of the world, by which phrase he means its power
simultaneously to attract and to betray. It betrays because
it is contingent, is limited in time and space, and so must
curtail the aspirations of man's mind. It attracts simply because man must live in and through his senses. Man must yield
to the attraction of the world; therefore he must experience
its betrayal. He is perpetually defeated by the inescapable
conditions of his existence. "My only crime was being a man
and living in the world of men," writes Jack Burden in *All the
King's Men,* "and you don't have to do special penance for that.
The crime and the penance, in that case, coincide perfectly.
They are identical." The same sense of guilty complicity in
a world they never made obsesses nearly all of Warren's important characters.

   Warren's characteristic vocabulary for dealing with the
condition of man in the world — guilt, sin, betrayal — suggests a strong, if secularized Calvinist sensibility. This
aspect of his imagination further manifests itself in a strong
ethical urge. Warren's heroes can only hope to find true happiness through right action. Willie Stark makes up his morality as he goes along. But there is another important class of
characters who seek to impose upon the world the language of
justice. Such men Warren describes as "men of the idea." In
sharp opposition to the men of action, they include Adam Stanton, Jeremiah Beaumont, Professor Ball, Seth Parton. Driven
to impose their ethical systems on the world, they are uniformly drawn into politics, with uniformly disastrous results.
Language can create moral systems; it cannot make them work in
the duplicitous world: it, too, has come to betray Warren.

   So Warren is brought to this painful paradox. Man is of
no worth unless he follows out his need for self-knowledge and
fulfilment; but in the very act of definition he will be betrayed. He will become part of the world, with all its attendant crime and guilt. And if he merely commits himself to the
joyful measure of necessity, he denies the ethical impulse
which is part of his humanity, and so delivers himself not to
freedom but to bondage. It is little wonder that he is driven
to speak, in *The Cave,* of "the deep, twisting strain of life"
— his interpretation of experience sees man as forced by his
nature and circumstances to seek his salvation along a path
which can lead only to pain and defeat. It is little wonder
that he construes acts of overpowering sensual violence as the
only means of breaking out of the vicious circle of man's dilemma.

   It is little wonder, too, that his style, under the pressure placed upon it, has disintegrated. In the recent books,

the tendency to polarity has become increasingly pronounced.
The warm rendering of the life of the senses has been concentrated into a series of brutally frank descriptions (obsessively returning to images of darkness), a slashing irony, a
batteringly active syntax. The characters are grouped into
mutually exclusive categories — the men of the pure idea, the
men of action, and those (satirically beyond the pale) who
have weakly abandoned the search for identity. The abstractions, no longer dramatically emerging from the narrative, are
resumed in a number of key nouns. Two of them occur in the
title, *World Enough and Time*. "Joy" comes to be the counter-
word for the ecstasy of even temporary self-fulfilment. More
usually, "guilt" and "betrayal" are the rewards of Warren's
seekers after identity, who desire simultaneously "involvement" and "responsibility." All of these have become shorthand terms by which Warren makes private reference to his
whole system of belief. Unfortunately their significance is
made clear only through an inspection of the whole canon; they
are not dramatically enacted novel by novel. Even those passages aimed at explicating Warren's themes too often, in his
later work, seem to be prejudged. The rhetoric which had previously restrained the tension between the two poles of Warren's style becomes more than anything else the embodiment of
rage and frustration. It even, unfairly, transfers some of
Warren's pain direct to his readers, without subjecting it to
the control and judgment of a significant literary form. The
recent failures of *The Cave* (1959) and *Band of Angels* (1955)
spring, in effect, from the increasingly desperate manoeuvres
of a novelist painfully honest to his understanding of his
material.

The plot of *The Cave* is derived from a minor episode in
the social history of America in the 1920s — the trapping of
Floyd Collins in a cave in Kentucky. Warren transfers the
situation to Tennessee in 1955; his man in the ground is Jasper Harrick, a Korean veteran who has failed to reach self-
knowledge even in the violence of combat. He returns to his
hillbilly home and takes to cave crawling. "Well," he says to
his mother, "in the ground at least a fellow has a chance of
knowing who he is." But in the cave Jasper finds, not the
answer to his questions, but death. It is not death by mis-
adventure but by the design of his friend, Isaac Sumpter, who
deliberately exploits Jasper's helplessness for his own purposes. Ike delays the rescue attempt in order to wring from
them their full publicity value. At the close of the novel
he leaves Tennessee for a successful career in the mass media.
He has committed himself to a kind of spiritual darkness, to
the amoral dictates of his pre-determined personality.

Grafted on to this central piece of duplicity are the
stories of a number of other characters, all caught up in Warren's typical dilemma. Nick Papadoupalos, a restaurant owner,
is beset by an impossible and seedy image of the film star,

Jean Harlow. Hoping to make his vision real, he has married a
cheap show girl, now fat and tubercular. Nick vents his rage
and disappointment at the discrepancy between fact and fancy,
at his inability to make the idea real in the world, through
violent sexual outbursts. Timothy Bingham, the bank manager,
is represented as something less than a man because he de-
clines to acknowledge the existence of any existential problem.
He has been defeated by respectability and by his wife. Jack
Harrick, now in the last stages of cancer, has always known
how to live; the bizarre tragedy of his son's entrapment in
the cave must teach him how to die.

The aim of *The Cave* is clear enough. The efforts of all
its characters, major and minor, are defined in Warren's comment on the wild orgy which breaks out when the news of Jasper's death is announced: "Thousands of people, he didn't know
how many, had come here because a poor boy had got caught in
the ground, and had lain there dying. They had wept, and
prayed, and boozed, and sung and fought, and fornicated, and
in all ways possible had striven to break through to the heart
of the mystery which was themselves. No, he thought, remembering Brother Sumpter with his arms lifted under the floodlights,
to break out of the dark mystery which was themselves." In
exploring the various forms of the human dilemma and the several attempts at a solution, Warren reveals an intellect possessing at once great force and great honesty. *The Cave* is
not a failure of mind or feeling. It is a failure of technique to transform the thoughts and feelings into valid fiction. Or perhaps the brutally sensuous melodrama is the only
mode now available to Warren's imagination.

Band of Angels is no less ingenious than *The Cave* in establishing a central plot designed to exhibit Warren's continual
preoccupations. Amantha Starr is brought up on a Kentucky
plantation, only to discover on her father's death that she is
half Negro. The question of identity is thrust immediately to
the foreground of the novel. Am I black or white? To whom do
I belong? — such are the questions that force themselves inescapably on Amantha's consciousness. Further, at the moment
that her identity is so shatteringly called into question,
she is sold into slavery, sent down the river to New Orleans,
bought by Hamish Bond. When Bond becomes her lover and brings
her a kind of peace, the paradox of Amantha's existence is
twisted into new shapes: What is freedom? What slavery? Can
a bondman be free in the centre of his being? To what dark
forces is the freeman enslaved? The revelation that Hamish
Bond's name is, in fact, Alec Hinks is a further blow struck
at Amantha; even language, the signs by which men identify
themselves, has failed her. Indeed, it is only in the short
final section of the novel that Amantha, with her lesser demands on life, achieves a measure of tranquillity. The world
redeems the idea, rather than the idea the world. Yet one
must have doubts about the worth of Amantha's final peace.

Throughout the book there is the sense of situations blatantly
manipulated; of a degree of contrivance in the plot which pre-
cludes its validity; of a straining violence which springs not
from character or situation but from Warren's outraged imagination.

It has taken Warren something like twenty years to travel
from *Night Rider* to *Band of Angels* and *The Cave*. By now, the
themes he discovered in writing his first novel have come to
exercise such a powerful hold on him that they dictate the
very terms and conventions of his art. It seems that he can
no longer bring together his images of the world and his generalized understanding except in a framework of violent rhetoric
and melodramatic action that affronts the conventions of realism by which the novel lives. But between the initial success
and the necessary failures lie two works which bring Warren
closest to major success — *World Enough and Time* (1950) and
All the King's Men (1946).

It is customary to include *World Enough and Time* in the
catalogue of Warren's failures: as, indeed, it should be, if
we bring to bear on it the normal canons of fictional judgment.
It displays all the characteristic traits of Warren's writing,
so necessary to the unfolding of his themes, so calculated to
bring his art to disaster. There is, for instance, the usual
programmatic development of the plot, enmeshing Jeremiah ever
more tightly in the web of the world. There is the usual violence of action and despair of mind. There is the usual rhetorical eloquence, less checked than in any other work by a
judging irony. If, then, we regard a close loyalty to direct
experience, some kind of "realism" in matter and manner, as
necessary to fiction, *World Enough and Time* is bad fiction.
But perhaps it is not fiction, or at least not a novel, at all.
On the title page, Warren has subscribed it "A Romantic Novel."
When an American as well versed in his literary past as Warren
so categorizes his work, it is fair to assume that he means it
is a narrative of a particular kind. Hawthorne and James have
established the "Romance" for Americans, as a distinct form
of prose narrative — what Philip Rahv in *Image and Idea* has
called "a preparatory scrutiny of experience" rather than a
direct report on reality. It may be difficult to conceive of
a work hovering somewhere between the novel and the romance,
but that is where *World Enough and Time* has its aesthetic existence.

All its technical devices work to produce the effect of
violence frozen into formal postures. "We see her," Warren
wrote of his heroine, Rachel, "like an allegorical figure of
autumn painted in a sentimental school"; and with those words
he defined the whole mode and perspective of *World Enough and
Time*. The very opening paragraph stresses the distance of the
author from the events he is recounting. His thoroughly un-
characteristic use of the first person plural pronoun unites
him with his readers rather than with his characters:

I can show you what is left. After the pride, passion,
agony, and bemused aspiration, what is left in our hands.
Here are the scraps of newspaper, more than a century old,
splotched and yellowed and huddled together in a library,
like November leaves abandoned by the wind.... Here is the
manuscript he himself wrote, day after day, as he waited
in his cell, telling his story. The letters of his script
lean forward in their haste. Haste toward what? The bold
stroke of the quill catches on the rough paper, fails,
resumes, moves on in its race against time, to leave time
behind, or in its rush to meet Time at last at the devoted
and appointed place. To whom was he writing, rising from
his mire or leaning from his flame to tell his story? The
answer is easy. He was writing to us.

At occasional moments throughout the narrative, Warren is at
pains to reinforce this early established sense of distance
between plot and reader, past and present. For the most part,
however, the narrative is shared between his own conscious eloquence and the high-flown rhetoric of Jeremiah's diary. Everything, that is, in *World Enough and Time* is aimed at making
the ethical frame of reference and the heroic vision acceptable as modes of the imagination. It is perhaps as much a comment on our century as on Warren that in *World Enough and Time,*
the work wherein he most single-mindedly examines the possibility of action motivated by virtue and honour, he felt compelled to set his plot in frontier Kentucky, to remove his
themes from the world of present actuality which is fiction
to the uneasy fringes of romance. Probably no modern author
could maintain such an unaccustomed aesthetic stance for as
long as *World Enough and Time* demands; Warren has come as
close to doing so as anyone.

Only in one full-length prose narrative has he managed to
project his obsessive concerns into the form of fiction, and
within that form to shape a dramatically viable solution: only
in *All the King's Men*. Somewhere in that book lies the secret
nexus which brought together Warren's images of the real world
and his abstraction from experience into a controlled and mature work of literature. Perhaps its secret lies in the Southern setting, in the historicity of its events (notoriously
based on the career of Huey P. Long), in the speech and action
of its vivid personalities, in the committed irony of its political reporting: in a word, in the concentrated presence of
those elements which have made possible the fragmentary successes of his other books. But clearly there is something
more at stake for Warren in the story of Willie Stark than the
opportunity of displaying his narrative talent or his gifts of
sensibility. In effect, the life and death of this political
demagogue provide a more adequate plot vehicle for Warren's
themes than any he has found since *Night Rider*. Here is a
story which, without the manipulation and bizarre contrivance

of *Band of Angels* and *The Cave,* embodies with extraordinary
completeness the chief issues which exercise his imagination.

Willie Stark, like Percy Munn, has the seeds of power
within him from the very start. But Willie is aware of their
presence and strives to awaken them through embarking on a
political career. His hour strikes in a moment of public tragedy; the collapse of a school-house fire-escape vindicates his
actions against those of the established politicians. Willie
for the first time has a taste of real power, and wants more.
He doesn't get any more until he learns how to release the
full hypnotic force of his being. This lesson he learns in
the splendid scene of the Upton political rally. Told of his
betrayal by his political associates, Willie goes to the barbe-
cue, completely drunk for the first time in his life. He abandons the ethical, statistical language of his prepared speech
in favour of the language of his hillbilly kind, and from that
moment the people of the state are his to do with as he will.

Through action, through non-thinking, Willie comes to
power: and through his knowledge of the world. Alone among
Warren's major characters, Stark understands the corruptive
power of the world from the very outset of his career; and
he uses his knowledge, is not used by it. "Man is conceived
in sin and born in corruption and he passeth from the stink
of the didie to the stench of the shroud" is his Calvinist-
tinged motto. And when his enemies resist the swelling force
of his personality, he merely sets Jack Burden to the un-
earthing of their pasts; he destroys them through their own
corruption. "You don't ever have to frame anybody," he says,
"because the truth is always sufficient." The ambiguity of
Willie's involvement with and contempt for humanity is magnificently summarized in his campaign slogan — "My study is the
heart of the people." It is a slogan which brings him to absolute control of the state and which engineers the remarkable
march of the mob on the Capitol during the attempted impeachment proceedings.

Beyond that point there can be no greater fulfilment of
the deep, wordless forces which move Willie Stark to action
and power. Indeed, after this moment of supreme triumph the
Boss begins to make new discoveries about himself and the
world. He comes to realize that the bonds of corruption that
tie him to humanity also tie him to responsibility; that every
act has its consequence as well as its cause. Stark, in other
words, is forced into an awareness of morality. Virtue at
first attracts him because it is the most vivid way of impressing himself on the world; then, because it cannot betray.
In his great debate with Adam Stanton he defines the morality
he can make out of the corrupt world: "Goodness. Yeah, just
plain simple goodness. Well, you can't inherit that from anybody. You got to make it, Doc. If you want it. And you got
to make it out of badness. Badness. And you know why, Doc?
Because there isn't anything else to make it out of." Willie

Stark is hastened along his path to honour and right action by
the injury to his son Tom, an event which is the necessary outcome of Willie's private and public life. But Willie learns
his lessons too late. Just as he bears the seeds of his power
and late-coming morality within him, so too does he carry the
cause of his own destruction. It is Willie who seeks out Adam
Stanton, the man of the idea, for his hospital. It is Willie
who becomes the lover of Adam's sister Anne, and so brings the
man of the idea to a full knowledge of experience. Adam reacts in the only way he knows how — he shoots Willie to death.
In the same moment, he falls under the bullets of Stark's bodyguard, Sugarboy.

Stated thus baldly, the plot of *All the King's Men* is
seen to display all the themes that Warren discovered in *Night
Rider;* further, its inexorable development towards catastrophe
dramatically embodies Warren's response to his themes in a way
not to be found in the earlier book. But the plot of *All the
King's Men* is not baldly stated. Indeed, it is made to submit
to the most complex of all the fictional structures that Warren has devised. Its time sequence is deliberately dislocated
to effect the sense of discovery of deep layers of self not
necessarily coincident with the march of external events.
Within the apparently naturalistic limits of the plot, the
characters are balanced in a manner that elegantly and powerfully outlines the thematic pattern. Above all, the entire
story is reported in the first person by Jack Burden. Burden
is perfectly equipped to record and comment on the career of
Willie Stark. He is, on the one hand, the close associate of
the Boss; he can describe the life of politics with all the
conviction of substantiated detail. On the other hand, he
is a (rather decayed) scion of an old Southern family, in the
tradition which places a high premium on ethics and honour.
He is the lifelong friend of Adam Stanton; he can report on
the motives of a murderer. And, for as long as he can remember, he has loved Anne Stanton.

Jack Burden, then, is magnificently situated to tell his
story. He is also finely equipped to display Warren's special
stylistic talents with real dramatic propriety. Before join-
ing the Boss's entourage, Burden has practiced two professions.
He has been a newspaper reporter. He has learnt, that is, the
uncommitted language which can report experience with salty
bravura without adding any abstracted interpretation. And he
has been a research historian. He has a passion for the truth,
for the past, and the intelligence to pass judgment on what he
discovers in the lives of men. All Warren's need to interpret
raw experience can validly get into *All the King's Men* through
the agency of Jack Burden's quick mind. But most important of
all, Burden avoids Warren's two major categories of existence.
The conflict between brute action and fanatical idealism is
played out between Willie Stark and Adam Stanton. For much of
the book Jack is the outsider, deliberately holding aloof from

any kind of commitment. His role as choric commentator is
perfectly symbolized in the scene of the attempted impeachment,
when he looks down on the mob from his high office window,
knowing all, but uninvolved. "I stood in the window of the
Capitol," he writes, "and hugged that knowledge like a thorny
secret, and did not think anything."

But not even Jack Burden can spend a lifetime uninvolved.
As the novel nears its close he writes, "This has been the
story of Willie Stark, but it is my story too." And he is
right. As much as anything else, *All the King's Men* is the
spiritual history of Jack Burden. It is the story of his journey from self-willed isolation back to mankind, to his acceptance of that common humanity which is punningly implied in
his name. In the career of Jack Burden, Warren seeks to reconcile all those opposites which so constantly tear at each
other in his fiction — past and present, public and private
life, ignorance and knowledge, good and evil. From the life
of Willie Stark Jack learns the force of the world; from his
ancestor, Cass Mastern, the need for justice; from Adam Stanton the strain of ethical responsibility; from them all, and
from Anne Stanton, the means of defining himself with honour
in the limited time at a man's disposal. Jack Burden represents the most successful, the most hopeful, and the most
realistic projection of Warren's themes into a single personality.

And, somehow or other, the success of the entire novel is
bound up with Warren's creation of Jack Burden, a Jack Burden
who exists as something more than a function of technical ex-
pertise. There can be felt in the narrator of *All the King's
Men* a vitality, the power of a liberated imagination, which
cannot be explained solely in terms of the controlling force
of a complex literary structure. The source of that vitality
(and the secret of the superiority of *All the King's Men* to
Warren's other novels) is suggested by Mary McCarthy in an
article "Characters in Fiction" (*Partisan Review,* 28, 2).
Miss McCarthy speaks of the immense popularity in modern fiction of the technique of first-person narration through an
invented character wholly alien to the author. "Much of modern literature," she writes, "might be defined as the search
for one's own diametrical opposite, which is then used as the
point-of-view." Such a procedure no doubt produces many admirable fictional structures, but the sense of rich creativity
will perhaps not be there. Miss McCarthy continues:

> The existentialist paradox — that we are subjects for our-
> selves and objects for others — cannot be resolved by tech-
> nical virtuosity. The best efforts, far from mastering
> the conundrum, merely result in the creation of characters
> — Benjy, Jason, Molly, Mr. Bloom, and so on — who are more
> or less "successful" in exactly the old sense, more or
> less "realized," concrete, objectively existent. What has

been lost, however, in the continuing experiment is the
power of the author to speak in his own voice or through
the undisguised voice of an alter ego, the hero, at once
known and unknown, a bearer of human freedom.

It is Warren's special achievement in *All the King's Men* to
have mastered the conundrum. Within the structural and stylistic terms of the novel, Jack Burden's final mastery over life
carries individual conviction. When he says, near the end,
"Then I thought how all knowledge that is worth anything is
maybe paid for by blood," he is speaking from a position which
has been dramatically tested and found true within a particular piece of fiction. He is also speaking with the voice of
Warren. For Jack Burden is not only a created character within a fictional structure; he is also Warren's alter ego. And
the claim does not violate the artistic autonomy of *All the
King's Men*. It is one of the very few modern novels which present a situation and an invented narrator-hero wholly conge-
nial to the author's cast of thought. In that fact lies the
peculiar importance of *All the King's Men,* the secret of its
creative vitality, liberated into a ripe maturity not to be
found in Warren's other work. It is perhaps a measure of our
century that it has been able to yield to Warren only one such
combination of hero and circumstance. It is certainly a measure of Warren's stature as a creative artist that he has not
merely repeated the empty forms of success, but has sought to
thrust his understanding into new areas of experience, even at
the expense of failure.

James H. Justus

The Uses of Gesture in *The Cave*

In his essay on *Nostromo,* Robert Penn Warren observes that
Conrad was more interested in the kind of experienced humanism
typified by Emilia than he was in the more flamboyant "radical
skepticism" of Decoud or Monygham. Such a humanism, he concludes, emerges only out of character-in-action, when the human will meets the hard, sometimes intractable facts of other
human wills in particular situations. From the clash, the
recoil and clash again, comes that reward of the active consciousness: an understanding of "the cost of awareness and the
difficulty of virtue."[1] The observation is useful for our
reading of *Nostromo,* of course, but the double fascination is
perhaps more Warren's than it is Conrad's.

In most of his novels, Warren sends his protagonist out of
an intensely private world, where commitment has been either
ill-defined or too easily pledged, into a public world where,
if he is strong, his experience will enrich and validate that
personal vision of self. The search for self-knowledge is a
response to two contradictory desires: the searcher's need for
a definition of his private being that will isolate him from
the mass and celebrate his uniqueness, and his need for immersion in the group, the cause, the spirit of community. If in
the search for self-knowledge he arrives at the clearing, the
needs of identity and community will have been harmonized.
The protagonist may succeed or, more often, fail, but in each
case he will come away from his experience with an apprecia-
tion of the high cost of awareness. From *Night Rider* (1939)
to *Flood* (1964), the protagonist resembles a Decoud or a Monygham more than he does an Emilia, a circumstance that sheds a
particular light on how, in Warren, the strenuousness of human
effort often outstrips its rewards. Perse Munn, Jerry Calhoun,
Jack Burden, Jeremiah Beaumont, Amantha Starr, Adam Rosenzweig,
Bradwell Tolliver — all achieve self-knowledge, but only after
the most painful, prolonged, and costly exertion, which is to
say that Warren, like Conrad, goes "naked into the pit, again

and again, to make the same old struggle for his truth" ("'The
Great Mirage,'" p.58).

None of Warren's novels demonstrates the strenuousness of
human effort, the defining of self through community, quite
so insistently as does *The Cave*.[2] Here, failure after great
struggle is still seen as a dismal fact of man's lot, but a
viable, even impressive success is dominant for the first time
in a Warren novel.[3] Because it is the only one of Warren's
novels which lacks a true protagonist, the structure of *The
Cave* suggests that all characters, however different they may
be, are equally illustrative of the theme. By exploring them
from multiple angles, Warren emphasizes both the strenuousness
and the reward of human effort. Reward commensurate with that
effort comes to no fewer than seven characters (Jo-Lea, Monty,
Jack and Celia Harrick, Brother Sumpter, Nick, Bingham). Two
minor characters (Nick's wife and Dorothy Cutlick) achieve
less, but their efforts are also less intense. One minor character (Mrs. Bingham) and one major (Isaac) make "wrong" peaces,
but they are exactly the right peaces inasmuch as these characters inevitably fulfill their separate natures.

The entire plot of *The Cave* is an exploitation of the problem of reality (announced clearly in Warren's epigraph from
Book VII of *The Republic*). It posits man's difficulty in separating shadow and substance and ominously suggests that even
the removes from reality are reality too. Warren's techniques
for this exploitation are therefore appropriate: the choice of
characters who often seem drawn from a ragbag of caricatures
and stereotypes; the language which, in juxtaposing cadences
of ceremony and the hokey folk idioms of realistic action,
ends up as stylized artifice unifying a vision of man that is
itself stylized; the mood created by a mannered prose richly
studded with the metaphors of reality-shadow (*image, shadow,
dream, ritual, fantasy, impromptu drama, the fusion...of the
dream and the actuality*). There are caves and typal caves —
all those cool, remote, pastoral glades and green back rooms
of houses and banks where Keats is either read or acted out
and where competing identities, personae and selves, are met
and clarified. These identities emerge by gesture, the expression of the personal and the particular in meaningful patterns, the personal and particular responses to given situations. Gesture, though it is Warren's most successful method
of delineating character, is also, in *The Cave,* the manifestation of the indirect, the oblique: gesture *shadows forth* the
reality of the gesturer.

Obvious difficulties arise for the reader. Warren here
lavishes his considerable energies on a created world that itself is almost an image of his customary world of politicians,
cranks, agrarian exploiters and reformers, and commercial
wizards and failures. However perfectly harmonious the novel
becomes on its own terms, the reader is forced to accept an

artistic artifact that is finally richer in statement than in
drama. He may refuse to accept it, of course, particularly if
he is impatient with an author who tends to transform a perfectly useful genre — the novel — into something resembling
the parable or morality play. To remember the work of others
who have appropriated the novel form for their own purposes
may not lessen his distaste. But the fact should be made
clear anyway: Warren's adaptations in *The Cave* suggest more
the occasional practice of, say, Kafka, Sartre, Faulkner,
Camus, Porter, and Golding than they do his own earlier practice — or, more accurately, that tradition of gamy Southern
naturalism into which many critics have been content to place
Warren. Stylization has always been a Warren hallmark; in *The
Cave* it guides characters and shapes their actions and knits
together both theme and structure into what is finally a co-
hesive, comprehensive work of art.

One of the more remarkable aspects of stylization in *The
Cave* is the structural, metaphorical, thematic figure of Jasper Harrick, a non-character almost in the same sense that
James's Mrs. Newsome of *The Ambassadors* is a non-character.
His compulsion as a separate identity we know only at second-
hand; yet we see the pervasive power of that compulsion informing the acts of every one who *is* a character. His experience
is the paradigm of self-definition. He is metaphorical, archetypal, mythical, bigger-than-life, even stereotypical; and it
is against him that "real" people test the validity of their
own more fragmented searches for self-definition. Jasper Harrick, it should be noted, never appears except in the flashbacks of other characters; he says very few things, even by
report, and only one statement is noteworthy: his mother remembers his explanation for being a compulsive caver — "'in
the ground at least a fellow has a chance of knowing who he
is'" (p.241).

This motive of self-definition becomes the impulse of all
the other principals; in Jasper's fatal act, his own entombment, the motive suddenly is manifested in a physical, tangible way, which in turn supplies the others with both motive
and act. Around the cave mouth Warren assembles his congeries
of searchers. Those who enter the cave in search of Jasper
do so frankly in hope of redefining their own identities; but
even those whose quest takes them no farther than the cave
mouth are searchers as well: they use Jasper's definitive gesture as a device for orienting their own attempts at self-
definition.

The assembly at the cave mouth is the central fact of the
action, the clearing where the paths of many searchers con-
verge and where all participate in a ceremony of identification and confirmation. It is the place of grand gestures,
where the two impulses toward identity and community are
either harmonized or permanently shattered.

These searches, moreover, are underpinned by earlier and

less grand gestures, which not only reveal motive of the acts
and speeches of the individual searcher, but also supply a
texture of motif that anticipates, corroborates, and intensifies the structural climax at the cave. The who-am-I theme
is imaged in characters who realize, however dimly, that their
present identity must be validated both verbally and physically.

In Warren's fictional world, speech accomplishes what it
has always done for man in the real world: it makes subjective
emotions external and objective facts internal. In answering
the double needs of a Warren protagonist — his impulses toward
identity and community — the verbal gesture possesses the double function of marking individual boundaries and erasing them.
It not only defines the gesturer, but also suggests something
of his dilemma in establishing intercourse between his private
world and the public world in which he seeks to justify himself.

Those Warren characters who are blessed (or cursed) with
the gift of vision, imagination, intelligence, or simply the
mysterious compulsion to do right by a standard equally mysterious, are those who place the most value on *saying,* as if
the words themselves may somehow act as agents for completing
an experience still in the future. This largely unconscious
use of verbal magic is an attempt not only to communicate
wishes and desires, but also to establish the word as a coex-
tension of the reality it names, to underscore the belief that
by saying certain things in certain agreed on ways, the *sayer*
can shape his future and force events to turn out the way he
wants them to. "Words," says Warren in a recent essay on
Dreiser, "are not only a threshold, a set of signs, but a fundamental aspect of meaning, absorbed into everything else."[4]

In *The Cave,* Jasper's entombment provides not only the
orienting scene, but also the chief orienting symbol by which
an individual's sense of his own identity is tested. The
entombment, for example, is the occasion for the restaurant
owner to assert his identity, to deny that *Nick Pappy,* even
though it is "what Johntown had decided was a good enough name
for Nicholas Papadoupalous" (p.41), is either proper or adequate. He asks Mrs. Harrick to pronounce his name, since no
one in Johntown had ever done that. His argument is as poignant as it is simple: "'they got things they call you. Like
Nick Pappy. But if it is not your right name, it looks like
sometime you don't know who you are, maybe'" (p.304). It is
Celia who remembers the shrug and the strange look of her son
as he had explained his need for proper identity. It is Celia
who sympathizes with, even though she cannot understand, the
central problem so massively symbolized by her son's gesture.
So even though she is "not handy with Greek," she tries three
times to pronounce *Papadoupalous,* and Nick is satisfied.

For Monty Harrick, the problem of identity is even greater
than it is for Jasper. He must not only live in the shadows

of a legendary father and a well-known brother; he must also
resist two versions of the public consensus: to the town generally that he is not even a chip like Jasper, and to the Bing-
hams, old blocks and chips notwithstanding, that he is still
a hillbilly. Monty's maneuver is to seize upon the epithet
hillbilly and force Jo-Lea to repeat it, as if an aggressive,
willed iteration will somehow substantiate his reality and
transform an epithet of alienation into one of acceptance and
union.

Monty's search for an identity that will satisfy both his
private and public needs is paralleled by Jo-Lea's insistence
that she and her father are separate identities. She can use
the phrase "I'm me" with repeated firmness and act upon it,
whereas Monty in the beginning qualifies the phrase for himself with "I don't know who I am." He remembers Jasper's assurance (rather, he literally interprets it) — "that trick of
being himself so completely" — and then falls into the self-
pitying depression of a younger brother because he "couldn't
even be himself, whatever that was" (p.19).

Jo-Lea's success and Monty's momentary failure in "naming"
an identity are similar to Goldie Goldstein's success and
Isaac's failure. Goldie can say firmly to Isaac, "'I want you
because you are you'" (p.113), but Isaac, who carries the burden of ill-defined identity, can respond only with indecision.
Like Monty to Jo-Lea, he confesses to Goldie that he does not
even have a sure identity to give her. And of all the characters in *The Cave,* Isaac is the one who is most concerned about
his name. Even before his embarrassment at being taken for a
Jew in college (Goldie is the first to call him "Ikey"), his
concern is more deep-seated. Because he has an obsessive fear
that he was named Isaac to be sacrificed, he taunts his father:
"'Personally, I don't think you'd be up to it.... Assuming
that you really heard the voice of God putting the bee on you,
would you really cut my throat?'" (pp.96-97). All his moments
of regret, however, when he wishes he were someone else, are
offset by his dreams of glory, of seeing his by-line over a
sensational story which he partly creates. He becomes, finally, shoddily, what he fears — the stereotyped Jew. His exploratory gestures before the mirror are a psychological rehearsal
for building up the shabby commercialism which attends the
search for Jasper:

> Isaac Sumpter drew himself up to his height, which was
> five feet, nine inches, straightened his good shoulders,
> curled his lip with the sardonic incisiveness, and with a
> tone that seemed to say that now he had, indeed, discov-
> ered all, said: "Isaac Sumpter."
> Then added, in a conniving whisper, with the pitying
> smile into the glass: "Ikey — Little Ikey."
> He shrugged, dropped his hands, palms outward, in a
> parody of the classic gesture of the Jew's resignation

and irony, and repeated, in the accent of the stage Jew:
"Ikey — Little Ikey." (pp.99-100)

The opportunity at the cave gone, Isaac flees to New York, fulfilling himself at last not in other individuals (an obviously
inadequate formula in itself) and not even in a stereotype,
but in his particular image of a stereotype. He breathes life
into a copy of a copy of his identity. The vision of himself
in the mirror is transferred to his mind as the defining name
and epithet by which he will complete his search for identity.
In a shockingly appropriate way, Isaac's search is successful.

Monty's success in establishing a clear identity is of a
different order. The words of Jasper should provide the principal impulse toward self-identity for the other characters,
but since his few speeches are reported from at least two removes — and deliberately faked as well — their importance is
diluted by charges, countercharges, and recriminations. Warren's scheme, using an almost non-character — long on symbolic
ramifications and short on realistic life — is a bold and imaginative one in the contextual drama of *The Cave;* but it is
also troublesome. The figure of Jasper, with his very absence,
his thinned-out abstractness, becomes in his life and death
less convincing for the reader, perhaps, than for the other
characters, whose full-bodied response may strike us as slightly disproportionate to Jasper as stimulus. Credibility — and
thus dramatic force — is strained. What is not strained, however, is the symbolic spinning-out of Jasper's role; and in
this Warren makes him a figure of impressive dimensions, a
mythic, though perhaps tawdry, hero capable of legend.

The task of verbally creating the symbol of transformation
finally falls to Monty, who in his improvised ballad sings
both for and about Jasper. Chapter VI is essentially Monty's;
here, for the first time, the guitar becomes the explicit vehicle for the gift of song, the talisman of creativity. Standing in new boots that are catalogue duplicates of Jasper's,
Monty takes the initiative by stationing himself at the cave
mouth; soon encouragement comes flowing from the bystanders,
some of whom had previously been friendly, some hostile or indifferent, some merely curious. As he dignifies his brother
in song, he simultaneously forges his identity, an independent
one that harmonizes both his separateness from and his continuity with Jasper's. The conclusion of this chapter is a kind
of premature Orphean triumph in which the entire assembly
rises to sing the stanzas which Monty has just created.

Names and epithets, then, enriching or diluting one's
sense of self, become significant indexes for several of these
searchers. For many of them, identity resides only tentatively, even uncomfortably, in the name. The restaurant owner
must be satisfied to be identified more by his yellow Cadillac
than by his name; his wife must answer to many ersatz identities required by both herself and Nick (*plain* Sarah Pumfret,

artiste Giselle Fontaine, *fantasy* Jean Harlow, *tubercular* Mrs. Pappy); Dorothy Cutlick can assign no more meaning to her own name than she can to the Latin declensions which she repeats silently during her dutiful sexual sessions with Nick ("a person's name is not a good enough name for the ache a person is" [p.40]); Jasper Harrick, vital as he is, struggles to retrieve an identity from the community's fiat that declares him the shadow of his father ("a chip off the old block"); and even the old blacksmith himself remembers the uncertain reality of the tribute paid to him in Johntown's legends for the identity he prizes ("old heller of high coves and hoot-owl hollows" [p. 135], since to Celia he is not Jack Harrick but John T., and since he himself doubts "who Jack Harrick was, or if Jack Harrick had ever existed" (p.148).

Words, whether used to cloak or to reveal, place their users in the position of declaring themselves; and when motives are made manifest, they stand as a defining trait of the characters who manifest them. The insistence on exploring names or epithets (most dramatically in the cases of Monty and Isaac) is the verbal gesture that particularizes the individual search for identity: the public correlative of a private need. But more: in Warren's dramas of confrontation, when the self seeks to focus more sharply its own blurred identity, words are not the only vehicle for this special communication. There is also the language of hands, the physical acknowledgment of the human need to know and to be known. The touch of a hand — or even the perfunctory handshake — possesses a certain residual value as a timeless symbol for human communion. In Warren's novels, such a touch functions literally — as physical gestures must in any novel. But Warren extends the literal gesture to its traditional symbolic function and then rings his own changes on that: the human touch may herald the visible need for that communion, the fear of it, or the doubt that communion is even possible. Its function is simultaneously literal and symbolic.

If entrapment in *The Cave* is the central metaphor for the difficulties of establishing personal identity, the human touch becomes the central metaphor for exploring the struggle to release, enrich, or redefine that identity. It can particularize a universal feeling of what might be called secular sacramentalism, the notion (more instinctive than rational) that not only one's health but also one's salvation depends on a right relationship with his fellows. It can also be used to pervert that notion and serve selfish purposes; even then, however, it reminds its user of what he should know at all times: that communion is possible but difficult. Touch symbolizes the greatest corporate virtue — human communion — but the rich, diverse, and complicated motives for touch dramatize the difficulty of that virtue.

Of all the characters who place importance on touch, Celia Harrick is consistently defined by that gesture. She sees the

touch of the hand as necessary for herself, to complete herself within the entire spectrum of humanity. She must declare
herself a part of the weakness of being human, and she offers
her own weakness as a test for others who would share their
strengths. She knows that touch is contaminating, but she
senses that it is also regenerative.

The love and devotion she feels for her husband are accompanied and undercut by a sympathy for his weakness, a spiritual weakness which is magnified by his disease. Since Jack
Harrick's image of himself — as hillbilly rouster — has never
included the intimation of weakness, he is the type (so Celia
reasons) who "does not know that he has a cracking point" (p.
152). She prays that she may be the one to hold his hand when
he does uncover that human flaw in himself. But her reiterated whisper, "'I want to hold his hand,'" is something more
than spiritual prayer. Verging also on the memory of sexual
desire, it reminds her of her own weakness, her own "breaking
point" in succumbing to the sensuality of Jack Harrick; and
the memory at one time causes her to bite the flesh on her arm
and at another to press closer in the arms of Nick Papadoupalous.

In moments of accusation, she blames Jack Harrick not only
for the blatant vulgarity of his heller role, but also for establishing the standards for Jasper, who, fulfilling expectations, became successively a favorite with the Johntown women,
a hero in Korea, and an obsessive caver. She condemns the social pressure from the town which forced Jasper to respond
appropriately to the nudgings and chuckles over "old Jack's
boy." And she remembers the touching: "'They would put their
hands on him — that awful old drunk Mr. Duckett, he put his
hands on him...'" (p.297). For Celia, this leering, winking,
joking relationship was the reason for Jasper's caving — "'To
get away from the hands on him'" (p.298). At the same time
she feels that she has failed Jasper precisely because she did
not reach out her hand and touch him: "If only she had touched
him. If only she had been able to reach out and touch him,
then everything might have been different" (p.241).

The difference here is not merely the difference between
the reactions of the wife and the mother. There is a kind of
maternal protectiveness about Celia, to be sure, but her desire to touch Jasper is essentially the same as her desire to
hold old Jack's hand; it comes from a simultaneous perception
of weakness — justifiable or not — and an impulse to ally her
own weakness with what Nick observes as "the humanness" of
these situations. In an early chapter, when the blacksmith
suddenly drops to his knees with a near-incoherent proposal,
the "heller of high coves" succumbs to the stereotyped humble
lover in need of encouragement from his lady. When the war
hero and carbon-copy heller suddenly turns serious, when his
pinched and quiet face looks as if he might cry out in anguish,
he communicates the need for touch even without words. In the

first case, Celia responds with a hand in the lover's hair.
In the second, she fails to put out her hand to touch her son.
This at least is Celia's point of view. The failure of that
gesture toward her son accounts in part for the intensity with
which she repeats that gesture toward her helpless husband in
his wheelchair. As they sit waiting in front of the cave, she
crouches beside Jack Harrick's wheelchair, "one hand on the
old man's right knee, supporting herself, comforting him, in
that contact defining their oneness in the moment of sad expectancy and tremulous hope..." (p.208). Touch, then, goes
out not only in response to human weakness, but also as the
manifestation of human weakness itself. The need is to be comforted as well as to comfort another:

> *This is my life*, the woman was thinking. *I can live
> it if he puts his hand on my head.*
> He laid his hand on her head. She had been staring
> toward the cave mouth and that touch on her head was a
> complete surprise. The tears were suddenly swimming in
> her eyes.... (p.208)

The aura about Celia extends to others. And as she becomes the focus for a kind of sacramental impulse, the touch-
stone which reveals human need in all its manifestations, so
Warren tactically transforms the gesture of touch into a radi-
al metaphor. The narrative is laced with hands that touch or
fail to touch. As a technique, this gesture functions both
literally and symbolically; and, diffused as it is among many
characters and episodes, it is most successful in establishing
coherence of theme. Warren begins with a commonplace, the
most obvious physical act in the social world, and ends with
an aesthetic device which, through parallels, repetitions, and
variations, makes a profound statement on man in a chaotic
world of competing realities.

At the entrance to the cave, for example, Celia cries out
that somebody must go after Jasper, and it is Isaac who agrees:
"'Yes, yes...'" and puts his arm around Mrs. Harrick's shoulder. "Then he jerked away from her, as though, very suddenly,
he couldn't bear to have his arm there" (p.227). For all his
own deliberate toying with human privation, even Isaac feels
the simultaneous need to comfort and to be comforted, but he
also feels guilty in his willfulness. Further, the display
of weakness threatens to tarnish the public image he has carefully created. Isaac's sense of deprivation, however illogi-
cal, suggests Celia's concern with having failed to reach out
her hand to touch Jasper. In both instances the gesture of
touching, if followed through, would have recognized the human
need and, in recognizing it, gone far toward satisfying it.
Isaac, however, is too committed to an image of himself to allow public airing of private fancies. Not even the momentary
guilt of being a manipulator of Jasper's accident can deter
him from that manipulation.

It is finally only Jack Harrick who can achieve a satisfactory reciprocity with Celia, and this can come only with his regeneration. Significantly enough, the closing scenes are sustained by a series of gestures of touching, where ambiguity is resolved in mutual recognition of human inadequacies. Old Jack Harrick reminds Jo-Lea that Monty, in the cave, "'will hold his Big Brother's hand, and tell him good-bye.'" He asks her to spend the night at his house with Celia "'and hold her hand'" (p.392). Since Jo-Lea is pregnant with Monty's child, this invitation marks the strengthening of a family relationship that has been endangered and fragmented for many years. Finally, once alone, Jack sings as he strums the guitar:

"He is lying under the land,
But I know he'll understand.
He is lying under the stone,
But he will not lie alone —
I'm coming, son, I'm coming, take your Pappy's hand."
                                                    (p.402)

And when Celia comes to him, he lays "his hand on her head, not the weight of it, just lightly." The respect for mutual weakness engenders its own strength: the strength of acceptance without despair.

The artistic strategy in *The Cave* is clear. In sacrificing a dominating protagonist, Warren chooses to divide the dramatic interest among seven major characters and a host of minor ones, all of whom share in varying degrees the common search for self-identity. The tactics used to implement this strategy are also clear. Warren attempts to solve a built-in narrative problem — an inevitable dispersion of dramatic force — by using a kind of conceptual shorthand which will thicken the thematic statement. Thus, he uses verbal and physical gesture to externalize individual dilemmas in accommodating private and public needs. It is a familiar Warren technique, observable in such an early work as *Night Rider* and used perhaps most effectively in *World Enough and Time*. His success with gesture as an artistic tool has always depended on a dual function: giving circumstantial fullness to an individual character, who, however much he shares in the strengths and weaknesses of the human community, emerges as an independent creature worthy of having a story told about him. He can be realistic-naturalistic in the machinery of his story and still posit characteristic stances of his species; he can be a reasonable imitation of a man and still come to be a viable symbol of Man. In this sense, *The Cave* is an important departure from Warren's previous novels, and the choice of multiple protagonists is more crucial than it first appears to be. One result of this technique is that the dramatic power is diminished, and "rich meaning" is forced to take up the slack. An important indication of this shift may be seen in the reiteration of gesture and its distribution, sometimes without effec-

tive discrimination, among all the characters. At their best,
they become more typal than human; at their worst, more stereotyped.

One of the more successful of these manipulations of
character types through physical gesture revolves about the
Sumpter-Isaac plot. From Brother Sumpter's point of view, the
entire struggle to save Jasper is merely an elaborate drama,
divinely ordained and staged, to save his son Isaac. It is
not clear whether Sumpter believes he is acting out of a fig-
ural Abraham role or not, but Isaac accuses him of it even before the incident occurs, and Sumpter says to himself: *"He is
my son, and he is beautiful, and God will give him back to me"*
(p.190). And, in an almost stupor-like voice, he says to
Celia and Jack Harrick: "'It is my son who will be saved'" (p.
206). But to whatever degree he is conscious of his role, the
drama does offer a testing of both father and son. Isaac has
accused his father of not having the courage to kill him as a
sacrifice in response to God's command and has speculated,
half-seriously, that "Little Ikey is the one better pray hard"
for a substitute sacrifice. He taunts his father with the possibility that there "'might be a snafu in the celestial bu-
reaucracy and somebody might not deliver that miraculous ram
in time to save bloody little miraculous Isaac's little neck'"
(p.97). Isaac gets his chance for salvation when Jasper in
the cave becomes the substitute sacrificial ram. But if this
is a miracle, Isaac never recognizes it. In manipulating the
occasion for his own material advantage, in transforming himself into a stereotyped Jewish opportunist, he further alien-
ates himself from the human communion.

Isaac's failure compels his father to go into the cave,
to act not out of, but against, his own faith and morality to
save Isaac: he lies and rearranges the evidence in the cave to
substantiate Isaac's lie. After his father emerges from the
cave with the report that Jasper is dead, Isaac reaches out
his hand to touch his father's arm:

>   The old man looked down at the demanding hand. Then,
>   effortlessly, he reached his own free hand around, lifted
>   his son's touch from him, meeting no resistance, and with-
>   out a word...rose into the open air beyond. (p.334)

There is more than a reversal of roles here. The old man does
not sacrifice himself for his son. Out of an overwhelming
love for Isaac, he sins against the merciful God in whose name
he preaches; he chooses human loyalty over divine loyalty,
and in that act tastes the bitterness of human weakness more
strongly than ever before. In the horror of his own act, however, he cannot yet show his solidarity with human weakness,
and he shrinks from the touch of it, even when it comes from
his own flesh. Even the love of his son is no excuse for the
guilt he feels. Isaac's sin is less than his own, and all
others' as well. Old Sumpter feels that all other people,

even with their imperfections, are superior to himself. When Nick tries to support him at the cave mouth, he jerks away, yelling, "'Don't touch me!... I am not worthy...of your touch!'" (p.349). And in the moment when he confronts old Jack, he asks him not to shake his hand but to spit on him.

That confession to Jack Harrick in turn stimulates old Jack's confession that he actually wanted to love his son. Such a confrontation, with its admission of error, paves the way for the regeneration of both men. Paradoxically, through his perception of weakness, when he recognizes his involvement in the human condition, Sumpter is better able to purge himself of spiritual pride and to attain a strength previously unknown to him. His sympathy for weakness can now gain for him a strength which will lead to his salvation. That sympathy, on the other hand, has only confirmed Isaac's scorn for weakness, including his own, and fostered an attitude that will lead him to codify the means for manipulating human weakness and to remove himself further from any hopes of salvation.

In *The Cave* more than in any of his other novels, Warren uses gesture — both verbal and physical — to objectify the personal response to moral challenges brought about by man's constant nature working itself out within necessary human contexts. On this matter Warren lavishes most of his energies, and though his particular interests do not give this novel the usual solid circumstantiality of Warren's world, they do go far in making *The Cave* a durable novel with its own impressive scaffolding. The *donnée* requires and receives from the reader not natural identification with the things and peoples of a "natural" place, but an astonished and even compassionate confirmation that psychic truths still coil and recoil in a natural world that has been imaginatively shattered and reassembled. The familiar Warren search for the "true" self continues, but here there is even more insistence (dramatically possible because of the large group of characters) that the "true" self lies in a mysterious but real concern for the nonself. Fathers must come to terms with sons, and sons with fathers; women with their men's adulteries, and men with their women's compromises; and brothers with their brothers' achievements and failures. In the shared commonality of weakness and imperfection lie strength and, perhaps, even regeneration.

---

1. "'The Great Mirage': Conrad and *Nostromo*," *Selected Essays* (New York, 1958), pp. 48-49.
2. *The Cave* (New York, 1959); page references are to this edition.
3. *The Cave* marks a crucial shift in Warren's technique. In *Wilderness* (1961) and *Flood* (1964), the same pattern emerges: the gray fact of existence resists man's control or even his understanding, but the dedicated human effort, in the midst of failure, can provide tentative success in the overwhelming concern for wholeness. Philosophically, Warren sees this success as being as difficult to attain as

that in *All the King's Men* and *World Enough and Time;* however, in its
dramatic working out, in its novelistic force, the success is much
easier: the hurdles come down against the reiterated onslaught of
rhetoric. This thickening of philosophic statement and the correspon-
ding dramatic thinning out have been cited most often as the reasons
for the relative failure of Warren's recent fiction. I believe that
an investigation of Warren's strategies in genre and his tactics in
technique will show that these later novels are more substantial than
has been generally believed, but the subject is not appropriate to
this essay. For the best presentation of Warren's weakness as a
"philosophic novelist," see Madison Jones, "The Novels of Robert Penn
Warren," *South Atlantic Quarterly,* 62 (1963), 488-98.
   4. "An American Tragedy," *Yale Review,* 52 (1962), 9.

Neil Nakadate

Identity, Dream, and Exploration:
Warren's Later Fiction

It is too easy to make generalizations about the writing
of Robert Penn Warren: He is a "Southerner" and a Formalist;
his writing is that of the critic as novelist, as poet. His
work is philosophical and intellectual; it is the literature
of irony and ambiguity and the search for self-knowledge.
In the case of Warren's fiction, the temptation to generalize
is particularly great, given the early and enduring success
of his third novel: The corpus is *All the King's Men* and "the
other fiction," all of which manages to exist in a critical
midregion somewhere between the austere judgments of the academy and the rewards of the marketplace. It is said that Warren's stories are always parables of sin and redemption; his
characters range from the folk to the allegorical, and are
inevitably engaged in an existential quest.

Such generalizations are useful, of course, but it is dangerous to take them for more than they are, and the danger of
presumed familiarity is nowhere more apparent than in reading
Meet Me in the Green Glen and *A Place to Come To,* Warren's two
novels of the seventies. Both novels contain echoes and after-
images from earlier novels, yet depart significantly from that
fiction almost as much as they contrast, in plot, tone, and
mode of expression, with each other. In the later fiction
(beginning as early as *Wilderness* but with *Flood* the apparent
turning point) Warren's chief concern is less with self-
knowledge per se — the need for it is not discovered here,
but assumed — than with the manner and mood of man's conscious
pursuit of understanding and verification of the meaning of
life. In the later fiction Warren's concern is with knowledge
as exploratory tool and with conscious need, sometimes pathetic and sometimes defiant, as vital fact. Ignorance and impul-
siveness, idealism, impatience, and the obsessions of youth
are no longer the urgent forces and major flaws of his characters. Rather, these men and women clearly, vexingly, possess

the maturity of lives lived more than understood, lives understood more than accepted. Warren's later protagonists engage
in probing, fitful, but patient quest of understanding and
acceptance (often self-acceptance) while burdened with the
ironies of maturity — their experience and "wisdom," their
intelligence and habits of mind, the sardonic vision of lives
suffered and endured (and sometimes inexplicably rewarded or
blessed). At best they see themselves as survivors, their
lives the curious legacies of others' passing; at worst they
view their lives as existences merely muddled through. The
urgency *to experience* has become in these people the commitment *to understand and embrace* that experience and to make it
comprehensible and acceptable to others.

I

> Time past and time future
> Allow but a little consciousness.
> To be conscious is not to be in time
> But only in time can the moment in the rose-garden,
> The moment in the arbour where the rain beat,
> Be remembered; involved with past and future.
> Only through time time is conquered.
>   Eliot, "Burnt Norton"

One would, of course, expect a writer of Warren's maturity
to have all the answers and to be willing to offer them up —
to profess. Yet in Warren's fiction the better part of maturity is to avoid pronouncement and the resulting implication
that he is offering any "final word." For him, as for Eliot,
being is "a little consciousness," a constant state of *becoming* in relation to past and future. *Flood* (1964) is a crucial
expression of this perceived need always to address the here-
and-now and to understand coming-into-being as process, especially insofar as that process is in direct conflict with
the depersonalization, fragmentation, and urgency of contemporary life.

For the novel's protagonist, Brad Tolliver, life is a suc-
cession of inexplicably contingent episodes that follow each
other in inexorable sequence; life is a collection of discrete
and successful gestures, the latest of which for him is the
writing of the screenplay for a film that will record the
flooding of his hometown by the waters of a government dam.
Tolliver is talented, fortunate, skilled, and successful, but
like the film's director, Yasha Jones, he is also a personal
failure, capable of pity (even self-pity) but not of the conviction that life (let alone Brad Tolliver) matters. Midway
on the road of life, Tolliver finds himself increasingly detached from others and from a sense of place, in confused and
purposeless transit and increasingly prone to step outside
time into the self-imposed solitude of the "high lonesome,"
"a strictly private booze-soak...undertaken for strictly phil-

osophical reasons. It is the nearest the State of Mississippi
comes to Zen. It is the nearest even the State of Tennessee
comes to Zen. It is the nearest Brad Tolliver comes to Zen,
and he is coming there now because, in this flood of moonlight
and memory, he is about to retire to the chamber where he, as
a boy, lay and, while moonlight strayed across his couch and
the mockingbird sang, indulged what the bard has so aptly
termed the long, long thoughts of youth."[1] Yet there is little consolation for Tolliver in the observation that "the
whole South is lonesome" or in the self-mockery with which he
tries to deflect narcissism; as the deputy warden of the nearby penitentiary remarks, solitary confinement is "the kind of
lonesomeness a man can't stand, for he can't stand just being
himself" (p.158). What Brad Tolliver seeks in returning to
Fiddlersburg, Tennessee, is some sense of his own significance
in the rush of time and circumstance. Despite his periodic
"retirements" he is engaged in what Warren has called "the effort of the alienated...to enter again the human communion."[2]

One reflection of Tolliver's dilemma in *Flood* is the multiplicity of styles in which his story is rendered — cinematic
landscapes, sardonic commentary, melodramatic dialogue, folk
wisdom, epistolary disquisition, and courtroom transcript,
to cite the most prominent. In fact, it is Tolliver's self-
consciousness, tied to his intelligence and skill at "existing" in terms of all the styles cited above, which causes him
to decide, perversely and perhaps desperately, to work on the
movie in the first place. His dilemma is that of the sensitive and intelligent man aware of his own pathos — his pathos
being his separation and relative isolation from "the world,"
the suffering caused by this separation, and the lack of a
sense of viable resolution to his malaise. He shares this
problem with Yasha Jones. "Yes, reality was the uncapturable,"
muses Jones. "That was why we need illusion. *Truth through
lie.... Only in the mirror, over your shoulder...does the
ghost appear*" (p.50). In other words, writing the screenplay
might make it possible for Tolliver to see the "ghost" of
truth after all, in spite of the illusions the task might require. Writing the screenplay, like his other half-conscious
probings — the search for Izzie Goldfarb, confrontations with
Calvin Fiddler, tryst with Leontine Purtle — might be an imaginative means to a real end. Failing that (and in mocking consolation) the screenplay might be an end in itself.

The need is there in Tolliver, even perhaps a sense of
obligation (to his spiritual father Izzie Goldfarb, to his
convicted friend Calvin Fiddler, to the memory of his "muskrat-
skinner" father, to himself), and there is no end to the
advice he gets from the more clear-headed and self-possessed.
His sister Maggie tells him, "You [simply] have to make your
you out of all that sliding and brokenness of things" (p.325),
and as Calvin finally realizes, "there is no *you* except in relation to all that unthinkableness that the world is" (p.412).

Tolliver, like these and the other displaced persons of Fiddlersburg, must frame a world view in order to have a world, a sense of community, and a self, at all. He must establish an identity and relationship with life in which things are, as Blanding Cottshill puts it, "tied together," in which there is a "spooky interpenetration of things, a mystic osmosis of being" (p.423).[3] The need is there, and in Tolliver a moment of awakening:

> He had run hither and yon, blaming Fiddlersburg because it was not the world and, therefore, was not real, and blaming the world because it was not Fiddlersburg and, therefore, was not real. For he had not trusted the secret and irrational life of man, which might be the truth of man.... For he, being a man, had lived, he knew, in the grinning calculus of the done and the undone.
>
> Therefore, in his inwardness, he said: *I cannot find the connection between what I was and what I am. I have not found the human necessity.*
>
> He knew that that was what he must try to find."
> (p.439)

Finally, Brad Tolliver accepts that life does not fit together like the contiguous frames of a reel of film, no matter how skillfully conceived and spliced; he accepts that (as Calvin Fiddler puts it) "time is the measure of life and life is the measure of time" (p.395). He accepts that further probings in life and time must be inward probings as well as outward, in an effort to eschew gesture and habit and achieve a life of integrity and "communion"; he knows that he must now pursue the probing without any sure sense of the ending. But though Tolliver recognizes the need to get beyond pity and self-pity, depression and despair, and though he recognizes that *"there is no country but the heart"* (p.440), the crisis and recognition are not enough. Fulfillment will come only in the course of time; the affirmative ending must still be earned. The people of Fiddlersburg will be relocated, and many seem on the verge of reconciliation, but he must once more be on the road, alone (as he was, literally, in the opening pages of the story), in search of his "proper relationship to the world."[4]

In the Warren canon Tolliver's *mezzo camin* quest for meaning, just seriously begun at the end of *Flood,* is picked up, years later, by Jediah Tewksbury in *A Place to Come To.*

II

> Time is a fluid condition which has no existence except in the momentary avatars of individual people. There is no such thing as *was* — only *is*. If was existed, there would be no grief or sorrow.
>
> Faulkner, *Paris Review* interview (1956)

Meet Me in the Green Glen (1971) follows *Flood;* it explores the psyche of a woman who, like Maggie Tolliver Fiddler,
tries to create a self "out of all that sliding and brokenness
of things" and in relation to "all that unthinkableness that
the world is." In *Meet Me in the Green Glen* Cassie Killigrew
Spottwood — by turns wife, child, nurse, lover, murderess,
failed prophet — fulfills "the human necessity." She lives
"the secret and irrational life of man."

Meet Me in the Green Glen is in the dream tradition of
American fiction — the tradition sustained by the obsessive
quest of Joe Christmas, the "longing" of Carrie Meeber, the demonic vision of Ahab, the erotic dream of Hester Prynne. It
is in a tradition of fiction in which dreaming demands action,
action involves moral choice, and the dream and the choice put
the dreamer in direct conflict with society. It is a tradition in which stasis is tantamount to death itself, a sign
of the failed life; it is a tradition in which to dream is to
act, and to act is to be. In the fiction of Faulkner, Dreiser,
Melville, and Hawthorne, the moral choices involve homicide,
infidelity, obsession, and carnal knowledge, and in each of
these the dreamer proves to be only human and vulnerable, one
from whom society demands, and exacts, compensation — apparently compensation for some violation of mores or error in calculation, but ultimately compensation for making an unequivocal,
unapologetic commitment to the dream itself. The dream may
of course breach convention and be socially condemned, or deny
reality and be impractical,' or involve an illusion and be un-
obtainable. Thus Christmas's defiant gestures, Carrie's unend-
ing desires, Ahab's misguided persecution, and Hester Prynne's
rebellious autonomy. But in a transformation wrought by innocence and error and what Dreiser called "emotional greatness," the dream defies reality, even conquers it. In the
fictions of the dream tradition, the dream's reality violates
and transcends the everyday world and, momentarily, vanquishes
time. As we are told at the end of *Meet Me in the Green Glen*
— ironically enough, through Murray Guilfort, the novel's
quintessential lost soul — the particular dream may be a "monstrous delusion," a lie, but the dreaming itself "is truth."[5]

Thus *Meet Me in the Green Glen* should be read not as a
novel (in the generic sense), but as a romance;[6] perhaps even
more than *Flood* it is "a romance of our time." *Green Glen* is
at once perverse, convoluted, existential, allegorical, and
affirmative; in the face of a world of pragmatism and judgment,
and despite the world's rejection of Cassie Spottwood's testimony, it affirms the vitality of dreams.

Cassie has the respect and indulgence of Spottwood Valley,
personified in the surreptitious chivalry of Murray Guilfort
and his dutiful monthly contribution to her welfare, only as
long as she lives a life of silent deprivation. Removed from
the vision of her community, Cassie remains "one of them" as
long as she nurses in faithful silence the paralytic frame of

Sunderland Spottwood, whose grotesque presence, nagging and offensive, seems only to magnify the inadequacies, demands, and betrayals of their long-dead marriage. Cassie's quotidian reality is one of mute devotion, unseen grief, and self-pity; it is the reality of insistent, overwhelming circumstance and isolation. Cassie's dream is her relationship (nocturnal, matutinal, erotic) with Angelo Passetto, the mysterious stranger (patent-leather shoes, city of Cleveland, Sicilian birth), whose arrival violates the sealed-off world of Spottwood Valley and the selfless existence of Cassie Spottwood. Cassie's dream is one of the rejection of life as "the way things went away from you, and left you standing" (p.73), of passivity in the face of changelessness, "inevitability," and others' needs. Her dream is one of being violated by Angelo, the generic "he," of later possessing him in her own need, and coming into being and identity as a creature of volition and will. Cassie's dream becomes the erotic reality which enables her to act — *"Now she come my room,* he thought. *Now, at night"* (p.129) — to make things change, to be: "She thought of the air touching her face all over, molding it, giving it a shape, making it alive. She thought how she had never thought that before. How you were a shape where the air was not, but the air touched you all around and its touching made the tingling that was your shape and made you know that you were alive and were you" (pp.151-52). And later, to Angelo, the catalyst of her awareness and passion: "I feel I just got born" (p.153).

Cassie's relationship with Angelo is, as Warren's Marvellian epigraph tells us, "begotten by Despair/ Upon Impossibility." It is at first perverse, clumsy, selfish; it is eventually joyous, transcendent, and fatal.

Dreams exist in the context of "reality" — that is, the simple presence and demands of others and the needs they see as truth, *their* dreams. Cassie Spottwood's dream is set against the realities of the world and of time, as represented by the men who most affect her later life — and whose lives are eventually ended because of that association. Sunderland Spottwood captured Cassie as a girl-bride who acted in "the hypnosis cast on her by the collusion between the tear-swimming gaze of Sunder's eyes in firelight and the ghostly breath of Cy Grinder" (p.85). Later paralyzed by a stroke, he lives only through the charity of Murray Guilfort and the hypnotic devotion of his wife; he is (as Angelo observes) "lying there now like dead, but worse than dead because you had to stay alive just to keep on suffering the being dead" (p.158). Once known for "directness, callousness, idiotic courage, and amiable bestiality" (p.83), Sunder lacks all human potential, each enormous hand resting spiderlike, in pale anticipation of death. Murray Guilfort is a man of ambitions (big Buick, state supreme court) and gratifications (Chicago, "a thousand Mildreds"), but one whose life, from the earliest days in the "good, decent house" of his childhood, has been "only nothing-

ness, a movement of shadows" (p.143). His only triumphs, merely pathetic in the end, are in the courtroom "vindication" of
the life he has led and the condemnation of Angelo Passetto —
and public rejection of Cassie's new reality. He can have his
own illusions — "Illusion," said his friend Milbank, "is the
only truth" (p.23) — only by denying other people's dreams.
Guilfort denies and is denied purpose and desire, and he is
ultimately alienated even from himself; he lacks all relationship to human need, even his own.

Angelo, having brought Cassie into being, begins to fear
the vitality and change his actions have brought about. He
seeks escape in the changelessness of sleep, "where nothing
had ever happened and nothing would ever happen" (p.125), and
in the cool, dry nothingness in the crawlspace beneath the
house. He seeks escape in ritual and habit: errands to Parker-
ton and the reading of moldering magazines; broken windows,
incubator, John Deere Model A; red dress, black stockings, rib-
ron, and radio. Angelo eventually seeks escape — or if not
escape, conflict and resolution — in his affair with Charlene
(at once Cassie's rival and symbolic "daughter," the mulatto
child of her husband and Arlita Benton). But Angelo gets nowhere; he always returns. "He hadn't been going anywhere" to
begin with, we are told. "There hadn't been any place to go,
and he had stayed right here, and that woman who had looked
at him out of her distance and indifference and age...was now
standing before him, but was somebody else" (p.175). In the
end Angelo becomes the victim of his own attempt to escape
from another dream, the nightmare of Guido Altocci, and of his
involvement in Cassie's dream-life and transformation.

> It was because she was both a girl and not a girl. She
> had been that old woman, in the brown sweater, all frozen
> up in her ignorance and hopelessness, and that fact had
> kept the girl inside her more innocent and tender and
> yearning than any girl who had ever been hidden that way
> inside an old woman could ever be.... That was it. For
> *la piccola* had only then, that very morning, come to exist.
> She had said: "I feel I just got born," and she was just
> born and didn't know anything.
>   In the end it was her ignorance that possessed him.
> (pp.176-77)

If one of the motives for Cassie's devotion to Sunder is
(as Angelo believes) her hatred of him, then loving Angelo and
no longer needing that hatred in order to live is one of her
motives for killing her husband. Another motive, of course,
is her despairing outrage at her lover's infidelity. When he
returns from town after having gotten himself beaten up for
trying to pass as "a Negro" (another perverse attempt to resolve his problematical existence), she tries to recover him
and protect her happiness by denying reality, blocking out
time. But the accumulated weight of repeated duplicity (Sun-

der and Arlita, Angelo and Charlene) overwhelms her; the pain
of her own self-consciousness claws at her inner being; Murray
threatens her with sending Angelo back to the penitentiary;
and, finally, irrevocably, Angelo locks her out of his room.
So finally the murder is Cassie's attempt to repossess Angelo
by publicly professing her love for him. In desperation she
commits an act calculated to affirm both her identity and her
love by thrusting her dream-life into the light of common day.
In killing Sunder she takes her love out of the protective
darkness of the "secret world of no-Time" (p.182) and forces
it into the world of Guilfort and Farhill and the court, the
public world in which it inevitably proves easier to make judgments than to affirm the significance of life.

     She learns that in the "real" world of the courtroom it is
not only Murray Guilfort who wants "one dago less in Tennessee"
(p.215); it is also Jack Farhill, Dr. Spurlin, and Judge Potts.
We learn that it is also Leroy Lancaster, the chevalier manqué
who sardonically recognizes himself as "the Conscience of Par-
kerton" (p.265), who wants Angelo to die.[7] Theoretically,
Cassie's confession brings the courtroom proceedings closer to
their ostensible goal, the truth. But the greater fact, the
fact which obscures the truth, is that her confession is also
a profession of love, and that Angelo himself stands and cries
out in public (*"Piccola mia — piccola mia!"*) and invites "the
hard, targeting eyes of all those people who...stared unforgiv-
ing at him from the thorny shadow of their own deprivations,
yearnings, and envies, as from a thicket" (p.275). Angelo's
crime is that he has outraged the sensibilities of Spottwood
Valley, not that he has killed Sunderland Spottwood. Cassie's
crime is that she has made their fantasies, their fears — a
life of passion, dreamlike and intense — her reality. In the
end the court is only (and obsessively) interested in legal
reality, not in emotional truth; it is interested in the sanctions that can pass for law, not the truth of passion or the
transcendent reality attested to by passion.[8]

     Like her namesake, the Trojan princess Cassandra, Cassie
is doomed never to be believed by those whose fates her words
have the greatest potential to redeem.[9] And like Coleridge's
Ancient Mariner, she is vexed by the paradox of the imagination; when her vision (truth, beauty, love) is rejected, the
public blessing becomes a personal curse.[10] Ultimately Cassie's testimony is extralegal, an affirmation of the love that
confirmed her reality; it is a testimony rejected by others
(with the exception of Miss Edwina, who functions, in the
"Mariner" context, as her shrieving Hermit) because they are
unable to understand and express their own needs, because, in
the end, they lack a sympathetic affinity for the imagination.
Without self-knowledge, Warren has often observed, there can
be no communion; and in this novel self-knowledge emerges only
from the dream which constitutes the process which gives that
knowledge life.

III

The search is what anyone would undertake if he were not
sunk in the everydayness of his own life.... To become
aware of the possibility of the search is to be onto something. Not to be onto something is to be in despair.
                              Walker Percy, *The Moviegoer*

In *A Place to Come To* (1977), as in *Meet Me in the Green
Glen,* process and purpose are fused. In the later novel, however, it is not dream, but the need for exploration which informs the narrative of Jediah Tewksbury. In the vein of *All
the King's Men* and *World Enough and Time, A Place to Come To*
is at once autobiography, apologia, and education novel. Yet
it is also a kind of communication that neither of those brilliant novels is; it is unstintingly different from Warren's
earlier fiction, and as critically challenging.
   To begin with, it is helpful to see that form and function
in *A Place to Come To* are fused at what we might call a rhetorical matrix; what the novel is and does is inseparable from
Jed's first-person narration, his presence of mind and the per-
plexing inadequacies of his prose, the mellowed ironies of his
past experience and his present relationship to the reader.
While *Meet Me in the Green Glen* was in the fictional tradition
of dream and romance, *A Place to Come To* is in the dual tradition of what Northrop Frye calls the "confession" and the "anatomy." In short, Warren's novel is a "confession" in that it
is both a kind of autobiography with *mea culpa* overtones and
an emotional and psychological history with an avowed "interest in ideas and theoretical statements." It is (in Frye's
formulation) both introverted in focus and intellectualized
in content. Warren's novel is an "anatomy" in that it is a
unique kind of "academic" discourse — one which deals with "intellectual themes and attitudes," and particularly with evil
and folly as "diseases of the intellect, as a kind of maddened
pedantry which the *philosophus gloriosus* at once symbolizes
and defines." It is both satirical and analytical in tone and
purpose, and stylistically "relies on the free play of intellectual fancy and the kind of humorous observation that produces caricature." It is an "anatomy" in that it is intellectualized and (paradoxically) extroverted. *A Place to Come To*
is a "confession" because to some extent it is Jed's "success
in integrating his mind...that makes him feel that his life
is worth writing about"; it is an "anatomy" in that Jed is
not only the subject but the object of his own narration, the
"pedantic target" of "an enormous amount of erudition" about
himself.[11]
   It is important to Jed Tewksbury, even therapeutic, to
tell us how he fought his way out of Dugton, Alabama, by virtue of football and Latin; how he triumphed at Chicago under
the tutelage of a remarkable mentor, Heinrich Stahlmann, who
committed suicide; how he served, and killed with, the Italian

partisans during World War II; how he returned, married, and
survived Agnes Andreson, a brilliant fellow student who died
of uterine cancer. It is important, even cathartic, to Jed to
tell us of how, because of Agnes's mortality, he was able to
write *Dante and the Metaphysics of Death;* of his indulgent, es-
capist, and futile affair with Rozelle Hardcastle Carrington,
formerly (and perpetually) "the queen of Dugton High"; of his
academic triumphs in Nashville, Chicago, and Rome; of his second marriage, to Dauphine Phillips Finkel, his fatherhood, his
divorce. To discourse on these things is for Jed both to validate their happening and to accept them. Beyond all this,
though, it is vital to Jed, and to us, to see that though his
life is the story of "my unfended weakness in the face of the
way the world was,"[12] he has lived it as he was and chose. It
is vital for us to see not only that he sustains the guilt of
the survivor who has done nothing to merit survival, but also
that, as he "proclaims" at the beginning of his narrative,
"Something is going on and will not stop. You are outside the
going on, and you are, at the same time, inside the going on.
In fact, the going on is what you are. Until you can understand that these things are different but are the same, you
know nothing about the nature of life" (p.3). Life is.
Despite his sense of inadequacy and remorse, errors of commission and omission, achievements and failures, Tewksbury —
beyond middle age but just now (as Jack Burden would say)
"entering Time" — affirms the reality of that which was and
is, for these are humanly and ineluctably the impure essence
of what is to be.

     Jed Tewksbury is engaged, as Walker Percy would say, in a
search, of which his narrative is commencement and core. That
search is at times rambling recollection and even Shandean
self-expression, but it has a weight of urgency and meaning;
at times the search seems a Conradian quest for an elusive
truth, but with the pessimism muted by a sense of the possibility of redemption in human affairs.[13] "How does a fact become operative except by the mind's recognition of its relation to a pattern?" he asks. "...We are all stuck with trying
to find the meaning of our lives, and the only thing we have
to work on, or with, is our past. This can be a question of
life or death" (p.19).

     In *A Place to Come To,* what Frye calls confession and an-
atomy become what a rhetorician might call an exploratory
novel.[14] For example, in discussing the anatomy, Frye points
out that "the short form of the anatomy is usually a dialogue
or colloquy, in which the dramatic interest is in a conflict
of ideas rather than of character"; in discussing exploratory
discourse, James Kinneavy writes that it is usually "plural
rather than monologual in form" and that "in written form,
the dialogue is a comfortable medium for exploration." Again,
Frye observes that "the intellectual structure built up from
the story makes for violent dislocations in the customary

logic of narrative, though the appearance of carelessness that
results reflects only *the carelessness of the reader or his
tendency to judge by a novel-centered conception of fiction*";
Kinneavy notes that in exploratory discourse "the general dialectical procedure can be interrupted by a flashback, for the
discussion of the moment may clarify something earlier left
indeterminate. Similarly, the present issue may suddenly establish relations which at the moment seem irrelevant to the
current topic and again the logical sequence may be interrupted by intuitions into the future. Such irregularities
make the final pattern of dialectic appear crude and unordered
in comparison with the rigid organization of science. Yet,
*this is desirably so, for the flashbacks and intuitive jumps
are as necessary to dialectic as its orderly deductive or in-
ductive progress.*"[15]

What Warren has done in *A Place to Come To* is internalize
the exploratory dialogue — the dialectical conflict of ideas —
in the mind of his narrator, and to reveal through him the "irregularities," intuitions, and violent dislocations of an intellect in search of the meaning of a life. Tewksbury is both
protagonist and antagonist in the cerebral conflict and search;
in Kinneavy's terms "there is a continual shifting of positions as the dialectic proceeds, and the hero of one stage of
the discussion may well be the goat of the next." Thus a double dialogue, a colloquy of sorts, is created in the narration,
the inner dialogue of Jed Tewksbury and the implied dialogue
between Jed and the reader.[16] Further, it should be clear
that what Warren has done cannot be clearly understood from
what Frye calls a "novel-centered" and Kinneavy a "scientific"
conception of discourse. Put simply, true exploratory discourse cannot result in a "well-made" novel. "Well-madeness"
is predicated on determinacy and order, and on the sureness of
the narrative voice. Yet Tewksbury is nothing if not unsure
of himself, and his story is clearly one of indeterminacy and
ambiguity.[17] Tewksbury himself might add that a well-made
novel cannot possibly be the product of a less than well made
life. Jed is what he is in relationship to everything else —
the identities and associations of the modern mind and world,
from Dugton to Sienna — in essentially idiosyncratic and un-
aesthetic association. His book, like his life, is marked by
"realism, wit, intellectual complication," which are the enemies of well-made novels and pure poetry. In defending his
life's story — on one hand "indefensible," on the other an
admirable gesture on behalf of lives still being lived — Jed
might cite Warren's now familiar observation (in which we can
substitute "exploratory novels" for "poems") that "Poetry
wants to be pure, but poems do not.... They are not even as
pure as they might be in this imperfect world. They mar themselves with cacophonies, jagged rhythms, ugly words and ugly
thoughts, colloquialisms, cliches, sterile technical terms,
headwork and argument, self-contradictions, clevernesses,

irony, realism — all things which call us back to the world
of prose and imperfection."[18]

For that, in fact, is what Jed Tewksbury wants: to have a
place to come to and to get there. It is a need that was born
in him as soon as he left the South for the first time and arrived in Chicago, where, lying on a cot in the YMCA and staring at the ceiling, "I felt reality flooding away from me on
all sides, like a retreating tide.... I lay on my cot and felt
a light-headed nausea of blankness — of placelessness, timelessness, of ultimate loneliness. I remember saying out loud:
'This is my life'" (p.54). Tewksbury wishes to be called back
— perhaps by his own recounting of how he has lived — from the
self-indulgence of loveless and timeless passion and from the
"elementary" and self-denying lesson "that work will fill up
Time" (p.374). He wishes to be reconciled to Claxton County,
Alabama, and to the father whose ignominious and comic demise
gave him a focus for his hatred of his home and of himself,
and to be reconciled to his mother, whose efforts to push him
out of Dugton, "this here durn hellhole" (p.24), began with
breaking his nose. He wants to be able to revisit the past
with a sense of its relationship to the present and future.
His exploratory narrative is the essence of that return.

By the end of the book, the reconciliation has, of course,
begun. Jed has acknowledged the mother whose funeral he did
not attend by "being" the son of the anonymous Italian woman
killed in Chicago: "And all the while I kept saying, *sì, sì,
sì,* which as everybody knows, means simply yes, and saying
that I'd seek to always be a *figlio buono,* and *non la lasci-
arei più, mai, mai,* which means I would never go away, never"
(p.388). Jed has spoken warmly with Perk Simms, surrogate
father and humble substitute for the Buck Tewksbury he never
really knew. He has made a gesture of reconciliation, self-
conscious and tender, toward Dauphine Finkel Tewksbury: "It
is that I cannot stand solitude.... I ask for your company for
what blessedness it is.... In all hope, Your (whether you like
it or not) JED." He has imagined that someday he will return
to Dugton with his son, so "I could point out to him all the
spots that I had dreamed of pointing out to him" (p.401). And
Jed has discovered that there is a kind of wholeness, a consistent pattern to his life. Near the end, as much earlier, he
is "still exploring the world I had stumbled into, was even
trying to understand why I was in it at all" (p.80). It may
be, as he says, that "every man has to lead his own life and
has little chance of knowing what it means, anyway" (p.356);
it may be that, as Rozelle once suggested, "you never know
what you are until you stumble on it" (p.136). The exploration, even the stumbling, will continue, for (as he has already observed) "there is only one place to go. Back into the
world of nags and half-measures" (p.221), back into the world,
"the past, the future, all values, vengeances, costs and pangs
of conscience" (p.204). He has, of course (and ironically

enough), at last discovered what he once called "the really commanding subject that would give shape to my life" (p.141), "an idea charged with passion...the kind of idea that touches life at the root" (p.332).

Warren's poetry and fiction corroborate each other and the search in line after line through the articles of faith that confirm the vision — passion, imagination, knowledge, dream. For Warren, to search, to explore is to be; to be is to know, in the manner of Audubon in pursuit of the birds of America, that all possibility lies before. "We are only ourselves," Warren tells us, but that is everything.

> We never know what we have lost, or what we have found.
> We are only ourselves, and that promise.
> Continue to walk in the world. Yes, love it!

He continued to walk in the world.[19]

---

1. Robert Penn Warren, *Flood: A Romance of Our Time* (New York: Random House, 1964), p. 54. Further page references will be incorporated into the text.
2. For Warren, as for Conrad, "the relation of man to the human communion" is everything, and the crisis of his story comes "when the hero recognizes the terms on which he may be saved, the moment...of the 'terror of the awakening.'" Robert Penn Warren, "'The Great Mirage': Conrad and *Nostromo*," in *Selected Essays* (New York: Random House, 1958), pp. 40-41.
3. A helpful discussion of the meaning of the "mystic osmosis of being" in Warren's work is Victor Strandberg, "Warren's Osmosis," reprinted in this collection.
4. Cf. Warren's remarks elsewhere: "Ultimately home is not a place, it's a state of spirit, it's a state of feeling, a state of mind, a proper relationship to the world.... Your world view in one sense is your home." Richard B. Sale, "An Interview in New Haven with Robert Penn Warren," *Studies in the Novel*, 2 (1970), 326. The contrast between this ending and the ending of *All the King's Men* is instructive. Tolliver, like Jack Burden, goes out into "the awful responsibility of Time," but he is unlike Jack in not yet being ready to reestablish "communion" through marriage (he has already failed twice). In fact, Brad seems only to be "reborn" in the final pages of *Flood,* and in need of further workings-out of his relationship to past and future, whereas Jack was "reborn" upon learning of the death (and identity) of his father — and at that moment began working out a viable relationship to what had happened (to Willie, Sugar-Boy, Anne and Adam Stanton) and what might yet be. The ending of *Flood* is heavy with pathos and need, but (in Tolliver's case) undercut by a lack of clear direction for the future.
5. Robert Penn Warren, *Meet Me in the Green Glen* (New York: Random House, 1971), pp. 369-70. Further page references will be incorporated into the text. In the novel's epilogue we learn that in his last conscious perception before a death brought on by sleeping capsules, Guilfort finally accepts the vitality of dreams: "He knew that he must undo it, he must go back and walk in the world, for that would

be enough, that would be bliss, merely to be in a world where people,
each walking in his dream, looked at you from within the individual
glow, and smiled at you, perhaps waved" (p.371).

6. It is useful to recall Northrop Frye's economical definition,
a part of his essay "Rhetorical Criticism: Theory of Genres," in *Anatomy of Criticism: Four Essays* (Princeton, N.J.: Princeton University
Press, 1957), pp. 304-5: "The romancer does not attempt to create
'real people' so much as stylized figures which expand into psychological archetypes. It is in the romance that we find Jung's libido,
anima, and shadow reflected in the hero, heroine, and villain respectively. That is why the romance so often radiates a glow of subjective intensity that the novel lacks, and why a suggestion of allegory
is constantly creeping in around its fringes. Certain elements of
character are released in the romance which make it naturally a more
revolutionary form than the novel.... The romancer deals with individuality, with characters *in vacuo* idealized by revery, and, however
conservative he may be, something nihilistic and untamable is likely
to keep breaking out of his pages."

7. The community's killing of Angelo because of its condemnation
of his relationship with Cassie is, of course, reminiscent of the de-
nouement of *Light in August,* in which Joe Christmas is killed for his
relationship with Joanna Burden. Warren's treatment of both race and
sexuality here is, like Faulkner's, aggressive, perhaps even liberating. In *Heiress of All the Ages: Sex and Sentiment in the Genteel
Tradition* (Minneapolis: University of Minnesota Press, 1959), pp. 114-
22, William Wasserstrom offers a provocative discussion of Warren's
early fiction in terms of its handling of sexuality.

8. This aspect of Warren's novel illustrates nicely D. H. Lawrence's observation, in *Pornography and Obscenity* (1930), on the relationship between innocence and guilt in the context of human sexuality: "Why a man should be held guilty of his conscious intentions,
and innocent of his unconscious intentions, I don't know, since every
man is more made up of unconscious intentions than of conscious ones.
I am what I am, not merely what I think I am."

9. Warren reinforces the classical allusion through the fitful
relationship between Cassie and Cy Grinder, whose bowhunting opens
the novel and who is, in modest degree, the novel's god of archery,
Apollo.

10. "The poetic imagination appears in a regenerative and healing
capacity, but in the end the hero, who has, presumably, been healed,
appears in one of his guises as the *poète maudit*. So we learn that
the imagination does not only bless, for even as it blesses it lays
on a curse. Though the Mariner brings the word which is salvation,
he cannot quite save himself and taste the full joy of the fellowship
he advertises. Society looks askance at him." Robert Penn Warren,
"A Poem of Pure Imagination: An Experiment in Reading," in *Selected
Essays,* p. 257. For a discussion of the significance of the Mariner
figure in Warren's work, see James H. Justus, "The Mariner and Robert
Penn Warren," reprinted in this collection.

11. Hence the book's ability to be both intro- and extroverted.
The references to and quotations from Frye are from *Anatomy of Criticism,* pp. 307-12.

12. Robert Penn Warren, *A Place to Come To* (New York: Random
House, 1977), p. 9. Further page references will be incorporated into
the text.

13. Indeed, from time to time Tewksbury's narration has the cast
of Marlow's voice at the end of his quest for Kurtz: "Droll thing life

is — that mysterious arrangement of merciless logic for a futile purpose. The most you can hope from it is some knowledge of yourself —
that comes too late — a crop of unextinguishable regrets." Yet Warren
has never been quite as horrified as Conrad (or as dark as Faulkner),
and his work is characterized by the degree to which he has lightened
the darkness of the Conradian vision. Hence Warren's stubbornly
hopeful, even defiant epigraph from Hopkins: "No, I'll not, carrion
comfort, Despair, not feast on thee;/ Not untwist — slack they may be
— these last strands of man/ In me or, most weary, cry *I can no more.*
I can;/ Can something, hope, wish day come, not choose not to be."

14. Specifically, for example, James L. Kinneavy, *A Theory of
Discourse* (Englewood Cliffs, N.J.: Prentice-Hall, 1971), pp. 96-104,
141-46, 162-66, 186-91. Another theoretical rhetoric central to the
discussion of exploration is Richard E. Young, Alton L. Becker, and
Kenneth L. Pike, *Rhetoric: Discovery and Change* (New York: Harcourt,
Brace, 1970). Common to both theories of "exploration" are close attention to heuristics and the concepts of "invention" and "discovery."

15. Frye, *Anatomy of Criticism,* p. 310; Kinneavy, *Theory of Discourse,* pp. 162-63. In both quotations, the italics are mine.

16. One of Kinneavy's observations seems particularly relevant and
ironic here, in light of Tewksbury's profession: "Partially because of
our more visual than oral-aural culture since the advent of printing,
much modern research is carried on in isolation — even in the midst of
cities and academic communities. In such cases, a man's dialogue may
often be with himself. He must sometimes even furnish his own opposition." *Theory of Discourse,* pp. 187, 188.

17. Kinneavy: One of the stages of the "logic of discovery" is
"indeterminacy"; one of the characteristics of exploration — "frequently a necessary virtue" — is ambiguity. *Theory of Discourse,* pp.
103, 189.

18. Robert Penn Warren, "Pure and Impure Poetry," in *Selected Essays,* pp. 4-6. Warren adds (p.7) that "the poetry arises from a re-
calcitrant and contradictory context" and so must inevitably *involve*
that context. Readers attentive to Warren's often symbolic use of
names will observe that the names in *A Place to Come To* — Jediah
Tewksbury, Rozelle Hardcastle, Dauphine Finkel, even Agnes Andreson,
to name the most prominent — seem to have been chosen less for their
symbolism than for their "impurity," their lack of symmetry and conso-
nance and rhythm.

19. Robert Penn Warren, *Audubon: A Vision* (New York: Random House,
1969), p. 19.

WRPW

POETRY

WRPWRPWRPWRPWRPWRPWRPWRPWRPWRPWRPWRPWRPWRPWRPWRPWRPWRPWRPWRPWRPWRPWRPWRPWRPWRPWRPWRPWRPWRPWRPWRPWRPWRPWRPWRPWRPWRPW

Hyatt H. Waggoner

Irony and Orthodoxy:
Robert Penn Warren

Even Robert Penn Warren's early poetry is much less well described by Ransom's theories than Tate's "Ode" is.[1] It is often ironic, but not constantly so. It is full of paradoxes; indeed paradox is at the center of it, but it moves generally toward the resolution of paradox. It is dense with specific images of "the world's body," but it wants always to do more than "see" the world more sharply, it wants to understand it. It is never patrician in tone or manner, as Ransom's is. It is regional only in the sense that Warren, born in Kentucky, returns again and again to personal memories of childhood, as he does in the series of poems called "Kentucky Mountain Farm." It makes no defense of the culture of the South as against that of some other region. It is not bookish, or learned, or primarily "mythic." So far as it is "orthodox," its orthodoxy appears to be a way of feeling and remembering, not a theoretical position adopted for prudential reasons. Ransom's justification of orthodoxy, by contrast, seems wholly prudential.

"Love's Parable" offers a way into the early poems that removes a good deal of their often-remarked obscurity. As Howard Nemerov has pointed out, the lovers in the poem are man and God. It is Warren's "Fortunate Fall" poem; the "prince whose tongue, not understood,/ Yet frames a new felicity" is Christ come to cure our alienation from ourselves and each other. The Fall occurs over and over, in each life and each period, but though a dreamed-of original innocence can never be restored, "weakness has become our strength" and hope arises from the "sullen elements" of "self that cankers at the bone," "for there are testaments/ That men, by prayer, have mastered grace."

There is nothing ironical about this poem, not even about these concluding lines, which it would be impossible to imagine either Ransom or Tate writing. The poem is open to the point of being defenseless. Its metaphysical quality is not

merely a literary manner but an expression of a way of thinking. Such images as "the fungus eyes/ Of misery" that "spore
in the night" are interpreted in generalized statements: "ripe
injustice," exploitation of nature, and "hatred of the good
once known" are more abstract ways of pointing to the outward
evidences of the Fall. The "inward sore/ Of self" produces
evil and allows us to see only evil, in ourselves and in nature. Here, as so often later in his career, Warren is in
effect rewriting Hawthorne for our time. The closest literary
parallel, thematically, to "Love's Parable," is "Young Goodman
Brown."

Like Hawthorne, Warren translates the received Faith into
psychological terms. C. G. Jung and Reinhold Niebuhr supply
all the theoretical framework necessary for drawing out the
largest meanings of many of the novels and most of the poems
through *Brother to Dragons* in 1953. Over and over, Warren retells the archetypal story of "My Kinsman, Major Molineux," in
which Hawthorne has his young man confront the ambiguities of
sin and sorrow, protest his innocence, discover his complicity,
and finally, Hawthorne at least permits us to believe, find a
more mature basis for hope than could be found in the Adamic
illusion of innocence. Warren's people, like Hawthorne's
break out of the prison of self only when they discover what
Hawthorne called "the brotherhood of guilt." As Warren puts
it, when man sees himself as a "brother to dragons," he is
ready to start moving toward the "glory" it is his destiny to
seek.

"Original Sin: A Short Story," a later poem than "Love's
Parable," is both less interesting for what it reveals of Warren's chief continuing preoccupations and attitudes, and more
typical of the voice we expect to hear in Warren's mature work.
A realistic allegory enriched by personal comment and observation, it personifies Original Sin as a repeated nightmare that
"takes no part in your classic prudence or fondled axiom" but
poisons them nevertheless. Original Sin is a nightmare connected in memory with the wen grandfather used to finger on
his forehead as though he treasured the deformity, a nightmare
that has grown so familiar it is no longer really frightening:

It tries the lock; you hear, but simply drowse:
There is nothing remarkable in that sound at the door.

There is irony in this poem, but, as so often in Eliot,
it is directed by the speaker at himself. He is grateful that
the nightmare figure never comes in the daylight to shame him
before his friends. He thinks it has nothing to do with "public experience or private reformation." Though he would like
to be rid of it, his attempts to escape it by moving and leaving no address have been ineffectual. Hoping to escape the
past, in which the nightmare figure mysteriously originated,
he finds himself taking "a sly pleasure" in hearing of "the

deaths of friends," but the pleasure does not last, and the "sense of cleansing and hope" it brings is delusory. By the end of the poem the speaker has become Everyman, seeking to maintain his innocence by projecting his guilt, denying it as a part of his own identity.

The new voice we hear in this poem is colloquial, easy, assured, humorous and serious in rapid shifts, moving between the folksy and the metaphysical. It takes its cadences from the rhythms of folk poetry while it gets its themes from philosophers and theologians. It moves constantly away from the poetic and the literary, returning only to make a fresh start away. The opening line of each stanza sets the pattern to be departed from.

Nodding, its great head rattling like a gourd...

Except for the initial trochee, this is a regular iambic line with five feet; but the final line of the stanza has moved, as though forced by the urgency of the need to speak, much closer to prose rhythms —

It acts like the old hound that used to snuffle
                your door and moan.

This is a long way from the voice we heard in "Love's Parable":

Then miracle was corner-cheap;
And we, like ignorant quarriers,
Ransacked the careless earth to heap
For highways our most precious ores;
Or like the blockhead masons who
Burnt Rome's best grandeur for its lime,
And for their slattern hovels threw
Down monuments of nobler time.

Between the two poems, Warren has found his own voice. But the change is nothing like the radical reversal we note between Tate's earlier work and "The Buried Lake." It is a matter, rather, of gradual self-discovery, gradual definition of the self-image.

"The Ballad of Billie Potts" is the triumph of Warren's new voice and manner, and, as it seems to me, one of the finest long poems in our literature. The mythic overtones in its tale of another Fall enacted in another "land between the rivers" are only lightly suggested in the background, played down by the poet's introductory note ("When I was a child I heard this story from an old lady..."), and countered by the tone both of the narrative itself and of the inserted authorial meditations on the action. Since *The Waste Land* we have tended to think of mythic poetry as "bookish," but the very last thing "Billie Potts" suggests is the library.

Vachel Lindsay in his "Simon Legree," the first poem in

his Booker T. Washington Trilogy, had used the folk rhythm
Warren adopted for the narrative sections of "Billie Potts."
As Lindsay handles the form, it sounds like this:

> Legree he sported a brass-buttoned coat,
> A snake-skin necktie, a blood-red shirt.
> Legree he had a beard like a goat,
> And a thick hairy neck, and eyes like dirt.
> His puffed-out cheeks were fish-belly white,
> He had great long teeth, and an appetite.
> He ate raw meat most every meal,
> And rolled his eyes till the cat would squeal.
> . . . .
> *But he went down to the Devil.*

Unfortunately, with a lapse of taste and feeling not un-
typical of him, Lindsay directs that this be read "in your own
variety of negro dialect." That the language is Southern dialect, having nothing to do with race or color, Warren knew
when he described Big Billie in the same folk language and the
same folk rhythms:

> Big Billie Potts was big and stout
> In the land between the rivers.
> His shoulders were wide and his gut stuck out
> Like a croker of nubbins and his holler and shout
> Made the bob-cat shiver and the black-jack leaves shake
> In the section between the rivers.
> He would slap you on your back and laugh.
> . . . .
> They had a big boy with fuzz on his chin
> So tall he ducked the door when he came in,
> A clabber-headed bastard with snot in his nose
> And big red wrists hanging out of his clothes....

Warren's handling of the form is a little freer than Lindsay's, a little less "literary." He is closer to his subject,
writing without any suggestion of the condescending attitude
that comes out in Lindsay's unfortunate note on the dialect in
his poem. (But Lindsay's condescension appears only in the
note, not in the poem itself.) If one had never read any of
Warren's verse and knew of him only as the third member of the
Ransom-Tate-Warren trio, a Vanderbilt man, contributor to *I'll
Take My Stand* and co-author of the most influential New Critical textbook, *Understanding Poetry,* he might be surprised by
"Billie Potts," which has behind it the work of Lindsay, Mark
Twain, and J. R. Lowell. Of the poets with whom he is most
commonly linked, Warren is at once, and paradoxically, the
most "liberal" and pragmatic, in ideas and attitudes, and the
most "traditional" in a literary sense, after his earliest
volume, in choosing to work within traditions developed by earlier American writers, rather than, for instance, those of the
French Symbolists or the English metaphysicals.

Traditionalism in this sense is as true of Warren's prose fiction as it is of his verse. His historical romances and allegories have their closest counterpart in the work of Hawthorne, as "Billie Potts" continues the work of Lindsay. Tate's early description of his friend as a "romantic" was prophetic. Despite Warren's continued suspicion of idealists who try to make the world fit a pattern in their mind, despite his affinity with the ironic vision of neo-orthodox theologians, for whom man is "fallen," there has always been a part of his sensibility that drew him toward our own nineteenth-century writers and away from Ransom and Modernist practice.

"The Ballad of Billie Potts" consists of two distinct parts, the folk legend itself and an enclosed, separate commentary, by the "I," set off by parentheses. The speaker is not in any significant sense a *persona* but the poet himself, who interrupts his narration to speculate on its meaning. The narrative tells of the murder of Little Billie by his parents, who didn't know who it was they were killing. The past is vividly present in the narrative sections, as little distant from us as the poet's art can make it. In the parenthetical commentaries the past recedes into the background while the present takes its place in the foreground. Imaginative identification is broken as the tale is acknowledged as remote, legendary, literally an old woman's tale, containing motives and meanings we can only partially understand and partially imagine:

> (Leaning and slow, you see them move
> In massive passion colder than any love:
> Their lips move but you do not hear the words....)

Ransom and other New Critics have thought that the formal unity of the poem is damaged by these breaks in the narrative in which the poet enters his own poem to address the reader directly, but it seems to me that to wish the author's comments away is to wish for a completely different kind of poem. Though the poem is called a "ballad," only the narrative parts could really be so described. Warren's assumption in the poem is the opposite of Pound's in the *Cantos:* the "facts," he knows and says, do *not* speak clearly, univocally, "for themselves." His method acknowledges his assumption. The manner of the poem is closer to Whittier's in "Snowbound" or Emerson's in "The Titmouse" than it is to Pound's.

The poem's subject is man (Billie Potts, Warren, the reader) trying to discover his identity, and so to understand his destiny, by defining the nature of his guilt and his innocence. "Billie Potts" is an exercise in moral philosophy executed in a form alternately narrative and meditative or discursive. No literary model for such a form existed, so that a judgment that it lacks formal "unity" cannot be drawn from an idea of the "requirements of the form," as several critics dissatisfied with the poem have tried to do. Traditional literary

genres begin to be meaningless with the English Romantic movement and have been increasingly inapplicable ever since, even
in British literature. In American literature, they have been
almost totally irrelevant since Emerson. In "Billie Potts,"
Warren created a new form involving a double focus, alternately bringing history close by imaginative identification, in
the narrative parts, and holding it at a distance so that it
may be understood by the mind, in the discursive parts. Put
yourself in Billie's place, the form says ("Think of yourself
riding away from the dawn"); but also, don't forget that the
limits of the poem are the limits of the imagination ("There
was a beginning but you cannot see it").

Between the narrative parts, which involve the reader directly, with an immediate and unselfconscious identification,
and the discursive parts, which turn the reader back upon himself, asking him to ponder what he is reading, asking him *why*
he has been identifying himself with the characters in the
poem, and what *that* means — between the verses in parentheses
and those outside, there are, nevertheless, all kinds of link-
ages. A single example will have to do. In the following
passage, we begin with the "I" of the poem commenting on the
remoteness in time and cultural conditions of his own characters, and end with his return to his narrative. The contrast
in diction, style, and formal *genre* between the part before
the parenthesis and the lines that follow is striking, but at
the same time an identity is suggested:

> Beyond your call or question now, they move
> . . . .
> And breathe the immaculate climate where
> The lucent leaf is lifted, lank beard fingered, by no
>   breeze,
> Rapt in the fabulous complacency of fresco, vase, or
>   frieze:
>
> And the testicles of the fathers hang down like old lace.)
>
> Little Billie was full of piss and vinegar
> And full of sap as a maple tree...

In general, the discursive parts utilize all the resources
of poetry to create the *stasis* of art, the stasis of a frieze
or fresco in which whatever seems to move, moves only in the
imagination. The characters, we feel in the discursive sections, are at once dead and immortal, living on only in the
"immaculate climate" of art. One thinks of Faulkner's use
of this theme — art as achieving its formal clarity only by
"lying" — in the opening story of *The Unvanquished,* and of
Aiken's repeated speculations on the theme in his early verse.
The shock of the lines about Little Billie that immediately
follow the parenthesis in the passage quoted above is functional. In the parenthetical lines omitted from the quotation,
the subject is defined as the relations of the generations,

and particularly of fathers and sons, each "betraying" the
other. The line about the testicles of the fathers gives us
the quintessence of the conflict in a single image. Now, after the parenthetical meditation, we return to the story that
has motivated the meditation, with the observation that lusty
young Billie, about to come into conflict with his father, is
"full of piss and vinegar" and "full of sap," folk ways of suggesting the connection of exuberant self-confidence and vitality with genital vigor. The folk expressions are at once less
vivid and, in context, more expressive than the last line within the parenthesis. Now that we have been prepared, we realize the poetry implicit in folk speech.

"The Ballad of Billie Potts" makes really clear for the
first time Warren's role as a bridging figure between the Fugitives and the more persistent and rooted romantic and transcendental tradition of Emerson, Whitman, Lindsay, Hart Crane, and
Cummings. Though the story he tells in the poem reminds us of
the archetype of the Fall, the "Original Sin" constantly re-
enacted by the generations, and so of the "orthodoxy" of Ransom and Tate, and before that of Eliot, the poem ends in hope,
not in resignation. It is not our guilt that needs definition.
For Warren, as for Hawthorne before him, *that* is obvious
enough, needing only to be admitted, not defined, not necessarily even "understood." It is our "innocence" that needs —
in this century at least, Warren thinks — "new definition":

> For the beginning is death and the end may be life,
> For the beginning was definition and the end may be
>   definition,
> And our innocence needs, perhaps, new definition,
> And the wick needs the flame
> But the flame needs the wick,
> And the father waits for the son.

Brother to Dragons is a reworking and expansion of "Billie
Potts" in both theme and form. Formally, the chief difference
is that Warren's comments no longer make up a separate poem
within the poem. Instead, he himself, in his own person as
"R.P.W.," has now become one of the characters in his own tale.
His commitment to his characters and to his art are now not
two things but one. In effect, the form of the poem says, art
is a process of self-discovery and self-realization, in which
man and artist cannot ultimately be separated. (As Cummings
said, "An artist I feel is a man." As Berryman said, referring to Eliot and others, poetry aims "at the reformation of
the poet." As Emerson said, poetry affords the poet, and his
readers, a "purchase" by which we may move life into a larger
circle.) The form of *Brother to Dragons* implies the artist's
double responsibility, to his art, and to himself as a person.
Insofar as it points toward the art as something "made" (the
tale is taken from history, but it can come alive for us only
through the poet's art), the form acknowledges the partial

truth of Modernist theory and practice. But insofar as
"R.P.W." takes personal responsibility as a man for what he
has made, and what he has "discovered," or "seen," in the
course of, and through, the making, the form of the poem re-
discovers our great tradition by going back to Emerson's idea
of the poet as *man naming,* just as the scholar is "man thinking."

Once again, as in "Billie Potts" and in most of the novels,
the central action of the poem is violent and terrible. Warren retells the story, which actually occurred, of how Jefferson's nephew, living in the "unspoiled" West among what ought
to have been, from the Adamic point of view, the purifying and
spiritually exalting influences of Nature, brutally murdered a
slave for a trivial offense. Warren departs from history only
to imagine motives, and to imagine the effect this event must
have had on Jefferson's thinking. (Actually, there is no mention of the event in Jefferson's papers, though he could not
have failed to be aware of the widely publicized infamy of his
sister's son. Could he not bring himself to face it?)

Again, as in "Billie Potts," the real concern, despite the
horror of the event itself, is not with "illustrating" man's
"guilt." Warren simply takes it for granted that we are all
guilty, and involved in each other's guilt, whether we choose
to think about it in psychological or in theological terms.
What the poem tries to discover, as "R.P.W." tells us toward
the end of his effort, is "an adequate definition" of the
"glory" involved in "the human effort." How can we recover a
sense of the self as transcendent? Is man, really and finally,
only a "brother to dragons," a physicochemical machine plagued
by a curiously unnecessary "inner monologue," or is he, potentially at least, "made in the image of God," and a son of God?
After Dickinson's doubts, Frost's diminutions, and Stevens' denials, must we, if we are to be honest, admit that the idea of
"the transcendent self" has been lost forever?

The title of the poem acknowledges the assumptions from
which such thinking as this starts and points in the direction
it will take. In the Book of Job, 30:29, Job says, "I am a
brother to dragons, and a companion to owls." The context
shows that this is not a humble admission but a bitter complaint: I am being *treated,* by God, as though I were such as
these, whereas in fact I am a just man deserving a better fate,
deserving particularly an answer to my questions. Everyone,
Job has said earlier in the chapter, holds me in derision, and
the Lord himself seems to be treating me as though I were nothing but dust and ashes. Who is guilty in my case, Job in effect is asking as he passionately asserts his innocence, who
but God himself?

Warren's poem starts by assuming that there is a real, and
not just apparent "problem of evil," as well as a "problem of
guilt." The "problem of evil" is the philosophers' and the
theologians' term for what is also called "the problem of

pain," which means the problem of unmerited suffering. Suffering that seems to be built into the nature of things becomes a "problem" when we think of nature as teleological. Melville had concentrated, at least insofar as he took Ahab's side, on the "problem of evil" in *Moby-Dick*. Hawthorne normally preferred simply to leave this problem a mystery and concentrate on the "problem of guilt," which is a metaphysical problem in the same sense that the problem of evil is *only* if we assume that man is "naturally good," or "unfallen."

As to the problem of guilt, the poem answers with Warren's idea of "complicity." We have all wished more evil than we have been able to do, as Hawthorne said long ago in "Fancy's Show-Box." Lilburne, the murderer, was peculiarly unfortunate chiefly in having the power and the opportunity to act out his wish. Still, it is also true that we have wished more good than we could accomplish, as well as more evil. We must believe in our responsibility, despite the cogency by which deterministic lines of thought may explain away Lilburne's guilt and our own.

As to the "problem of evil," again Warren bridges the gap between Emerson and Melville, or Cummings and Eliot. God never explained to Job. He merely overwhelmed him with his power and glory. Reason provides no clear or certain answer to this problem, which, as Gabriel Marcel has insisted, is not properly called a "problem" at all but a "mystery." Nevertheless, to say that the question of why there is unmerited suffering is "meaningless," as Sidney Hook has recently said it is to ask "What is the meaning of life?" is to stultify the human effort before it begins.

The "moral order" and the "natural order" are not the same order, Warren's poem says:

No, what great moral order we may posit
For old Kentucky, or the world at large,
Will scarcely account for geodetic shifts.
There was an earthquake, sure. But it just came.

In the moral order, self-transcendence depends first upon the recognition and acceptance of personal guilt, and then on moving toward the ideal. As Jefferson says, after he has first been forced by the crime to lose his faith in natural goodness and fall into despair, and then to think and feel his way back toward hope:

                    To find? Oh, no!
To think to find it as a given condition of man
Would be but to repeat, I now see,
My old error. I have suffered enough for that.
Oh, no, if there is to be reason, we must
Create the possibility
Of reason, and we can create it only
From the circumstances of our most evil despair.

We must strike the steel of wrath on the stone of guilt,
And hope to provoke, thus, in the midst of our coiling
    darkness
The incandescence of the heart's great flare.
And in that illumination I should hope to see
How all creation validates itself,
For whatever you create, you create yourself by it,
And in creating yourself you will create
The whole wide world and gleaming West anew.

Or as "R.P.W." puts essentially the same conclusion in
more general and inclusive terms,

We have yearned in the heart for some identification
With the glory of the human effort, and have yearned
For an adequate definition of that glory.
To make that definition would be, in itself,
Of the nature of glory. This is not paradox.
It is not paradox, but the best hope.

It is the best hope, because we have,
Each, experienced what it is to be men.
We have lain on the bed and devised evil in the heart.
. . . .
But we must argue the necessity of virtue:

In so far as man has the simplest vanity of self,
There is no escape from the movement toward fulfillment.
And since all kind but fulfills its own kind,
Fulfillment is only in the degree of recognition
Of the common lot of our kind. And that is the death of
    vanity,
And that is the beginning of virtue.

The recognition of complicity is the beginning of
    innocence.
The recognition of necessity is the beginning of freedom.
The recognition of direction of fulfillment is the death
    of the self,
And the death of the self is the beginning of selfhood.
All else is surrogate of hope and destitution of spirit.

Brother to Dragons is a philosophic poem cast in the form
of dramatic narrative. The first question to ask about a
philosophic poem is, what does it mean? This is the enabling
question. The poem seems not to have been widely understood,
judging from most of the comment it has elicited. But whatever its success as a poem may ultimately seem to be, it is
certainly a central *document* in American poetry. It represents, I strongly suspect, a conscious effort at accommodation
and synthesis of the several strands of American literary tradition.
    At any rate, whether Warren consciously aimed at such an
effect or not, his poem achieves it. Whether we use the his-

torian's labels, the "Jeffersonian" and the "Hamiltonian," or
the philosopher's "idealist" and "realist," or such reminders
of a divided past as the "light" and the "dark" traditions, or
"the party of hope" and "the party of memory," or the "liberal"
and the "conservative" — however we name the chief traditions
in our culture, they all are remembered and reconsidered, and
drawn upon for whatever insight they embodied that still seems
valid, in this poem. The only "tradition" positively dis-
missed as without value is the recent one of deterministic
naturalism.

Brother to Dragons aspires to greatness and almost reaches
it. It seems to me that its only significant flaw lies in its
partial failure to take us fully enough, and sympathetically
enough, into the mind of Lilburne. We are asked to recognize
our complicity with him by virtue of a shared nature; but our
temptation, recognized in the poem and philosophically, but
not, with complete success, I think, *aesthetically* countered,
is to dismiss Lilburne as mad, or a mere victim, or else a
fiend. Insofar as we either deny him any responsibility, or
think of him as pure satanic intention, we are denying him his
humanity, denying that he is "like us." Warren says we must
not do this, and we feel the wisdom of his advice, but we may
still guard our secret reservation: but *I* wouldn't have done
that, we say. Perhaps Warren would have done better to have
followed Coleridge's example in "Rime of the Ancient Mariner"
and invented a less terrible crime, instead of using the historical one that seems to cast its perpetrator in the role of
maniac. History is often hard to imagine and even harder to
believe.

The three volumes Warren has so far published since *Brother to Dragons* continue his steady progress toward the romantic,
the direct, the personal, and the visionary in poetry. They
have been widely condemned by reviewers for carelessness in
technique, for addressing the reader directly with an appeal
for intuitive understanding, and for implying that their author believes a poem is something *said* rather than something
made — for their "romanticism," in short.

That some real tendency in Warren's poetry is being pointed to in all these complaints is clear, whether the tendency
should be cause for complaint or not. The first poem in *You,
Emperors, and Others,* for instance, is titled "Clearly About
You," and begins this way,

> Whoever you are, this poem is clearly about you,
> For there's nothing else in the world it could be about.
> Whatever it says, this poem is clearly true,
> For truth is all we are born to, and the truth's out.

If this, the first of a series of eight poems under the
general heading of "A Garland for You" — that is, for every
reader — seems to violate the proprieties of "Impersonal"
poetry as we have been taught them, the last poem of a later

series called "Some Quiet, Plain Poems" does so even more violently in its undisguised offering of the *personal. What,* no
persona? the critic asks, when he reads,

> Long since that time I have walked night streets, heel-
> iron
> Clicking the stone, and in dark in windows have stared.
> Question, quarry, dream — I have vented my ire on
> My own heart that, ignorant and untoward,
> Yearns for an absolute that Time would, I thought, have
> prepared,
>
> But has not yet. Well, let us debate
> The issue. But under a tight roof, clutching a toy,
> My son now sleeps, and when the hour grows late,
> I shall go forth where the cold constellations deploy
> And lift up my eyes to consider more strictly the
> appalling logic of joy.

Or looking for the "wit," "irony," and "paradox," and
finding none in the poems gathered as "Short Thoughts on Long
Nights," the reviewer whose only criteria are Modernist and
New Critical wonders what to say about "Nightmare of Mouse":

> It was there, but I said it couldn't be true in daylight.
> It was there, but I said it was only a trick of starlight.
> It was there, but I said to believe it would take a fool,
> And I wasn't, so didn't — till teeth crunched on my skull.

Or about the poem that follows, "Nightmare of Man":

> I assembled, marshaled, my data, deployed them expertly.
> My induction was perfect, as far as induction may be.
> But the formula failed in the test tube, despite all my
> skill,
> For I'd thought of the death of my mother, and wept; and
> weep still.

The reviewer might of course say that they "move" him, but
that would be "impressionistic." What would *Understanding
Poetry,* in the stern purity of its first edition, have said
about these poems? It would be an amusing and profitable exercise to write out a destructive analysis of "Nightmare of
Mouse" and "Nightmare of Man," complete with unexplained references to the damaging effect on the poems of their lack of
irony and to the embarrassing directness of their statements,
in the manner of the Brooks and Warren textbook that pioneered
in bringing New Critical doctrine to the teachers of literature.

When Warren's later poems *are* ironic or ambiguous, the
irony or the ambiguity seems not to be a matter of style, a
device invented in the making of the poem, to make it "work"
better, but a concession style makes to the nature of nature.
Thus the negative statements in "The Necessity for Belief,"

the last poem in *Promises,* suggest their opposites, as though
they were merely "willed"; and the third and last lines are so
nicely balanced on the razor edge of ambiguity that we hardly
know whether to read "scarcely" as "just barely" or as "not
quite." But these ambiguities have been thoroughly prepared
for in the earlier poems in the book, and now they seem not so
much a manner of style as a recognition of fact. "Belief" is
unquestionably necessary, the poem says, and yet, in our time,
hardly possible, or, perhaps, not quite impossible:

> The sun is red, and the sky does not scream.
> The sun is red, and the sky does not scream.
>
> There is much that is scarcely to be believed.
>
> The moon is in the sky, and there is no weeping.
> The moon is in the sky, and there is no weeping.
>
> Much is told that is scarcely to be believed.

However we take this, the poems in Warren's recent volumes
are the work of a man on the move, a seeker, of a seeker in
personal memory, in personal experience, in the sight of his
children sleeping, or in the images of nature, for clues to
an adequate definition of the glory that potentially is man's.
At times his search seems to be taking him, despite his respect for pragmatic ways of thinking, back to something like
the conviction of Edward Taylor, who might have written one of
the lines in "Go It, Granny — Go It, Hog!" — which is part of
one of Warren's finest late poems, "Ballad of a Sweet Dream of
Peace." The hogs, the devourers, *time* made incarnate in *flesh,*
are eating Granny, or the ghost of Granny, again, or still, or
always, in the middle of Central Park. The realistic or skeptical mind rejects the possibility:

> *Any hogs that I slopped are long years dead,*
> *And eaten by somebody and evacuated,*
> *So it's simply absurd, what you said.*

But the believing mind, which is also the imaginative and
dreaming mind, replies, and this is the line that Taylor might
almost, with some stylistic and some theological changes, have
written:

> You fool, poor fool, all Time is a dream, and we're
>   all one Flesh, at last....

Of course Taylor would have wanted to exclude Unbelievers
from the "we," and he would have used "one Flesh" as a conceit
for the Body of Christ in Heaven, or the Church Triumphant.
But he and Warren would understand each other if they stood in
colloquy.

The new poems in Warren's 1966 volume, *New and Selected
Poems,* provide the most striking evidence that this poet ought
to be thought of in terms of the metaphor for the poet favored

by Emerson, Whitman, and Gabriel Marcel, man on the road, *Homo Viator*. "Homage to Emerson: On Night Flight to New York," in this volume, shows us a poet who has long understood Taylor now seeking to understand Emerson also. Emerson's essays lie open on the lap of the speaker in the poems as he flies eastward in the pressurized cabin at 38,000 feet. How can he square the hope they speak of with his present experience?

Warren's most recent poems ask us whether it is possible, honestly, for us to reverse the trend toward rationalistic alienation that has been dominant for the past century among our poets, who are, for Warren, as for Emerson, our *seers,* our *diviners*. In "Emerson's Smile," and in the Emerson series as a whole, the poet asks whether there is any real *reason* to smile. If there is, can *we* find Emerson's secret?

Of R. P. Warren it ought to be said, as Robert Frost once said of himself, that the career of this one-time "Fugitive" suggests "not a flight but a seeking."

---

1. John Crowe Ransom's literary theories, as expressed in *God Without Thunder* (1930) and *The World's Body* (1938), are discussed in an earlier section of Waggoner's study, as is Allen Tate's "Ode to the Confederate Dead." — Ed.

John Crowe Ransom

The Inklings of "Original Sin"

Of more than seasonal magnitude is the literary event
which gives to the public the whole staple of Robert Penn Warren's poetry. For ten years my head has rung with magnificent
phrases out of the five poems which he contributed to a Special Poetic Supplement in *The American Review* of March, 1934.
I felt they must have made a great commotion (as I knew they
had not) and established him at once as a ranking poet; they
were so distinctive, those poems of twenty lines each, with
their peculiar strain of horror, and their clean-cut eloquence
and technical accomplishments. But evidently the rating of
the poet waits upon the trial of his big book. The five poems
are in the present book, and serve very well as its center,
though some later ones may define a little better the special
object of this poet's tragic sense.

For a text I will try the easiest of the five, "Aubade for
Hope." The speaker (or hero: sometimes he is in the third person) appears to be an adapted and adult man waking, in the company of his bride it would seem in the Kentucky farmhouse on a
winter morning:

Dawn: and foot on the cold stair treading or
Thump of wood on the unswept hearthstone is
Comment on the margin of consciousness,
A dirty thumb-smear by the printed page.

Thumb-smear: nay, other, for the blessed light
Acclaimed thus, as a ducal progress by
The scared cur, wakes them that wallowed in
The unaimed faceless appetite of dream.

All night, the ice sought out the rotten bough:
In sleep they heard. And now they stir, as east
Beyond the formal gleam of landscape sun
Has struck the senatorial hooded hill.

A review of *Selected Poems: 1923-1943* — Ed.

Light: the groaning stair; the match aflame;
The Negro woman's hand, horned gray with cold,
That lit the wood — oh, merciless great eyes
Blank as the sea — I name some things that shall

As voices speaking from a further room,
Muffled, bespeak us yet for time and hope:
For hope that like a blockhead grandam ever
Above the ash and spittle croaks and leans.

The waking is out of a dream in which the speaker was faced
with some nameless evil, and he is glad to be woken; and the
dawn to which he wakes is a symbol of hope though sadly short
of brilliant in its accessories and triumphant. The waking
or rational world does not altogether displace the dark world
of the unconscious. The "merciless great eyes" that are addressed in parentheses bring a difficulty of identification;
they are new in the present version, having displaced some
less telling original item. But in the light of other poems
I should hazard that they belong to an ancestor, or a ghostly
mentor, and survive from the dream as a counterpoise to hope,
and attend their victim much as the Furies would attend the
Greek hero under a curse. We feel they will not be propiti-
ated though the citizen start punctually on his round of moral
daylight activities.

But what is his curse? "Aubade for Hope" is of the very
type of the Warren poems, whose situations are always fundamentally the same. It is true that the poet is fertile, and I
find quite a few titles to suggest his range of variation upon
the one tragic theme; as, "Terror," "Pursuit," "Crime," "Letter from a Coward to a Hero," "History," "End of Season," "Ransom," "Aged Man Surveys Past Time," "Toward Rationality," "To
a Friend Parting," "Eidolon," "Revelation," "Variation: Ode
to Fear," "Monologue at Midnight," "Picnic Remembered," "Man
Coming of Age," and the Marvellian "The Garden." It is the
quality of a noble poetry that it can fixate powerful living
images of the human crisis, and be received of us with every
sense of the familiar, yet evade us badly if we would define
its issue; and that is why poetry, intuitive in its form like
religion, involves us in endless disputation when we try to
philosophize it. I proceed with peril, but I rely on a conviction that Warren's version of horror is not only consistent,
but more elemental and purer than that of other poets. For
there was Poe, for example, with whom it was almost vulgarly
"literary" and supernatural; and Baudelaire, for whom it recorded his implication with the monstrous and obscene, and his
detestation and disgust. The terror they felt was perhaps
chiefly for crazy breaches of the common moral code, but ours
here is stranger and yet far more universal than that.

The recent poem, "Original Sin: A Short Story," furnishes
us with a philosophical term, or at least a theological one,

which we should use provided we remember that the poet has
not put all his secrets into one word.

> Nodding, its great head rattling like a gourd,
> And locks like seawood strung on the stinking stone,
> The nightmare stumbles past, and you have heard
> It fumble your door before it whimpers and is gone:
> It acts like the old hound that used to snuffle your door
>   and moan.

> You thought you had lost it when you left Omaha,
> For it seemed connected then with your grandpa, who
> Had a wen on his forehead and sat on the verandah
> To finger the precious protuberance, as was his habit
>   to do,
> Which glinted in sun like rough garnet or the rich old
>   brain bulging through.

But this nightmare, the vague, inept, and not very presentable
ancestral ghost, is not to be exorcised. It appears even in
Harvard Yard, for the victim's handsome secular progress has
led him so far, where the ghost is ill at ease indeed. But
you must not think the illusion of the ghost is the form of
the speaker's simple nostalgia, for that is painful, too, but
goes away:

> You were almost kindly then in your first homesickness,
> As it tortured its stiff face to speak, but scarcely mewed;
> Since then you have outlived all your homesickness,
> But have met it in many another distempered latitude:
> Oh, nothing is lost, ever lost! at last you understood.

This ghost will not be laid. Yet it is an ineffectual ghost,
unlike that portentous apparition of Hamlet the Elder, which
knew so much about "theatre," including how to time and how to
make an entrance: our ghost does not interfere with the actions of the living.

> But it never came in the quantum glare of sun
> To shame you before your friends, and had nothing to do
> With your public experience or private reformation:
> But it thought no bed too narrow — it stood with lips
>   askew
> And shook its great head sadly like the abstract Jew.

> Never met you in the lyric arsenical meadows
> When children call and your heart goes stone in the bosom:
> At the orchard anguish never, nor ovoid horror,
> Which is furred like a peach or avid like the delicious
>   plum.
> It takes no part in your classic prudence or fondled axiom.

> We must return to the title, and take its consequences:
Original Sin. And here it may be of some moment that we our-

selves have had dire personal inklings of Original Sin, hus-
tled and busybody creatures as we are yet perhaps painfully
sensible of our treachery to some earlier and more innocent
plan of existence; or, on the other hand, that we know it by
theology and literature. The poets and priests who dramatize
it in Adam's Fall seem to have known it precisely in the same
sense with Warren's protagonist; and historically it has
proved too formidable an incubus to rate as an idle "metaphysical" entity, for it can infect the whole series of our human
successes with shame and guilt. Briefly, Original Sin is the
betrayal of our original nature that we commit in the interest
of our rational evolution and progress. Anthropologists may
well imagine — if they are imaginative — that the guilt-feel-
ing of Original Sin, though it opposes no specific adaptation
or "conditioning" of the pliant human spirit, might yet have
some business on the premises as an unassimilated core of resistance and therefore stability; so precarious would seem the
unique biological experiment of equipping an animal species
with reason instead of the law of its own nature. Original
Sin obtains a sort of poetic justification when we consider
the peculiar horror to which the strict regimen of medieval
monks exposed them; acedia; the paralysis of will. Or, for
that matter, the horror which has most shaken the moderns in
their accelerating progress: the sense of psychic disintegration, that is, of having a personality which has been casually
acquired, and is still subject to alteration, therefore hollow
and insincere.

By the present account Original Sin seems to be nearly
related to the Origin of Species — of that species at least
which is most self-determining of its behavior. It may be
tempting to assume, and dogmatic theology at its nadir of un-
realism is apt to assume, that the blame falls only on Adam,
and we are answerable only in some formalistic sense to Adam's
ghost. But here we should take into account the phenomenon of
"recapitulation"; for it is understood that individually we re-
enact the evolution of species. We do it physiologically, but
there is a conscious side to it too. We have a nature, and
proceed to "condition" it; and more and more, from age to age,
are subjected to the rule of reason, first the public reason
which "educates" us, and then, when we have lost our native
spirits, our own reason which draws corollaries to the public
reason. If we may venture now upon a critical impertinence,
and commit the biographical fallacy, we will refer the nightmare of our poet's verse to the admirable public datum of his
life, to see what edification it will bring. As follows. The
South Kentucky country of his nativity is distinctive among
landscapes, and the sense of it is intimate and constitutive
in the consciousness of its inhabitants; and his breed, the
population of that country, acknowledges more firmly than another the two bonds of blood and native scene, which individu-
ate it. If then the ancestral ghost really haunts the mature

poet, as the poetry professes, it might be said to have this
excuse, that the circumstance of his origin is without visible
consequence upon his social adaptiveness, which is supple and
charming, or upon his capacity for such scholarship and industry as his professional occasions may demand, which is exem-
plary. The poetic torment of his sensibility is private, and
yet here it is, published. But we need not think it something
very special. The effect is universal as philosophers use
that term: it is the way a fine native sensibility works, in
those who have the sensibility and keep it.

Besides the poetry, Warren has a well-known body of fiction, including an important recent novel; the aforesaid
nightmare of Original Sin showing in the fiction too. But the
poetry, I think, is superior to the fiction, for a curious reason. Warren has fallen in increasingly with the vogue of the
"naturalistic" novel; and this means that he likes to take low
life, or at any rate life with a mediocre grade of vitality,
for his material. His characters are mean, and inarticulate
too, though their futilities and defeats furnish him faithfully with documents of the fateful Original Sin. But they do
not know what tune they are playing, and the novelist has the
embarrassment of having to speak for them. In the recent novel, *At Heaven's Gate,* he has to contrive a quaint though mar-
velously realized rural saint, to furnish a significant commentary; and it is not very organically connected with the action
of the plot.

I mention this because Wareen begins to import the naturalistic method into his verse; as in the Kentucky ballad of "Billie Potts," the most substantial poem in the present volume.
With great skill he expands the primitive ballad form (in this
case the loose and vernacular American form) without quite
breaking it down, though he goes much farther than Coleridge
did in his "Ancient Mariner." The story is of how Young Billie
left Old Billie (and his old mother, too) behind in Kentucky,
and went West to make his fortune on his own power (and his
own reason) with scarcely a backward look. The Pottses, incidentally, are most unsympathetic characters; they are a nest
of Kentucky rattlesnakes. But after ten years' success Young
Billie has a sort of "conversion," and returns to the ancestral rooftree; where his parents promptly kill him; for one
cannot return. It is true that they do not recognize him, but
the accident is at least the symbol of the intention. To interpret all this in terms of his thesis Warren uses long parentheses, filled with his own matter and language, and that is
a gloss far more implausible than that which Coleridge wrote
upon his margins.

I suggest that this is not the best strategy of composition. And I would add something else, which for me is of par-
amount importance: I wish we had a way of holding this poet,
whose verse is so beautiful when it is at his own height of
expression, to a level no lower than this height.

Robert Penn Warren

The Way *Brother to Dragons*
Was Written

You ask me to say something about the composition of
"Brother to Dragons." I don't have much in the way of great
generalization about long poems. For one thing, I reckon I
am still too close to the particular problems encountered in
trying to write this particular long poem. But I may mention
some of those.

About ten years ago, I got the notion of doing something
with the story of Thomas Jefferson's family in Kentucky. The
story is a shocker.

At first, I wasn't sure what caught my fancy. Then I knew:
It was that this was Jefferson's family. The philosopher of
our liberties and the architect of our country and the prophet
of human perfectibility had this in the family blood. Bit by
bit, the thing began to take thematic shape. But the form
didn't get settled.

First I thought of a novel. But this wouldn't do — the
historical material doesn't have the structure of a novel, it
doesn't fulfill itself circumstantially, it spreads out and
doesn't pull in at the end. A novel, too, couldn't bear the
burden of comment probably necessary to interpret the material.

Next I started a collaboration for a play in which Jefferson would serve as a commentator, a chorus, brooding over the
affair. But again, the plot problem appeared. And also we
discovered that the role of Jefferson would be disproportionate for a play. So we abandoned that.

Then, at last, I struck on the notion of using the form
of a dramatic dialogue — not a play but a dialogue of all the
characters, including Jefferson, at some unspecified place and
time — really "no place" and "no time." This would allow me,
I hoped, to get out of the box of mere chronology, and of incidental circumstantiality. In this form I might be able to

Warren here responds to the request of the *New York Times Book
Review* — Ed.

keep alive the issues among the various participants — all the
actors of the old horror — and keep a dramatic relation between them and Jefferson. But I wanted to give the thing a
wider perspective than even Jefferson, or the ghost of Jefferson, would provide. I wanted a sense of the modern man's relation to the business. So I slipped in another character — the
"poet" — R.P.W., as a kind of interlocutor. But more and more
Jefferson became the real protagonist, the person who had to
come to terms with something.

I needed provocation for Jefferson's redemption from mere
shock and mere repudiation of his old dream. So I developed
Lucy, his sister, and I introduced Meriwether Lewis, who had
stood, in fact, in a sort of filial relation to Jefferson, and
was the cousin of the tragic Lilburn and Isham. I shan't explain this further now, except to say that Meriwether's story
of the opening of the West to the Pacific, and of his death by
suicide (if it was suicide) form a parallel, and a contrast to
the story of his cousins, Lilburn and Isham — who also went
"West." In other words, these are all among our "Founding
Fathers."

One problem that I found more and more fascinating, and
more distressing, as composition proceeded, was that of keeping episode as sharp as possible in a symbolic as well as a
narrative sense. In all fiction, of course, even the most
realistic fiction, there is such a problem — though "symbolic"
is probably not a good word here. But in a poem, I'm sure,
the problem gets more acute, as you can't depend on mere narrative interest and logic, and must pare away the merely circumstantial interest — but keep enough for conviction.

Another problem in this particular poem was that of language, or languages, suitable for the various characters.
This couldn't be literally done, of course. A matter of slant
and flavor. And I'm still too close to the thing to know how
this came out. Last, there was the big problem, enclosing all
other problems — that of keeping interest and readability at
the level of action and debate and at the same time keeping
that inwardness that is the central fact of poetry.

Frederick P. W. McDowell

Psychology and Theme in *Brother to Dragons*

    Warren's novel in verse, *Brother to Dragons,* is most notable in its philosophy and psychology and summarizes vividly his continuing metaphysical and ethical themes. Aware in his moralist's zeal "that poetry is more than fantasy and is committed to the obligation of trying to say something about the human condition," Warren is in this work more than ever haunted by an anguished sense of the disparity in man between recurrent beatific vision and the ubiquitous evil which blights it. Accounting for the force of the book are Warren's realization of character, his flair for the arresting image and apt phrase, his evocation of situation and atmosphere, and his instinct for the telling structural contrast. Indispensable as are these aspects of literary talent to the precise rendition of value through form, they are all subordinate to Warren's tense brooding over human motivation and human destiny.
    Despite his cavils against oversimplified abstract thinking in his critique of "The Ancient Mariner" and elsewhere, abstract speculation has come to absorb Warren. He has, however, eschewed the dangers he warns against — the abstract, the general, the universal is always related forcibly, even violently, to the concrete, the particular, the local. Warren achieves a sensible, sometimes drily pragmatic balance, then, between the relative and the absolute, the mutable and the permanent, the fact and the archetype. In *Brother to Dragons,* the combined reflections of the several interested persons, including the author as R.P.W., yield a valid disinterested truth, since its roots are in their immediate experience. The localizing of his narratives in history achieves a similar purpose. Viewing dispassionately the dilemmas of individuals in history, Warren has a specific perspective upon which to focus his ranging intelligence. To reach exact definitions of elusive moral and metaphysical values, to reach befitting conclusions as to the provenance of good and evil, Warren also utilizes in *Brother*

to Dragons an incident from out of the past, one drawn from
the annals of the Jefferson family.

The central figure in this episode is Jefferson's nephew,
Lilburn Lewis, who, after his mother's death, butchers his
Negro valet, George, when the latter breaks a pitcher once be-
longing to the mother. Since a maniacal self-love and a maniacal Oedipus complex consume him, Lilburn must at all costs
secure vengeance for an imputed spiteful violation of his mother's memory by George and the other household Negroes. The
senselessness of Lilburn's crime and the sinister forces it
epitomizes all but overwhelm the hapless idealist, Thomas Jefferson, who had not, in his aspiration, fully considered the
evil in all men. With his eventual if somewhat reluctant attainment of a more valid knowledge — presupposing right reason,
infused by the spirit, or else creative imagination, informed
by the sense of fact — he is then able to effect a fruitful
reconciliation between aspiration and reality, between the
disparities, in general, of his experience. As a result, he
achieves wholeness of spirit.

Warren is even more insistent in *Brother to Dragons* than
in his other work upon the transforming influence of the true
spiritual principle and the nefarious influence of perverted
spirituality. Both Lilburn and the early Jefferson illustrate
a familiar pattern in Warren's work: the individual's search
for spiritual peace by side-stepping his inner difficulties
and by subservience to an abstract ideal only indirectly related to them. Unable to find peace within, through his lack
of internal resources and through his too easy disregard of
the truths to be found in religious tradition, such an individual searches for it too aggressively outside the self — in the
empirically derived configurations of his experience or in
nature. From these sources, he seeks some kind of absolute
which can always command allegiance, but an absolute personally defined and designed to further his own interested motives,
whether he will admit to this tacit hypocrisy or not. Such
anodyne for inner insecurity is only temporary since too much
is expected from it. Unless conversion to a different mode of
being has finally occurred, disillusionment and violence rather than meaningful insights into reality result from a quest
thus histrionically self-centered and self-sufficiently pursued. The aborted spirituality which may derive from such
activity often has dire consequences, since if prideful man
alone provides the measure for all values there is nothing to
prevent him from going to any length, even to crime, to make
his vision prevail. Barring a conversion from such self-
righteousness, the typical Warren character is unable — or
unwilling — to lose his soul to find it.

In purport *Brother to Dragons* does not depart markedly
from Warren's previous work, but its exacerbated tone and persistent undercurrents of violence reveal Warren's increasingly
urgent sense that the provenance of original sin is universal

and that it is inescapable. The potential acedia of spirit
resulting from our possible despair at such a prospect Warren
condemns, however, at the same time that he shows how little
room there can be for complacent acceptance of human nature
as it is. If human nature in itself is seen to be ultimately
monstrous, and if we are lost in its labyrinthine fastnesses,
there can also transpire, through the accession of Grace, an
enlargement of our possibilities beyond those predicated by
any superficially optimistic philosophy. The succinct definition of these possibilities and of the positive values that
man, in his fallen condition, may yet embrace is Warren's most
distinctive achievement in *Brother to Dragons*.

   I

   A psychology which distorts the facts of experience by
assimilating them into a self-generated obsession betrays Lilburn Lewis. Consumed by Oedipal attraction, he idealizes Lucy
Lewis and makes of mother-love a worshipful abstraction, to be
put forward regardless of the consequences. This intense, abstract benevolence ultimately leads to crime, enforcing Warren's judgment that this is a tragedy of "our sad virtues."
In Lilburn we see the most frightening aspect of our moral history, that all too often "evil's done for good, and in good's
name" and that a single-faceted idealism can be tragic. Lilburn has made no compact with the devil, Warren says — he has
not had to go that far afield. He has only had to follow the
good impulse, love of his mother, to be corrupted. If, after
his mother's death, Lilburn had been humble in his sufferings,
he might have escaped the degradation which ensues when he insists that all others revere his mother's memory as he does.
When the household Negroes, in particular, seem to forget Lucy
Lewis, Lilburn's fury works at odds with the affection that
prompts it. He finds to his horror that love diminishes to
the degree that he asserts it strenuously and desires to preserve it intact. In its place, injured pride and fear lest
the organizing principle of his life be destroyed now fanatically motivate him. Like the Ancient Mariner in Warren's interpretation, Lilburn is the victim of self-deception as to
his own motives, judging the morality of an act in terms of
its advantage to him while pretending to be dispassionate.
The good impulse, conceived in self-interest apart from Christian restraints, can become through its induced intensity more
uncontrollable than calculated evil and eventually more destructive. When self-knowledge or "definition" eludes Lilburn,
he adheres to his mistaken idea of the good and does the worst.
Following a reductive principle, Lilburn tries, with fearful
results, to define the human, to give order, violently, to
chaotic flux. In such wrenching of the spirit to preconceived
ends, all hint of humility evaporates. Such eager defense of
his self-locked love for his mother from contamination in the

outside world blinds Lilburn to his mother's greatness of soul
and causes him more and more to fix upon the letter of his affection for her.

To implement this ruling devotion to his mother's memory,
Lilburn develops a passion for the pure act motivated by the
pure idea and untouched by embarrassing reality. Afraid that
the facts might rout his cherished ideal, he raises it above
them to an absolute and assures himself that its importance
justifies his realization of it beyond the limits of the eth-
ically permissible. "The dear redemption of simplicity" in
such abstracted activity becomes his solace despite its un-
truth and the anguish it fosters. To others, the gratuitous
act inspired by unreasoned fervor is forcible but not ethical-
ly justifiable. When they then react sharply against it, Lilburn is only the more confirmed in his self-righteous vision.

Lilburn's desire for others to meet his impossible standards prevents, first of all, a normal sexual relationship
with Laetitia. Something she describes as "awful" transpires
in their relationship shortly after their marriage. Though we
are not told definitely what has happened, some sort of sexual
violence has undoubtedly occurred. Lilburn seems to force the
apparently inexperienced Laetitia against her will and then
holds this fact against her, particularly after he compels her
the next night to tell what she thinks has happened. Irration-
ally, he resents the fact that she is spoiled at his own hands
and would not remain "pure" despite her helplessness before
his violence. His "angelic" Laetitia is an ordinary mortal
after all; she has, he is sure, liked stepping in "dung."
Shock from her violent experience deepens in Laetitia to fri-
gidity, so that, after the mockery of their marriage, she cannot respond to the husband whose contempt for her increases
nor help him when he most needs her.

Because obsessive love for his mother excludes the possibility of other emotional commitments, Lilburn uproots the
love that might have steadied him after her death. After he
spurns Laetitia, he becomes yet more tortured, more unfeeling,
more inhumane. He beats his servant George, whom Lucy sent
out to bring him home following a three-day drunk when Laetitia had disappointed him. Having resisted the affection of
Laetitia and George before Lucy's death, he is led, in his
overwrought fixation upon his mother, to repudiate, after her
death, both Aunt Cat and his hound. Since these two love him
most unquestioningly, he derives sadistic pleasure from sense-
lessly repulsing them. Poetic justice is served when they
betray him after his crime — though such betrayal is paradoxically also Lilburn's "deepest will" — the dog unwittingly,
Aunt Cat by clever design. By killing love, Lilburn attains
"the desiderated and ice-locked anguish of isolation" which
then frightens him, a security breeding insecurity. He asks
love, yet he cannot bear to be loved, since it magnifies his
guilt; he must then destroy what disturbs him. Symbolic of

his confusion and incipient degradation is Lilburn's hatred
at his mother's grave for the encroaching grass which destroys
her memory among men. In view of the raw, cold, cruel, pure
fact of his love, he wishes her grave to remain bare and open
as a fresh wound, to be a perpetual reminder to him of his
loss.

In order to break through to a reality whose force, however, diminishes in proportion to his frantic efforts to reach
it, Lilburn is led, Macbeth-like, from one crime against man
and nature to others still more harrowing. Now that any other
love except that for his mother seems desecration to him, he
instinctively kicks the hound which comes fawning to him at
the grave. The resulting rapture of conflicting joy and sorrow brings catharsis in cruelty for his festering grief. When
he kicks the hound the second time, Lilburn is not surprised
but soothed. Distraught by his mother's image, he feels no
joy "of the soul's restoration" in reconciliation with the
hound. Terror and violence besiege the homestead, while the
Negro victims counter with supernal cunning. He rages inwardly and broods upon insatiate revenge, trusting that inward
force will vindicate the self by vindicating what the self
most reveres.

At no time does Lilburn question the rightness of his acts,
since their absolute rationale forbids any vacillation. The
only necessity he now feels is to remain true to the light
within, to a self-appointed destiny. Defining thus expedi-
tiously his own necessity, Lilburn resembles Warren's other
uncritically self-confident characters like Slim Sarrett in
At Heaven's Gate, Willie Stark and Adam Stanton in *All the
King's Men,* and Jeremiah Beaumont in *World Enough and Time.*
Like them, once Lilburn tastes the spiritual security inherent
in a self-generated absolute principle, he has no power to remain aloof from its demands. To compensate for deficient inner resources, which had earlier made him discontented with
the frontier, he now enshrines at all costs the ideal which
orders his life. In contrast with his previous states of in-
certitude, Lilburn is now perfectly adjusted, if occasionally
still unsure of himself. As he waits for the "thrilling abso-
luteness/ Of the pure act to come," Lilburn is unaware of the
price he has paid for this assurance, the snuffing out of intervening benevolent instincts. Forcible and self-willed, he
abrogates the intelligence and attains to a ruminative peace
like that which any monster might feel, sunk deep in nature,
such peace as Warren depicts in his poem "Crime" as "past despair and past the uncouth/ Violation." Linked to Lilburn's
suprahuman surety is the motionless, insensate catfish with
its brute face and complacent adaptation to the channel-mud
as it hibernates under the Mississippi ice. In his complete
harmony with amoral nature, of Lilburn as well as of the catfish it might be said, "How can there be/ Sensation where
there is perfect adjustment?" The result is that Lilburn

is unconscious of the barbarity of his crime, since his own
nature justifies it.

His crime moves him one step nearer a more perfect realization of self as he has been able, delusively, to define it.
The fact that he has now completely left the world of actuality behind him is implied in his inability to kill a huge moth
which comes in the window and which distracts him only momentarily from concentrating upon his vision of his self-imagined
destiny. With the help of Isham after the crime, he awaits
then, in his half-joyful abandonment to the currents of the
self, the grand hour when he can still more completely fulfill
his nature, "the hour of the Pentecostal intuition." In his
impatience, he moves to bring this time about more quickly
when he gets Isham to agree to a mutual death pact. Because
Lilburn savors the full pleasure of this abstracted moment —
the grandest of moments because the farthest removed from the
distracting realities of life — and because he wishes to enjoy
to the full his "sweet alienation" and the sense of injustice
done him previously, he counts slowly while Isham stands before him with a pistol. He then betrays Isham by himself not
firing, since he knows that the law will take care of Isham.
Monomania induces the "death of the heart," despite the fact
that a heart too sensitive to confront the reality had induced
the monomania.

II

At a more intellectual level, Thomas Jefferson in Warren's
view is also initially motivated by the oversimplified abstraction. His ruling passion is the idealistic destiny he fore-
sees for man, for he grasps the fact that man in his median
position between God and beast aspires to the God-like. He is
too anxious, however, to believe this aspiration exists pure,
and he discounts too readily and vehemently the beast-like
within man, as he himself admits later. Subscribing to this
self-defined "rational hope" and leaping beyond man's "natural
bourne and constitution" to envisage his glorious future, Jefferson denies, until too late, the discomfiting reality. At
first, he looks upon the evil in man as a blot upon his shining nature, which the centuries have all but erased. With its
clean lines and simple harmonies, the Romanesque cathedral at
Nîmes is a symbol of ideal human fulfillment and of Jefferson's noble vision. If man would but strike off his shackles,
his divine innocence would then "dance" amid the oppressive
realities of the world which tend to stifle it. Because one
must struggle with some of the realities of the world to attain to inner integrity, one cannot, as Jefferson tends to do,
deny them all. "The eternal/ Light of just proportion and the
heart's harmony," which Jefferson so insatiably hungers for,
is, accordingly, ironically extinguished in his fanatical crav-
ing to achieve it. As Warren presents him, Jefferson is, in

220 Frederick P. W. McDowell

his early phase, as fervent in his idealism and as insensitive
to pragmatic realities as Jeremiah Beaumont in *World Enough
and Time*. As a result, Jefferson cannot see that he desires
too unmixed a good, impossible under the imperfect conditions
of this world, just as Jeremiah Beaumont cannot see that if
his antagonist, Cassius Fort, once did evil he might yet be,
on the whole, a good man. Neither character realizes until he
has been inexorably reoriented by tragedy that beatitude for
man — a partial realization at best of all that he aspires to
— is possible only through humble contrition and dispassionate
love. Such a transcendence of reality must be earned through
suffering, through divine Grace, instead of merely being asserted by the intellect as a cherished aim.

Warren shows how close Jefferson's psychology is to Lilburn's despite their different purposes in life. Both seek
to define the human through the self-determined abstraction,
and both wish to assert an innocence consonant with it. Both
lack in large part a sense for tangible realities, and both
become enslaved to an overpowering vision. Both are romantic
in that they tend to transform by wishful thinking things as
they are into what they are not. As with so many of Warren's
misguided characters, they both wish a too easily attained coherent explanation for an essentially incoherent world. Hate,
the result of a naive emotionalism in Lilburn's case, and
nobility, the result of a misguided intellectuality in Jefferson's, are, as Warren explains, but different "thrust[s] toward Timelessness, in Time." The only valid motivation, Warren implies, is just the opposite: with one's intuited sense
of the eternal, one must work toward time, the actual, the objective, and bring one's sense of the ideal always back to the
reality. Life without saving illusion is a mockery, but a
life given over to furthering at all costs the self-righteous
illusion can be calamitous. Neither Jefferson of the early
hopeful stage nor Lilburn could realize that the "impalpable"
is not the ideal and that the ideal, in becoming too nebulous
and disembodied, is in danger of being distorted.

The difference between Jefferson and Lilburn is in sensitivity, the contrast Warren had made memorable in *World Enough
and Time* between Jeremiah Beaumont and Skrogg. Despite the
fact that he meets a violent death, Jeremiah could ultimately
be saved in a spiritual sense after a wasted life because he
had spiritual receptivity, whereas Skrogg had deliberately
snuffed out his soul. This kind of sensitivity also underlies
the bluff exterior of Jack Burden in *All the King's Men* and
allows him finally to decide between the conflicting claims
of the illusion and the reality, of the self and the world of
other men. The education of a misguided protagonist to the
truth is thus a constant theme in Warren. In *Brother to Dragons* both Lucy Lewis and Jefferson are educated by tragedy, Jefferson the more slowly because his mistaken vision is so inflexible, Jefferson's conversion from a restrictive idealism

to a more integral view of life is the chief situation explored in this verse-novel. It is significant that Lucy Lewis,
reborn through her death — the result of her inability to cope
with reality — redeems Jefferson by making him aware of realities outside those apparent to the intellect when it perceives
only what it is interested in perceiving. For most of the
novel, Jefferson is in the first period of his redemption —
when he has become disillusioned with his earlier ideals and
has come to realize the universality of evil in men. Only at
its end, through Lucy's intervention, does he reach a decisive
spiritual poise and the second period of his redemption — when
he can acknowledge original sin without recrimination.

In the first stage, Jefferson is haunted by the fact that
human nature too often turns its back upon the glories of
which it is capable to revel instead in the evil act. Like
Lilburn, Jefferson lacks to a large degree the spiritual reserves, the stabilizing philosophy he needs to combat the evil
which destroys his perfectibilist vision. Heartfelt joy in
his vision leads to Jefferson's sense of betrayal, then, when
one of his own blood, through the absolutely evil act, extin-
guishes it. Trying to order reality according to his own
ideals, Jefferson continually fails to grasp the circumstances
under which it may be ordered. Like Jeremiah Beaumont or Adam
Stanton, Jefferson at this point both overemphasizes and under-
plays the intellect; he worships an intellectualized abstraction while disregarding the critical function of reason except
as it reinforces his interested idealism. Jefferson becomes
bewildered, disillusioned, almost cynical in outlook. In this
phase, this induced pessimism is so powerful as to becloud his
earlier humanism. In a world where evil is apparently supreme
and obliterates by greater force the serene good, Jefferson
even comes to feel that violence alone gives truth. He now
assumes that "all values are abrogated in blankness," and he
reproves his sister for not having struck George after he had
turned from Lilburn's beating. At this stage, Jefferson does
not understand how close this counsel is to that suggested to
Lilburn by his own unleashed nature before the crime. From
Lilburn's brand of violence Jefferson had, indeed, recoiled
in loathing. The fact that redemption often derives from violence through the polar connection existing between a strongly
negative evil and a strongly positive good does not justify
this counsel of Jefferson's to Lucy, although he is right in
feeling that the violence he recommends is preferable to the
inertia of Charles Lewis, for example. Jefferson does not perceive, moreover, that Lucy's inability at this point to con-
quer pride and assert the love which inwardly prompts her is
her real sin and the ultimate cause for her son's tragedy.

In his first stage of regeneration, Jefferson cannot see
past the fact of human evil, which has paralyzed his soul. In
his obsession with its prevalence, he is as unreasoning in his
denial of aspiration as he had been devoted to it previously.

At a time of crisis, the inflexible philosophy of life, whether it stresses demonic pride in Lilburn or angelic aspiration in Jefferson, fails to comprehend the complexities of experience. In recoil from the reality he misunderstood, Jefferson now condemns love as "but a mask to hide the brute face of fact,/ And that face is the immitigable ferocity of self." Unrealistic also is his present despair over humanity itself: "I'd said there's no defense of the human definition." This agonized pessimism is actually as intense and as uncritical as the optimism of his unregenerate days had been.

Since he has had to relinquish the perfectionist enthusiasm which motivated him at the First Continental Congress, Jefferson now recognizes "the darkness of the self" and its labyrinthine wilderness. At the height of his dreams, he had been realist enough to acknowledge the fact of evil, but he had tried to minimize it. He knew from his reading of history, for instance, that there lurked horror in its "farther room" and that the act and the motive are not always ballasted by the good deed and the good intention respectively. He also had known that all men are not innocent despite his belief in Innocence as an ideal. His disillusion, however, makes him perceptive where he had been merely suspicious. Correctly but reluctantly gauging evil, even if unnerved by it to an unreasoned denial of the good, he now sees that it can be passive, since all things come to it and seek it out in magnetic attraction. He sees the lurking beast within us all, a minotaur to be found at the last turn of the spirit's labyrinth. This beast, "our brother, our darling brother," is not, in Warren's view, to be denied by any mere effort of the will; his insidious promptings can be finally overcome only by effort of the will if one can force himself to make it. Like Pasiphaë with her unnatural lust, we can become enamored of our evil. This Jefferson now sees. At the height of indulgence, we catch, like her, in the same sneaking way, a glimpse of our beatific innocence in childhood, and thereby rationalize our evil acts. Except for the reductive premises in each case, Jefferson's initial vision of man's preternatural innocence was the obverse of Pasiphaë's. She was evil but rationalized her evil by the fleeting vision of the innocent good, while Jefferson thought of man as innocent only to find him besmirched with evil. Thus the lie was given to Jefferson's earlier "towering definition, angelic, arrogant, abstract,/ Greaved in glory, thewed with light." That earth's monsters are innocent in their lack of knowledge Jefferson had always realized; but that man, capable of knowledge and self-definition, could be a "master-monster" and exhibit only a blank, ignorant innocence Jefferson had not realized. Neither had his nephew, Meriwether Lewis, comprehended "the tracklessness of the human heart" until the facts of experience forced him to do so.

Now that his original conception of man has been proved wrong, Jefferson would have stressed the truth about man at

all costs, he asserts, had he known then what he knows now:
he would have run with "the hot coals" of that truth till they
had burned through his flesh to the bone. That evil is progressive, that one deed of horror can poison all else, is Jefferson's sickening conclusion. When he still tries to cling
tenaciously to "the general human fulfilment," he finds that
violent evil obtrudes in his thoughts and proliferates emotion-
ally. In his near-hysteria, therefore, Jefferson looks upon
Lilburn's deed as the reigning archetype of human psychology,
as the microcosm of the evil which infects all hope and which
lies like a cloud and curse over the land he had once loved.
To Jefferson, all social injustice and all crime are, in fact,
somehow inherent in the fall of the meat-axe, in the fact that
his nephew could commit his crime and that other people might
commit similar crimes. That one must not only shudder at evil
but try actively to understand it Jefferson doesn't realize until later, nor the fact that suffering, in some degree, atones
for it. He is impatient at its persistence, failing to see
that it can be only partly overcome and that one must not
shirk the struggle to master it.

The second stage of Jefferson's education provides the
poem with its central meaning. Under the guidance of Lucy
Lewis, Jefferson accommodates his original resplendent vision
of man's nobility to the actual facts of human existence, especially to the cardinal fact of original sin, and mitigates
the harsh abstractness of this ideal with the exertion of his
sensibility. A grander nobility than Jefferson's initial conception consists, Lucy claims, in testing that conception in
the world. His redemption is assured when his faith in the
Idea is renewed, once a "deep distress" has humanized it and
once he relates it to mankind. The dream — or idea — of the
future, Jefferson concludes, requires for complement the fact
of the past:

> Now I should hope to find the courage to say
> That the dream of the future is not
> Better than the fact of the past, no matter how terrible.
> For without the fact of the past we cannot dream the fu-
> ture.

Since lack of self-knowledge is original sin in either Lilburn or Jefferson, and since complete self-knowledge is impossible, original sin is universal, and we are all implicated in
it and with each other. As a gesture indicating he now understands that he and all men are involved in Lilburn's crime,
Lucy insists that Jefferson take his hand. Evasion will no
longer do, for Jefferson can't escape our universal complicity
in sin, "our common crime," as Warren phrases it in "End of
Summer." As commentator on the action, "R.P.W." stresses
throughout our complicity in the tragedy. It contains us, he
says, and it "is contained by us," for we in our fallen condition are all guilty of it in being human. We are guilty, fur-

thermore, in being too complacent about evil, since we are
only too anxious to adjust ourselves comfortably and snugly to
it. As to the crime which so unnerves Jefferson, R.P.W. explains that it is not so special as he thinks. It is but one
episode in the long pageant of man's sinfulness down the ages
and is "impressive chiefly for its senselessness" as all evil
acts tend to be. The earthquake which followed the crime
struck fear into the hearts of guilty men who had had no knowledge of Lilburn's act — they were simply guilty of it by extension, by being human, and by being capable in their worst moments of kindred atrocity. Guilt is common enough, therefore,
to make any one day appropriate for the Judgment, even as this
present hour would be. R.P.W. expresses, however, the ironical fear that the modern age might be too "advanced" to pray
for deliverance from its guilt or to fear God's wrath, just as
men in 1811 had got used both to the repeated quakes and to
the "horror" of being men. In any event, Jefferson's complicity in original sin through his use of black labor to build
that citadel of freedom, Monticello, is real, if at first un-
acknowledged by him. The fact that evil exists should not attract us nor repel us, but should interest us since we all are,
for better or worse, involved in it. When the evil is done is
the question R.P.W. would explore, for all who face up bravely
to life must solve that question, must analyze the anguish and
the agony involved in bringing the evil act to its full birth.
Unless we have that curiosity, we can never attain to saving
knowledge, R.P.W. would insist.

In a noble speech Lucy tells Jefferson that she in her
love brought disaster to her son, just as he in his aspiration
brought disaster to Meriwether Lewis. "Our best gifts," she
says, carry some ineradicable taint, and we corrupt even as we
freely give — Jefferson like Lilburn has done evil in the name
of good by interfusing his altruism with pride of self. This
burden of our shame should always confront us, and while it
should not inhibit us, it should make us bestow our gifts with
humility. Lilburn's face, Jefferson must realize, is but a
"mirror of your possibilities." To the criminal we are linked
by the terror we all must feel at our own demonic propensities
which, without our careful scrutiny, will project outward into
the evil act: Lilburn's last indefensible hour is simply "the
sum of all the defensible hours/ We have lived through." Jefferson has squelched his fear that he, too, might be capable
of all evil in being capable of any evil. As R.P.W. expresses
it, Jefferson had forgotten that even the wicked man seeks God
according to his own lights and fulfillment as he can find it.
Along with his disillusion and his cynicism, Jefferson is
forced to see that his rejection of Lilburn is too summary.
Now that his confidence in himself and in his Utopian dreams
has been shaken through Lilburn's crime, Jefferson rejects his
nephew principally out of pique. There is some truth, then,
to Meriwether's charge that Jefferson had originally contrived

his "noble lie" for his own comfort and to feed his own vanity.
Jefferson has a sure sense for the horror of Lilburn's crime,
but hardly sees, in his revulsion, its application to himself:

> For Lilburn is an absolute of our essential
> Condition, and as such, would ingurgitate
> All, and all you'd give, all hope, all heart,
> Would only be disbursed down that rat hole of the
>   ultimate horror.

In commenting upon the action and characters, R.P.W. insists that evil — at least its germ — is universal. Modern
Smithland, a village near the site of decayed Rocky Hill, is
to Warren a symbol for universal sin and universal suffering,
by virtue of the sin and suffering it does contain. The mino-
taur-in-labyrinth image, so forcibly presented by Jefferson
early in the poem, also becomes a symbol which dominates the
poem in vividly suggesting the lurking evil in the dark heart
of man. In greater or less degree, all the characters in the
poem sin, and they all suffer because they cannot transcend
their failings and emerge completely from the darkness of
their inner selves. None of them are as wholly innocent and
glorious as Jefferson had initially imagined the men at the
First Continental Congress to be; rather they all resemble his
colleagues as Jefferson describes them in a revised estimate:

>   lost
> Each man lost in some blind lobby, hall, enclave,
> Crank cul-de-sac, couloir, or corridor of Time.
> Of Time. Or self: and in that dark no thread...

Lucy Lewis, radiant as she is, is prevented by pride from making toward George in his suffering the spontaneous gesture
which would alleviate it and result in her own fulfillment:
"the small/ Obligation fulfilled had swayed the weight of the
world." Similarly, Laetitia is prevented from making toward
Lilburn at Lucy's death the gesture which would gain his love
forever through her willingness to forgive his past violence
to her. Actually, Laetitia had in part willed Lilburn's violation of her, and in one sense, therefore, merits the scorn of
her husband for imputed impurity — at least she could not, and
hardly wanted to, tell Lilburn to stop. Betrayed by her innocence into a fascination with the evil she shrinks from, Laetitia in her psychology at the time of her defilement by Lilburn
is not unlike Pasiphaë, as Warren describes her, at the time
of her submission to the plunging bull.

Our common complicity in evil Warren elaborates upon still
further in his analysis of Laetitia's brother, of Isham, of
Aunt Cat, and of George. Laetitia's brother is indignant when
he learns that Lilburn had forcibly used Laetitia, and he proclaims loudly how sweeping would have been his revenge if he
had known. Laetitia acutely says that he would not have
avenged her out of love, but out of pride at accomplishing

the deed — at best, out of desire to protect the family honor.
Aunt Cat, Lilburn's colored mammy, really loves him, but in
her love there is calculation too, manifested for years in the
silent but tense struggle between her and Lucy Lewis for Lilburn's affection. To a degree she also merits what she gets
when Lilburn, in a fit of fury at the time of his mother's
death, pretends to disgorge the black milk he had been nursed
upon. Isham, too, is as guilty of George's butchering as his
brother, for Isham knew instinctively what was going to happen
and did nothing to prevent it. In that he seemed half-willing
to meet his fate, George was, in some part, an accomplice in
the deed. He almost wills, with obscene pleasure, the fatal
stroke, and seems more in love with the "sweet injustice to
himself" than fearful of death. Even though he keeps running
away, George is also drawn back hypnotically again and again
to Lilburn in a continuing attraction-repulsion pattern.
R.P.W. admits this notion of George's complicity is, in some
degree, fantastical, since nothing can really excuse Lilburn's
crime. But R.P.W.'s observations are true, he would assert,
to the extent that "we're all each other's victim./ Potentially, at least."

III

Jefferson has failed to see, in short, that positive good
presupposes positive evil, that the two are closely related,
and that Lilburn's motivation is really the need, as R.P.W.
maintains, "to name his evil good." That moral and psychological values are complex Jefferson is unwilling to admit, because of his zeal to preserve the integrity of his vision.
That ambiguity is the indispensable feature of the moral life,
that philosophical truth is to be measured in terms of an adjustment of the discordancies of experience, that illusion
must be squared with a multiform actuality has somehow escaped
Jefferson, as it had also escaped the unintellectual Lilburn.
In describing the crime, R.P.W. had addressed the night as a
symbol of the absoluteness of vision that Lilburn — and Jefferson — aspired toward. The night would obliterate in its uni-
form blackness "the impudent daylight's velleities," that is,
the concrete actualities of our experience. Once they are obscured, it is tempting to define the Absolute by an interested
exertion of the will alone rather than by the vigorous reconciliation of the Many to the One. The mixture of good and
evil in humanity is something that Jefferson had realized in
his intellect, but he had not given the concept his emotional
assent. Jefferson's psychology is essentially too simple — in
his disillusion he rejects, for instance, the innocence of the
newborn babe because of the evil that human nature can also
perpetrate. He then denies the generous act because it can
never exist pure, because it is always tainted inescapably by
the self. The omnipresence of malignant evil disturbs his in-

ner poise to the extent that he all but denies the worth of
the ideals he had once cherished. Though love, for example,
has an admixture of pride in it and is scarcely ever disinterested, Jefferson fails to see, notwithstanding, that it is
truly estimable. The all-or-none point of view is thus per-
nicious in overlooking the truth that every act and emotion
carries within it not only its own impulsions but its contrary
possibility. A fervently accepted good, therefore, has more
possible evil in it than a lukewarm virtue, while an unabashed
evil carries within it latent violences that augur the possibility of heartfelt conversion.

Every act, moreover, implies a choice among motives for
it to become the act, implies a resolving of "the essential
polarity of possibility" contained within it. The act has a
finality "in the mere fact of achieved definition," therefore,
a degree of purity and simplification at variance with its
confused intent. Even though such choice among motives is
made and a large degree of purity is thereby attained, the act
still carries within its secret core other latent impulsions.
If it represents a simplification of our swarming experience,
the origins of the act are never clear-cut, but rather a "hell-
broth of paradox and internecine/ Complex of motive." It must,
accordingly, be exhaustively analyzed, not merely accepted at
its apparent value for the relief it brings the doer. Lilburn's evil deed, for instance, must be judged not only for
its destructiveness but also as misguided creation. The
wicked man, says R.P.W., is, after all, but seeking for his
crimes some outward rationale which the good man would term
God.

The paradoxical substratum underlying all our acts is var-
iously emphasized in the poem. One aspect of the tangled nature of reality is suggested by Charles Lewis — though Warren
shows more contempt for him than for anyone else — the fact
that madness is "the cancer of truth" and has more affinity
with the actuality than has a deadened complacency. For this
same reason, Warren values violence more highly than timid
conformity to convention. Even Jefferson realizes this truth
when in his disillusion he says that "all truth is bought with
blood," except that he then is too much obsessed with the
blood to realize that violence is only one avenue to renewal.
At the very least, violence will exorcize unreality, will
expose the fraudulence of "the pious mind" to whom "our history's nothing if not refined." Only when violence is pursued
with self-interest, as with Lilburn, does it become the supreme evil. Since reality is thus elusive and multiple, R.P.W.
maintains that a balance of qualities, educed by the supple intelligence, is the essential of wisdom. Grace, pity, and charity we all need from God, but that does not mean that free-
will can be set aside. The glorious possibility acknowledges
the despair which hems it round, and derives its strength from
that honesty. But it does not give in to this pessimism. The

complexity of existence is again emphasized when R.P.W. asserts that it is through isolation that we grasp "the human bond" and at length define the self — in "separateness," Warren has declared in his poem "Revelation," "does love learn definition" — while at our peril we reject our fellow man completely. If we withdraw from society to gain a greater inner irradiation, we must, thus fortified, return to it and seek our place in it. Failure to see that a personally determined moral code has weight only when it comprehends the self in relation to other men was, after all, Jefferson's original mistake as it had also been Lilburn's.

Of the many ambiguities explored in the poem, the most striking concerns the natural world. On the one hand, Warren stresses the malignancy and impersonality of nature. The fact that the white inhabitants have unfairly wrested the land from the Indians places a curse upon it, so that moral unhealth hangs like miasma over the wilderness, and its shadows enter the souls of the pioneers. Both sons of Lucy Lewis come under its dark spell; both have become victims of "the ignorant torpor/ That breathed from the dark land." After his crime, moreover, Lilburn feels only at home in "the unredeemed dark of the wild land." Raised on the edge of the wilderness, Jefferson had also come to feel over and through him "the shadow of the forest," sinister and foreboding. Even then, he had felt that man must redeem nature, for nature is too harsh and unfeeling for it to serve as moral ministrant to erring, aspiring man. As she did in 1811, nature will likely as not visit mankind with earthquakes, floods, and sickness to add to his discomfort and perplexity. As measure of her hostility to living creatures, she causes the dog-fox to drown in protracted agony in a flood, or she causes the oak tree, like Jacob, to struggle all night in anguish with "the incessant/ And pitiless angel of air." In a perfect adjustment to nature, there is either overplus of misdirected feeling or inability to feel at all. In its "idiot-ignorance" nature obliterates the purely human and the moral law which alone can educe the human. Feeling strongly this need for other than naturalistic values in their undiluted form, Warren asserted in his poem "Monologue at Midnight" that "Our mathematic yet has use/ For the integers of blessedness." The grandeur of nature, Warren maintains in the concluding lines of the verse-novel, can give us an "image" only for our destiny, but can in no sense give us a "confirmation" of it. That must be sought from within the soul itself.

If nature "as an image of lethal purity" is a symbol of evil, it is also a symbol of reality and truth; it is both malignant and beautiful, soul-benumbing and life-inspiriting, giving rise to heartfelt joy despite the infinite darkness at its heart, as Warren also tells us in "Picnic Remembered." The beauty of the springtide upon the untracked forest, its "heart-breaking new delicacy of green," is an emblem of such

ambiguity. If we follow the promptings of nature too closely,
we can lose our humanity; but, paradoxically, it can also as-
suage our sufferings deriving from the evils which follow the
loss in others of that humanity. By making such men contempti-
ble and insignificant in comparison with its power, it can comfort us for the violence and cruelty they may instigate. It
can bedwarf even the monstrous and endow us with the vital energy that can alone enable us to transcend the "human trauma."
Lilburn is as if driven onward by the raging wind, as if in
the whirlwind of senseless force. Yet if he is so closely
part of nature, it is only by escaping from him out into "the
glimmering night scene" that we can regain proportion and san-
ity. After his crime Lilburn, so much a part of nature in his
unrestrained violence, can no longer respond to its spiritual
influence. He inhabits then a somber inner landscape "of
forms fixed and hieratic," and abjures the promiscuous promise
of joy in newly wakening nature.

Nature is in essence spiritual and a source for deep reality provided its power is used to strengthen the innately spiritual and not substituted for it. Warren can say, therefore,
that in spite of "all naturalistic considerations" or because
of them, we must believe in virtue — nature can both extin-
guish the human impulse and reinforce it. We ought not to regard nature abstractly by naming its objects out of their context, for they are more than mere names: they are symbols of
inner spiritual facts, so that a snake is really a symbol of
evil, violence, darkness, and terror, though science would
call it only "Elaphe obsoleta obsoleta." Such a rationalist
approach to nature impoverishes it, yet Warren's earlier emotional fervor for it, as recounted in the poem, is also unreal.
The joy he had felt as a boy in holding tight the objects of
the sense provides an easy faith that cannot last. Neither an
easy nor an exclusive faith in nature is tenable, yet Warren
does quote Lucretius to the effect that the order underlying
nature, the ranging of natural phenomena under natural law,
may dispel the "darkness of the mind" and lead to inner light.
A true knowledge of nature, fortified by our sense of the human, can dispel our morbid fears and the darkness and terror
that haunt the innermost soul of man, while an unconditioned
emotional response to its promptings can intensify those fears
and that darkness and terror. Man is at once part of nature
and above it, and should, in his adjustments to it, be mindful
of this paradox. A security or joy obtained, like Jefferson's,
by a denial of inconvenient natural fact is as reprehensible
as Lilburn's blind immersion in nature.

IV

More than any of his other poems, *Brother to Dragons* represents a mature if sometimes muted statement of Warren's own
values. From his narrative Warren elicits certain conclusions

about human life which he is always careful to clothe, however, in the specific symbol or to educe from the concrete situation. While for Warren the absolutes of tradition have an independent existence, he avoids sentimentality and provides for their inevitable definition by allowing them to emerge from a specific milieu.

Chief among these positive values is glory, which alone makes life worthwhile, fearful as the experience of it may become. It is a dynamic spiritual harmony, the exaltation attendant upon salvation, the sense of being attuned to both the natural and the supernatural. Failing to cultivate such a mystique as it illuminates his experiences, man fails to live as deeply as he could, Warren asserts. Despite this truth, it is with reluctance that we face the necessity of being saved, of surrendering ourselves to the radiance of glory and permitting it to determine the quality of our lives. As the chief reality in our lives to be reverenced, glory will, once its provenance is admitted, reorient us positively; "for it knocks society's values to a cocked hat." Glory is what the soul is best capable of, contrasting with the abstract idealism which becomes hardened to formula and withers rather than elicits the potentialities of the soul. If we are identified with all other men in guilt, we are also identified with them in their troubled aspirations after glory.

To know the farthest reaches of the spirit demands an emotional sensitivity toward others, a realization that it is fatal only to love and to love well, and not to love well enough. In these terms Lucy Lewis describes her own failure with respect to the family tragedy. Unable because of fear to extend her hand to George in kindness and love, she soon collapses physically and morally. Her death retributively follows her inability to live the life her instincts countenance. Because she fails in love toward George, she fails in love toward her son. She learns that love is the most valuable human trait and represents "definition"; once expressed it can never again be denied, unless one would die spiritually, the same point that Warren had made in his poem "Love's Parable." As we have seen, Laetitia does not love Lilburn enough, either, to minister to him at the time of Lucy's death. She is right in feeling that a change of heart in herself would have availed her husband; in her pride, however, she is unregenerate and cannot attain to selfless love. Lilburn is in a sense betrayed by the women who love him — Lucy, Laetitia, and Aunt Cat — because they do not love him strongly enough to stand by him when he needs them most and to instruct him in "the mystery of the heart." In the modern age, we also deny ourselves too often to others. As we speed down the highway, we can too easily forget, for instance, the loveless eye, which glares at us from a hovel and reminds us of our inhumanity; we merely press the accelerator "and quick you're gone/ Beyond forgiveness, pity, hope, hate, love."

Closely allied to Warren's reverence for both love and glory is that for virtue and its concomitant, humility. There is no possibility of our not believing in virtue, for our conscience is always with us and will not be silenced, Warren asserts. Virtue is tougher and more "remorseless" than any of our other attributes, for it isolates the human amongst the other forms of life. Virtue, if disregarded, will lie in wait murderously, like "the lethal mantis at his prayer," to pounce upon the heart that denies it. It is also the necessary rationale for all human anguish. Without anguish, virtue could not be so clearly delimited as to command our absolute allegiance: anguish gives to virtue its local habitation so that it does not become intolerably abstracted from reality.

> I think I begin to see the forging of the future.
> It will be forged beneath the hammer of truth
> On the anvil of our anguish. We shall be forged
> Beneath the hammer of truth on the anvil of anguish.
> It would be terrible to think that truth is lost.
> It would be worse to think that anguish is lost, ever.

Virtue purifies from pride and induces in the more sensitive characters of the poem needed humility, a sacramental vision of the universe such as the regenerate Ancient Mariner also embraces in Warren's interpretation of the poem. Through thus dying to the self, real selfhood alone will be achieved, says Warren in his own poem. As to Jefferson, he remains cynical until Lucy can prevail upon him to cease dwelling upon the outrage of Lilburn's crime and to accept him. When he finally acknowledges Lilburn, the pride inseparable from the judging of another by one's own standards disappears. Jefferson then attains the humility needed for the inner balance his near-hysteria had heretofore destroyed. The other chief characters, Laetitia, Lucy, and Aunt Cat, are, as we have seen, all prevented by varying kinds of pride from being true to their instinctive sympathies. Only when they accept in humility rather than reject in pride are they serene. The forms of pride, Warren argues, are many and treacherous. Even the act of forgiveness stems in large part from injured self-esteem, and allows us to placate the wounded self. Heroism, declares the knowledgeful Jefferson, this time speaking for Warren, is more often motivated by pride in putting down the monster than by any altruism. The usual hero is potentially more evil than the monsters he vanquishes, because vainglory encourages him to reject normal human limitations in an aggrandizement of self: "man puts down the bad and then feels good," says Warren. The black snake that R.P.W. sees outside at Rocky Hill is not only the traditional symbol for the evil and violence that have brooded there, but it is conversely a symbol of the fact that forgiveness for such evil is necessary, of the fact that by humility and love we gain wisdom to oppose the influence of furtive evil. Like man at his ideal moral and spiritual fulfillment, the snake both forgives and asks forgiveness.

An activist cluster of values also informs the poem. As
members of the human race, Warren insists, we must be morally
responsible — our connections with other men are so subtle and
so pervasive that we deny them at our peril. Because we are
all in some degree the victims of history and of our environment, we have no right, Warren alleges, to disavow responsibility:

> For if responsibility is not
> The thing given but the thing to be achieved,
> There is still no way out of the responsibility
> Of trying to achieve responsibility
> So like it or lump it, you are stuck.

Jefferson's rejection of Lilburn is simply his rejection of
what is unpleasant, says Lucy, Warren's mouthpiece. In his
presentation of Charles Lewis, Warren even more directly in-
culcates the need to assume gratefully and without evasion our
responsibilities. Lewis had fled his moral obligations in Virginia in the hope of finding peace in a new land; but since he
brought his inner weakness and hollowness with him, he is, if
anything, more at loose ends on the frontier than he had been
in Virginia. By his repudiation of family responsibility,
his descendants are left, without light, to degenerate on the
frontier.

Coming to Kentucky to seek reality, to become once more
"part of human effort and man's hope," Charles does not find
it because his soul is shrivelled. After Lucy's death,
Charles in fact sometimes thinks he is empty so that he is
surprised to find his footprint in the earth. At that time he
feels relief, as well as sorrow, that he need no longer seek
reality. It demands too much uncomfortable effort now that
the one person to whom he was in any way real has gone. He
hopes that her remains will rot quickly "into the absolute
oblivion" and that she may soon be the nothingness he has already become. He goes back to Virginia to fulfill a barren,
hollow destiny amid the artifices of civilization where the
reality — as well as the stark evil — of the dark land will
not so rudely challenge him, where he will be safe from disturbing violence, and where he can pursue, unimpeded, a mater-
ialist "success." Like his nephew Meriwether, Charles Lewis
had also found that the foulness of savage men had more vitality than the artifice of "civilized" man, but Charles lacks
the vigor to break out of his moral torpor. He cannot escape
the lie he lives because he brings it with him from Virginia
to the Kentucky wilderness. The milieu he fled, he sees, is
intolerable simply because it had nothing intolerable in it.
His desire to find some new "tension and test, perhaps terror"
in the West is thwarted because he tells the only lie that a
man cannot embrace and still live, "the lie that justifies."
Lilburn and Jefferson — and in his wake, Meriwether Lewis —

also tell the lie that justifies. Tragic violence, disheart-
ening disillusion, and suicide are the respective results.
This kind of lie is simply a rationale for irresponsibility:
in each case, the critical sense, or, as R.P.W. calls it, "a
certain pragmatic perspective," is lacking.

The effort of the will to achieve definition is ultimately
necessary if the individual is to attain spiritual clarity.
One cannot arrive at the reasons for George's anguish and Lilburn's degradation by thought alone, says the reborn Jefferson,
but one must create the possibility for such a reason by a directed resolution, wherein strength is modulated by charity.
This, the only knowledge worth possessing, is so elusive as to
be almost impossible to possess fully. Understanding — even
understanding a crime — requires an active exertion of the
will, not merely a passive analysis by the intellect. One cannot define abstractly the inscrutable, but one must participate, at least vicariously, in its manifestations: "what is
any knowledge/ Without the intrinsic mediation of the heart?"
Above all, we have to realize that such intuitive sympathy demands that we also acknowledge, unflinchingly, the worst that
can happen:

> We must strike the steel of wrath on the stone of guilt,
> And hope to provoke, thus, in the midst of our coiling
>   darkness
> The incandescence of the heart's great flare.
> And in that illumination I should hope to see
> How all creation validates itself,
> For whatever you create, you create yourself by it,
> And in creating yourself you will create
> The whole wide world and gleaming West anew.

To translate idea into action demands a courage which Warren's characters do not usually possess, though they may recognize its desirability. Lucy and Laetitia, for example, are
unable to realize in actuality what their hearts tell them is
right. Warren says that bravery is the quality which counts
most, for only those who meet moral tests without cowering
have a true knowledge of life. The reasons which prompt the
Lilburns to evil will become apparent alone to those who have
striven, for they alone will be aware of the suffering involved in translating the evil impulse into the actual evil
act. Warren, as we have seen, quotes Lucretius to the effect
that, in dispelling the "darkness of mind," the law and aspect
of nature is needed: this implies a patient perusal and endurance of the tests it offers. Stoic endurance is also necessary for the expunging of vanities: it is needed, for example,
says Warren, in accepting our fathers' reconciliations to experience, which we can do only when we do not set ourselves
above our fathers and when we can accept our own failure to
achieve their triumphs. Recounting his experiences in the
West, Meriwether Lewis stresses how greatly fortitude was re-

quired, a quality, moreover, which eluded him in his own
adjustments to life. His sentiment that "pride in endurance
is one pride that shall not be denied men" is surely, in its
clear emphasis, Warren's own. Aunt Cat also illustrates the
tenacious fortitude that Warren values so highly, for she has
the stability which permits her to survive to a ripe old age,
to outlast the rest of the people at Rocky Hill who are either
physically dead or blighted inwardly.

Warren is poised in his general view of things between an
outright pessimism, which is most intense when due to self-
dramatized frustrations, and a too easy optimism, which feels
it can control to its own advantage the conditions of life.
Warren is pessimistic to the degree that he feels life is possible only because we do not have to face realities too often.
He condemns both Lilburn and the earlier Jefferson for not facing them at all, yet he knows also that mankind cannot stand
too much reality. Life is possible only because of its "discontinuity." A partial glimpse of the truth is about all that
we can ordinarily endure. Otherwise the pressures upon us
might cause us to go mad. In the conduct of life, discretion
is all-important, for it is an outward sign of inner balance.
Jefferson's ultimate reasoned position and, by extension, Warren's own is a qualified optimism or a meliorative pessimism:
"we are condemned to some hope," says Jefferson at the last to
contrast with the fulsomeness of his earlier utterances and
with the blackness of his intervening despair. The fact that
Grace is possible, that a modicum of knowledge may be attained,
that tentative definition is possible implies that a construc-
tive point of view is, in part, valid. Extreme optimism or
extreme pessimism are both false since they both falsify the
facts. Warren is not sure, however, how far he ought to stand
from either pole. Lucy Lewis is his avatar: the spaciousness
of her personality, superior to both transient enthusiasm and
soured despair, induced in the slaves under her control an
enthusiastic loyalty which to them — and to Warren — represented a serenity that transcended in value their love for her
and her love for them.

Neil Nakadate

The Function of Colloquy
in *Brother to Dragons*

At the end of *All the King's Men* (1946), when Jack Burden
goes "out of history into history and the awful responsibility
of Time," he is inspired by an author whose own stance toward
the material of his fictions has shifted considerably from
that of his earlier years. From this point on, neither Burden
nor Robert Penn Warren will be as distanced from the world of
liability and fact as he was before confronting the awesome
presence of Willie Stark. In the case of Burden, inertia and
illusion, sarcasm and disdain have given way to action and
accountability in the world of men. In the case of Warren,
where (in *Night Rider,* for example) the distance was more
aesthetic than ethical, the implied stance of the invisible
author gives way to the acknowledged presence of the writer
in his work, both rhetorically and philosophically. There is
much of Warren in the narrator-historian of *World Enough and
Time* (1950), for example, and in *Promises: Poems 1954-1956*
(1957), the voice of the poet-father could hardly be more
poignant or clear. In *Brother to Dragons: A Tale in Verse
and Voices* (1953), the foreshortening of narrative distance
and the surfacing of direct philosophical statement result
in a compelling colloquy unique in Warren's *oeuvre*.

The crux of the tale and subject of the colloquy is the
murder, dismemberment, and cremation of a Negro slave by
Lilburn and Isham Lewis — a shocking, even repulsive event.
(Next to this, the barn-burning of *Night Rider,* the assassi-
nations of *All the King's Men,* and the passion and murder
of *World Enough and Time* seem easy enough to comprehend — and
acknowledge.) The incident is so repulsive, in fact, as to resist assessment; even as homicide, the crime seems particularly wanton and inexplicable. We could reject it as "inhuman."
It is typical of Warren, however, that he insists on explicating the issues raised and develops a viable form for doing so.

The issues emerge for him because the killers in this case were nephews of Thomas Jefferson: "The philosopher of our liberties and the architect of our country and the prophet of human perfectibility had this in the family blood."[1]   Warren is interested in what Enlightenment man might say when informed of his darkest potentialities, reflected in the actions of countrymen and kin; he is eager to examine the incongruity between our elusive ideals and immediate reality, and the self-deception and error to which this often leads.   As D. H. Lawrence once observed, "You can't idealize the essential brute blood-activity, the brute blood desires, the basic, sardonic blood-knowledge."[2]   The verse colloquium, the form of the poem, emerges in order to make such "blood-knowledge" possible. "Violence is a component of our experience," Warren tells us. "It is a component of ourselves.   Therefore, we are involved in the tale of violence."   But it is crucial, he adds, "to know the nature of our involvement — discover it bit by bit — the context of our involvement.   And...the effective thing is when you begin to sense the context...the thing that's there, mirroring your own possibilities."[3]   The tale of *Brother to Dragons* is such that while one voice is sufficient to cite the facts, several are needed to frame their context and reveal their implications — and ultimately to accept the knowledge they offer.   As his historical "Notes" remind us, and as is often the case in Warren, it is a confrontation with the past which gives rise to this book (the murder occurred in 1811); but in the end Warren's primary concern in *Brother to Dragons* is with the meaning of the tale and the manner of discovering that meaning.   Here, as in *World Enough and Time* and *All the King's Men,* his impulse is philosophical and his mode is inquisition.   As always in Warren's work, at the heart of the discussion are human sin and suffering and the need to seek redemption through knowledge: suffering must be understood so that wisdom might be possible.[4]

It is only through trial and error that Warren arrives at a form which will enable him to articulate his interest in the tale.   He starts and rejects novelistic and dramatic versions, and then begins a narrative poem, in the manner of his "Ballad of Billie Potts" (1944).   But the "folk simplicity" of this form will not do.

> For the beauty of such simplicity is only
> That the action is always and perfectly self-contained.
> And is an image that comes as its own perfect explanation
> In shock or sweetness to the innocent heart.

The ballad treatment is tempting but inadequate, for the action of Lilburn's story can only be explained

> by our most murderous
> Complicities, and our sad virtue, too.
> No, the action is not self-contained, but contains

Us too, and is contained by us, and is
Only an image of the issue of our most distressful self-
    definition.[5]

The explanation, the self-definition, lies in man, not the
long-dead figures of the historical past; the appropriate form
must contain "us." Warren finally decides to construct a
verse colloquium, "a dialogue of all the characters, including
Jefferson, at some unspecified place and time — really 'no
place' and 'no time.' This would allow me, I hoped, to get
out of the box of mere chronology, and of incidental circumstantiality."[6] He summons what Jeremiah Beaumont, the confused idealist of *World Enough and Time,* would call "a great
chorus of truth in many voices" in order to affirm the brotherhood of democrat and dragon, suicide and slave, and of these
several with the poet.
    The colloquium structure allows Warren to escape the trou-
blesome flatness of the very documents which inspired the poem,
and it enables him, as the "R.P.W." of the poem, to ask questions, forge definitions, and influence intellectual direction.
He becomes a participant in a discussion in which he has more
than an academic investment and more than token control, and
his overt willingness to give up authorial omniscience is a
subterfuge both calculated and humane; it is the enabling tactic in the creation of a dialogue. At the same time, the Jefferson to whom Warren addresses himself has lost the self-
possession which once enabled him to create. Having witnessed
the outrages of American as well as family history, he is disillusioned and alienated. Like the Adam Stanton who refuses
to take charge of Willie Stark's hospital, he now rejects in
disdain that which he would earlier have embraced. "'It is because he is a romantic, and has a picture of the world in his
head,'" says Jack Burden of Adam, "'and when the world doesn't
conform in any respect to the picture, he wants to throw the
world away. Even if that means throwing out the baby with the
bath.'"[7] Jefferson's definition of man, his "picture," like
his description of the Maison Quarrée at Nîmes, was based on
precision, proportion, and harmony; "the Square House spoke to
my heart of some fair time/ Beyond the Roman tax-squeeze, and
the imperial/ Licentiousness, and the Gothic Dark" (41). Like
his French contemporary, Condorcet, he voiced a deep faith in
the progress of the human spirit; he lived, however, in "a
pride past pride,/ In my identity with the definition of man"
(6). His definition was incomplete, and hence his faith; he
did not perceive the doubleness of the promise, the complexity
of potential, the irony of experience. "And thus my minotaur,"
Jefferson declares;

                    better, indeed,
Had it been the manifest beast and the circumstantial
Avatar of destruction. But no beast then: the towering
Definition, angelic, arrogant, abstract,

> Greaved in glory, thewed with light, the bright
> Brow tall as dawn. I could not see the eyes.
> . . . .
> I did not know its eyes were blind.   (9-10)

Rather than discipline and design, Jefferson has seen dispro-
portion, chaos, and the grotesque contortions of the meathouse
murder. The "Shade of the Gothic night" (39) can eclipse "the
law of Rome and the eternal/ Light of just proportion and the
heart's harmony" (40). Overwhelming the firm assertions and
measured phrases of the Declaration is the time-transcending
scream of the murdered slave.

Outraged and disgusted by his nephews' crime, Jefferson
has plunged from self-confident prophecy to self-indulgent
hindsight. He can only repudiate as meaningless gestures in
a metaphysical swamp his own humanitarian efforts and those of
others — "Marmosets in mantles, beasts in boots, parrots in
pantaloons" (6) — to define the glory of human effort. He
would acknowledge only the possibility of animality, corruption, and terror:

> beyond some groped-at corner, hulked
> In the blind dark, hock-deep in ordure, its beard
> And shag foul-scabbed, and when the hoof heaves —
> Listen! — the foulness sucks like mire.
>
> The beast waits. He is the infamy of Crete.
> He is the midnight's enormity. He is
> Our brother, our darling brother.   (7)

And Jefferson would admit of only one reality: "Pain, and from
that inexhaustible superflux/ We may give other pain as our
prime definition — " (132). At this point Jefferson comprehends the brotherhood of man with Minotaur and dragon; he does
not understand the significance of the kinship or the nature
of filial responsibility.

Warren, however, refuses to take Jefferson as seriously
in his self-indulgence as Jefferson takes himself. It is the
poet who senses the incompleteness of the President's vision
and the selfishness of his repudiations. And it will be the
poet who, by means of the colloquy, calls the President back
from his heresy of despair. Quick, tough, ironic, and totally
aware of the perverse appeal of quiet desperation, R.P.W. establishes his intense, inquisitive stance and then goes on to
voice the central paradox of the poem:

> ...Despite all naturalistic considerations,
> Or in the end because of naturalistic considerations,
> We must believe in virtue. There is no
> Escape.

In the end, "virtue is/ Only the irremediable logic of all
the anguish/ Your cunning could invent or heart devise" (29,

30). Of course Jefferson would like to believe that naturalistic forces prevail, for if "philosophic resignation" can be
equated with "the fatigue of the relaxed nerve," then catfish
can be likened to hog snake and both to Lilburn Lewis, and all
can be exorcised from the President's mind. "There's no forgiveness for our being human," says Jefferson; "It is the in-
expugnable error" (24). And later:

> Nothing would change nothing!
> For Lilburn is an absolute of our essential
> Condition, and as such, would ingurgitate
> All, and all you'd give, all hope, all heart,
> Would only be disbursed down that rat hole of the ultimate
>   horror.
> Nothing would change.   (93)

Clearly Lilburn *is* disgusting — in committing the axe-
murder itself, in the sadism he practices on brother (Isham),
wife (Laetitia), surrogate mother (Aunt Cat), and dog, and
later in his solipsistic sorrow when "He craves the sight of
the wounded earth" (103) — and it is this which at first makes
it easy on Jefferson, R.P.W., and us. But as Warren repeatedly reminds us, both here and elsewhere, if alteration of our
humanness is impossible, then the search for or offering of
"forgiveness" for this condition is a source of "obscene grat-
ification," a cheap catharsis. The rhetoric of "forgiveness"
distracts us from the fact that where error is a condition of
existence, innocence and guilt are relative terms. If we know
anything of the mystery of the heart, it is that all actions
are a matter of will, of decision and choice — both Lilburn's
and ours.

> ...The accomplished was once the unaccomplished
> And the existing was once the non-existing.
> And that transition was the agony of will
> And anguish of option — or such it seems
> To any man who has striven in the hot day and glare of
>   contingency
> Or who has heard the breath of darkness stop
> At the moment of revelation.   (111)

The question is whether one is to exploit "the agony of will/
And anguish of option" in the interest of good (as does R.P.W.)
or ignore it to the benefit of evil (Lilburn and, in his own
way, Jefferson).
  A proper stance toward agony and anguish is achieved
through perspective, and here it is the perspective of the
poet which clarifies for us virtue's "irremediable logic."
The grotesque murder was "Just an episode in the long drift
of the human/ Narrative," Warren tells Laetitia Lewis:

> there's always and forever
> Enough of guilt to rise and coil like miasma

From the fat sump and cess of common consciousness
To make any particular hour seem most appropriate
For Gabriel's big tootle.   (64)

As Jefferson later learns through Laetitia herself, human experience contains myriad unnamed anxieties and acts (they need
not, like Lilburn's Oedipal drive, be dramatized), but chaos
and despair should not hold sway simply because we do not understand them. Warren will neither wallow in Lilburn's corruption nor join in Jefferson's lament. He waits for Jefferson to accept knowledge with his pain. In the meantime the
poet warns his complacent reader to refrain from judging and
rejecting Jefferson for his error. It is the voice of self-
irony which asks in speaking of Lilburn, "Why does he suffer
and understand nothing?/ Were we in his place, we should surely understand./ For we are instructed in the mystery of the
heart..." (103). The self-irony must apply when we speak of
Jefferson, too. Warren the teacher knows that instruction
does not always lead to understanding, or understanding to
knowledge, and that at best modern man is open to both the advantages and the temptations of historical hindsight. He asks
us if tales like this are intriguing only because their melodramatic cast excuses us from all responsibility for guilt;
he asks if we relish the search for the scapegoat-killer only
because this means that we ourselves will never be accused.
He asks how might we, the heirs to Jefferson's dream, also be
brothers to the dragon, Lilburn Lewis. If we are to rejoice
in the benevolent possibilities of will, then we must also acknowledge its darkest needs. "We have to want to kill King
Duncan," Warren remarks elsewhere, "to enjoy *Macbeth*."[8] It is
possible, R.P.W. allows, "That George himself was quite responsible" (138), that the slave was a self-styled victim and in a
sense victimized Lilburn; however, he reminds Jefferson, this
is only "A way to say we're all each other's victim./ Potentially, at least" (140).

But by now Jefferson has withdrawn from the world of men,
and it is not until the arrival of Meriwether Lewis, his nephew and spiritual son, that he is forced to respond (though not
yet constructively) to the challenge of the colloquy.[9] Apparently a victim of his own despairing hand somewhere in the
Natchez Trace, Meriwether comes to accuse his kinsman: "I am
the man you did give the bullet to./ I am the man you killed."
And he adds: "It was your lie that sent me forth, in hope"
(176-77). It was Meriwether who co-led the great expedition
to wilderness and "Shining Mountains," unknown beasts and rigorous seasons, Pacific vision (*"O Ocian in view! O! the joy!"*),
and the return. And it was Meriwether, once more in the company of "civil" men, and serving as governor of the Territory
he had explored, who became a victim of his own naiveté and
others' evil. Having been falsely accused of embezzlement and
mismanagement, and having taken his own life because of it,

Meriwether now rejects as a lie Jefferson's claim "that men
are capable/ Of the brotherhood of justice" (182).

> Had I not loved, and lived, your lie, then I
> Had not been sent unbuckled and unbraced
> To find the end — oh, the wilderness was easy! —
> But to find, in the end, the tracklessness of the human
>   heart.   (184)

If the black slave George was the victim of Lilburn's love,
then Meriwether is the victim of Jefferson's virtue and vanity.
The accusation is direct and unequivocal, but Jefferson responds by denying responsibility, just as he has already rejected Lilburn.

It is Lucy Lewis, speaking out of her love for both Lilburn (her son) and Jefferson (her brother), who finally makes
the accusation stick:

> We had hoped to escape complicity,
> You and I, dear Brother. But we have seen the unfolding
> Of Time and complicity, and I, even in my love,
> And in the milk of my breast, was in guilty involvement,
> And my son died. And you, even in your aspiration,
> Could prime the charge for our poor Meriwether.
> And this is why in our best gifts we could give
> Only the worst. It is because my love and your aspiration
> Could not help but carry some burden of ourselves,
> And to be innocent of that burden, at last,
> You must take his hand, and recognize, at last,
> That his face is only a mirror of your possibilities,
> And recognize that you
> Have deeper need of him than he of you,
> For whatever hope we have is not by repudiation,
> And whatever health we have is not by denial,
> But in confronting the terror of our condition.
> All else is a lie.   (191-92)

Any abstract ideal ("my love and your aspiration") is insufficient in itself, for exposed to the uncertain world of men
("the unfolding/ Of Time and complicity") it is open to distortion, misuse, and betrayal — in short, to destruction and failure. Articulation of an ideal does not guarantee noninvolve-
ment and innocence, and at its worst (e.g., as in Jefferson
here) it simply betrays an urge toward willful ignorance of
culpability and choice. It is not true that, as Jefferson argues, once having given a project his blessing, he need not be
concerned with its practical effects; the argument is as bankrupt for him as it is for such other Warren protagonists as
John Brown, Perse Munn, Willie Stark, and Jeremiah Beaumont.
Lucy suggests that it is only by acknowledging his own worst
possibilities in the disgusting figure of Lilburn ("You must
take his hand") can he define the dream to suit men's needs.
Confronted by R.P.W. as interrogator and Lucy and Meri-

wether as witnesses, Jefferson's bitterness gives way to weariness and confusion; he fumbles for the phrase with which to voice his sadness.

>   Yes, Meriwether said I lied,
> But long since I had lost the strength for that lie,
> But cannot yet find the strength to endure without it,
> But can affirm my need only in the curse and rejection
> Of him who had robbed me of the comfort of the lie.
> I am tired.   (192)

But Lucy, like R.P.W., would have him cast off his resignation; she strengthens him with a reassertion. "We are human," she says, "and must work/ In the shade of our human condition. The dream remains" (193), she adds, but only in that context. At last Jefferson, recalling an old letter to John Adams, acknowledges "That the dream of the future is not/ Better than the fact of the past, no matter how terrible./ For without the fact of the past we cannot dream the future" (193). (The narrator of *All the King's Men* had said, "If you could not accept the past and its burden there was no future.") Finally Jefferson acknowledges that "we are condemned to reach yet for a reason" for our anguish and guilt. "We are condemned to some hope" (194). The emphasis here is on the word "yet," for creation is not a finite act, but an ongoing gesture which characterizes the vitality of the human condition. The declaration of possibility must be remade and revitalized, for

>   if there is to be reason, we must
> Create the possibility
> Of reason, and we can create it only
> From the circumstances of our most evil despair.
> We must strike the steel of wrath on the stone of guilt,
> And hope to provide, thus, in the midst of our coiling
>   darkness
> The incandescence of the heart's great flare.
> And in that illumination I should hope to see
> How all creation validates itself,
> For whatever you create, you create yourself by it,
> And in creating yourself you will create
> The whole wide world and gleaming West anew.   (194-95)

Like Jeremiah Beaumont and Jack Burden, Jefferson revises his conception of human potential and responsibility, and in doing so, redefines himself. Knowledge is the seed of creation, and re-creation itself is the definitive act. In *Brother to Dragons,* Jefferson engages, haltingly but in the end successfully, in the fundamental New World impulse to transform and redefine the self.

At the end the poem is more Warren's than Jefferson's, a matter of reconciliation of man in the present rather than re-creation of men of the past. The last dozen pages of *Brother to Dragons* concern the man earlier described as "A fellow of

forty, a stranger, and a fool,/ Red-headed, freckled, lean, a
little stooped,/ Who yearned to be understood, to make communication..." (26). And it is Warren, scholar and teacher, who
claims along with Jefferson that

> nothing we had,
> Nothing we were,
> Is lost.
> All is redeemed,
> In knowledge.   (195)

Now, having reconciled Jefferson to Lilburn, the poet must
reconcile himself to Jefferson; "that most happy and difficult
conclusion," he had called it, "To be reconciled to the father's own reconciliation" (28). For to be reconciled metaphysically to the forefather is to be reconciled to his own father's
father, whose now-vanished house and whatever "hope or hapless-
ness" it once held is itself "a fiction of human/ Possibility
past" (204). Revisiting the site of the Lewis house, this
time in the dead of winter, the poet reinforces at his own expense (not Lilburn's now, not Jefferson's) our awareness that
creation and fabrication are often confused and that the im-
posing images of the mind's eye, whether of President or poet,
are often only the products of our expectations and need.
He recalls his first visit, in an earlier July, and how he
"damned the heat and briar,/ Saw-vine, love-vine, and rose"
and

> clambered through
> The tall, hot gloom of oak and ironweed,
> Where grapevine, big as boas, had shagged and looped
> Jungle convolvement and visceral delight.   (207)

Yet he sees that in reality the thicket is meager and "scrag-
gly-thin," and the "piddling" trees scattered and bare. Of
course "winter makes things small. All things draw in"; but
even granting this, he confesses, "I had plain misremembered,/
Or dreamed a world appropriate for the tale" (208). Even now
Warren, again like Jefferson, must guard against offering his
own sweeping vision "'as the image and confirmation/ Of some
faith past our consistent failure, and the filth we strew'"
(210). He must, in other words, resist the temptation to see
radiance in the grandeur of nature and the nature of words,
rather than in man himself, for

> whatever the gleam of massive magnificence or glimmer
>   of shy joy
> May be, it can only resemble the moon
> And is but mirror to the human heart's steadfast and
>   central illumination.

Magnificence is ours, Warren asserts, and also responsibility:

> If there is glory, the burden, then, is ours.
> If there is virtue, the burden, then, is ours.   (211)

We cannot escape our burden of guilt, he has told us; the tale
of kinsman and dragon compels us to acknowledge that, like
Lewis and Jefferson, "We have lifted the meat-axe in the elation of love and justice" (213). Now he also accepts a redeeming burden, our obligation to "argue the necessity of virtue"
(214). It is the burden he has persuaded Jefferson to bear.

Finally R.P.W.'s rigorous treatment of Jefferson is another way of demanding much of himself, his invocation of Lilburn, Meriwether, and the rest a voicing of his need (better:
obligation) to know himself. For finally it is the obligation
of the separate self to acknowledge separateness and struggle
with the texture of experience — past and present and past-in-
present — in order to come to terms with it. "Isolation is
the common lot," he asserts, "And paradoxically, it is only
by/ That isolation that we know how to name/ The human bond
and thus define the self" (205-206).[10] In *Brother to Dragons*
Warren elicits the confirmatory testimony (alienation, disillusionment, despair) of men like Lilburn, Jefferson, and
Meriwether as witness to his (and our) own separateness; he
elicits Lucy's demanding spirit of responsibility and love in
order to strengthen his own. In their respective combinations
of confusion, illusion, and hope they confirm what is common
to the lot of man. Finally acknowledgement of our common involvement is made possible by a community of voices — a community of voices makes possible a community of man. "Whatever
you create," Jefferson had finally realized, "you can create
yourself by it."

The form of a work of literature, Warren tells us, "the
organic relation among all the elements of the work," is a
vision of our experience too. In *Brother to Dragons,* it is by
invoking a chorus of voices from a century and a half ago, and
making the voices render the meaning of their history, that
Warren fully realizes his image of man. "The form is a vision
of experience, but of experience fulfilled and redeemed in
knowledge, the ugly with the beautiful, the slayer with the
slain, what was known as shape now known as time, what was
known in time now known as shape, a new knowledge. It is not
a thing detached from the world but a thing springing from the
deep engagement of spirit with the world."[11] In his "tale in
verse and voices" Warren achieves "identification/ With the
glory of the human effort" (213) and a revelation of complicity, necessity, and the direction of fulfillment. The achievement enables Jefferson, Warren, and the reader "to go into the
world of action and liability" (215), to confront the world of
men.

1. Robert Penn Warren, "The Way It Was Written," *New York Times
Book Review* 58 (Aug. 23, 1953), 6.
2. *Studies in Classic American Literature* (New York: Viking,

1964), 105. We might also recall that elsewhere (62) Lawrence describes "the essential American soul" as "hard, isolate, stoic, and a killer."

3. Robert Penn Warren, in "Violence in Literature" [A Symposium, with William Styron, Robert Coles and Theodore Solotaroff], *American Scholar* 37 (Summer 1968), 490. Later in this discussion Warren observes that it is a specific brand of violence which has long preoccupied his imagination. "I equated long ago with a world where violence was quite common, was always intensely personal, was based on a personal grievance, a personal thwarting of some kind; but it had to do with the ego, or as they called it in sociology in those days, 'status homicide' — as opposed to homicide for gain" (493).

4. Readers of both Faulkner and Warren should recognize interesting similarities between *Absalom, Absalom!* and *Brother to Dragons*. The relentless R.P.W. recalls Shreve McCannon, for example, and the pained Jefferson shares much with Quentin Compson. Both books are, of course, colloquies with a historical focus.

5. Robert Penn Warren, *Brother to Dragons: A Tale in Verse and Voices* (New York: Random, 1953), 43. Subsequent page references will be incorporated into the text.

6. Warren, "The Way It Was Written," 6. Cf. the complementary remarks of John L. Stewart, *The Burden of Time: The Fugitives and Agrarians* (Princeton: Princeton Univ. Press, 1965), 510-12.

7. Robert Penn Warren, *All the King's Men* (New York: Harcourt Brace, 1946), 262. Frederick P. W. McDowell provides a useful summary of Jefferson's case in "Psychology and Theme in *Brother to Dragons*," *PMLA* 70 (Sept. 1955), 577-78.

8. Warren, "Violence in Literature," 490.

9. And, according to Stewart, it is not until this point that Warren comes to fullest terms with the writing of the poem itself. "Meriwether's accusation, for Warren, was the turning point of the poem. He had the shape of his meaning." *The Burden of Time,* 512.

10. In his early poem "Revelation" Warren had said: "In separateness only does love learn definition." Here the context is different, but the conviction is sustained. For a discussion of "The Persona RPW in Warren's *Brother to Dragons*," see Dennis M. Dooley, *Mississippi Quarterly* 25 (Winter 1971), 19-30.

11. Robert Penn Warren, "Knowledge and the Image of Man," *Sewanee Review* 62 (Spring 1955), 191-92.

Victor Strandberg

Warren's Osmosis

To thread forth a central theme out of a writer's whole
corpus can be risky business: Ernest Hemingway's resentment
of the "psychic wound" interpretation of his novels is a case
in point. To isolate such a theme in a writer like Robert
Penn Warren is even riskier. Author of eight novels, four
major volumes of poetry, four non-fiction books, and innumerable other writings, Warren is more complex and variegated
than most writers, both in form and theme. Nevertheless running through that wide scope of fiction and poetry, and even
through the non-fiction studies, a central vision does stand
forth. In a phrase, Warren's theme is the osmosis of being.
     The phrase is Warren's own, articulated most elaborately
in his essay, "Knowledge and the Image of Man" (*Sewanee Review,* Winter, 1955, p.186): "[Man is] in the world with continual and intimate interpenetration, an inevitable osmosis of
being, which in the end does not deny, but affirms, his identity." It is also articulated in most of Warren's creative
writing, usually implicitly, as when a character in *Promises*
is awakened to the book's highest promise, "You fool, poor
fool, all Time is a dream, and we're all one Flesh, at last,"
but sometimes explicitly, as when Blanding Cottshill tells
Bradwell Tolliver (*Flood,* p.353), "Things are tied together.
... There's some spooky interpenetration of things, a mystic
osmosis of being, you might say."*
     The central importance of osmosis of being in Warren's
work is seen in connection with his predominant theme of identity or self-definition. For such osmosis is the final answer
to the problem of identity, and is indeed the only answer in
the world, as Warren sees it. An awakening to this truth is
what normally provides the structure for Warren's fiction and

     *Since I quote so widely and frequently in this discussion, I
thought it best to incorporate page references into my main text and
so avoid excessive footnoting. All page references refer to the books
listed in my bibliography.

poetry. For example, it is this osmosis of being that finally
requires Jack Burden in *All the King's Men* to accept responsibility for history; that causes Thomas Jefferson in *Brother to
Dragons* to accept complicity in murder; that leads a long series of Warren characters in all his novels towards acceptance
of a father figure, however shabby or tainted; and that draws
forth the theme of a reconciliation within the self, between
conscious and unconscious zones of the psyche, in much of Warren's poetry. And ultimately, it is this osmosis of being
that imparts whatever meaning the self may have in the light
of eternity; that absorbs the self into the totality of time
and nature with the consoling promise, often repeated in Warren's work, that "nothing is ever lost."

Hence, Warren's osmosis has moral, metaphysical, and psychological ramifications; it is his contribution to modern religious thought, having an ethic and a mystical dimension.
Looking back over Warren's career with hindsight, moreover, we
may find that osmosis was there all the time, much like T. S.
Eliot's Christianity, implicit in the early works and explicit
later on. Like Eliot's Christianity, again, Warren's osmosis
is evoked in the early work by negative implication: the naturalistic fragmentation of the world is intolerable and cries
out for some sense of oneness. In "Mexico Is a Foreign Country: Five Studies in Naturalism," a poem written about 1943,
a narrator watches some soldiers marching — "And I am I, and
they are they,/ And this is this, and that is that" — with a
vain wish that "everything/ Take hands with us and pace the
music in a ring." And in the fiction, likewise, osmosis of
being is what Warren's characters should be seeking, relating
themselves to the totality of time and nature and society,
whereas they characteristically are observed bent towards opposite ends, narrowing their identity to a basis of fame, sexual
prowess, success in business, or membership in a philosophical,
religious, or political sect.

I

To define the meaning and importance of osmosis in Warren's work, then, I should like to examine in turn its three
major dimensions: psychological, social, and metaphysical.
Let us begin with the workings of osmosis within the individual psyche, where, Warren feels, something is badly wrong in
the way of self-definition. What is wrong, precisely, is that
the Freudian id, or Jungian shadow — which is mainly what Warren is getting at in his recurrent motif of "original sin" —
this darker, more bestial part of the psyche has been denied
its place in reality. An innocent, idealistic figure like
Thomas Jefferson (in *Brother to Dragons*), seriously undertaking to remake the human project from scratch and to do it
right this time; or Tobias Sears, the utopian Transcendental-
ist in *Band of Angels;* or Adam (the name is deliberately cho-

sen) Stanton, the physician to the poor in *All the King's Men*
— such high-minded humanists are not about to think themselves
brothers to dragons or indeed to concede any reality to a
monster-self within.

But the reality of evil, though denied for a time, will
finally make its presence known. As Carl Gustav Jung says,
in *The Undiscovered Self* (pp.107-8): "The evil that comes to
light in man and that undoubtedly dwells within him is of
gigantic proportions.... We are always, thanks to our human
nature, potential criminals.... None of us stands outside humanity's black collective shadow." In Warren's narratives,
humanity's black collective shadow is bodied forth in some of
his most memorable characters and episodes: in the two hatchet-
wielders, Lilburn Lewis (*Brother to Dragons*) and Big Billie
Potts of "The Ballad of Billie Potts"; in the gradually esca-
lating violence of "The Free Farmers' Brotherhood of Protection and Control" in *Night Rider;* in the degrading trip to Big
Hump's island in *World Enough and Time;* in the horrific episode of the slave raid into Africa in *Band of Angels;* in the
frenzied sexual orgy following Brother Sumpter's preaching in
The Cave; in the callous butchery of Negroes by whites during
the New York draft riots of 1863 as portrayed in *Wilderness;*
in the swamprat animalism of Frog-Eye in *Flood*. And actual
history, as discussed in Warren's books, adds confirming evidence. Warren's first book, *John Brown: The Making of a Martyr* (1929), shows the famous abolitionist to be a murderous
fanatic, an obvious forebear of Warren's recurring fictional
killers who lift rifle or meat-axe in an elation of justice,
while his most recent book, *Who Speaks for the Negro?* (1965),
identifies Malcolm X as the monster self in the inner dark:
"Malcolm X can evoke, in the Negro, even in Martin Luther King,
that self with which he, too, must deal, in shock and fright,
or in manic elation.... Malcolm X is many things, He is the
face not seen in the mirror.... He is the nightmare self. He
is the secret sharer" (p.266). (In saying this, shortly before Malcolm X's assassination, Warren was thinking particularly of the Negro leader's statement at a Harlem rally, "We
need a Mau Mau to win freedom!" — p.265.)

From the beginning, Warren saw this discovery of a beast
within the self as a basic structure in his work. Away back
in his first novel, *Night Rider,* a piously Bible-quoting Professor Ball is heard to say (p.142), "Yes, sir, I'm a man of
peace. But it's surprising to a man what he'll find in himself sometimes." What Professor Ball comes to find in himself
is murder, cowardice, and betrayal, causing the death of the
book's main character, Percy Munn. And in the next novel, the
masterful *At Heaven's Gate,* Slim Sarrett likewise traces out
the melancholy curve of self-discovery. Early in the book,
Slim is the artist-intellectual writing of literature and self-
knowledge ("Bacon wrote: Knowledge is power.... Shakespeare
wrote: Self-knowledge is power" — p.191), but when his own

self-knowledge comes to include the murder-cowardice-betrayal
syndrome, Slim writes ruefully not of power but of a dark un-
banishable being within the self:

> It came from your mother's womb, and she screamed at the
>   moment of egress.
> The family doctor slapped breath in, relighted his bitten
>   cigar
> While the old nurse washed it and washed it, without com-
>   plete success.

And in Warren's most recent novel, *Flood,* the main character
feels a beast within himself quite literally: "Then, in the
inner darkness of himself...the black beast heaved at him...
that black beast with cold fur like hairy ice that drowsed in
the deepest inner dark, or woke to snuffle about, or even, as
now, might heave unexpectedly at him and breathe upon him"
(p.336).

And if Warren's fiction hints at a beast — a darker being
or pollution of "original sin" within the self — Warren's poetry describes it much more explicitly. "And our innocence
needs, perhaps, new definition," Warren said at the end of
"Billie Potts," and it is pretty clear that this new definition of innocence must embrace, like osmosis, the guilt that
"always and forever [will] rise and coil like miasma/ From
the fat sump and cess of common consciousness," as R.P.W.
describes it in *Brother to Dragons* (p.64). In all his major
volumes of poetry, Warren refers to this guilt in the common
consciousness, which Jung calls "humanity's black collective
shadow," in terms of animal imagery. *Eleven Poems on the Same
Theme* (1942) takes the acknowledgment of this shadow self as
its major structure. The conscious ego, sanctimonious and
sure of an innocent identity, locks the shadow self out of the
house of the psyche in a poem called "Original Sin: A Short
Story," where the darker self acts like a loyal though rejected animal: "you have heard/ It fumble your door before it
whimpers and is gone:/ It acts like the old hound that used to
snuffle your door and moan," and later, "it goes to the back-
yard and stands like an old horse cold in the pasture." In
"Crime," the conscious ego, finding that the shadow self simply won't go away, murders and buries it in the cellar, only
to have it rise again: "...memory drips, a pipe in the cellar-
dark/ And in its hutch and hole.../ The cold heart heaves like
a toad." And so the *Eleven Poems* ends with "Terror," a poem
in which the shadow self that had seemed so docile and easily
repudiated earlier now assumes, genie-like, terrifying dimensions in the reality of actual history (circa 1940), where
"the face.../ Bends to the bombsight over bitter Helsingfors"
and "the brute crowd roars...in the Wilhelmplatz," while "you
now, guiltless, sink/ To rest in lobbies."

In Warren's next major poetic work, *Brother to Dragons,*
Thomas Jefferson also thinks himself "guiltless" until his

sister and R.P.W. finally get him to clasp his murderous nephew's hand and so accept oneness with Lilburn, the emblem (together with minotaur, catfish, and serpent) of man's darker
self within. The key embodiment of the shadow self in *Brother
to Dragons* is borne by the serpent that scares R.P.W. in his
summer visit to what's left of the Lewis house. And though
R.P.W. calls it "just a snake," it turns out to have suspi-
ciously human characteristics linking it to the "old hound"
and "old horse" metaphors (noted above) of *Eleven Poems on the
Same Theme:*

> ...he reared
> Up high, and scared me, for a fact. But then
> The bloat head sagged an inch, the tongue withdrew,
> And on the top of that strong stalk the head
> Wagged slow, benevolent and sad and sage,
> As though it understood our human pitifulness
> And forgave all, and asked forgiveness, too.   (p.35)

That last line states what the relationship between the conscious ego and the shadow self should be, but isn't (until
the very end) in Jefferson's case: "I still reject, cast out,
repudiate,/ And squeeze from my blood the blood of Lilburn"
(p.62). In *Promises,* too, man's natural revulsion towards the
shadow self is implicit in the slaying of a snake by some men
getting hay:

> ...a black snake rears big in his ruined room.
> . . . .
> Men shout, ring around. He can't get away.
> Yes, they are men, and a stone is there.
>
> Snagged high on a pitchfork tine, he will make
> Slow arabesque till the bullbats wake.
> An old man, standing stooped, detached,
> Spits once, says, "Hell, just another snake."
> ("The Snake")

But of course the beast within the self is not exorcised by
such impulsive destruction of other creatures, though men are
prone to locate evil anywhere outside the self and then move
ahead with the destruction, whether of snake, octopus (similarly slain elsewhere in *Promises*), or human enemies.
   Warren's most recent collection of poems, *You, Emperors,
and Others* (1960), speaks of a beast in the psyche in many
places. The emperors Warren writes of are Domitian and Tiber-
ius, whom the Roman historian Suetonius considered monstrous
criminals for using their imperial power in the service of
greed, murder, incest, and unlimited orgiastic pleasures.
The "You" in Warren's title, however, is not greatly superior
to the emperors, having a tainted ancestry ("Your mother preferred the more baroque positions./ Your father's legerdemain
marks the vestry accounts.") and a criminal character of trou-

blesome if not imperial proportions, as is illustrated in "The
Letter About Money, Love, or Other Comfort, If Any," in which
the narrator pursues a beastly alter ego from place to place
("you had blown, the rent in arrears, your bathroom a sty")
and from crime to crime ("your Llewellin setter/ was found in
the woodshed, starved to death" and "you fooled with the female Fulbrights/ at the Deux Magots and the Flore,/ until the
police caught you dead to rights —"). The reality of evil
within the self, then, is set forth in a long and vividly memorable series of vile characters, violent episodes, and beast
images throughout Warren's work, and the acceptance of that
reality is the first step toward psychic wholeness — an internal osmosis of being, as it were.

II

Proceeding from the inner caverns of self to the outer
world of other people, we find an equally long series of technical devices — plot, character, imagery, allusion, irony, and
so forth — sustaining the idea of osmosis on a family and social level. The repeated summons towards a father figure —
felt by Sukie Christian in *Night Rider* (1939), Jerry Calhoun
in *At Heaven's Gate* (1943), Billie Potts in the "Ballad"
(1943), Jack Burden in *All the King's Men* (1946), Jeremiah
Beaumont in *World Enough and Time* (1950), R.P.W. in *Brother
to Dragons* (1953), Rau-Ru (alias Oliver Cromwell Jones) and
Amantha Starr in *Band of Angels* (1955), Ikey Sumpter in *The
Cave* (1959), Adam Rosenzweig in *Wilderness* (1961), and Bradwell Tolliver in *Flood* (1964) — this call to acceptance of a
father is especially fundamental to Warren's work because it
grounds the osmosis of being in physiological fact. As Jack
Burden puts it in *All the King's Men* (p.39): "The child comes
home and the parent puts the hooks in him. The old man, or
the woman, as the case may be, hasn't got anything to say to
the child. All he wants is to have that child sit in a chair
for a couple of hours and then go off to bed under the same
roof.... This thing in itself is not love. It is just something in the blood. It is a kind of blood greed, and it is
the fate of a man. It is the thing which man has which distinguishes him from the happy brute creation. When you get
born your father and mother lost something out of themselves,
and they are going to bust a hame trying to get it back, and
you are it. They know they can't get it all back but they
will get as big a chunk out of you as they can."

It follows, then, that the true villains in Warren's work
are not the hatchet-murderers like Big Billie Potts and Lilburn Lewis so much as those characters who willfully reject
the claims of osmosis. Among these truly damned are Ikey Sumpter in *The Cave* and Slim Sarrett in *At Heaven's Gate,* both of
whom renounced the father, cut all their human ties, and vanished into the vicious and glittering isolation of New York

City. Or sometimes the temptation is more subtle and human
than that offered by New York, like the rich and powerful substitute fathers Bogan Murdock in *At Heaven's Gate* and Aaron
Blaustein in *Wilderness,* glamorous figures who nearly seduce
Jerry Calhoun and Adam Rosenzweig from the memory of their
real fathers, the stooped and shabby ones. Or maybe the sin
of rejection is committed in pride of modernity, as with the
brash young fellow in "Ballad of a Sweet Dream of Peace" in
Promises, who keeps calling his grandma "old fool" and "old
bitch" until some supernatural hogs abruptly appear to chomp
them both into the "oneness of Flesh" that is the book's mystical vision. And sometimes the osmosis is shunned not by
reason of ignorance or a temptation towards wealth and glamour,
but out of a fear of contamination. Thomas Jefferson's reluctance to shake Lilburn's hand with "the blood slick on it" is
a case in point, and similar fear of contamination is delight-
fully portrayed in "Two Studies in Idealism," a poem in *You,
Emperors, and Others* in which a Union soldier, a Harvard graduate of 1861, complains bitterly how a filthy old geezer fighting for the other side had the gall to forgive his death at
the hands of the speaker:

> I tried to slay without rancor, and often succeeded.
> I tried to keep the heart pure, though the hand took stain.
> . . . .
> But they grinned in the dark — they grinned — and I yet
>   see
> That last one. At woods-edge we held, and over the
>   stubble they came with bayonet.
>
> He uttered his yell, he was there! — teeth yellow, some
>   missing.
> *Why, he's old as my father,* I thought, finger frozen on
>   trigger.
> I saw the ambeer on his whiskers, heard the old breath
>   hissing.
> The puncture came small on his chest. 'Twas nothing.
>   The stain then got bigger.
>
> And he said: "Why, son you done done it — I figgered I'd
>   skeered ye."
> Said: "Son, you look puke-pale. Buck up! If it hadn't
>   been you,
> Some other young squirt would a-done it."

Like the serpent who "forgave all, and asked forgiveness, too"
in *Brother to Dragons,* this rebel soldier offers a human communion transcending his loathesome appearance. To be sure,
the Harvard graduate is too clothed in the Right of the Union
Cause ("Touch pitch: be defiled" in his social creed) to accept the old geezer's dying gesture. But such acceptance of
a human communion beyond right and wrong is what he needs to
be saved, nonetheless, as opposed to his dependence on the

"Treasury of Virtue," which is Warren's term for the North's enduring sense of merit in having fought for Right in the Civil War.

Warren's osmosis, then, postulates an ethic of community transcending self and family and tribe, and transcending too the separations worked by time or sin or ignorance. And in the end, the Warren protagonist must accept osmosis even as Jack Burden does, after the deep isolation of his Great Sleep and Great Twitch and Going West periods in *All the King's Men*. Having witnessed a procession of unsatisfactory father figures stream through his life — the Scholarly Attorney, the Tycoon, the Count, the Young Executive, the Judge — Jack Burden comes to accept the first (though not his biological) father in this Whitmanesque parenthesis (p.462): "So now I live in the house which my father left me. With me is my wife, Anne Stanton, and the old man who was once married to my mother.... (Does he think that I am his son? I cannot be sure. Nor can I feel that it matters, for each of us is the son of a million fathers.)"

The consummation of such osmosis of being on a social or family level is seen most strikingly in *Promises,* in a series of lyrics called "Ballad of a Sweet Dream of Peace." Here, in a macabre transition zone between the living and the dead, a brash young initiate is instructed in the mysteries of osmosis. In the following exchange between the initiate and his guide (whose role is much like Virgil's in Dante's *Inferno*), the initiate's speech is in italics, his guide's in regular print:

> *Out there in the dark, what's that horrible chomping?*
> Oh, nothing, just hogs that forage for mast,
> And if you call, "Hoo-pig!" they'll squeal and come
>   romping,
> For they'll know from your voice you're the boy who
>   slopped them in dear, dead days long past.
> *Any hogs that I slopped are long years dead,*
> *And eaten by somebody and evacuated,*
> *So it's simply absurd, what you said.*
> You fool, poor fool, all Time is a dream, and we're
>   all one Flesh, at last,
> And the hogs know that, and that's why they wait....
> > ("Go It Granny — Go It Hog!")

What the hogs wait for is to chomp one and all into the "one Flesh, at last" which their most fleshly of bodies symbolize. They begin, in the above poem, by devouring the initiate's grandma (the skeleton granny he had earlier called "old fool" and "old bitch"), and proceed thence — alarmingly — to the initiate himself, in a poem called "I Guess You Ought to Know Who You Are":

> *...But look, in God's name, I am me!*
> If you are, there's the letter a hog has in charge,

With a gold coronet, and your own name writ large,
And in French, most politely, "Répondez s'il vous plaît."

Our last view of the initiate shows him submitting at last to
the doctrine of "one Flesh," as he meets the hour of his death
in the traditional posture of humility —

Now don't be alarmed we are late.
What's time to a hog? We'll just let them wait.
But for when you are ready, our clients usually say
That to shut the eyes tight and get down on the knees
    is the quickest and easiest way.

Devouring their former devourers, these supernatural hogs provide in the otherworldly dark a universal eucharist, a compul-
sory last supper to which the guest comes to be eaten and absorbed into a collective final identity. This is real osmosis
of being, then, its final object being a transubstantiation
that merges (to return to Warren's *Sewanee Review* essay) "the
ugly with the beautiful, the slayer with the slain," producing
— in whoever can see this — "such a sublimation that the world
which once provoked...fear and disgust may now be totally
loved."

    III

    And so we come to the third major facet of Warren's os-
mosis: the metaphysical dimension, which is the most momentous
in its price and rewards. The immediate price of osmosis is
humility, which, seriously considered (as in Thomas Jefferson's case), is not easily come by; and the ultimate price is
death: a permanent consignment of self to the oneness of Time
and Flesh. This may well involve a final annihilation of the
conscious ego, putting an end to that temporary and prideful
separation from the larger collective being, but such a condition may prove desirable, and is in any case inevitable.
    Part of Warren's concern with the father-son relationship
bears upon this need to accept one's extinction, for in the
natural world the father always comes bearing the gift of life
in one hand and (this is the final meaning of the Billie Potts
saga) a hatchet in the other: "What gift — oh, father, father
— from that dissevering hand?" "The father waits for the son,"
Warren says at the end of "The Ballad of Billie Potts," and so
the son comes, at last, back to what looks like prenatal unconsciousness: "Back to the silence, back to the pool, back/ To
the high pool, motionless, and the unmurmuring dream." And if
he understands osmosis of being properly, he will come unwill-
ingly, when he must, to bow his head to the hatchet-blow:

And you, wanderer, back,
. . . .
To kneel
Here in the evening empty of wind or bird,

> To kneel in the sacramental silence of evening
> At the feet of the old man
> Who is evil and ignorant and old....

Similar illustrations of acceptance appear in Warren's fiction.
In *The Cave,* Jack Harrick, stricken with cancer, at first resents his wife and son living on while he must die: "Old Jack
Harrick wished she were dead, dead so he could love her, and
not hate her as he did when he thought of her lying alone in
her bed on a June night with moon coming in the window, and...
her struggling against the need for a man-shape, simply a man-
shape in the dark, not him, not Jack Harrick" (p.144) and "I
wanted my own son to die" (p.361). But Jack comes to accept
his extinction after he learns of his son's death in the cave.
And in *Promises,* Warren's own parents, Ruth and Robert Warren,
accept the price of osmosis, willing in their deaths that the
generations supplant one another. "Child," the two skeletons
tell their son in his vision at their gravesite, "We died only
that every promise might be fulfilled." Later in *Promises* the
skeleton granny who is devoured by hogs repeats this acceptance of sacrificial death: "I died for love."
     Commitment to one Flesh is further enacted by a series of
Christ figures in Warren's work, such as Jasper Harrick, the
youth who dies in *The Cave* to "save" others (such as Ikey
Sumpter: "*I'm saved,* he thought, and his heart overflowed with
gratitude to Jasper Harrick who had saved him" — p.272) and
to bear guilt for their iniquity (Jasper is blamed for his
younger brother's fornication). And most recently, Brother
Potts in *Flood* makes the Christlike commitment, praying for
a Negro convict who had spat on him without even wiping the
spit away ("and it was running down some. It was a good gob,
to run down...." — p.202), and spending his last days not in
fear for the cancer that has already cost him an arm but
preaching that "the life they had lived was blessed" (p.355).
Clearly, then, Warren's osmosis requires acceptance of one's
annihilation: granny's whisper, "I died for love," means that
she saw the self as a tool to be used and discarded to the advantage of a larger being that goes on and on.
     But if the price of osmosis is high, meaning death for the
conscious ego, the rewards are also high, meaning a kind of
immortality through the ministrations of that shadow self so
often shunned and loathed and locked out of the house of the
psyche. For the shadow self, as made known in dream or animal
intuition, is perfectly at ease in that infinitude of time and
space which smites the conscious mind with anxiety that man
and his Earth are a bubble in a cosmic ocean. The indestructi-
bility of this deeper self was implied in its survival through
Eleven Poems, despite the murder and burial in the cellar, and
this immortality seems even clearer in *Brother to Dragons,*
with particular reference to the serpent and catfish metaphors.
In having "the face of the last torturer," the catfish is

clearly associated with the "original sin" aspect of Warren's thought, but it also has redemptive possibilities not given to the conscious ego. (The ice in the following passage appears to divide the world of light and time and consciousness, above ice, from the timeless, totally dark world of unconsciousness — "unpulsing blackness" — under ice.)

> And the year drove on. Winter. And from the Dakotas
> The wind veers, gathers itself in ice-glitter
> And star-gleam of dark, and finds the long sweep of the
>   valley.
> A thousand miles and the fabulous river is ice in the
>   starlight.
> The ice is a foot thick, and beneath, the water slides
>   black like a dream,
> And in the interior of that unpulsing blackness and
>   thrilled zero
> The big channel-cat sleeps with eye lidless, and the brute
>   face
> Is the face of the last torturer, and the white belly
> Brushes the delicious and icy blackness of mud.
> But there is no sensation. How can there be
> Sensation when there is perfect adjustment?   (p.94)

"Perfect adjustment" despite the awful cold and dark under ice is something the conscious self, in fear of naturalistic oblivion, might well envy. Warren becomes very Jungian indeed in what follows the above passage, for just as Jung saw the deeper self as both divine and demonic ("the unconscious [is] the only accessible source of religious experience," Jung says in *The Undiscovered Self,* even though it also embodies "the general proclivity to evil...lodged in human nature itself" — pp. 101,110), Warren sees this creature with the brute face of a torturer as being, in its total osmosis with its environment, enviably "at one with God":

> 　　　　　　　　　　...The blood
> Of the creature is but the temperature of the sustaining
>   flow:
> The catfish is in the Mississippi and
> The Mississippi is in the catfish and
> Under the ice both are at one with God.
> Would that we were!

We are now clearly in the area of metaphysical speculation. In its oneness with the total darkness under ice, the catfish need not fear, as the conscious ego must, the awesome infinitude of time and cosmos above the ice, where "the stars are arctic and/ Their gleam comes earthward down uncounted light-years of disdain" (p.95). The catfish's brother image, the serpent, likewise evinces intimation of an immortality transcending the naturalistic winter at the end of the book, where the snake, "looped and snug," survives in "earth's dark inward-

ness" (p.208) underneath the pitiful ruins of the Lewis house,
those "huddled stones of ruin" which "say the human had been
here and gone/ And never would come back, though the bright
stars/ Shall weary not in their appointed watch" (p.32).   Jasper Harrick gives human embodiment to these metaphysical speculations when he describes the cave as a place resembling the
catfish's dark and timeless realm under ice: "'It's a nice tem-
perature down there,' he had said. 'It is not summer and it
is not winter. There aren't any seasons to bother about down
there,' he had said, and laughed.... 'Blizzard or hot spell,'
he had said, 'a lot of things don't matter down there'" (pp.
227-28). And Jasper goes on to state yet another advantage
of that dark underworld: it, and only it, can yield forth the
secret of final identity, the search for which has provided
Warren's most recurrent theme over the decades: "He had said,
'Well, in the ground at least a fellow has a chance of knowing
who he is'" (p.229).

"Perfect adjustment," being "at one with God," and knowing
at last who you are — such are the final rewards of Warren's
osmosis, though its final price is the death of the conscious
ego. "And the death of the self is the beginning of selfhood,"
R.P.W. had said in *Brother to Dragons* (p.215), but the new
selfhood appears clearly superior to the old. Back in "The
Ballad of Billie Potts," Warren had indicated this supremacy
of the unconscious over the conscious self in a pair of memorable passages. The first lists several modes of establishing
a conscious identity as the world knows it:

> Though your luck held and the market was always satis-
>   factory,
> Though the letter always came and your lovers were always
>   true,
> Though you always received the respect due to your posi-
>   tion,
> Though your hand never failed of its cunning, and your
>   glands always thoroughly knew their business,
> Though your conscience was easy and you were assured of
>   your innocence,
> You became gradually aware that something was missing from
>   the picture,
> And upon closer inspection exclaimed: "Why, I'm not in it
>   at all!"
> Which was perfectly true.

But in contrast to the unease of the conscious self on finding
"that something was missing from the picture," the unconscious
— as usual, embodied in a series of animal images — shapes the
direction and meaning of life through its secret, intuitive
knowledge:

> (The bee knows, and the eel's cold ganglia burn,
> And the sad head lifting to the long return,
> Through brumal deeps, in the great unsolsticed coil,

Carries its knowledge, navigator without star,
And under the stars, pure in its clamorous toil,
The goose hoots north where the starlit marshes are.
The salmon heaves at the fall, and wanderer, you
Heave at the great fall of Time....)

Like these creatures, Billie crosses from the realm of conscious to unconscious direction in coming home to his father and thus to death and eternity ("homeland of no-Time"): "You come, weary of greetings and the new friend's smile,/ ...Weary of innocence and the husks of Time,/ Prodigal, back to the homeland of no-Time."

Like "The Ballad of Billie Potts" and *Eleven Poems, You, Emperors, and Others* (a book very ignorantly reviewed, for the most part) is very effective in setting off the conscious as against the unconscious identities, to the great advantage of the latter. "Lullaby: Exercise in Human Charity and Self-Knowledge," for example, is addressed to a sleeper who, being unconscious, has lapsed out of the false identity provided in his conscious life by name (Stanza 1), face (Stanza 2), and sex (Stanza 3), and who therefore, in his unconsciousness, has access to an osmosis of being blending his identity with the whole universe: "And your sweet identity/ Fills like vapor, pale in moonlight, all the infinite night sky." Further emphasis on the superiority of the unconscious to conscious reality appears in the poet's advice in "A Real Question Calling for Solution," where conscious life is so chaotic that "There is only one way, then, to make things hang together,/ Which is to accept the logic of dream" rather than such things of consciousness as "Night air, politics, French sauces, autumn weather,/ And the thought that, on your awaking, identity may be destroyed." Warren's headnotes sometimes prove relevant, too, as when he refers to "a Roman citizen of no historical importance" and to Walter Winchell's Mr. and Mrs. North and South America. According to Warren's osmosis of being, all citizens are of historical importance — or else none are — and even Mr. Winchell's phrase, as referring to a collective self, might hold a meaning its originator never understood.

You, Emperors, and Others is especially concerned with imparting a sense of power and vision through dream or animal intuition. "In the Turpitude of Time" states overtly man's need for such animal intuition: "Can we — oh could we only — believe/ What annelid and osprey know,/ And the stone, nightlong, groans to divulge?" And "Prognosis" (the prognosis is that you will die) tells quite plainly the advantage of knowing what annelid and osprey know. Here a woman doomed with cancer sleeps, after a horrible day, and "...past despair,/ Dreamed a field of white lilies wind-shimmering, slow,/ And wept, wept for joy...." Fear of death, moreover, is as irrelevant at this level of consciousness as it was to the catfish in his "unpulsing blackness" under ice; thus the woman

says of her impending death: "and I do not grieve to be lost
in whatever awfulness of dark...." Intuition ventures past
the awfulness of dark in some of the "Nursery Rhymes" like
"The Bramble Bush," where the speaker "now saw past the far-
therest stars" and "heard the joy/ Of flesh singing on the
bone." The last word on osmosis of being is given by a grasshopper in the final poem of *You, Emperors, and Others*. Unlike
Ikey Sumpter or Slim Sarrett, who cut all their ties and fled
East (in *The Cave* and *At Heaven's Gate*), the insect in "Grasshopper Tries to Break Solipsism" is trying to establish connections: his grasshopper song is evidence of the humblest
creatures' need for each other. Solipsism, or the theory that
the self is the only existent thing, is the obvious enemy of
osmosis, and as such, merits the effort to "Break Solipsism"
with which this book of poems closes.

IV

It is only just that we conclude this essay with a few
lines from the master of osmosis, Walt Whitman. In a conversation we once had, Mr. Warren expressed misgivings about
Whitman's work because of its undue optimism — its lack of a
sense of sin such as Hawthorne and Melville often gave expression. And certainly Warren's own continuing preoccupation
with delusion, betrayal, and depravity — or "original sin" —
makes some of Whitman's ringing affirmations seem innocent and
sentimental by contrast. Warren distrusted Whitman, I think,
because Whitman's osmosis has no internal dimension, no psychological level of conflict and reconciliation within the
self between conscious ego and humanity's black collective
shadow. But on the other two levels, social and metaphysical,
no one has ever proclaimed the osmosis of being with the effi-
cacy of Walt Whitman. "And these tend inward to me, and I
tend outward to them," Whitman says in *Song of Myself* after
embracing all manner of folk in a tremendous catalogue: "The
pure contralto sings in the organ loft... The deacons are or-
dain'd with cross'd hands at the altar... The lunatic is carried at last to the asylum a confirm'd case,/ (He will never
sleep any more as he did in his mother's bedroom)... The mal-
form'd limbs are tied to the surgeon's table/ What is removed
drops horribly in a pail... The youth lies awake in the cedar-
roof'd garret and harks to the musical rain... The old husband
sleeps by his wife and the young husband sleeps by his wife...
And of these one and all I weave the song of myself" (Stanza
15). Whitman's osmosis, like Warren's, embraces creatures
long dead as well as those of the present: "In vain the mas-
todon retreats beneath its own powder'd bones." And most
strikingly, Whitman's metaphysics are at one with Warren's
in seeing one's cobweb connections to the entirety of past
and future and in accepting the gift of death gracefully,
as a welcome fulfillment or release into ultimate identity:

Afar down I see the huge first Nothing, I know I was even
    there,
. . . .
Cycles ferried my cradle, rowing and rowing like cheerful
    boatmen,
. . . .
For it [my embryo] the nebula cohered to an orb,
The long slow strata piled to rest it on,
Vast vegetables gave it sustenance,
Monstrous sauroids transported it in their mouths and de-
    posited it with care.   (*Song of Myself,* Stanza 44)

Like Warren's creatures under ice or his sleepers who do
not fear "whatever awfulness of dark," Whitman is enabled by
his osmosis to accept return to the oblivion that bred him:

A few quadrillions of eras, a few octillions of cubic
    leagues...
They are but parts, any thing is but a part.

See ever so far, there is limitless space outside of that,
Count ever so much, there is limitless time around that.
                                                    (Stanza 45)

And I say to any man or woman, Let your soul stand cool
    and composed before a million universes.
. . . .
(No array of terms can say how much I am at peace about
    God and about death.)   (Stanza 48)

And as in Warren's metaphysics, this acceptance of death comes
through the ministrations of an unconscious self, perceiving a
pattern and meaning not available to the conscious ego:

There is that in me — I do not know what it is — but I
    know it is in me.

Wrench'd and sweaty — calm and cool then my body becomes,
I sleep — I sleep long.

I do not know it — it is without name — it is a word
    unsaid,
It is not in any dictionary, utterance, symbol.
. . . .
It is not chaos or death — it is form, union, plan — it
    is eternal life....   (Stanza 50)

Moved by these intuitions from the unconscious, Whitman can
bend his will, even as Warren's parents or old granny did in
Promises, to commit his identity to the osmosis of being: "I
bequeath myself to the dirt to grow from the grass I love,/
If you want me again look for me under your boot-soles." And
as *Song of Myself* ends, even greater oneness is pending: "I
stop somewhere waiting for you."
    Osmosis of being, in various manifestations, is not a new

idea. It obviously motivated Emerson's conception of an Over-
soul, for example, as well as Wordsworth's pantheistic mysti-
cism, his vision of "a spirit that...rolls through all things"
(*Tintern Abbey*). Ultimately, it dates back to sacred writ; an
idea of osmosis underlies both the biblical ethic of brotherhood, as preached by Isaiah and Jesus, and the Hindu metaphysics of *Atman* (the soul), as seen in the *Bhagavad-Gita:* "I am
the Atman that dwells in the heart of every creature: I am the
beginning, the life-span, and the end of all...I am the divine
seed of all lives... Know only that I exist, and that one atom
of myself sustains the universe" (Part IX — "The Yoga of Mysti-
cism"). With the declining influence of sacred writ such as
this in modern times, people look more than ever to the artist
for help in finding the meaning of their lives. One could do
worse, I think, than look to Warren's osmosis of being as a
possible source of meaning.

BIBLIOGRAPHY

   I. Writings of Robert Penn Warren, Chronologically Arranged

Night Rider. Houghton-Mifflin, 1939, and Random House, 1948 (my copy).
At Heaven's Gate. Harcourt, Brace and Co., 1943, and Signet paperback,
       1949 (my copy).
Selected Poems, 1923-1943. Harcourt, Brace and Co., 1944 (includes
       Eleven Poems on the Same Theme and "The Ballad of Billie Potts").
All the King's Men. Harcourt, Brace and Co., 1946, and Random House,
       1953 (my copy).
World Enough and Time. Random House, 1950.
Brother to Dragons. Random House, 1953.
Band of Angels. Random House, 1955.
"Knowledge and the Image of Man," *Sewanee Review,* 63 (Winter 1955),
       182-192.
Promises: Poems 1954-1956. Random House, 1957.
The Cave. Random House, 1959, and Signet paperback, 1960 (my copy).
You, Emperors, and Others: Poems 1957-1960. Random House, 1960.
The Legacy of the Civil War: Meditations on the Centennial. Random
       House, 1961.
Wilderness: A Tale of the Civil War. Random House, 1961, and Signet
       paperback, 1965 (my copy).
Flood: A Romance of Our Time. Random House, 1964, and Signet paper-
       back, 1965 (my copy).
Who Speaks for the Negro? Random House, 1965.

   II. Other Writings

Bhagavad-Gita: The Song of God. Mentor Religious Classic (paperback),
       1954.
C. G. Jung, *The Undiscovered Self*. Mentor Books (paperback), 1959.
Walt Whitman, *Song of Myself*. Any edition.

James Wright

The Stiff Smile of Mr. Warren

Although it is possible, generally speaking, to discover
certain consistently developing themes in Mr. Warren's work
— prose and verse alike — it is nevertheless impossible to
know just what he will do next. In our own century he is perhaps the only American writer who, having already established
his major importance, remains unpredictable. If anyone has
noted any similarity between Mr. Warren and, say, Dickens, I
should be surprised and delighted. But the two authors share
the power — it is a very great power, and perhaps it is the
heart of the poetic imagination — of unpredictability. A
critic is right in being a little hesitant about such a writer.
But how explain the neglect of Mr. Warren's poems when we compare it with the critical concern with his novels? I use the
word "neglect" when I speak of the poems, simply because I
have a hunch that they contain the best seedings and harvests
of his imagination.

I

A good many reviewers of *Promises* have been taken aback by
the violent distortions of language. But one reviewer is Mr.
James Dickey, in the *Sewanee Review,* who describes and clarifies my own response to the book.

The first point concerns the distortions of language, and
the critic felt that most of them were flaws: "Warren has his
failings: his are a liking for the over-inflated, or 'bombast'
as Longinus defines it; he indulges in examples of pathetic
fallacy so outrageous that they should, certainly, become
classic instances of the misuse of this device. Phrases like
'the irrelevant anguish of air,' and 'the malfeasance of nature or the filth of fate' come only as embarrassments to the
reader already entirely committed to Warren's dark and toiling

A review of *Promises: Poems 1954-1956* — Ed.

spell." I think this is a pretty fair description of the
kinds of awkwardness that frequently appear in *Promises*. However, the really curious and exciting quality of the book is
the way in which so many of the poems can almost drag the reader, by the scruff of the neck, into the experiences which they
are trying to shape and understand.

But this very triumph of imaginative force over awkward
language is Mr. Dickey's second point, and the critic states
it eloquently: "Warren's verse is so deeply and compellingly
linked to man's ageless, age-old drive toward self-discovery,
self-determination, that it makes all discussion of line-
endings, metrical variants, and the rest of poetry's parapher-
nalia appear hopelessly beside the point."

Yet, so very often in this new book, Mr. Warren simply
will not allow the reader to consider the rhetorical devices
of language "hopelessly beside the point." That he is capable
of a smoothly formal versification in some poems, and of a
delicate musical variation in others, he has shown many times
in the past. We are not dealing with a raw, genuine, and un-
trained talent, but with a skilled and highly sophisticated
student of traditional prosody. In effect, a major writer at
the height of his fame has chosen, not to write his good poems
over again, but to break his own rules, to shatter his words
and try to recreate them, to fight through and beyond his own
craftsmanship in order to revitalize his language at the
sources of tenderness and horror. One of the innumerable
ironies which hound writers, I suppose, is the fact that the
very competence which a man may struggle for years to master
can suddenly and treacherously stiffen into a mere *armor
against experience* instead of an instrument for contending
with that experience. No wonder so many poets quit while
they're still behind. What makes Mr. Warren excitingly important is his refusal to quit even while he's ahead. In *Promises,* it seems to me, he has deliberately shed the armor of
competence — a finely meshed and expensive armor, forged at
heaven knows how many bitter intellectual fires — and has gone
out to fight with the ungovernable tide. I mean no disrespect
— on the contrary — when I say that few of the poems in this
book can match several of his previous single poems. Yet I
think there is every reason to believe that his willingness
to do violence to one stage in the development of his craftsmanship is not the least of the promises which his book contains. I do not wish to argue about any of the poems in *Promises* which I consider at the moment to be failures, though I
shall mention one of them. But I think that a book such as
this — a book whose main importance, I believe, is the further
evidence it provides for the unceasing and furious growth of
a considerable artist — deserves an attention quite as close
as that which we conventionally accord to the same author's
more frequently accomplished poems of the past.

II

The distortion of language in the new book is almost
always demonstrably deliberate. When it is successful, it
appears not as an accidental coarseness, but rather as an extreme exaggeration of a very formal style. The poetic function of the distortion is to mediate between the two distinct
moods of tenderness and horror. This strategy — in which formality is driven, as it were, to distraction — does not always
succeed. It is dishonest critical damnation, and not critical
praise, to tell a gifted imaginative writer that he has already scaled Olympus when, as a matter of frequent fact, he
has taken a nose-dive into the ditch. The truest praise, in
my opinion, is in the critic's effort to keep his eye on the
poet's imaginative strategy, especially if the poet is still
alive and still growing. I think that the failure of Mr.
Warren's strategy is most glaring when the material which he
dares to explore will somehow not allow him to establish one
of the two essentially dramatic moods — the tenderness and the
horror of which I spoke above. An example of this failure is
the poem "School Lesson Based on Word of Tragic Death of Entire Gillum Family." The horror is stated, and the reality of
horror is a lesson which everyone must learn, as the poet implies in the last line. But there is no tenderness against
which the horror can be dramatically drawn, and there is no
dramatic reason that I can discern for presenting the ice-pick
murder of the Gillum family. Now, I am sure the reader will
allow me to claim a human concern for the Gillum family, wherever and whoever they were. All I am saying is that they are
not here: that is, their death seems to me a capricious horror;
and the distorted language, in spite of its magnificent attempt to achieve a folklike barrenness and force, remains a
capricious awkwardness.

My speaking of "failure" in a poet of so much stature is
of course tempered by my statement of a conviction which constantly grows on me: that a failure like the "School Lesson"
is worth more than the ten thousand safe and competent versi-
fyings produced by our current crop of punks in America. I
am spared the usual but boring critical courtesy of mentioning
names by the fact that we all know who we are. But I am not
comparing Mr. Warren's performance in *Promises* with the performance of us safe boys. I am trying to compare it with his
capacities. I want to look somewhat closely at a poem in *Promises* in which the poet's exploration past facility into violent distortion ends in discovery. I suppose there are five
or six fine poems of this sort in the book, but I will settle
for a reading of one of them.

The poem is called "The Child Next Door." I hope that my
reader will take time, at this point, to read aloud to himself
the entire sequence of poems in *Promises* entitled "To a Little
Girl, One Year Old, in a Ruined Fortress." Furthermore, since

there can be no harm in our simply taking the poet at his word
(and where else can we begin?) the reader had better read the
dedication aloud also.

III

There are two kinds of violent distortion in "The Child
Next Door" — one of rhythm and one of syntax. I invite the
reader to discover, if he can, some regularity of scansion in
the following representative lines of the poem:

Took a pill, or did something to herself she thought would
    not hurt....

Is it hate? — in my heart. Fool, doesn't she know that
    the process....

I think of your goldness, of joy, how empires grind,
    stars are hurled....

I smile stiff, saying *ciao,* saying *ciao,* and think: this
    is the world.....

I find no regularity of metrical stresses. Now, one reviewer
has suggested an affinity between Mr. Warren's new verse and
the verse of Hopkins. Suppose we were to read the above
quoted lines according to Hopkins's system (I quote from one
of the famous letters to R. W. Dixon): "It consists in scan-
ning by accents or stresses alone, without any account of the
number of syllables, so that a foot may be one strong syllable
or it may be many light and one strong." (These are, of
course, Hopkins's somewhat desperately oversimplifying words
to a puzzled admirer.) The system seems promising, but even
this way of reading Mr. Warren's lines does not reveal a regular pattern. Playing the above lines by ear, I can hear six
strong stresses in the first line, six in the second, seven in
the third, and seven in the fourth. Yet I am not sure; and my
uncertainty, instead of being an annoyance, is haunting. Moreover, there are eighteen lines in the whole poem, and my feeling is that nearly all of the lines (mainly with the exception
of the above) can be read aloud according to a system of five
strong stresses. Here, for example, is the first line of the
poem: "The child next door is defective because the mother...."
I hesitate slightly over the word "next," but, with a little
straining to get past it, I think I can find clearly strong
stresses in "child," "door," the middle syllable of "defective," the second syllable of "because," and the first syllable of "mother." And so on. The regularity becomes clear
only if the reader is willing to strain his senses a bit — to
give his physical response to the rhythm, as it were, a kind
of "body-English." We find the poet like the tennis player
keeping his balance and not taking a fall, and feel some kind
of relief which is at the same time a fulfillment. I get this

kind of physical sensation in reading "The Child Next Door,"
a poem in which a skilled performer is always daring to expose
his balance to chaos and always regaining the balance. In
plain English, the rhythm of this poem may be described as a
formality which is deliberately driven to test itself, and
which seems imaginatively designed to disturb the reader into
auditory exaggerations of his own. Perhaps what is occurring
in the rhythm of this poem is a peculiar kind of counterpoint.
We have "counterpoint," said Hopkins to Dixon, when "each line
(or nearly so) has two different coexisting scansions." But
these words explain only a part of Mr. Warren's counterpoint.
I propose the hypothesis that one can hear in the poem two
movements of language: a strong formal regularity, which can
be identified with a little struggle, but which is driven so
fiercely by the poet that one starts to hear beyond it the approach of an unpredictable and hence discomforting second movement, which can be identified as something chaotic, something
very powerful but unorganized. It is the halting, stammering
movement of an ordinarily articulate man who has been shocked.
The order and the chaos move side by side; and, as the poem
proceeds, I get the feeling that each movement becomes a little stronger, and together they help to produce an echoing
violence in the syntax.

   Some of the later lines do indeed sound something like
Hopkins; but that is an accidental and, I think, essentially
irrelevant echo. The lines have their own dramatic justification, which I shall try to show in a moment:

   Can it bind or loose, that beauty in that kind,
   Beauty of benediction? I trust our hope to prevail
   That heart-joy in beauty be wisdom before beauty fail.

The syntax in the earlier lines of the poem seems to be recognizably more regular:

   The child next door is defective because the mother,
   Seven brats already in that purlieu of dirt,
   Took a pill.

If the reader grants that the syntax of these earlier lines is
fairly normal and regular as compared with the syntax of the
passage beginning "Can it bind or loose," then I think he can
identify the two kinds of distortion which I have mentioned:
a distortion of rhythm, and a distortion of a syntax. But
each distortion, however strong, is accompanied by an equally
strong regularity. And in each case the violence of the distortion is identifiable as an exaggeration of the regularity
itself.

   What a neat stylistic formulation! And how dead, compared
with the poem!

IV

Now, to say that the sound of a poem is not identical with
its sense is different from saying that the two may not exist
in rhetorical harmony with each other. I believe that the exaggerated formality of sound in Mr. Warren's poem is justified
by the dramatic occasion of the poem itself. Let us consider
the poem's dramatic occasion by limiting ourselves, at least
temporarily, to the references which we can find within it,
or in the title of the sequence of which it is a part.

First, the speaker is addressing a one-year-old child.
He has told us so in the title of the sequence. Moreover, the
fact that in this particular poem he is not merely brooding on
things in general is made clear to us by his explicitly addressing the child in the next-to-last line: "I think of your
goldness...." In addressing the child he first points out
something that exists in the external world; then he describes
his own feelings about this thing; and finally he tries to convey the significance of what he sees in relation to the one-
year-old child herself. It might be objected, either to the
poem or to my reading of it, that a one-year-old child could
not conceivably understand either the physical horror of what
the speaker points out or the confused and confusing significance which he has to extract from it. She is defended
against its horror by her youth. But the speaker is also
incapable of grasping what he shows the child. And he has
no defense. He is exposed to an almost unspeakably hideous
reality which he can neither escape nor deny.

Indeed, what makes reality in nature seem hideous is that
it is both alluring and uncontrollable. Once a man is committed to it in love, he is going to be made to suffer. "Children sweeten labours," said Bacon, "but they make misfortunes
more bitter." The reason is that children tear away, if anything can, a man's final defense against the indifferent cruelty of the natural world into which he has somehow blundered
and awakened. The speaker in Mr. Warren's poem speaks to his
own appallingly precious child about another child who seems
blindly and meaninglessly lamed and halted by something in nature itself for which it is absurd to assign anything so simple as mere blame. I would find it hard to imagine a dramatic
situation in which the loving commitments of the speaker are
subjected to more severe tensions than this one. And conceiv-
ing, as I do, that the speaker is an *actor* in this drama, and
not merely a *spectator* of it, I would say that his "pathetic
fallacy" of attributing "malfeasance" to nature and "filth" to
fate is his dramatically justifiable attempt to defend himself
against something more horrible than malfeasance and filth —
i.e., the indifference of nature and fate alike.

The speaker cannot escape the contemplation of this horror
because of the very child whom he addresses. The tenderness
with which he regards this child ("I think of your goldness,

of joy") is the very emotion which exposes him to the living
and physical evidence of the horror which man and child contemplate together, which neither can understand, but which the
man is trapped by his tenderness into acknowledging.

For the horror (embodied in the defective child, the child
next door) in its vast and terrible innocence of its own nature actually *greets* the speaker. He cannot ignore the greeting; for he, too, has a child — not defective, but nevertheless unknowingly exposed to all the possibilities, all the
contingencies and promises (of course, Mr. Warren knows very
well, and dramatizes in this poem with surpassing power, that
not all promises are sentimental assurances of a return to
Eden), the utterly mindless and brutal accidents of a fallen
world. So every child, in a sense which is fundamental to the
loving and moral agony of this poem, is defective — and the
speaker himself is such a child. Perhaps the real "child next
door" is the reader of the book.

The fallen world is chiefly characterized, in the poet's
vision, by a tragic truth: that man's very capacity for tenderness is what exposes him to horrors which cannot be escaped
without the assumption of an indifference which, to be sufficiently comforting, would also require the loss of tenderness
itself, perhaps even the loss of *all* feeling — even the loss
of hatred. The beautiful sister in the poem is not in agony,
and her face is not stiff with anger, or contorted with tenderness. Her face is pure, calm. Her face is, in the most
literal sense, unbearable. "She smiles her smile without
taint." Without taint! To give my sense of the dramatic and
human appropriateness of the poet's outburst against the mad-
dening and untainted smile, I can only say that, if the speaker in the poem had not damned her for a fool, I would have
written a letter to Mr. Warren and damned her on my own hook.

The speaker is trapped in his necessity of choice; and yet
he cannot choose. Between the necessity and the incapacity
the speaker is driven to a point where the outraged snarl of
an animal would have been justified by the dramatic context.
But this is where the imaginative courage of Mr. Warren's continuous explorations comes in. Instead of following the music
of his lines and the intensity of his drama into chaos, he suddenly rides the pendulum back to formality — but this time the
formality of the rhythm includes the formality of the drama,
and I think that the strategy is superbly successful. Instead
of snarling, the speaker acknowledges the horror's greeting.
He faces the horror, and his acknowledgement is a perfect embodiment of what earlier I called a severe and exaggerated
formality. Consider the emotions that the speaker must simultaneously bear in his consciousness: frightened and helpless
tenderness toward his own child; horror at the idiot; rage at
the calm face of the sister. His problem is like the lesson
in Frost's poem: "how to be unhappy yet polite." And the

speaker smiles — stiffly: "I smile stiff, saying *ciao,* saying
ciao." The stiffness of that smile, I think, is what we must
attend to. It is the exaggerated formality with which a man
faces and acknowledges the concrete and inescapable existence
of an utterly innocent (and therefore utterly ruthless) reality which is quite capable not only of crushing him, but also
of letting him linger contemplatively over the sound of his
own bones breaking. And the exaggerated formality is, in the
sound and syntax of the poem, that violence of language which
I have described, and which many reviewers of the poems have
found discomforting. I admit that the distortions, which
swing on the living pendulum of the poet's imagination between
the sound and the sense of the poem "The Child Next Door," are
discomforting. All I suggest is that they dramatically illuminate each other, and that they are therefore rhetorically
harmonious parts of a single created experience: a successful,
though disturbing, poem.

M. Bernetta Quinn

Robert Penn Warren's Promised Land

Since his Vanderbilt days, Robert Penn Warren's poetry has
charted a movement toward that country to which everyone gives
a name of his choosing, Warren's being the Promised Land. Un-
fettered by adherence to schools of verse (Black Mountain, Ob-
jectivist, neo-Romantic), Warren has left behind conceits and
witty ironies, "little magazine" academic pieces in the Augus-
tan vein, ever deepening and simplifying until the present
when "His years like landscape lie,"* as he once wrote of his
grandfather. Whether looking backward or forward he now can
view an interior terrain which need yield to no other in American writing in its power to create the sense of place, and
never "of this place only."

All his professional life, until recently, Warren the novelist and critic has overshadowed Warren the poet. During the
forties, playing the second role, he composed the essay "A
Poem of Pure Imagination: An Experiment in Reading" on *The
Ancient Mariner,* a landmark deserving to rank with that of
Lowes on "Kubla Khan" or Brooks on "Ode on a Grecian Urn."
The distinctions he there makes between symbol and allegory
help in appreciating his own work. Following Coleridge, he
attributes symbol to the imagination, allegory to the understanding (Warren's edition of *The Rime of the Ancient Mariner,*
p.74). His differentiation rests on the same kind of idealism
whereby Coleridge defines the primary imagination as "the perception which produces our ordinary world of the senses" (p.
68), with the secondary imagination adding what makes life
worthwhile. Further dividing the primary, Warren contrasts
symbols of necessity, running through all cultures (for example, the wind in *The Ancient Mariner*) with symbols of congruence, resulting from an artist's manipulation of an image
within a special context, like Byzantium in Yeats. Of Warren's symbols of congruence, the most prominent is the cedar
tree, named over thirty times and always with resonances of

*Quotations from Warren's verses are from *Selected Poems New and
Old, 1923-1966* unless otherwise indicated.

mortality far beyond those of its cousins the yew and the cypress. Sun and moon, storm, gull, and river are among his symbols of necessity, but none has the importance of the West, or Promised Land.

Landscapes of Nature, dream, and memory abound in Warren's writing. In the accents of Auden he speaks of "the wide landscape of probability," a Mexican setting in a poem the title of which evokes an oil or watercolor: "Small Soldiers with Drum in Large Landscape." Elsewhere, he becomes a small child, day by day staring out of a classroom window studying the "accustomed landscape" of "School Lesson Based on Word of Tragic Death of Entire Gillum Family." Like Randall Jarrell, he finds the word useful for life itself: "the landscape of his [Warren's father's] early experience" (p.205) in *Brother to Dragons*. Characteristically he identifies inner and outer scenes, as in that moving line "And a gray light prevailed and both landscape and heart were subdued" ("What Was the Promise That Smiled from the Maples at Evening?"). The major motif of his recognition that a bond of spirit exists between man and environment takes the form of Canaan, sensible of its own joyousness, a state of freedom where "natural innocence would dance like sunlight over the delighted landscape" (*Brother to Dragons,* p.41).

Next to *All the King's Men,* the best-known of Warren's novels is *World Enough and Time*. In his youth, Kentucky was for him world enough, as it remains in memories and dreams, an Eden to which he occasionally returns, only to be saddened by its decline: "The World of Daniel Boone," which he contributed to the December, 1963, issue of *Holiday,* describes it as "a beautiful country even now. It was once thought to be Eden" (p.160). When tracing the advance of the Kentucky pioneer's party into Blue Grass territory he says: "They were moving into the Promised Land." But the aboriginal glory vanished: "In the heart of Eden the palisades were rotting down. Soon Boonesborough itself, the first incorporated town in the commonwealth, was to disappear, that 'land of heart's desire,' Boone's dream" (*In the American Grain,* p.139).

Warren often sets poems around his birthplace — Guthrie, Kentucky — subjecting them to the many transformations of the light after the manner of Giovanni Bellini in treating the Italian *paese*: "Bellini's landscapes are the supreme instances of natural facts transfigured through love" (*Encyclopedia of World Art,* IX,15). At times he uses light, especially that at day's end, to express a complex affection for his native soil and to translate into a universal language various truths that in boyhood he half-comprehended and in manhood came to understand: such wisdom underlies the choice of title, *Incarnations,* for his 1968 collection of verse. In other instances, light becomes a tool of irony to render foreboding, as in *Brother to Dragons,* which notes "a trick of light on the late landscape" (p.7), *late* possibly meaning dead.

Once we have fully "received" a landscape, Warren believes,
it lives forever, or at least as long as we do, captured in
the "impeccable unspeaking line of art" ("For a Self-Possessed
Friend," *Thirty-Six Poems,* p.61). Stevens voices the same intuition about permanence in Part Three of "Peter Quince at the
Clavier"; Yeats, in "Sailing to Byzantium"; Keats, in "Ode on
a Grecian Urn." Unfortunately excised from the Bollingen
Award book, "The Cardinal" of the Kentucky Mountain Farm series sets to dignified music a Promised Land unthreatened by
change:

> Here is a bough where you can perch, and preen
> Your scarlet that from its landscape shall not fall,
> Lapped in the cool of the mind's undated shade.
> In a whispering tree, like cedar, evergreen.   (Ibid.,p.8)

Here the cardinal is addressed in Marvellian terms as
"lover of cedar and shade." Warren contrasts its flamboyant
"vision of scarlet" with "Rock and gold is the land in the
pulsing noon," a hostile backdrop from which his mind, like a
tree, will perennially shelter the bird after summer's lizard,
"carved" on the lichen-covered limestone, has fled like the
last breath of the season. Thus he himself becomes the cedar
casting shadows, the blue tones of memory. Here four concen-
tric images constitute the landscape of oasis: (1) its heart,
the tiny reptile as sacred icon; (2) the actual Kentucky scene
as an artistic whole; (3) the depiction of this scene in "The
Cardinal"; and (4) Warren's mind as origin and Omega.
   Typical of the Judaic Promised Land is the Garden, inseparable from its serpent. Part Four of "Boy's Will, Joyful Labor without Pay, the Harvest Home (1918)," like the story
"Blackberry Winter," flings an adolescent up against the problem of evil, here the stoning of a black snake by farmhands.
The aftermath is chilling:

> Against the wounded evening matched,
> Snagged high on a pitchfork tine, he will make
> Slow arabesques till the bullbats wake.

The action of these scriptural vultures focuses the ugliness
of a boy's awakening to cruelty, pain, the destruction of
beauty. Taking, like Judas, his earned silver, the protagonist goes to bed only to toss about imagining the blameless
creature being torn to pieces while still alive. He continues
to see this down the years, more vivid than the tangible
things about him. Even the brilliance of the European vaca-
tion land wherein he composes the lyric cannot distract him
from this gruesome object lesson, softened though it be by the
starlight over the barnyard after the harvesters' departure:

> And I shut my eyes and I see that scene
> And name each item, but cannot think
> What, in their urgency, they must mean,

But know, even now, on this foreign shore,
In blaze of sun and the sea's stare,
A heart-stab blessed past joy or despair,
As I see, in the mind's dark, once more,
That field, pale, under starlit air.

The boy (later, the man) recreates this autumnal landscape,
analogous in its symbolism to Albert Pinkham Ryder's *Death on
a Pale Horse,* where a skeleton rides a dark steed around a
race track while a snake undulates in the foreground. In his
Mediterranean landscape the sea flames up as his child's joy
did; at the same time, like a threatening monster, it stares
at him, lying in wait to strike. The poet recalls how the
farm looked after the snake kill: the cooling tractor under
that tree of death, the cedar; the work mule described as
saurian, drooping under the night's splendor. "White now, the
evening star hangs to preside over woods and dark water and
countryside," shining on in his thoughts long after "The little blood that smeared the stone" has dried. Forever and forever, "In the star-pale field, the propped pitchfork lifts its
burden, hung black, to the white star." Bethlehem and Calvary,
the star and the cross, haunt the pilgrim-poet as he searches
his way back to the paradise he once inhabited, before the
scene that has acquired for him the horror of a ritual murder.

     Another remembered landscape of man's involvement in the
mystery of original sin comprises "Small White House," a poem
which, as if it were the painting its title suggests, remains
stark and unchanging in the gallery of Warren's private past.
Possessed of all the details, he even so cannot remember
"where, in what state" (ambivalently, mind or place) he encountered the house upon which the July sun beats down until
it "Swims in that dazzle of no-Time," the world of retained
sensation. The second line touches greatness: "The pasture
is brown-bright as brass, and like brass, sings with heat":
chiasmus and synaesthesia heighten the sense of an unbearable
metallic midsummer drought. Behind the house, the hills "shudder, withdraw into distance," to which Warren adds "Like paranoia," an instance of the Auden influence he has never quite
shaken off. While this yoking of abstract and concrete (*hills,
paranoia*) is as old as Pope ("And sometimes counsel takes and
sometimes tea"), it seems slightly contrived here where no
witty effect is intended but rather a Münch-like horror.
Again the omnipresent cedar appears: "— And the wax-wing's
beak slices the blue cedar-berry, which is blue as distance,"
that death into which the hills have retreated. Subtly, Warren introduces the color of the horizon as identical to the
blue cedar-berry's. The river, tiny because of its remoteness
in the background, is patently symbolic: "The river, far off,
shrinks among the hot boulders, no glister, looks dead as a
discarded snake skin —"; the simile condenses not only time,
the serpent-river, but also lost innocence and everything else

signified by the dark portent of the snake in the harvest poem
above.

   Less merciless, though still in a somber vein, "Picnic Remembered" returns us to a Promised Land, even though its existence belongs to an unreachable tense. A luminous conversation with self held long after the joyous outing, these seven
stanzas of Warren's seem more intricately woven than they actually are. A certain freedom in rhyme reduces that Marvellian
symmetry which dominates a first response, though diction
throughout remains more seventeenth-century than contemporary.
Its three chief landscape features — leaf, hill, sky — gain
structural harmony as the two picnickers look upward through
waves of light, hungering for an impossible retention of joy.
In the October, 1948, *South Atlantic Quarterly,* John L. Stewart connects agrarian primitivism with Freudian psychology in
commenting on Warren's submarine landscapes, wherein water represents "the state of innocence for which man longs" (p.568).
"Picnic Remembered" is executed as a poetic canvas of an underwater episode ("We stood among the painted trees: The amber
light laved them, and us"). Then, suddenly, stasis — the artist conceives the light as being so solid that the human beings are flies in amber. In the third stanza he releases his
characters into motion again, further developing the seascape:

> Joy, strongest medium, then buoyed
> Us when we moved, as swimmers, who,
> Relaxed, resign them to the flow
> And pause of their unstained flood.

   Warren's first book-length critic, Leonard Casper, couples
this lyric with "Bearded Oaks" — a poem a man might be born to
write — in which "the lovers lie submerged in the diminishing
sea-light beneath the trees, symbolic of the urge to be unborn,
unbothered, unnamed" (*The Dark and Bloody Ground,* p.65). The
day, like all days, ends:

> But darkness on the landscape grew
> As in our bosoms darkness, too;
> And that was what we took away.

Light will come again to the natural landscape but not to
their hearts, where the darkness that ebbs before sunrise in
"the region happier mapped" streams into the bosoms of these
picnickers once night has dropped in front of their view like
a black stage curtain, turning the amber light that laved them
into "that brackish tide." Yet were these persons to return,
seasonal conditions being equal, to the Promised Land, the
light would still be as purely gold as in Warren's translation
of their bliss into art which is the poem.

   Another use of the submarine landscape occurs in "Fall
Comes to Back County, Vermont": the lounging eagle "Shoulders
like spray" the last light before his dive to the mountain.
Wherever Warren goes, from the Louisiana of "Bearded Oaks,"

with its meadow over which currents of bright air roll, to the
secluded retreat of Stratton, Vermont, focus of more recent
poems, he experiences moments when place takes on the Edenic
qualities of Atlantis. First mentioned by Plato in the fourth
century B.C., this sunken continent has, according to a favorite theory, long been believed to be the location of the biblical Paradise.

Robert Penn Warren rewrites the Fall in "Composition in
Red and Gold," which belongs securely to submarine landscape
through its splendid image of the tail of the cat (an animal
traditionally used by the devil as a disguise): "gold plume
of sea-weed in that tide of light." Its pictorial character
is established in the title, reminiscent of Demuth's abstract
portrait of William Carlos Williams, *I Saw the Figure Five in
Gold*. Its author accents the importance of this lyric by
including it in the series "Notes on a Life to be Lived."
Color effects build up, beginning with the general word *light,*
through *sunlight* (used twice), *golden* and *flame* (twice each),
gold (eleven times) to *red-gold,* until they climax in *flame-
gold,* which "Completes the composition." Warren emphasizes
how the landscape is an actor in his drama by humanizing the
brook, brown-gold like the hair of the watching little girl
who sees the cat kill the chipmunk, which braids its waters
as if they were tresses. The mountain in the background, de-
serted by its solitary eagle after the crime, may possibly be
a symbol of Calvary at the end of Good Friday; the fish leaning hidden against an icy current in the alder-shaded stream,
a reminder of Christ. Here, the Promised Land ironically
wears a garment of flooding gold, just as the earth in Rilke's
"Evening" wraps itself in a vesture of darkness.

The psychological equivalent of a terrestrial heaven is
emotional delight. In the series of lyrics so named, Warren
telescopes time, as he has done elsewhere, in a way typical of
medieval masterpieces. He transforms the past considered as
landscape into the present moment, *then* becoming *now* in a manner impossible to a society manipulated by clocks and calendars. The poet in "Delight," Part V, addresses some children,
possibly his own, possibly vanished companions of his Guthrie
boyhood:

> ...Oh, children,

> Now to me sing, I see
> Forever on the leaf the light. Snow
> On the pine-leaf, against the bright blue
> Forever of my mind, like breath
> Balances.

His memory of a certain winter scene resembles a canvas
painted a shocking blue behind its snowy pine trees. This
landscape, like Edward Hopper's relentless *Cape Cod Morning,*
will not change. Both this excerpt from "Two Poems about Suddenly and a Rose" and the recollection from which it springs

have a permanence beyond leaves, snow, sunlight — matter in
general. Warren calls to the children to look at the dew, a
symbolic bead of light on the bloodred petal, the same juxtaposition as in "Composition in Red and Gold":

> ...Light,
>
> Suddenly, on any morning, is, and somewhere,
> In a garden you will never
> See, dew, in fracture of light
> And lunacy of gleam-glory, glitters on
> A petal red as blood, and
>
> The rose dies, laughing.

The verb *is* predicates of light a universal present: this gar-
denscape will exist independent of addressee and artist.   The
four closing words constitute a poem in themselves: "The rose
dies, laughing."
     The total impression of "Delight," Part V, recalls Flan-
nery O'Connor's death scenes, wherein the characters do not
wholly die. We tend to feel as we grow older that whatever
awaits us beyond the grave is better than what we used to suppose, a truth which the rose has penetrated, if only we could
come upon its secret. The participle *laughing* stands for the
exultation (hilarity in the Poundian sense) of Hopkins in dying: "I am so happy, so happy!" Part VI of "Delight," if it
retracts the Jesuit's affirmation, does so only to return to
it again in a meditation where Warren, gazing at a marine landscape, inquires:

> If this, now, is truly the day's end, or
>
> If, in a new shift of mist,
> The light may break through yonder
> To stab gold to the gray sea, and twist
> Your heart to a last delight — or at least, to wonder.
>
> ("Finesterre")

The mark of Gerard Manley Hopkins lies upon these last two
lines, as well as on the diction and prosody throughout the
three most recent Warren books.
     Two of the ten "Notes on a Life to Be Lived" have been
discussed. The third in this opening section of the Bollingen Award winner, "Blow, West Wind, Blow," is one of the
best poems of the century, destined to rank with its author's
"Bearded Oaks." The cedar tree in it, besides presaging grief,
serves as Aladdin's lamp to summon up from the past three
crises, two of which appear as painted landscapes. Like the
blackbird looked at thirteen ways by Stevens, the cedar tree
remains a crucial symbol from poem to poem even when these are
not explicitly joined. In Warren's ode to the west wind, his
allusion to it is redeemed from gloom by the fact that besides
physical death it connotes, as Michel Jacobs remarks in *Colour*

in *Landscape Painting,* the positive values of faith, victory,
contemplation, and immortality.

The first two lines condense the theme: "I know, I know —
though the evidence is lost, and the last who might speak are
dead." What the speaker knows is human transience, forgotten
so quickly, with the evidence lost. We don't really believe
that we shall die, except in moments of heightened awareness,
symbolized here by wind and cedar imagery, when we are possessed by a simpler process than rational conviction:

> Blow, west wind, blow, and the evidence, O,
>
> Is lost, and wind shakes the cedar, and O
> I know how the kestrel hung over Wyoming,
> Breast reddened in sunset....

Coming from the direction of death, the west wind shakes the
cedar, that "golden bough." Warren's whole lyric is a highly
melodic tissue of vowel identities or approximations: by ending his third and fourth lines with "O" and repeating the cry
in the sixth, he communicates a triple anguish. The sound of
the west wind brings back to him that setting in Wyoming when
the sun wounded the breast of that gallant bird suspended, but
not for long, over the landscape. With the second rub of the
lamp, the cedar trembling in the wind returns with the remembered sensation of a final kiss: "...and I know how cold was
the sweat on my father's mouth, dead." Finally, the wind and
cedar reinvoke his Kentucky childhood at a moment fraught with
a significance which then was out of his range of prophecy,
considered as the gift of looking deeply into the reality of
the present:

> Blow, west wind, blow, shake the cedar, I know
>
> How once I, a boy, crouching at creekside,
> Watched, in the sunlight, a handful of water
> Drip, drip, from my hand. The drops — they were bright!

The evidence — kestrel, sunset, Wyoming skyline, shining
creek — is gone because of the irreplaceable uniqueness of
every instant, the remoteness of the poet, the subsequent
deaths of any other persons who might have been participants
in this three-act drama. Only the constants, west wind and
cedar, persist, with their variations on the theme of time:
to all appearances permanent, they function as warnings of
impermanence. Expanding his skepticism through the pronoun
you, Warren concludes: "But you believe nothing, with the evidence lost."

"Blow, West Wind, Blow" exemplifies what J. B. Leishman
says about Rilke in introducing a group of translations:
"More and more his poetry became the expression of a kind of
interior landscape, the 'transformation' by inwardness, into
a kind of higher *visibility,* of an intensely seen outwardness"

(Rilke's *Poems 1906-1926,* p.33). Contemplation to the point
of trance changes a windblown tree (the only object indisputably "there") into first a sunset mountainscape, then a death-
bed scene, and thirdly, a Kentucky brookside. All of these
metamorphoses catch at the fleeting nature of life while at
the same time implying a radiance just beyond the tangible
which teases us out of thought, like a glimpse of the Promised
Land.

"A Vision: Circa 1880" is a sort of elegy wherein Warren
sees his father as a boy in Trigg County, Kentucky. The season is spring, though he himself recalls only the scorching
summer or the fall, times when outside this "apparition" he
tries to visualize the region where it transpired:

> ....and so the scene
> I had seen just now in the mind's eye, vernal,
> Is altered, and I strive to cry across the dry pasture,
> But cannot, nor move, for my feet, like dry corn-roots,
>   cleave
> Into the hard earth, and my tongue makes only the dry,
> Slight sound of wind on the autumn corn-blade.

As if through binoculars ("Down the tube and darkening corridor of Time"), the son stares at that "sunlit space" between
woods ("green shadow") and pasture ("sun-green"), an immortal
landscape inhabited by the father-as-child whom he never knew.

In "The Ballad of Billie Potts" the narrator defines Time
as "the new place," "West," all of which can be related to the
Canaan symbol. *Brother to Dragons* also conceives Time as a
setting, with its characters meeting at "no place," "any time,"
the alternation of personae held together in the mind of a
storyteller who spins reflections about a labyrinthine landscape:

> Deep in the world of winter, snow on the brown leaves,
> Far in Kentucky there, I raised my eyes
> And thought of the track a man may take through Time,
> And how our hither-coming never knows the hence-going.
> (p.209)

As Warren writes earlier in this play for voices, his father,
Moses-like, had climbed his years as if they were mountains,
giving those who followed him an example impossible to evade:

> But still, despite all naturalistic considerations,
> Or in the end because of naturalistic considerations,
> We must believe in virtue. There is no
> Escape. No inland path around that rocky
> And spume-nagged promontory.   (p.29)

Just as writers construct the anti-Utopias competently dissected in Kingsley Amis's *New Maps of Hell,* so do they create
warped Canaans. Warren's "Place and Time" is given over to
his Richard Cory, Dr. Knox, who mysteriously commits suicide.

Its landscape in whites conveys the nightmare terror of German
Expressionism, the sun filling the sky with a scream of whiteness. Two moments unite into a single flare: that immediately
before the event which happened when the poet at nine was walking along a dusty road daydreaming, and a hallucinatory moment
during a return visit as an adult to this town aptly called
Cerulean Springs:

> But to resume:
> heat-dazzle, dust-whiteness — an image in sleep,
>
> or in the brain behind the eyeball,
> as now, in the light of this other day,
> and year, the eyeball stunned by that inner
> blaze, sees nothing, can nothing see
>
> outward whatsoever — only
> the white dust of that street, and it
> is always August, is 3 P.M.,
> the mercury 95....

Both moments lack the "water to wash the world away" ("And All
That Came Thereafter"), mentioned in the series probing into
the reasons behind the doctor's death. Here, the cleansing,
sacramental waters are symbolized by the child's anticipated
swimming haunt shaded by silver willows. When Warren the boy
asks his grandfather why Dr. Knox hanged himself, the Civil
War veteran begins a reply but breaks off his discourse to
gaze out beyond the fennel, the peeling fence, and the cedars:

> The land, in sunlight,
> swam, with the meadow the color of rust,
> and distance the blue of Time....
> ("A Confederate Veteran Tries to Explain the Event")

Rust is one of the many scriptural allusions in Warren: in comparison to timelessness, the meadows that hypnotize the old
man belong to the things that rust corrupts.

In taking Time as a landscape, Warren resembles his friend
and younger contemporary Randall Jarrell, an affinity especially clear in their dreamscapes. "Vision under the October Mountain: A Love Poem," one of his newer achievements, is set near
Stratton, Vermont, where he, with his wife, son Gabriel, and
daughter Rosanna, spend holidays. The mountain appears to his
uplifted eyes to drift slowly through the sunset so beautiful-
ly that he thrice asks his companion if it springs from a
shared prenatal dream:

> ...did we
> once in the womb dream, dream
> a gold mountain in gold
> air floating....

Here he restricts the meaning of the mountain, almost making
it an emblem rather than a symbol: "it is the image of author-

ity, of reality." Though doubt of its power immediately intrudes ("oh, is it?"), the mutual gaze of the watchers drives
it away.

   Brother to Dragons, which has so many fine passages, includes among them the anti-paradisial dream of Lilburn's sister, Laetitia, who after Lucy's death sees him in terms of a
landscape — again such as Ryder might have devised, Ryder with
his grotesque forms and limited palette:

> I turned and saw him — something on his face
> Grew like a stain in water, and it spread,
> And grew like darkness when the moon sinks down
> And creeks and valleys dark, and the trees get black,
> And grew like recollections in the night
> When you wake up cold and all you did seems awful....
>   (p.86)

Lilburn's father also thinks of him as if he were a nocturnal
painting: *"I have looked in the eyes of my first-born son and
have seen/ The landscape of shadow and the shore of night"* (p.
98). Lucy herself, just before or after she has entered eternity, views her child in the same way. *Brother to Dragons,*
like *Our Town,* regards life and death as more flexible conditions than the rigidly separate ones we know, thus leaving
open the interpretation of her state:

> But I, I made the repudiation. I died.
> I lay and knew the end, and then I saw
> His face. But a wide world between, like a valley,
> Like a wide valley, and the rain fell steady between,
> So steady and gray and you hardly see beyond
> Where the far hill is, and far across the valley
> So full of the rain falling. I saw his [Lilburn's] face.
> It was big as the hill, but the hill was small with dis-
>   tance,
> And distance was dim and the rain without ceasing.
> The distance was but to the bed-foot, but a great
> Distance, and a wide valley where the rain fell.   (p.73)

Babette Deutsch in evaluating the tale for the *Yale Review*
calls its symbolic background, of which the above may stand as
"a figure in the carpet," a witness to, even analogue of, the
human condition itself (vol.43, p.278).

   When Billie Potts, in the second longest of Warren's poetic narratives, rides back whistling in the sun toward his
birthplace after ten years out West, it is the narrator who
sees the white peak beneath which Billy as prodigal son dis-
mounts to stand and spit, sees it as the Hebrews did the
Promised Land "that glittered like a dream." When Billie's
parents in their greed unwittingly murder him, a Sophoclean
"messenger" (frontiersman Joe Drew) reveals to them their macabre mistake. Looking into the dark mirror of the forest
pool after his ugly slaying, the narrator, true prophet who

penetrates happenings, drinks at its waters of experience but rises without the innocence he seeks: "And years it lies here and dreams in the depth and grieves/ More faithful than mother or father in the light or dark of the leaves," innocence here personified as cursed by what "Letter to a Friend" calls the "dream without fruition."

Bearing in mind Warren's distinction between allegory as generated in the understanding, and symbol as constructed by the imagination, one can discern in this excerpt from his famous essay on Coleridge why he chose the dream-device for landscape epiphanies: "In his swound the Mariner receives a fuller revelation of his situation and of the nature of the forces operating about him. He learns these things, it is important to notice, in the dream — just as the fellow-mariners had received the first intimation of the presence of the Polar Spirit through dreams. And the symbolic significance of this fact is the same: The dream is not at the level of the 'understanding,' but is the mode by which the special kind of knowledge of the imagination should be revealed" (pp.97-98). The Oriental scenery of "Kubla Khan" demonstrates such a revelatory character, a controlled imaginary fabrication far from the phantasmagoria of surrealism.

Though as a child in Kentucky Warren briefly took art lessons from a Sister Luke, he has never been a practitioner, yet he has cultivated "the painter's eye" to the extent that he regularly sees Nature as landscape. "Aubade for Hope" conceives sunrise to be a view from a window out of which no one is looking:

> And now they stir, as east
> Beyond the formal gleam of landscape sun
> Has struck the senatorial hooded hill.
> (*Thirty-Six Poems*, p.47)

More appropriate to the Canaan theme is Jefferson's "vision" of Kentucky in *Brother to Dragons*:

> I saw all,
> Swale and savannah and the tulip-tree
> Immortally blossoming to May,
> Hawthorn and haw,
> Valleys extended and prairies idle and the land's
> Long westward languor lifting toward the flaming escarp-
>   ment at the end of day.   (p.11)

Jefferson's dream of the Promised Land ends in a nameless paradisial isle in the Pacific (counterpart of Saint Brendan's, west of Ireland), where the black seal barks, knowing that eventually the seekers will arrive ("And on the western rock, wracked in the clang and smother,/ The black seal barks, and loves us, knowing we will come").

Warren in the first twenty years of his lifespan drew less heavily, if at all, upon a Kentucky which was perhaps then too

close to be seen as source material. "The Garden" is subtitled "On prospect of a fine day in early autumn," placing
it in the category of landscape art where *prospect* is a common if archaic term. Modeled on Marvell's lyric of the same
name, it shows the Fugitive reaction from Georgian verse, as
well as movement toward metaphysical stanzaic tightness and a
severely concentrated diction. Despite the absence of a focus
of narration, the reader gets the impression of someone enjoy-
ing the sight of a garden, sparkling with frost, wherein
leaves have become blossoms, his vantage point that best
suited to "prove" or test aesthetically "The grace of this
imperial grove":

> But branches interlace to frame
> The avenue of stately flame
> Where yonder, far more bold and pure
> Than marble, gleams the sycamore....

The other trees, bent to a fiery arch, precede the sycamore,
the shining trunk of which duplicates the cold but beautiful
effect of a cathedral: "Of argent torso and cunning shaft/
Propped nobler than the sculptor's craft." No one acquainted
with Yeats can help thinking of that writer's Galway "laboratory," Coole Park.
    In summer, lovers before kissing could see the consumma-
tion of their relationship portrayed in the ripe peach:

> The hand that crooked upon the spade
> Here plucked the peach, and thirst allayed;
> Here lovers paused before the kiss,
> Instructed of what ripeness is.

Edenic overtones inform the quarrel of Warren's familiar jay
and cardinal, as these dispute over the ruined garden, its
Adam and Eve departed. To the beholder, standing alone at the
entrance, autumn is more rewarding than the sensual summer or
the ominous winter, even though he is not happy: the garden,
once a "rank plot," is referred to as "precincts," the first
noun suggesting some traitorous conspiracy and the second its
prison dénouement. A milder sun than August's will bring its
blessing of peace:

> Only for him these precincts wait
> In sacrament that can translate
> All things that fed luxurious sense
> From appetite to innocence.

Purified sacramentally, the protagonist can here recover the
"lost country" of his youth, akin to the virgin Kentucky of
frontier America.
    Though Jefferson's portrayal of a vista within the Louisi-
ana Purchase in *Brother to Dragons* is perhaps the most prominent nature description turned landscape by heroic perception,
other passages treat settings as synecdoche. At times the

"golden glade" figure gleams more brilliantly because of a juxtaposed foil, as in Laetitia's thoughts after Lucy's death. It is dusk, "With night coming on and the gray light filling the land," which only the day previous was gold from the sun on the sweetgum:

> ...and I could see out the window,
> Way down the bluff and over the flat land, way off.
> The river was there and had a kind of gleam-like,
> Not sun, for the sun was shady and night nigh,
> But just like the river gave off some light and it cold,
> Like a knife that lies in the shadow and the blade
> Gives off a light with a gleam-like, so still and cold.
> And grayness was slow over all the flat land,
> And I tried not to think but be still like the land and
>   the gray light.   (p.76)

Laetitia (what name could be less appropriate?) finds in this gray light not only an exact replica of her emotional state but also some sort of answer to the riddle of existence. Desolate as she is, she remembers "yesterday/ When sunshine made the sweet-gum all gold," and even though the river has become for her a knife lying ready in shadow, in her subconscious she expects the apotheosis of this gray light, remembering that "light changes old landscape," as Warren has affirmed in "A Real Question Calling for Solution."

Another instance of exterior landscape turned interior in *Brother to Dragons* is a double presentation of a certain Kentucky scene. In July heat, the narrator toils up a hill, struggling through plants and shrubs tangled "like a dream," until suddenly green serenity breaks upon him. The only *locus* such a place now has is *dove sta memoria:* it has become "that landscape lost in the heart's homely deep" of "Moonlight that Lingers." When he revisits it in cold weather, the bluff does not look so high. Out of the past there rises the way it used to be:

> July it was — and I damned the heat and briar,
> Saw-vine, love-vine, and rose, then clambered through
> The tall, hot gloom of oak and ironwood,
> Where grapevine, big as boas, had shagged and looped
> Jungle convolvement and visceral delight.
> For that's the way I had remembered it.
> But no, it's not like that. At least, not now,
> And never was, I guess, but in my head.   (p.207)

One reason we can't go home again is the unlikelihood that the home we think we came from ever existed.

What the speaker sees before him on the second trip matches the first landscape point by point, except for seasonal change:

> There is some thicket, yes, and grapevine, sure,
> But scraggly-thin and hanging like it's tired

> From trees gone leafless now, and not so tall.
> So I'm prepared for what I find up yonder.   (pp.207-8)

His discovery upon reaching the crest is that the Promised
Land has withered into the Waste Land:

> The ruin all shrunken to a little heap
> Of stone that grass and earth pre-empt again
> And those fine beech trees that I'd celebrated —
> They just aren't there at all, and all I find
> Is piddling shag-barks, walnuts, two or three,
> And two oaks, scrub to middling, not to brag on.
> So winter makes things small.   (p.208)

On the dead leaves rests a little covering of snow. The climb-
er meditates, raising his eyes beyond the bluff and plain to
the river, which in a younger year was another river. Then
comes the miracle: the happiness he has known between the summer of scene one and the winter of scene two allows him to endure this parody of Eden with a mature and tranquil courage
("Since then I have made new acquaintance with the nature of
joy"). He has learned that the kingdom of God is within him.

Not always is an "examination of conscience" in terms of
life as landscape dominated by the peace of this passage from
Brother to Dragons. Also in the valley-orchard-garden pattern,
"Aged Man Surveys the Past Time" shows a man weeping over
missed opportunities as he contemplates the western view of
his unfruited trees at sunset, his tears like twilight rain —
a touch of sentimentality which, together with strained inver-
sions, may have prompted Warren's later rejection of this
lyric published in *Thirty-Six Poems*. As the protagonist
stands there "in diminished light," he reads his entire autobiography in the farm before him. It is winter. The catbird,
counterfeit of spring's songsters, mocks him. Gazing out at
his barn, he notes how the light pales behind it, even as it
has died out in his own career, and he sees himself as a
lightning-struck oak: "Light fails behind the barn and blasted
oak." Like a strumpet, April with her spray of green and her
crocuses has deceived him, as she will again in the year to
come. All his days have been a journey downward into a private hell: "Time has no mathematic. Could Orpheus map/ The
rocky and bituminous descent?" The concluding words ("Thy
godless summer and the dusty road!") summarize the misery of
this modern Pontius Pilate, to whom the poem has compared him.

In "Garden Waters," all night, "Noisy and silver, over the
moon-dark stone," a stream falls, unlike the waters of dream
in that it possesses sound (*Selected Poems, 1923-1943*, p.101).
In contrast to this silver-streaked fantasy, outside this superficially Edenic nocturne lies a world where "men by crags
have stopped against the loud/ Torn cataract or hollow-bosomed
flood," appalled by the similarity to the sea of the tumult
within their veins, just as violent but "voiceless." The long-

est study of Robert Penn Warren's poetry to date is Victor
Strandberg's *A Colder Fire,* which finds rich meaning in these
microcosm–macrocosm landscapes: "This complexity of water
imagery in 'Garden Waters' shows the deepening complexity of
Warren's perspective in his search for identity. His effort
to define the self, as this poem demonstrates, employs both
the inward and the outward look, both the groping downward
through the inward labyrinth, wherein Warren most affirms the
Romantic tradition, and the venturing into the outer landscape,
so as to measure and evaluate, in the Classical tradition, the
civilization that has shaped the raw material of self" (p.70).
The speaker in "Garden Waters" and the aged man surveying his
land recognize catastrophe in the "dead leaf." They must
mourn their failures in silence, like the blood within the
body, denied the release of the ocean: "More terrible breaks
the torrent with no song."

All of the poems analyzed thus far are in the mainstream
of literature, which since Coleridge has leaned more and more
toward *paysage moralisé,* as Herbert Marshall McLuhan has
pointed out in his essay "The Aesthetic Moment in Poetry":
"Beginning with Thomson's *Seasons* the poets appropriated landscape as a means of evoking and defining states of mind" (*English Institute Essays,* 1951, p.171). Rimbaud, Poe, Eliot,
and Crane are examples. Conflict within the mind resulting
from original sin, a concept which can rise from either secular or sacred convictions, runs through both the fiction and
the verse of Robert Penn Warren. His great exegesis of *The
Rime of the Ancient Mariner* is based on the Fall of Man. In
the old sailor's narrative the sun and moon share the adventures of the crew: mirrors of mood, malevolent or beneficent
influences. The cause of estrangement from grace and token of
reconciliation is the sacramental Albatross, which Warren defines as a "moon-bird" (p.91). His trial over, the Mariner
"gets home, in the moonlight, which, we recall, is the light
of imagination, and in the end he celebrates the chain of
love which binds human society together, and the universe"
(p.104). Naturalistic novelists lower man to the level of non-
rational animals through symbol; Warren, on the contrary, ele-
vates even the non-organic as a result of his belief in the
oneness of the universe in the redemptive plan, as it links
the first Paradise to the final.

By associating himself (a figure of Everyman, though re-
taining uniqueness) with Billie Potts the outlaw, Warren affirms again the solidarity of the race. Like Faulkner, he
thinks of a unity, vertical and horizontal, among men, so that
guilt incurred by a segment, as in slavery, affects all. Thirteen times "The Ballad of Billie Potts" mentions its setting
in the land "between the rivers," as Kentuckians know the region separating the Cumberland and Tennessee. Sometimes Warren returns here in dream to contemplate the terrain. The
remembered shagbark and tulip tree have vanished, along with

an old cabin, but the low hills, the oak, the slough, the tangled cane, the muskrat, and the bluejay remain:

> But the land is still there, and as you top a rise,
> Beyond you all the landscape steams and simmers
> — The hills, now gutted, red, cane-brake and black-jack
>   yet.
> The oak leaf steams under the powerful sun.

Throughout the yarn, Billie is the storyteller's double:
"Think of yourself at dawn: Which one are you?" When Billie
returns to die at the hands of his parents in a landscape of
evil, Warren balances against this scene the innocent pasture
so prevalent in his writing: "The stars are shining and the
meadow is bright." The spring which had served as a mirror
the morning Billie left home is now "black as ink." Terrible,
and yet somehow regenerative, this father-son crime (like the
mother-son horror in *Oedipus*) becomes a step in the drama begun at Billie's disinterment in the light of a pine knot, a
ceremony which awakens the long-quenched tenderness of Big
Billie and his wife for their only son. Billie himself dies
kneeling at the symbolic pool "in the sacramental silence of
evening."

"To a Face in the Crowd" brings this insight of man's solidarity up to date by inquiring quite simply of a passing
stranger: "Where will you one day be buried?" Various landscapes which might serve are put in the form of questions:

> Brother, my brother, whither do you pass?
> Unto what hill at dawn, unto what glen,
> Where among the rocks the faint lascivious grass
> Fingers in lust the arrogant bones of men?

Moving backward in time, Warren speculates in terms of a ma-
rinescape what the nameless other will suffer during his life:

> Beside what bitter waters will you go
> Where the lean gulls of your heart along the shore
> Rehearse to the cliffs the rhetoric of their woe?

Both he and the stranger derive through the centuries from
"the chosen people": "We are the children of an ancient band/
Broken between the mountains and the sea," whose pilgrimage is
recorded in *Tale of Time,* subtitle for the 1960-1966 lyrics in
the Bollingen Award collection. They become pilgrims explicitly in the lines:

> Renounce the night as I, and we must meet
> As weary nomads in this desert at last,
> Borne in the lost procession of these feet.

The convergence of men in this procession which is history depends upon choice: to renounce the powers of darkness, to keep
on toward the promise. "To a Face in the Crowd" must have un-

usual strength in Warren's opinion, since it ends his most
complete book of verse — must indeed, as he there says in the
Prefatory note, lie on the main line of his impulse.

Since we come upon our goal while looking for something
quite different, Saul in one of the "Holy Writ" poems finds
not his father's asses, as he expects, but destiny when he en-
counters Samuel on the desert's edge. Event and environment
blend: "Fate is the air we breathe." Saul's backdrop is a
lion-colored landscape of noon-blazing stones resembling the
droppings of lions, a wilderness of dry thorns, and a yelping
wind. He walks toward the old man who will anoint him king.
Samuel as prophet sees them frozen in the ritual of consecra-
tion, the locale fragile as his sensory assimilation of it:

> The far hills, white light on gypsum, dazzle.
> The hills waver like salt dissolving in water. Swim
> In the dazzle of my eyes.

These hills do not waver any more than the ones in "Small
White House" shuddered: perception intensified by high emotion alters their existence (cf. "Modification of Landscape").
When Saul leaves, Samuel, watching him, thinks of how his own
consciousness is the desert through which the younger man
travels:

> He moved from me in the white light.
> The black dwindle in distance which now he
> Was, was upheld by
> White light as by
> A hand. He moved across distance, as across
> The broad palm of my knowing.
> The palm of my hand was as
> Wide as the world and the
> Blaze of distance.

Here, the ambivalent *palm* demonstrates Warren's mature skill
in the use of metaphysical conceit. In his mind, Samuel pictures the future monarch arriving at the south shoulder of the
pass in the greyness before dawn, where a stone-grey stallion
will stand to bear him to Gilboa, the place preordained for
his death.

No object in Creation exists in isolation: man and Nature
are looped together by a band of light which symbolizes the
common destiny of a mortal world awaiting its fulfillment.
Robert Penn Warren's vision, including *Incarnations* and *Audubon: A Vision,* is basically affirmative. "The Last Metaphor,"
from *Thirty-Six Poems* (pp.52-53), opens with one of his least
hopeful statements; though the end brightens, it is with a
facile optimism which perhaps led to the exclusion of this
lyric from later collections. In it, a man goes out in a chil-
ly twilight to seek bare trees, shadow-colored rock, a lonely
wind, rather than the soaring birds of a gentler day:

He passed by a water, profound and cold,
Whereon remotely gleamed the violent west.
Stark rose a wood above a rocky crest.

Unlike the stripped trees of this grove, he is a tree from
which tenaciously hang "memories of the phantom spring's decay." The real trees on the horizon represent the stoicism
he desires:

How flat and black the trees stand on the sky
Unreminiscent of the year's frail verdure.
Purged of the green that kept so frail a tenure
They are made strong; no leaf clings mortally.

Alternately the man looks up at the grim hills or down at "the
violent west" (the adjective not promising) gleaming across
the icy depths of water, as if mocking him by Nature's indifference. His heart counsels him to be instructed by this
bleakness, and in the end he is:

Before he went a final metaphor
Not passionate this, he gave to the chill air,
Thinking that when the leaves no more abide
The stiff trees rear not up in strength and pride
But lift unto the gradual dark in prayer.

In spring it is easy to feel a joy of renewal; in summer, of
triumph and mastery; when not only wind and dark but also cold
come on, the spirit faints. In "The Last Metaphor" the plea
for supernatural help as assuagement for grief is unconvincing
because unprepared for.

The moods of this lyric are incidental, however, as
against the cumulative Promised Land of Warren, a writer
thoroughly conversant with the Bible as a source of symbol.
Though the concept of Canaan is broader than Old Testament
references to it, acquaintance with the latter helps, in the
way that Genesis is relevant to a critic of *East of Eden*. The
term began in Judeo-Christian tradition with Abraham's departure from Ur for Canaan. Centuries later the Hebrews, captive
in Egypt, kept on trusting in God's pledge to him (Gen.17:8)
as to their ultimate joy. When Moses led them out of bondage
across the Red Sea, their entrance into the Promised Land
might have been accomplished had not fearfulness over exaggerated reports of scouts doomed them to wander until Moses, at
the age of one hundred and twenty, died within sight of his
dream and was replaced by the warrior Joshua. Gradually, the
entire twenty-six thousand acres west of the Jordan came to be
considered the Promised Land, under the name of Palestine.
The second stanza of "Swing Low, Sweet Chariot," — "I looked
over Jordan and what did I see,/ Waiting for to carry me home,
/ A band of angels coming after me" — reflects the transfiguration of this small nation into Paradise itself. Its phrase

band of angels brings to mind Warren's novel of that title.
"History" concerns itself directly with this Promised Land:

And now
We see, below,
The delicate landscape furled,
A world
Of ripeness blent, and green,
The fruited earth....

Throughout Warren's verse, Canaan, as in this passage, takes
on the character of an "innocent pasture." The religious tone
of this episode in the migration toward the West, as recorded
by an eyewitness, has a Psalmist ring. "Much man can bear,"
the poem says, listing the chastisements of the Bride: arduous
travel, hunger, no water or fodder, cold, ulcers, cracked lips.
The travelers descend to take the Promised Land by storm, but
not in anger.

The lyric "The Letter about Money, Love or Other Comfort,
If Any" treats of a personal, not a communal, Promised Land.
Its biblical inspiration is clear from the metonymy of its sub-
head: "'In the beginning was the word, — THE GOSPEL ACCORDING
TO ST. JOHN.'" The "word" is a letter marked BY HAND ONLY
which the protagonist in a Kafkaesque tragicomic series of attempts, delivers for a stranger resembling the one in "Blackberry Winter." He goes on and on, everywhere meeting trials
but persevering until he climbs a high cliff, where he buries
the letter like a body. His mission over, he plunges back into the darkness of trees, to emerge into an enchanted sunrise:

I stand, bewildered, breath-bated and lame,
at the edge of a clearing, to hear, as first birds
    stir, life lift now night's hasp,
then see, in first dawn's drench and drama, the snow
       peak go gory,
and the eagle will unlatch, crag-clasp,
fall, and at breaking of wing-furl, bark glory,
and by that new light I shall seek
the way, and my peace with God....

Among Warren's Eden enclaves, "Gold Glade" is unquestionably one of the most exquisite. The poet thinks of the landscape with a sense of "Is this real or imagined? What state
(even literally, as on a map of the United States) is it in?"
The splendor of "Gold Glade" resembles that surrounding Stratton, Vermont, or the magic mountain of "October Vision." Yet
actually the spot exists in a Kentucky remembered from his boyhood, when he was not as yet capable of realizing that his aimless hunting expedition had brought him right to the edge of
a woodland beauty which was Canaan in symbol, a place looking
backward to Eden and forward to Paradise. After spending his
holiday climbing under the black cedars, the young huntsman

gains the crest of a limestone ridge from which he can gaze
down and picture in his mind's eye the hidden "white water tum-
bling" over "stone wet-black." This landscape of gorges, seen
at the start of evening, is "sublime" and perhaps to some extent more a source of the fright the boy feels than the danger
facing him in clambering down slick boulders: it is hazardous
to approach perfection.

Between the lad and the Promised Land is a level beech
grove; after he has crossed it he comes out upon a magical
"theater in the round":

> The glade was geometric, circular, gold,
> No brush or weed breaking that bright gold of leaf-fall.
> In the center it stood, absolute and bold
> Beyond any heart-hurt, or eye's grief fall.
> Gold-massy the beech stood in that gold light-fall.
>
> There was no stir of air, no leaf now gold-falling,
> No tooth-stitch of squirrel, or any far fox-bark,
> No woodpecker coding, or late jay calling.
> Silence: gray-shagged, the great shagbark
> Gave forth gold light. There could be no dark.

The gold-gleaming midpoint of this circle is a beech. Unlike
Hopkins's golden grove, these trees are too still for unleaf-
ing, holding themselves separate foom the sorrows of a beholder's heart or the tears in his eyes. Typically, the landscape
of this moment is silence: the highest landscape effects in
Warren occur in scenes devoid of sound or motion. A deleted
version limits the Promised Land here to a definite place, not
an elusive dream such as Poe's Eldorado or Yeats's garden of
the golden apples of the sun and silver apples of the moon,
but a particular glade the location of which he has forgotten;

> No, no! in no mansion under earth,
> Nor imagination's domain of bright air,
> But solid in soil that gave its birth,
> It stands, wherever it is, but somewhere.
> I shall set my foot and go there.   (Promises, p.25)

Warren's dropping this passage might be interpreted as a loss
of faith in a certain form of primitivism. No longer does he
expect to recover the pure bliss of natural loveliness which
thrilled him in boyhood and young manhood. Moreover, with the
lengthening of the river of consciousness, he finds it increasingly difficult to distinguish reality from imagination. Yet
though he comes to such things colder, this Kentucky landscape
recollected embodies a revelation too piercing ever to be lost. .
The speaker in "Gold Glade," unable to decide whether its
perfection belongs to Tennessee or Kentucky (and if the latter,
to Montgomery, to Todd, or to Christian county), ends by wondering: "Is it merely an image that keeps haunting me?" In
symbolism the *paysage* is very near to Frost's "Nothing Gold

Can Stay," which I have analyzed for landscape meaning in the
English Journal (55, 621-24). *Gold* is Warren's favorite word,
as a concordance will one day substantiate. What he says
about Frost in *Selected Essays* might just as easily apply to
himself: "The poet has undertaken to define for us [in 'Birch-
es'] both the distinction between and the interpenetration of
two worlds, the world of nature and the world of the ideal,
the heaven and the earth, the human and the non-human (oppositions which appear in various relationships), by descriptive
level or reference to the symbolic level of reference" (p.135).
Gold is as symbolic for Warren as for Saint Matthew in the
text concerning the gifts of the Wise Men.

"Gold Glade" looks to the west for its transfiguration.
The American West started much farther from the Pacific Ocean
than the twentieth century thinks. Its Moses was Jefferson,
who led his people to Canaan though he never entered it, possibly because of the confusion in morals dramatized by William
Wells Brown's novel *Clotel*. In *Brother to Dragons* he presents
himself in that biblical role:

> It was great Canaan's grander counterfeit.
> Bold Louisiana,
> It was the landfall of my soul.   (p.11)

From the top of Mount Nebo, God showed Moses a panoramic view
of the Israelites' terrestrial paradise. Jefferson identifies
Kentucky and beyond with what Moses saw:

> But it was my West, the West I bought and gave and never
> Saw, or but like the Israelite,
> From some high pass or crazy crag of mind, saw....

More fortunate than Jefferson, the narrator, R.P.W. (in *Brother to Dragons*), crosses the frontier:

> There was the quiet, high glade.
> Blue grass set round with beeches, the quietest tree.
> The air was suddenly sweet, a hint of cool,
> And even the sun's blaze could abate its fervor,
> And I stood in the new silence while my heart was beating.
> Some cattle gazed like peace from the farther shade.
>
> (p.32)

As in a "picturesque" painting, the ruined dwellings of departed farmers only enhance the Romantic art of this day in a
vanished July.

Toward the end of *Brother to Dragons,* Warren introduces as
a last "voice" Meriwether Lewis, companion of Boone, who experiences the same exhilaration as Jefferson as he looks out over
the virgin landscape: "We entered the land of the enormousness
of air./ For a year we moved toward the land of the Shining
Mountains" (p.178). The excitement of Cortez vibrates through
his response to unbelievable serenity:

And the snow on the far peak glared blue
In excess of light, and no track of beast on the unruffled
White of the high plain, no wing-flash in high air,
And in that glittering silence of the continent
I heard my heart beating distinctly, and I said,
Is this delight? Is this the name of delight?   (p.179)

The word *delight,* title of a seven-poem sequence in the 1966
volume, relies upon its second syllable to render visible the
ecstasies which, unannounced, pierce man the explorer.

Incarnations, although it contains "Treasure Hunt" with
its proclamation that all promises are kept, even happiness,
has nothing to offer by way of explicit Canaan imagery. *Audubon: A Vision,* too, does not develop this figure directly:
only its hero binds it to Kentucky, where the bird artist
knows the most supreme of emotions, caught up in a state in
which dream and reality are indistinguishable. In a letter
of September 20, 1969, Warren has given Eudora Welty's story
"A Still Moment" as in all likelihood the germ for this latest
book: after twenty years, even he can't be positive. Miss
Welty imagines Audubon thus: "Coming upon the Trace, he looked
at the high cedars, azure and still as distant smoke overhead,
with their silver roots trailing down on either side like the
veins of deepness in this place, and he noted some fact to his
memory — this earth that wears but will not crumble or slide
or turn to dust, they say it exists in one spot in the world,
Egypt — and then forgot it" (*The Wide Net,* p.82). Even closer
to Warren's overall intentions in his vision is the excerpt a
few pages on: "O secret life, he thought — is it true that the
secret is withdrawn from the true disclosure, that man is a
cave man, and that the openness I see, the ways through for-
ests, the rivers brimming light, the wide arches where the
birds fly, are dreams of freedom? If my origin is withheld
from me, is my end to be unknown too? Is the radiance I see
closed into an interval between two darks, or can it not illuminate them both and discover at last, though it cannot be
spoken, what was thought hidden and lost?" (pp.85-86).

The Middle Ages looked on Nature as the Book of the Creatures. Audubon, Warren, all of us in these still moments of
shalom come close to reading its secret. The closest analogue
to such a "dream/ Of a season past all seasons" (p.29) is a
reappearance of the golden glade:

The spring is circular and surrounded by gold leaves
Which are fallen from the beech tree.

Not even a skitter-bug disturbs the gloss
Of the surface tension. The sky

Is reflected below in absolute clarity.
If you stare into the water you may know

That nothing disturbs the infinite blue of the sky. (p.21)

George P. Garrett has said of this poet: "He stands almost alone in the sense of continued growth and change in his poetry" (in *Robert Penn Warren: A Collection of Critical Essays*, pp.223-24). In the years ahead, Warren's readers can logically expect that each lyric, by the keeping of its unique promise, will be a step forward toward its maker's Promised Land.

William Tjenos

The Art to Transfigure

The effort of Robert Penn Warren's poetry is to discover
the way in which consciousness engages experience and makes
it respond to human desire. In an interview of 1966, Warren
describes the need for "a mental experience that gives a sense
of moving from disorder to order, to a moment of poise....
It's a liberation. Not, I should emphasize, because of particular 'solutions' offered, but because the process is an image of the possibility of meaning growing from experience."[1]
Warren's poems enact the movements of a consciousness working
to arrest the flow of events and to define experience. The
growth of meaning depends on one's ability to construct bases
of relationship between the present and the total scope of
his mental experience. Until an experience is given definite
bounds and is placed in a particular conscious context, it remains alien, chaotic and unintelligible. The acceptance of an
experience into one's field of consciousness does not consist
merely of matching it with a pre-determined category. For Warren, consciousness should not only be broadened and enriched
by the present, it should be continually reformed by it. The
meanings of past experiences are by no means fixed; and if the
present is to have potential for more than the reiteration of
the past, the past must remain volatile, responsive to new possibilities for understanding. Warren has described this as
the way in which "cause flows backward from effect," the way
in which the past is given form by the present.

The poems, then, show the poet's labor of incorporating
experience into the life of his consciousness, of setting the
past and the present in living dialogue. The end of this action, as Warren says, is the achievement of a moment of poise
in which the process, momentarily suspended, reveals its meaning.

"Homage to Emerson," from *Tale of Time: 1960-1966*,[2] is a
good representative of Warren's poetic method. In the last
several lines of the poem there arises what appears to be an
intrusion of the authorial voice:

> ...There is the city, the sky
> Glows, glows above it, there must be
> A way by which the process of living can become Truth.
> Let us move toward the city. Do you think you could
>   tell me
> What constitutes the human bond?

If we see the "process of living" as presented in the uncertain progress of the poem, the outbreak of desire for "Truth" becomes a natural expression within the process of consciousness — the poem — which has been striving to transcend itself, that is, to achieve a definite order. The truth of the human bond as the conscious goal toward which the poem reaches is developed in the permutations of the poem's subject, and does not exist as such until it is articulated in the very last lines. The intention of the poem, in Warren's words, "is closer to the result than to the cause." The implications of the question are dependent upon the context from which they arise, but also achieve an independence in that they conceptualize what previously has been working in a multiplicity of perceptions. Is the human bond that which unifies man with nature, other men and himself; or is it that which holds man in bondage, that isolates him from nature and other men?

The first two stanzas of Part I, "His Smile," image the speaker's perceptions as his attention moves from without to within the "pressurized gloom" of the aircraft cabin. The perspective on the earth, "by snow like sputum smeared," as it moves into darkness is transposed onto the condition within the cabin, in which the "finger/ Of light" shines down on the field of the page. The environments, however, are of opposite natures: the sliding earth is characterized by process and irregularity while the sealed cabin is a glowing, but gloomy, stasis — there is no change, "No sin. Not even error." Essentially the same movement of attention occurs between the third and fourth stanzas. The relationship of the plane to the night atmosphere is interiorized by the speaker. The night hissing "on the glass" of the plane's tubular body becomes the wind whistling over the abstract glass of the subject's heart: "an empty/ Coca-Cola bottle." These stanzas express an increasing sense of isolation and disembodiment; the collective sense of "we" and "our" in the first perceptions becomes a focused concentration on "My heart," which is presented as a personal, "pressurized gloom." The heart, the center of being, is pictured as a passive container, a glass whose content is the passing image that is imperfectly reflected through it.

The image of Emerson, whose essays "lie" in the static light, is now summoned. He is portrayed with sustained irony:[3] "he walked in the greenwood./ He walked lightly, his toes out, his body/ Swaying in the dappled shade." Emerson, like the poet's abstracted heart, accepts all without discrimination:

"For he had forgiven God everything." Names and identities
are superfluous; there is "no error." There is, however, a
definite tension imposed between the first four stanzas and
the description of Emerson. The pressure and confinement of
the speaker's personal condition, which is described in harsh
technological language — "sand-blast," "ammoniac blast" — is
completely absent from the pastoral picturing of Emerson. The
rhythm of the two scenes also expresses this tension. The
speaker's world is one of abrupt piston-like movement: "A fin-
ger/ Of light, in our pressurized gloom, strikes down,/ Like
God, to poke the page, the page glows." The breakdown of sentences into isolated phrases, sharp alliteration, and the use
of few conjunctions presents a world of independent, mechanistic parts. Emerson, as he tells us himself in "Nature," exists in a world of lyric flow.

Briefly, the consciousness of the speaker establishes itself in a field of relationships that suggests its previous
engagement in a particular essay by Emerson: "Nature." The
superimposition of Emerson's vision on the subject's immediate
situation, however, has a disruptive effect. The comical depiction of Emerson, which is clear in its relation to the
first four stanzas, and the ironic suggestiveness of the words
"lie" and "dead right" indicate a current of emotion that finally erupts in the disassociated sentence: "When I was a boy
I had a wart on the right forefinger." Fundamentally, this
is the assertion of the individual, corporeal existence of the
speaker which has been hitherto denied.

Sections Two, Three, and the major portion of Four involve
the subject in a contextualizing of images and events from his
personal past into the conflict generated in section One. The
warted finger, which appeared so abruptly and unexpectedly is,
in "The Wart," integrated more smoothly into the ongoing movement of the poem. The desire for specificity, for a substantial identity, expresses itself in a short, frenetic narration
of a childhood memory. The event is drawn by simple association; the form of the recounting of that event, however, is
the source of its significance. In opposition to the piece-
meal type of construction in section One, in which images are
placed side to side and exert no vital influence on one another, "The Wart" is a sustained flow that is carried on by a
momentum that builds from the exigency of its need "to be something specific." There are no end stops within the development which moves between tenses — present to past to present
— as well as linearly within the past. The sense of one substantial reality impressing another substantial reality is
also conveyed in the definiteness with which the dialogue is
presented: "he said, *Son/ You quit that jack-off, and that
thing go away,/* And I said *Quit what,* and he giggled *He-he,*
and he/ Said...." This sense of concrete identity, however,
"At 38,000 feet" is only an evanescent image reflected in the
abstract heart. So, the second part, like the first, ends

with a fragmented sentence, a disruption that moves the poem
forward.

The return to crystalline indistinctness expressed in "The
Spider" is effected by a redirection of the subject's attention toward the immensity of space; the particularity of the
wart is lost in the infinity of the heavens. The stars — the
spider's eyes — recall a past dream: "I used to dream that God
was a spider, or/ Vice versa." (We remember that for Warren
dreaming may signify a conscious activity.) Even God and the
spider are indistinguishable; there is no substance, only
reflection. The funnel, of which "it is easier/ To dream,"
gives momentary shape to the fumeless and "Clear liquid" that
is the indefinite and indistinct "you." The lines are diffused on the page, and there is a sense of stasis about the
description, even though it centers on the act of pouring.
The elements, as is the situation in "His Smile," are arranged
in a quiescent order: "The liquid glimmers in darkness, you/
Are happy, it pours easily, without fume." This passive receptivity which represses the solid movement expressed in "The
Wart" again, as in part One, generates the pivot of its over-
throw: "All you have to do is not argue."

Argument, as it is taken up in the next section, "One
Drunk Allegory," is the manner in which the passivity of the
funneled liquid is resisted; it is the means for members of
"the kind," "human-kind," "to be...whatever you are." The
assertion of one's particular shape, or identity, is defined
by the shape of one's experience; identity exists in concrete
engagement with other identities. Abstraction again is com-
bated by the summoning of memory; it is not so much the content of the event, we remember, as the form which it takes in
the recounting that is of significance. The speaker's selection of the particular event probably arises from a conjunc-
tion of geographical placement — shortly West of Kentucky:
New Orleans — and the previous thoughts of a clear, pouring
liquid: Absinthe. But as the liqueur clouds in its solution
with water, so voices become distinct and bodies substantial
when attention is focused on the particular. "In New Orleans,
in French Town, in/ Front of the Old Absinthe House, and it/
Was Saturday night, was 2 a.m."

The narrative rhythm of "One Drunk Allegory" parallels
that of "The Wart"; there are few end stops, and the momentum
of the consciousness conjoins tenses and thoughts that syn-
tactical logic would have separate. Also, there is the presence of another voice which is distinct in its manner of
speech, as was the dialect of the Southern black in section
Two, from that of the narrator: "*Prithee,* the voice/ Expensive-
ly said." The account of the event, however, moves into the
realm of allegorization; that is, its substantiality is called
into doubt: "Emerson thought that significance shines through
everything." The subject tries to harbor simultaneously the
conflicting perceptions of identity and non-identity, opacity

and transparency, which previously have been mutually exclusive states of consciousness. This attempt at synthesis informs the speaker's next perception, which follows the narration without a grammatical break. "If it was, it was sure-God
one drunk allegory, and/ Somewhere in the womb-gloom of the
DC-8/ A baby is crying. The cry seems to have a reality/ Independent of the baby. The cry/ Is like a small white worm
in my brain." The image of birth, of breaking out into the
experience of newness and otherness, is undercut by images of
confinement and death. The child's voice is disembodied and
lives as an agent of decay in the subject's consciousness.
The meshing together of the contrary modes of perception has
resulted in their transformation into a single predicament: if
everything is only something through which significance shines,
all that we know lives only in our minds. One is entombed in
a subjectivity that knows no otherness; reality exists independently of the world of particular things. The speaker attends
to the immensity of space: "To my right, far over Kentucky,
the stars are shining."

Section Five, "Multiplication Table," begins with the
speaker in essentially the same perspective as we saw him at
the beginning of the poem: from the plane window he is contemplating the irregular patterns strewn over the earth's surface.
Unlike the first vision, however, this perception is not inter-
nalized; rather, he elaborates it with idiosyncratic metaphor,
the particularity of which indicates a desire to affirm familiarity with the texture of the earth. When the field of
vision is exhausted, the regions of darkness, previously left
as mere blankness, are lit by memory: "but/ Beyond the lights
it is dark, and one night in winter, I/ Stood at the end of a
pier at Coney Island." The rhythm of the first two stanzas of
the section is similar in its momentum of exigency to sections
Two and Four; the desire for particularity, to establish a personal context, is still manifested as a struggle.

As the aircraft descends, however, the sense of disruptive
immediacy wans and the earth shows individuality and life:
"Individual lights can be seen throbbing like nerve ends."
The animate image expresses, again, the identification of particularity with life. The perspective opening the section is
repeated: "I have friends down there, and their lives have
strange shapes/ Like eggs splattered on the kitchen floor."
But this time, as the distance between the subject and the
earth diminishes, the world is wholly personal; it is a home.
The relaxation accompanying this reassuring sense of identity
and relationship is expressed in the leisurely tone and rhythm
of the stanza. There is, though, a surfacing sense of unwar-
ranted complacency: "I love them, I think." The use of the
collective pronoun echoes Emerson's indiscriminate love for
the nameless violet. This realization breaks through in the
disrupting last sentence: "In a room, somewhere, a telephone
keeps ringing." The connection has not yet been made.

Born out of the "pressurized gloom" of the aircraft, the subject is hit by a tempest of sensations: "The wind comes off the Sound, smelling/ Of ice. It smells/ Of fish and burned gasoline... The air/ Shivers, it shakes like Jello with the roar of jets." Section Six, "Wind," is clearly an analogue to section Three, "The Spider"; the denatured liquid and the all-consuming thunder both deny the distinct. In this largely technological whirlwind, how is the particular to preserve itself against the "roar of jets." The "infinitesimal scrape" of the newspaper, however, is that to which one must hold, "forever"; for it is upon that scraping that identity hangs. What was true at 38,000 feet is also true at sea-level; particularity, individual identity, is contingent upon a context of other particulars.

The interior dialogue with the indefinite and unresponding "you" that begins in the latter part of "Wind" is the form that follows through to the poem's finish. The dialectic between abstraction and particularity which was carried on by the vehicle of the plane's trajectory, but which failed to achieve a correspondent synthesis at the plane's touchdown, now becomes explicit within the speaker's consciousness as a conversation with a nonspecific other. The opening stanza of section Seven is an ironic re-vision of the unshakeable order attributed to Emerson's essays — which, we remember, "lie." To endow an envelope of life insurance with the power to put the "All" of one's life in order involves the same reductionism expressed in "The Spider": the distilled liquid is replaced by money. The real problem of ordering life involves the very progress of the poem; it is the "process of living" which must be fashioned into order, the journey and not a presealed end. The three images that follow: the gulls on the night sea, the stars falling in eternal darkness, and the black ice of memory, recall the problem of establishing a context for identity. Against the immense sea of blackness, how are the flecks of life to be understood; do they have a place, or is everything falling freely in the darkness?

The final question, "Do you ever think/ Of a face half in shadow," focuses on one of the glimmerings in the dark. Clearly, the face is that of the speaker who has been with us since his first appearance over Peoria. However, the manner in which the question is presented, much like a riddle, suggests that it is of a hypothetical nature; it thus loses the context of the entire poem. The formation of this question, then, achieves the "poise" described by Warren. The conflict has not been resolved; rather, the tension is held in suspension. The final image is both moving to transcend the process of the poem, and calling on the authority — that is, the context — of the poem to dispel the shadow. We see then that the desire to know the truth of the "human bond" is, in many ways, the success of the poem's process. The question is a generalized query that has arisen from an engagement with concrete

experience, and which, by its ambiguous direction — "bond" implying both a uniting and an isolating function — is truthful
to the complexity of that experience. The section ends, like
the preceding ones, with a dissociated and disruptive comment:
"Is it merely a delusion that they seem to smile?" The answer
to this question, like all the others, is forthcoming; no final word can be given as long as life remains a process: "For
nothing is ever all, and nothing is ever all."[4]

In proposing this reading of "Homage to Emerson," I do not
mean to suggest that each of Warren's poems is involved in a
similar movement of amorphous perception into a progressively
defined conception. In "Ornithology in a World of Flux" and
"The True Nature of Time," a single image from the past is
juxtaposed with the present, the two images forming a diptych
whose meaning derives from the reflection of one time upon the
other. "Homage to Theodore Dreiser" begins with an examination of Dreiser's psyche, which is then viewed from the increasing perspectives of social environment and the human condition in general. The sequence of *Promises: To Gabriel* is
the effort of the author to understand himself, and by that
his son, in terms of the progress of generations. Times past,
present, and future are confronted by consciousness in "the
act/ To transfigure all fact" into the "story" of life.

In *Audubon: A Vision,* Warren writes that Jean Jacques
"dreamed of hunting with Boone, from imagination painted his
portrait." The effort of the narrator of the volume is to
paint a true, imaginative portrait of Audubon, and thus to
hunt with him. To do this, it is necessary to pare off the
encrustations of myth which obscure tha real passion of Audubon: "what/ Is man but his passion?" The volume begins with
the discarding of the last myth in which he was swathed —
that he was the lost Dauphin — and works to the heart of the
man by imaginatively subjecting Audubon's consciousness to the
world in which he walked. The truth of a person "can only be
enacted." The volume ends with the narrator affirming a "season past all seasons" — the season of the imagination — in
which one can participate in the vision, the passion, of Audubon. The forms of Warren's poems develop according to the
particular nature of the conscious experience from which they
are generated; there is no formula. The effort of his poetry,
however, is consistent; it is to create a "life record" by
meeting the world of flux and making it answer to human desire.

> All items listed above belong in the world
> In which all things are continuous,
> And are parts of the original dream which
> I am now trying to discover the logic of. This
> Is the process whereby pain of the past in its pastness
> May be converted into the future tense
> Of joy.[5]

301   *The Art to Transfigure*

. Frank Gado, ed., *First Person: Conversations on Writers & Writing* (New York: Union College Press, 1973), p. 76.

2. Robert Penn Warren, *Selected Poems, New and Old, 1923-1966* (New York: Random House, 1966), pp. 40-49.

3. A pose suggestive of the famous "transparent eyeball" passage in the essay "Nature."

4. *Selected Poems,* p. 233.

5. Robert Penn Warren, *Or Else — Poem/Poems 1968-1974* (New York: Random House, 1974), p. 22.

A. L. Clements

Sacramental Vision

For the abundance, range, variety, and high achievement in both fiction and poetry, one thinks back to Lawrence and Hardy for comparisons with Robert Penn Warren. There are important differences too, to be sure. Whereas Hardy wrote most of his poetry only after he abandoned novel-writing, Warren, who published his first book of poems a few years before his first novel, has continued to write in both genres throughout his lifetime, his tenth novel, *A Place to Come To,* being published the same year as his eleventh volume of poetry, *Selected Poems 1923-1975* (New York: Random House, 1977). (That this is his third *Selected Poems* — previous ones appeared in 1944 and 1966 — is in itself an extraordinary mark of accomplishment.) And whereas Lawrence, who produced magnificent poetry as well as bald assertions wigged out typographically in the shape of printed poems, will always be acclaimed a greater novelist than poet, Warren may finally be considered a better poet than novelist, especially if literary honors and awards are any sign of judgment to come. His first major recognition was the Pulitzer Prize for *All the King's Men* (1946), but in the past twenty years the awards, a long list of them, have been for his poetry: another Pulitzer in 1957, followed by the National Book Award, the Edna St. Vincent Millay Prize, the Bollingen Prize, the Van Wyck Brooks Award, and the Copernicus Award from the Academy of American Poets, among other recognitions. And one may reasonably expect other equally and more prestigious awards to follow.

In addition to his poetry and novels, Warren (like Lawrence) has published numerous other books: a play, short stories, biographies, influential criticism and textbooks, editions of other poets, and historical work, so that some critics consider him the most accomplished and distinguished living American man of letters. It is fortunate to have this other body of writing because, among other reasons, much of Warren's own poetry may best be regarded in the light of his

own articulate criticism. We are familiar with his view that
a poem is an organic system of relationships and that the poetic quality should not be understood as consisting in one or
more elements taken in isolation but rather in relation to
each other and to the total organization, the *structure,* of
the poem. Decades ago, Warren opposed theories of "pure" poetry, which tend to legislate out of poetry certain elements
that might qualify or contradict the original impulse of the
poem.[1] He has, furthermore, always sought some connection
between "my central and obsessive concern with 'poetry'...and
the 'real' world." In an interview published in *Writers at
Work,* he describes poetry as "a vital activity...related to
ideas and life."[2] His essay on Coleridge records the view
that "...the truth is implicit in the poetic act as such...
the moral concern and the aesthetic concern are aspects of the
same activity, the creative activity, and...this activity is
expressive of the whole mind."[3] And his most recent essay,
Democracy and Poetry (1975), observes that the central "fact"
of poetry is the concept of the self, which he defines as "in
individuation, the felt principle of significant unity," *significant* implying both continuity and responsibility: that is,
"the self as a development in time, with a past and a future"
and "the self as a moral identity, recognizing itself as capable of action worthy of praise or blame.... What poetry most
significantly celebrates is the capacity of man to face the
deep, dark inwardness of his nature and his fate."[4] Thus his
expository prose spells out what we recognize in his fiction
and poetry to be his major triune theme of self, time, and
moral responsibility, and reveals what for him is the vital
purpose of poetry.

   With this critical focus from his own essays, we may more
clearly and pertinently review Warren's prolific poetic career,
a career that is divisible into three distinct periods: 1923-
1943, 1943-1960, and 1960-1975. Many poems of each period
have a decidedly philosophic and religious content, being preoccupied with his major tripartite theme as well as with guilt
and innocence, love and the imagination, death and rebirth.
But Warren avoids dogmatism, often minimizes explicit commentary, qualifies ironically, balances tensions. His poetry
moves over the years toward "sacramental vision," expressed
increasingly in sequences and in the "principle of interrelatedness."

   I

   Warren's latest volume of poetry, *Selected Poems 1923-1975,*
reprints 23 of the 42 poems published in *Selected Poems 1923-
1943,* which was largely composed of *Thirty-six Poems* (1935)
and *Eleven Poems on the Same Theme* (1942). Astute critic that
he is, Warren has made essentially the right choices. Reminders of his association with the Fugitives, of the Ransom and

Tate manners, of the Metaphysicals (particularly Donne and Marvell), and Eliot-like devices and diction remain, beside his
own distinctive signature. Common to this poetic company are
the much discussed complexity of attitude, psychological sub-
tlety, strong dramatic sense, textural density, abrupt transi-
tions and shifts of tone, juxtaposition of abstract, meditative lines and concrete colloquial passages, and even metrical
alternation from smooth to harsh and from tight to loose lines;
most of these being modes of contrast, tension, and inclusion.
Lines from the powerful early poem on the death of the poet's
mother, "The Return: An Elegy," illustrate some of these characteristics:

It will be the season when milkweed blossoms burn.

    The old bitch is dead
    what have I said!
    I have only said what the wind said...

    turn backward turn backward O time in your flight
    and make me a child again just for tonight
    good lord he's wet the bed come bring a light...

Warren has kept ten of the *Eleven Poems on the Same Theme,*
but these have been radically re-arranged and interspersed
among the eleven poems remaining from *Thirty-six Poems*. Nevertheless, groups of juxtaposed poems, most very formally pat-
terned, emerge and, together with "Mexico Is a Foreign Country:
Four Studies in Naturalism" (originally Five Studies), adum-
brate a developing interest in writing and arranging thematically and technically echoic poems into sequences (much more
about that later). The opening lines alone of "Monologue at
Midnight," "Picnic Remembered," and the much explicated and
anthologized "Bearded Oaks," for example, reveal a ready similarity of setting and subject. "Terror," "Pursuit," "Original
Sin: A Short Story," and "Crime," still another group, are not
only "on the same theme" but so uniformly dense, minimally generalized, and tightly organized in the successive images of
their formal stanzas that F. O. Matthiessen in his 1944 review
and Victor Strandberg on the very first page of his 1965 book
on Warren's poetry remarked upon the "obscurity" of these and
other poems. Today we do not see them quite so. The "you" at
the center of each of the four poems has in "Terror" "no adequate definition of terror." This poem pictures an age of neu-
rotic anxieties and a world spending itself in its own destruction, repeating "The crime of Onan, spilled upon the ground,"
while genuine terror seems a pre-condition for salvation.
The wholly noncommitted person, the one with the "darling and
inept" terrors, equally as guilty as the sensation-seeking
destroyers of self and the world, sees nothing, heeds nothing,
does not "ask tonight where sleeps/ That head which hooped
the jewel Fideltiy" — that is, is faithful to nothing; on the
other hand, "the conscience-stricken stare/ Kisses the terror."

"Pursuit" also concerns search for meaning, in particular "The secret you are seeking" to eradicate deeply buried pain. You cannot buy the secret with charitable purchases, so you take your pain to a doctor, the usurper of priest and poet, who does not know you carry your pain very deep inside you. Hence his prescription: "you simply need a change of scene." Seeking the secret in Florida, you consider nature in the form of the flamingo; that form, returning no answer, takes the shape of a question. Looking for the answers from the other guests, even from the innocent child, is finally fruitless. You are thus left sitting alone, "which is the beginning of error," for "solution, perhaps, is public, despair personal." Though you will continue fruitless wandering, unless you see the inwardness of your disease, there may yet be a palliative, hope maybe, and even perhaps rebirth through commitment to some external support: "the little old lady in black...rattles her crutch, which may put forth a small bloom, perhaps white," "perhaps" being a frequent qualifier in Warren's poetry. His perception of the human condition does not permit expectations of vast or easily affected changes.

In "Crime" Warren ironically invites us to "Envy the mad killer," because he, with a kind of childlike innocence, has buried his crime, cannot even remember it. Nor can he "formulate the delicious/ And smooth convolution of terror, like whipped cream." In "Original Sin: A Short Story" the pursuing "you" of "Pursuit" becomes the pursued; "the nightmare," original sin, is now the pursuer and cannot be buried. As in "Pursuit," changing places does not alter the darkness in the very nature of man, the partially fixed and inherited capacity for evil and irrationality. "There must be a new innocence for us to be stayed by," but this poem does not "endeavor definition." Naive utopianism and easy panaceas evaporate when to the tentativeness of "may...small...perhaps" and the restraint and qualification of other poems, like "Ransom," is added the knowledge that the nightmare is never entirely lost.

The most ambitious, longest, and best poem from *Selected Poems 1923-1943* still is "The Ballad of Billie Potts," still placed at the head of the selection, but now slightly revised. Many of Warren's persistent essential themes inform the poem, a structural unit that integrates a colloquial narrative section and a choric, meditative section, an effective combination of Warren's strong story-telling and speculative abilities. These themes and the double-thread form appear in *At Heaven's Gate* and *All the King's Men,* novels nearly contemporaneous with the poem, and propose a view of reality as dialectical process rather than static perfection. Uniting contrary impulses and discordant elements, "The Ballad" is rich, gritty, funny, pitiful, and tragic, and (together with "Mexico Is a Foreign Country," a poem of hearty and humorous coarseness) it marked a breaking away from the mannered, purely intellectualized modes that were popular some decades ago.

The story element of "The Ballad of Billie Potts," based
on material Warren heard in his youth and acquiring mythic
proportions through his treatment, concerns an inn-keeping family: Big Billie Potts, his "dark and little" wife, and their
son, Little Billie, "A clabber-headed bastard with snot in his
nose," who have a lucrative side-business of robbing their former customers on the road. Little Billie attempts to commit
a robbery himself, fails at it, is wounded and, for safety's
sake, is sent out West by his parents. The Prodigal returns
ten years later but is not recognized by his parents, who sink
a hatchet into his head for his money and then learn too late
what they have done. Such is the simple narrative outline.
But the various thematic implications are not as easily set
down. The lines

     (There was a beginning but you cannot see it.
     There will be an end but you cannot see it....)

suggest a recurrent interest of Warren's: man's predicament
of lacking sufficient knowledge in time. The context of these
lines indicates that the beginning is with the father, a variation on the doctrine of Original Sin. Little Billie tries to
escape West and find himself; but as seen in other poems you
cannot escape what is always pursuing you, and you must stay,
face responsibility, and earn definition.

     There is always another name and another face...
     The name and the face are you.
     The name and the face are always new...
     For they have been dipped in the redeeming blood.
     For they have been dipped in Time.

In this sacramental vision, a man in Time cannot know the end,
cannot know until he is out of Time. But, another edge to the
irony, a man can be redeemed only in Time. The poem remarks
that innocence, associated by Warren with childhood as it always mythically is associated, was lost long ago, and it concludes with this image of "you, wanderer, back,"

     To kneel in the sacramental silence of evening
     At the feet of the old man
     Who is evil and ignorant and old,
     To kneel
     With the little black mark under your heart,
     Which is your name,
     Which is shaped for luck.
     Which is your luck.)

As in "Original Sin," Warren affirms the need for a new innocence, but again he does not here attempt definition. There
are only "hints and guesses" and the direction taken in the
poems of Warren's middle and late periods.

II

In the decade after *Selected Poems 1923-1943,* Warren was preoccupied with writing and publishing several volumes of fiction and his "novel in verse," *Brother to Dragons* (1953). He returned to the "short" form in *Promises: Poems 1954-1956,* widely regarded as more successful than the experimental *You, Emperors, and Others: Poems 1957-1960.* After considerably reducing this later volume for *Selected Poems 1923-1966,* Warren has made further cuts so that only about half of *You, Emperors, and Others* now appears in *Selected Poems 1923-1975.* Still, unsatisfactory poems remain, such as "Switzerland" and especially "Man in the Street" with its jarring jingling rimes. "Mortmain," one of several groups of poems, is the most effective and moving in *You, Emperors,* its subject being the poet's father and the father's death, developed in five poems with a shifting time scheme that proceeds achronologically from the 1950s to the 1880s. On the whole, however, *You, Emperors* must be regarded as a largely failed experiment, Warren's least impressive book of poetry.

Except for the very short last poem, "The Necessity for Belief," all of the extraordinary *Promises* has been reprinted in *Selected Poems 1923-1975.* The subject of childhood and Warren's bent for twofoldness are again evident in *Promises,* which is divided into two sections. The first and smaller section, "To a Little Girl, One Year Old, in a Ruined Fortress," dedicated to his daughter, has a Mediterranean setting in a season which moves from summer toward autumn. The second, longer section, "Promises," dedicated to his son, is itself of a twofold nature: most of these poems draw their material from Warren's recollections of his childhood in Kentucky during the early years of this century, and other poems are addressed and applicable to his son. The basic subject matter of childhood helps give thematic continuity to the book's quest for self-discovery, contemporary childhood contrasting and interacting with recollected childhood, and encourages a ranging from intense personal feelings to historical and universal implications.

In his criticism of "The Rime of the Ancient Mariner," Warren writes that there are two themes, the primary theme of sacramental vision or of "One Life" and the secondary theme of the imagination; sacramental vision and the imagination are construed as distinguishable aspects of the same reality. He approaches the secondary theme through the symbol of different kinds of light, discussing the constant contrast between moonlight, symbolizing the imagination, and sunlight, symbolizing the "mere reflective faculty" which, Coleridge said, partakes of "Death." Warren points out that in the poem the good events occur under the aegis of the moon, and the bad events, under that of the sun. The issue is a bit complicated in that the operation and effect of the imagination can be both joyous

and terrifying. In his own poetry, Warren makes similar use
of light imagery and the themes of sacramental vision and imagination, though he often substitutes starlight for moonlight
in his later poetry.

Recollections are present imaginings of the past. In
"Court-Martial," written in short couplets and triplets, the
speaker recalls his grandfather's story of the hangings of
bushwhackers during the Civil War. "I see him now, as once
seen." The grandfather and grandson sit in the shade of an
evergreen, "withdrawn from the heat of the sun," the light of
which dapples the objects under the boughs. The old cavalry-
man's story is itself a recollection — a history, in one sense,
the significance of which the speaker tries to discover:

> I sought, somehow, to untie
> The knot of History,
> For in our shade I knew
> That only the Truth is true,
> That life is only the act
> To transfigure all fact,
> And life is only a story
> And death is only the glory
> Of the telling of the story,
> And the *done* and the *to-be-done*
> In that timelessness were one
> Beyond the poor *being done*.

While raising questions concerning History, Truth, Time,
the poem suggests that the final reality is somehow involved
with the imagination. Just after the old man has concluded
his story and before the poem ends, the speaker turns away and
sees his grandfather, "not old now — but young," riding out of
the sky. This is imagined in detail: the saddle, the cavalry
boots, the hanged men with outraged faces taking shape behind
the rider. The poem concludes:

> The horseman does not look back.
> Blank-eyed, he continues his track,
> Riding toward me there,
> Through the darkening air.

> The world is real. It is there.

What, considered in its context, is the world referred to in
the last line; what is the referent of "there"? The world external to the mind or the world as transfigured by the deific
imagination? The answer may well be both. But internal considerations lead to the conclusion that "world" and "there"
refer in a special sense to the world shaped by the speaker's
imagination: History, Truth, and Time are functions of the
creative imagination, which has a value-giving capacity. The
external world or natural order is devoid of values. Taken by
itself, there is no one thing in the natural order that is bet-

ter than any other thing. The poem (and particularly the line,
"life is only a story") does not empty reality of its content;
it makes it clear that the content is given value and meaning
by the imagination.

Just as in this poem of recollection so in "Lullaby: Smile
in Sleep" the theme of imagination as a kind of ultimate, transcendental (in Kant's sense) shaping force finds expression.
Lulling his infant son, the speaker says "You will dream the
world anew." Awake, the boy in years to come will see a violent world, the truth perverted, and love betrayed; thus is
his obligation greater to "Dream perfection": the more imperfect the world the greater is the human need for perfection.
The image serves to re-create and to perfect imperfect reality
and gives "our hope new patent to/ Enfranchise the human possibility./ Grace undreamed is grace forgone./ Dream grace, son."
The tension of lullaby juxtaposed against images of violence
is resolved in the last stanza:

> There's never need to fear
> Violence of the poor world's abstract storm.
> For now you dream Reality.
> Matter groans to touch your hand.
> Matter lifts now like the sea
> Toward that cold moon that is your dream's command.
> Dream the power coming on.

The implications are clear: as the moon influences the sea,
so the dream or image, which is the working of the imagination,
shapes inferior matter. Warren's conception of the imagination is precisely Coleridgean. The imagination organizes what
otherwise would be chaotic sensation, and, contrariwise, it
anchors the reason in images of sensation, so that the imagination repeats "in the finite mind...the eternal act of creation in the infinite I am." The primary imagination creates
the world and the self; the secondary imagination is the value-
creating capacity; and one knows by creating.

The child as well as the poem is a "promise"; both renew
the world. In Warren, childhood has much of the same prominence and significance that it does in Henry Vaughan and Thomas Traherne. The Infant Boy at Midcentury, we read in a poem
of that title, enters "our world at scarcely its finest hour...
in the year when promises are broken," when the need for renewal is great. Thus the poet has attempted to order and set
down meanings wrung from early experience as a legacy to the
child. Though there will be "modification of landscape... And
expansion, we trust, of the human heart-hope, and hand-scope,"
Warren does not sentimentally anticipate vast changes or
changes easily effected. The poems of recollection present
images of a violent and terror-ridden world: a summer storm
bringing havoc to a county; the founding fathers in their de-
fects; some unidentifiable evil terrifying another county; a
father murdering his entire family. The same dark and hidden

forces that, submerged, lie waiting to spring and do spring in one generation do not simply disappear in the next. Thus

> The new age will need the old lies, as our own more than
>   once did;
> For death is ten thousand nights — yes, it's only the
>   process
> Of accommodating flesh to idea, but there's natural
>   distress
> In learning to face Truth's glare-glory, from which our
>   eyes are long hid.   ("Infant Boy at Midcentury")

The need of finding Truth to live by is related to Warren's pervasive theme of the need for self-definition; he who has discovered and defined himself in finding a Truth by which to live an integrated life can face "the awful responsibility of Time."

The difficult problem of truth-finding is further complicated by the elusiveness of the meanings of experiences. Such elusiveness preoccupies several poems: "Dark Woods," "Country Burying (1919)," "School Lesson...," "Dark Night of the Soul," and others. In "The Dogwood," the second section of "Dark Woods," the speaker is walking in, not merely stopping by, the dark woods at night. These were the woods of his childhood. Now suddenly he comes across a dogwood tree, "White-floating in darkness...white bloom in dark air." He experiences a mixture of feelings: first joy, and then wrath so that he would have struck the tree if a stick had been handy.

> But one wasn't handy, so there on the path then, breath
>   scant,
> You stood, you stood there, and oh, could the poor heart's
>   absurd
> Cry for wisdom, for wisdom, ever be answered? Triumphant,
> All night, the tree glimmered in darkness, and uttered no
>   word.

This object of white in dark should, it seems to the speaker, have held the key to meaning; but the speaker remains outside the still moment, not entering into intuitive illumination. As with other tree imagery, the dogwood in the night, a contrast of opposites, is both a symbol of reality and of the speaker's wish for insight into it.

It is this insight, resulting in the silent state of being "blessed past joy or despair" (from "Boy's Will...") that the poems, finally, move toward. On the word "blessedness," which in its different grammatical forms appears repeatedly in the later poetry, Walter Stace remarks: "Whatever may be the root and derivation of this word in common language, it is now a wholly religious and mystical word, and not a part of the common naturalistic vocabulary at all."[5]   The ultimate symbolizandum of Warren's poetry, as of all religious language, is the mystical or transcendental or peak experience. That this

is so is clearly evidenced in the sacramental vision and the
principle of interrelatedness of the more recent poems of *Tale
of Time: New Poems 1960-1966, Incarnations: Poems 1966-1968,
Audubon: A Vision* (1969), *Or Else — Poem/Poems 1968-1974,* and
"Can I See Arcturus from Where I Stand? Poems 1975."

III

While a number of pieces have been moved to *Or Else,* only
six poems from Warren's previous four volumes have not been reproduced in *Selected Poems 1923-1975,* more than half of which
(188 of 325 pages) consists of poems written between 1960-1975,
clear and accurate recognition by Warren himself of the general superiority of his later poems over his earliest work. He
has been increasingly both a more prolific poet and a remarkably better one.
These four recent volumes as well as "Can I See Arcturus
from Where I Stand?," the ten new poems published in *Selected
Poems 1923-1975,* demonstrate both poetic continuity and development in a poetry stylistically more lucid, firm, and powerful, with somewhat less tentativeness and qualification. The
strokes are bolder and yet the nuances more subtle and various,
usually through a directness of poetic narrative, more frequent use of the long line, and added emphasis on the colloquial, though sometimes the language is plainly too flat.
Warren's later poetry is less metaphysically knotty and dense
than his early work but no less complex in significance. He
can still delight us with echoes of the Metaphysical manner,
with "glittering ambiguity" and a "more complex/ Version of
Zeno's paradox" ("Paradox" in "Can I See Arcturus..."), but
that of course was never his own major mode so much as a part
of a more various, inclusive style and of his insight into
a diverse range of writers and traditions. His later poetry
is intellectual without being intellectualized, with few ex-
ceptions idea not being purposelessly substituted for image.
Warren is now as accomplished at presenting descriptive images
which "effortlessly" expand into metaphor and meaning as he is
at developing narrative, always his great strength. Exceptionally vivid descriptions and extraordinarily pleasing sounds
frequently appear as integral parts of a poem's progress (see,
for example, "Forever O'Clock" and "Composition in Gold and
Red-Gold" in *Or Else*). The later poems are generally less formally arranged in meter, line length, and rime, but Warren has
developed enormous skill in the syntax of the sentence, the
placement of the words in the line, the use of spacing, and
the rhythms thereby and otherwise produced. While he takes
radical risks in language, thought, and structure, the poetry
achieves seemingly stunningly simple and often powerfully direct effects.
Many of Warren's later poems are remarkable for the quality of unanticipated yet just and engaging, sometimes over-

whelmingly effective and memorable last lines. The ring, reason, and rhythm of these last lines remain long after reading
within the reader's memory. It will not do to quote only a
few lines in illustration. For (and herein lies the principle
of interrelatedness), the lines must be taken and understood
in context, and by "context" is meant not only the poem of
which the last line or lines are a part, but also the sequence
of which the poem is a part, the volume of which the sequence
is a part, and the total body of Warren's poetry of which any
one volume is a part. This principle of interrelatedness functions as the major formal and technical aspect of his more recent poetry as well as a major semantic dimension of his sacramental vision and the subsumed central themes of time, self,
responsibility, love, death, rebirth, and joy.

Since the publication in 1942 of *Eleven Poems on the Same
Theme,* Warren has been writing in groups of poems, increasingly so from *Promises* on forward, as just a glance at the table
of contents in *Selected Poems 1923-1975* readily though only
partially indicates. Not only grouping and repeated subjects
and thematic concerns but also full sequences with the recurrence of certain words and images conduce to the sense of
continuity and integration. *Audubon: A Vision* reads as a single long poem composed of shorter poems. And in a foreword,
Warren has said exactly that about *Or Else:* "this book is conceived as a single poem composed of a number of shorter poems
or sections or chapters." Simplifying slightly, *Or Else,* preoccupied with remembrance of things past ("Time is the mirror
into which you stare"), begins in summer, progresses soon
thereafter from very frequent images of snow to thaw near the
end of the book, from death to rebirth, from parent to self
to son and blessedness ("For what blessing may a man hope for
but/ An immortality in/ The loving vigilance of death?"), from
uncertainty about the self (*"Is this really me?"*) to rediscovery of the self. The words *dream* and *see* (and their grammatical variations) keep reappearing, often associated with the
past, the imagination, and sacramental vision. Images of
mountains and especially of stars ("Man lives by images," we
read in "Reading Late at Night, Thermometer Falling," a marvelous and moving poem on Warren's father) abound in this volume.
They do also in "Can I See Arcturus from Where I Stand?" which
has eight of its ten poems star-lit or night-set and which
takes its epigraph, "Is *was* but a word for wisdom, its price?"
from a poem in *Or Else*.

Warren employs a number of other means for indicating interrelatedness both within and between sequences and volumes.
For example, in the later poetry, he vastly increases the
number of run-on lines, not only from line to line but also
between stanzas, sections, and even whole poems within a sequence. For another example, *Tale of Time,* which asserts "To
know is, always, all," has one poem in the title sequence that
ends with the question "What is love?"; the next poem con-

cludes "You have not answered my question." The answer or
rather one answer comes two volumes later in *Audubon: A Vision,*
in the poem "Love and Knowledge," which tells us about the
birds Audubon painted that

> He put them where they are, and there we see them:
> In our imagination.

And then the poem concludes:

> What is love?

> One name for it is knowledge.

Knowledge here being Audubon's loving, creative, imaginative
apprehension and rendering of his birds and perhaps also the
viewers', "our," imaginative perception.

Added significance and purpose obtain in Warren's poetic
sequences because his metaphysic regards reality as relational
or interrelated. As *Incarnations* reads, "Truth lives only in
relation," and from one of the Arcturus poems: "you are a part/
Of everything, and your heart bleeds far/ Beyond the outermost
pulsar." (It is now an ecological truism that everything is
ultimately connected to everything else; science has finally
confirmed what poets and mystics have intuited and experienced
— actually sensed and felt — for centuries.) Like the world's
body, each poem is itself an organic system of relationships,
and each poem, as each creature, object, and event in the
world, has full meaning, value, and being not separately in
isolation from but interdependently in relation to all others.
Form and content, especially in Warren's later work, are themselves inextricably interwoven.

In "Holy Writ," from *Tale of Time,* the biblical Samuel,
concerned about his "son," expresses a view of time to be
found throughout Warren's poetry and novels too:

> I am the past time, am old, but
> Am, too, the time to come, for I,
> In my knowledge, close my eyes, and am
> The membrane between the past and the future,
>   am thin, and
> That thinness is the present time, the membrane
> Is only my anguish, through which
> The past seeps, penetrates, is absorbed into
> The future, through which
> The future bleeds into, becomes, the past even before
> It ceases to be
> The future.

Earlier in the same volume, Warren had written that "Truth"

> Is all. But
> I must learn to speak it
> Slowly, in a whisper.
> Truth, in the end, can never be spoken aloud,

For the future is always unpredictable.
But so is the past...   ("Insomnia")

In *Incarnations* we read that "The world"

Is fruitful, and I, too,
In that I am the father
Of my father's father's father. I,
Of my father, have set the teeth on edge. But
By what grape? I have cried out in the night.
                              ("The Leaf")

Similarly, in *All the King's Men,* Jack Burden, who comes to
realize that "all times are one time" and "nothing is ever
lost," says "I eat a persimmon and the teeth of a tinker in
Tibet are put on edge." The allusion in both the poetry and
prose is of course to the biblical "the fathers have eaten a
sour grape and their children's teeth are set on edge" (Jer.
31:29; Ezek.18:2), which is one succinct formulation of the
doctrine of Original Sin. "All times are one time" in the
sense that, as Samuel's words suggest, any event in time is
meaningful only in relation to past and future events. The
past is not separate and completed in itself but an ever-
developing part of a changing present and future. Once this
knowledge is learned, one's individual life and all life may
be seen to fall into coherent and inevitable patterns which
give meaning to the past, present, and future. We all have
and are a multiplicity of fathers because we inherit all of
the past and we bequeath our lifetime.
    Warren's conception of the self parallels his view of time:
a past self or a past life is never simply over, for the past
exists not only as past but simultaneously with the present
in the sense that, being a part of the present self, it influences the present, as it and the present shape the future.
Hence the importance and recurrence in Warren's work of history, recollecting the past, childhood, relationships between
generations. Warren further distinguishes between two selves:
a surface, spurious, temporal self and a deeper, essential,
and eternal (that is, timeless) self (Warren has used the
terms "ideal" and "regenerate" self). The first self or ego
is one's conception of oneself, the role one assumes and is
assigned to play, the known created object, not the knowing,
imaginative, creative Act. As shown, for example, by "Interjection #5: Solipsism and Theology," with its repeated "Wild
with ego," the ego is a prideful sense of separate existence,
a rather abstract and conventional notion of oneself rather
than the actual, concrete, living reality. To be in touch
with this latter nontemporal real self, which paradoxically
develops only in time and in vital relation to community, is
to be blessed. Warren writes of Jean Jacques Audubon:

His life, at the end, seemed — even the anguish — simple.
Simple, at least, in that it had to be,

Simply, what it was, as he was,
In the end, himself and not what
He had known he ought to be. The blessedness! —

To wake in some dawn and see,
As though down a rifle barrel, lined up
Like sights, the self that was, the self that is, and
     there,
Far off but in range, completing that alignment, your
     fate.

Hold your breath, let the trigger-squeeze be slow and
     steady.

The quarry lifts, in the halo of gold leaves, its noble
     head.

This is not a dimension of Time.
                          ("The Sign Whereby He Knew")

Various succinct though incomplete expressions of Warren's
complex sacramental vision appear throughout his poetry, such
as in the problematic, prosy "Interjection #4" from *Or Else:*

                    If blood
Was shed, it was, in a way, sacramental, redeeming...
                    Dear God, we pray
To be restored to that purity of heart
That sanctifies the shedding of blood.

More clearly and certainly: "we are all one flesh," "The world/
Is a parable and we are/ The meaning," "do you truly, truly,/
Know what flesh is, and if it is...really sacred?" from *Incarnations,* one of whose epigraphs is from Nehemiah 5, "Yet now
our flesh is as the flesh of our brethren." And "have you...
eaten the flesh of your own heart?" and "the dream of the eating of human flesh" from *Tale of Time*. The last phrase is
from the title poem "Tale of Time," which centrally concerns
the death of the speaker's mother, just as many of Warren's
later poems dwell or touch upon death. "Tale of Time" also
provides this fuller expression of sacramental vision:

But the solution: You
Must eat the dead.
You must eat them completely, bone, blood, flesh, gristle,
     even
Such hair as can be forced. You
Must undertake this in the dark of the moon, but
At your plenilune of anguish.

Immortality is not impossible,
Even joy.

History, all time, and the cruel, inescapable fact of death
are to be incorporated in and by the living. Acceptance, indeed affirmation, of the past and of change or transience, is

essential to successful self definition, that is, to knowing
one's deep, regenerate self, that "unself which was self,"
"that darkness of sleep which/ Is the past, and is/ The self."
Self-knowledge, in turn, gives direction to the future and induces in one, as in Audubon, a capacity more fully to love and
sympathize.

Self-knowledge, however, is never completed; it is a process of continuous becoming because the self is always in the
process of becoming a new self, of coming into new relations
with others. "You are not you," one of Warren's novels reads,
"except in terms of relation to other people." Self-knowledge
is difficult because the self is not so much just a knowable
object but rather a series of relations in time. Hence the
necessity of sacramentally eating the dead, incorporating the
past and all time in a kind of communion, to discover one's
larger, eternal self and thereby attain "Immortality... Even
joy."

Something of the principle of interrelatedness as method
and of an end of sacramental vision appears in *Or Else* in the
remarkable "Interjection #2: Caveat":

Necessarily, we must think of the
world as continuous, for if it were
not so I would have told you, for I have
bled for this knowledge, and every man
is a sort of Jesus...

The poem moves from a prosy "metaphysical" beginning on continuity and discontinuity to contrasting plain, subtle statement, even understatement, describing a highway under construction with miles of crushed rock and recommending that you "fix
your eyes firmly on/ one fragment of crushed rock," highway
and fragment becoming metaphors for continuity and discontinuity. At first the rock "only/ glows a little," then it glit-
ters and vibrates, the earth underfoot twitches,

                        the bright sun
jerks like a spastic, and all things seem to
be spinning away from the univer-
sal center that the single fragment of
crushed rock has ineluctably become....

                    at last, the object screams

in an ecstasy of

being.

The poem leads suddenly to overwhelming vision, makes us see.
In other words, another aspect of Warren's sacramental vision
obtains in the illuminated, imaginative perceptions into
reality as joyous and sacred, when *every/ Ulcer in love's
lazaret may, like a dawn-stung gem, sing — or even/ burst into
whoops of, perhaps, holiness,*" as we read in "There's a Grand-

father's Clock in the Hall," a poem which attains grace beyond
the reach of art.

At times the divine is seen as incarnate in the world.
In such perfect moments, or epiphanic spots of time, ordinary,
everyday events and entities appear extraordinary and transcendent, become charged through the creative imagination with
enormous physical, emotional, and spiritual meanings, are more
fully created or brought into fuller being. "All the things
of the universe," as Whitman says, "are seen as perfect mira-
cles." Or as Zen puts it, "How marvelous, how supernatural,
I draw water and carry wood!" Emerson also, as Warren remarks
in his sequence "Homage to Emerson," "thought that significance shines through everything." Examples abound in Warren's
later poetry, often associated with images of light, such as
the exceptionally fine "Two Poems about Suddenly and a Rose"
from the sequence "Delight" in *Tale of Time,* which lead us to
see that "The rose dies laughing, suddenly."

"Trying to Tell You Something" and "Brotherhood in Pain,"
two companion poems in "Can I See Arcturus...," develop the
idea that "All things lean at you, and some are/ Trying to
tell you something," and conclude that any chance object you
fix your eyes on will "smile shyly, and try to love you."
In *Or Else,* "The mountains lean. They watch. They know"
("Little Boy And Lost Shoe"). In the same volume, the speaker recalls the time he looked at the stars and cried out

> "O reality!" The stars
> Love me. I love them. I wish they
>
> Loved God, too. I truly wish that.   ("Stargazing")

And he remembers

> How once I, a boy, crouching at creekside,
> Watched, in the sunlight, a handful of water
> Drip, drip, from my hand. The drops — they were
>   bright!   ("Blow, West Wind")

Not uncharacteristically, Warren concludes this poem with a
balancing ironic tension, "But you believe nothing, with the
evidence lost." Nevertheless, sacramental vision exists also
in present time without irony or contradiction. From *Incarnations,* we read

> When there is a strong swell, you may, if you surrender
>   to it, experience
> A sense, in the act, of mystic unity with that rhythm.
>   Your peace is the sea's will.

This poem, "Masts at Dawn," indicating that imaginative loving
(an act of enlightened loving apprehension) leads to seeing
the incarnate divine, concludes "We must try/ To love so well
the world that we may believe, in the end, in God." And, finally, this instance of "dream"-like or imaginative, illumi-

nated, joyful vision beyond the rational knowing of the "mere
reflective faculty," with the consequent "perfect stillness,"
from *Audubon:*

> The world declares itself. That voice
> Is vaulted in — oh, arch on arch — redundancy of joy,
>   its end
> Is its beginning, necessity
> Blooms like a rose. Why,
>
> Therefore, is truth the only thing that cannot
> Be spoken?
>
> It can only be enacted, and that in dream,
> Or in the dream become, as though unconsciously, action...
>
> He walked in the world. He was sometimes seen to stand
> In perfect stillness, when no leaf stirred.
>   ("The Sign Whereby He Knew")

If Warren's poetry thus affirms life and its moments of
perfect stillness, it does so only after its journey through
the valley of the suffering and the dead, only after spending
its season in hell. Audubon comes to his vision some time
after witnessing the violent death by hanging of a woman and
her two sons, described with precise detail. He who "felt
the splendor of God..., loved the world...and wrote: 'in my
sleep I continually dream of birds'" knew also that the world
"though wicked in all conscience is *perhaps* as good as worlds
unknown." Affirmation thus obtains through the tentativeness
of the italicized qualifier *perhaps* and after various means
of balanced ironic tension. Similarly, *Incarnations* contains
both the long poetic sequence "Internal Injuries," which concerns the death by execution of a convict and the death by
automobile accident of his mother, and also such balancing
seemingly contradictory yet all "true" statements as "The
world means only itself," "the world is a metaphor," "the
world is a parable and we are the meaning," and "only Nothingness is real and is a sea of light," this last being one of
several expressions of the mystical *via negativa* to be found
in Warren's poetry. A good number of poems in *Or Else* and several poetic sequences in *Tale of Time* likewise centrally involve violence and death, including one death by suicide. In
short, Warren's joyful, interrelated, sacramental vision is
not an easy or facilely optimistic one but one gained through
judicious qualification and hard, unblinking, recurrent recognition, even a pervasive sense, of pain, darkness, and death.
Thus *Incarnations:* "The terror is, all promises are kept.
Even happiness"; "and there is no joy without some pain."
The rose dies laughing, suddenly.

> All items listed above belong in the world
> In which all things are continuous,
> And are parts of the original dream which

I am now trying to discover the logic of. This
Is the process whereby pain of the past in its pastness
May be converted into the future tense

Of joy.
    ("I Am Dreaming of a White Christmas..." in *Or Else*)

IV

We may say finally of Warren exactly what he has written
of Audubon: "He yearns to be able to frame a definition of
joy." And exactly what he has written of Flaubert:

                his heart
burst with a solemn thanksgiving to God for
the fact he could perceive the worth of the
world with such joy.   ("Flaubert in Egypt" in *Or Else*)

For Warren knows, as Yeats has written:

When such as I cast out remorse
So great a sweetness flows into the breast
We must laugh and we must sing,
We are blest by everything,
Everything we look upon is blest.

In Warren's later poems, the sense of human limitations is as
strong as in his early poems, but the sense of the possibilities of joy and blessedness is somewhat greater. His poems
point to and progress toward the joyous and blessed experience
in which lies the perfect repose of silence. "Silence, in
timelessness, gives forth/ Time, and receives it again" ("The
True Nature of Time"). *Incarnations* contains the prayer "Forgive us — oh, give us! — our joy," this one subsequent statement among many on rebirth, "There comes a time for us all
when we want to begin a new life," and near the end of the volume these lines, "Light rises... All, all/ Is here, no other
where. The heart, in this silence, beats." *Or Else* contains
a poem, "Interjection #8," that describes the ubiquitous and
"unsleeping principle of delight." *Audubon* concludes with the
perfect stillness of Audubon and the petition "Tell me a story
of deep delight." And *Tale of Time* ends with a sequence of
poems entitled "Delight." Warren's poetry, like much poetry
of great or important poets, begins in pain, makes its progress through darkness to death, and then, perfectly aware of
the often inexplicable violence and suffering that human flesh
is heir to, through its earned and integrated vision ends in
rebirth, truth, selfhood, even joy.

----

    1. "Pure and Impure Poetry," *Selected Essays* (New York: Random
House, 1958), pp. 22f.

2. *Writers at Work,* ed. Malcolm Cowley (New York: Viking Press, 1959), p. 192.

3. "A Poem of Pure Imagination: An Experiment in Reading," *The Rime of the Ancient Mariner* (New York: Reynal & Hitchcock, 1946), p. 103.   See also his "Knowledge and the Image of Man" in *Robert Penn Warren: A Collection of Critical Essays,* ed. John L. Longley, Jr. (New York Univ. Press, 1965), pp. 237-246.

4. *Democracy and Poetry* (Cambridge, Mass.: Harvard Univ. Press, 1975), pp. xii-xiii, 31.

5. *Time and Eternity* (Princeton: Princeton Univ. Press, 1952), p. 104.

A Selected Checklist of Criticism
on Robert Penn Warren

This is a highly selective checklist of criticism and commentary on Robert Penn Warren's work. The list is broken down into three major divisions: section A, Interviews and Symposia; section B, Booklength Studies, Special Issues of Journals, and Collections of Criticism; section C, Articles, Reviews, and Chapters in Books. An attempt has been made to include commentary on aspects of Warren's writing not extensively addressed in this collection — that is, his criticism and nonfictional prose works. As a general rule, a piece which has been revised and reprinted is cited in its later version, especially when that version is more easily obtainable than the original. Items included in this volume are not cited in the checklist.

Readers who are particularly interested in *All the King's Men* should consult the annotated checklist on that novel, covering criticism through 1972, compiled by James A. Grimshaw, Jr. (cited in section C below). A comprehensive chronological bibliography on Warren through 1975 can be found in my *Robert Penn Warren: A Reference Guide* (cited in section B).

A. Interviews and Symposia

Baker, John. "Robert Penn Warren." Interview. In *Conversations with Writers, I*. Ed. Matthew J. Bruccoli, et al. Detroit: Gale Research, 1977, pp. 279–302.

Ellison, Ralph, and Eugene Walter. "The Art of Fiction XVIII: Robert Penn Warren." *Paris Review,* No.16 (Spring–Summer 1957), pp. 112–40. Repr. in *Writers at Work: The Paris Review Interviews,* First Series. Ed. Malcolm Cowley. New York: Viking Press, 1958, pp. 183–207.

————, William Styron, Robert Penn Warren, and C. Vann Woodward. "The Uses of History in Fiction." Panel discussion. *Southern Literary Journal,* No.2 (Spring 1969), pp. 57–90.

Farrell, David. "Reminiscences: A Conversation with Robert Penn
Warren." *Southern Review,* NS 16 (1980), 782-98.
"Interview with Eleanor Clark and Robert Penn Warren." *New England
Review,* 1 (1978), 49-70.
Purdy, Rob Roy, ed. *Fugitives' Reunion: Conversations at Vanderbilt,
May 3-5, 1956.* Nashville, Tenn.: Vanderbilt Univ. Press, 1959.
Sale, Richard B. "An Interview in New Haven with Robert Penn War-
ren." *Studies in the Novel,* 2 (1970), 325-54.
Stitt, Peter, "An Interview with Robert Penn Warren." *Sewanee Re-
view* 85 (1977), 467-77.
Walker, Marshall. "Robert Penn Warren: An Interview." *Journal of
American Studies,* 8 (1974), 229-45.
Warren, Robert Penn. "A Conversation with Cleanth Brooks." In *The
Possibilities of Order: Cleanth Brooks and His Work.* Ed. Lewis
P. Simpson. Baton Rouge: Louisiana State Univ. Press, 1976, pp.
1-124.
————, William Styron, Robert Coles, and Theodore Solotaroff.
"Violence in Literature." Symposium. *American Scholar,* 37
(1968), 482-96.
Watkins, Floyd C. "A Dialogue with Robert Penn Warren on *Brother to
Dragons.*" *Southern Review,* NS 16 (1980), 1-17.

B. *Booklength Studies of Warren, Special Issues of Journals,
and Collections of Criticism*

"All the King's Men": A Symposium. Carnegie Series in English, No.3.
Pittsburgh: Carnegie Institute of Technology, 1957. Contains
7 essays.
Beebe, Maurice, et al., eds. *Modern Fiction Studies,* 6 (Spring 1960).
Robert Penn Warren number. Contains 7 essays.
————, and Leslie A. Field, eds. *"All the King's Men": A Critical
Handbook.* Belmont, Cal.: Wadsworth Publishing Co., 1966.
Bohner, Charles H. *Robert Penn Warren.* New York: Twayne Publishers,
1964.
Casper, Leonard. *Robert Penn Warren: The Dark and Bloody Ground.*
Seattle: Univ. of Washington Press, 1960. The first booklength
discussion of Warren's work as a whole.
Chambers, Robert H., ed. *Twentieth Century Interpretations of "All
the King's Men": A Collection of Critical Essays.* Englewood
Cliffs, N.J.: Prentice-Hall, 1977.
Guttenberg, Barnett. *Web of Being: The Novels of Robert Penn Warren.*
Nashville, Tenn.: Vanderbilt Univ. Press, 1974.
Huff, Mary Nance, comp. *Robert Penn Warren: A Bibliography.* New
York: David Lewis, 1968.
Keenan, John J., and J. D. McClatchy, eds. *Four Quarters,* 21 (May
1972). Robert Penn Warren issue. Contains 11 essays and an in-
terview.
Light, James F., ed. *The Merrill Studies in "All the King's Men."*
Columbus, Ohio: Charles E. Merrill, 1971. Contains 14 essays
relevant to *All the King's Men.*
Longley, John Lewis, Jr. *Robert Penn Warren.* Southern Writers Series,
No.2. Austin, Tex.: Steck-Vaughn, 1969.
————, ed. *Robert Penn Warren: A Collection of Critical Essays.*
New York: New York Univ. Press, 1965.

Moore, L. Hugh, Jr. *Robert Penn Warren and History: "The Big Myth We Live."* The Hague: Mouton, 1970.

Nakadate, Neil. *Robert Penn Warren: A Reference Guide.* Boston: G. K. Hall & Co., 1977. Covers work on Warren through 1975.

Strandberg, Victor H. *A Colder Fire: The Poetry of Robert Penn Warren.* Lexington: Univ. of Kentucky Press, 1965.

──────. *The Poetic Vision of Robert Penn Warren.* Lexington: Univ. Press of Kentucky, 1977.

Walker, Marshall. *Robert Penn Warren: A Vision Earned.* New York: Barnes & Noble, 1979.

West, Paul. *Robert Penn Warren.* University of Minnesota Pamphlets on American Writers, No.44. Minneapolis: Univ. of Minnesota Press, 1964.

C. Articles, Reviews, and Chapters in Books

"All the King's Men: A Symposium." Folio, 15 (May 1950), 2-22. Contains 5 essays.

Anderson, Charles R. "Violence and Order in the Novels of Robert Penn Warren." *Hopkins Review,* 6 (1953), 88-105.

Arrowsmith, William. "Robert Penn Warren: *Selected Poems, 1923-1943.*" Review. *Chimera,* 2 (Summer 1944), 44-45.

Bentley, Eric. "The Meaning of Robert Penn Warren's Novels." *Kenyon Review,* 10 (1948), 407-24. Discusses the novels through *All the King's Men.*

Berner, Robert. "The Required Past: *World Enough and Time.*" *Modern Fiction Studies,* 6 (1960), 55-64.

Blum, Morgan. "Promises as Fulfillment." *Kenyon Review,* 21 (1959), 97-120.

Bonds, Diane S. "Vision and Being in *A Place to Come To.*" *Southern Review,* NS 16 (1980), 816-28.

Bradbury, John M. *The Fugitives: A Critical Account.* Chapel Hill: Univ. of North Carolina Press, 1958, pp. 172-255 and passim. Chapters 12-14 cover Warren as poet, writer of fiction, and critic.

Brooks, Cleanth, Jr. *The Hidden God: Studies in Hemingway, Faulkner, Yeats, Eliot, and Warren.* New Haven, Conn.: Yale Univ. Press, 1963, pp. 98-127.

──────. "The Modern Southern Poet and Tradition." *Virginia Quarterly Review,* 11 (1935), 305-20. Rev. and repr. in his *Modern Poetry and the Tradition.* New York: Oxford Univ. Press, 1965, pp. 77-87.

Campbell, Harry Modean. "Warren as Philosopher in *World Enough and Time.*" *Hopkins Review,* 6 (1953), 106-16.

Cargill, Oscar. "Anatomist of Monsters." *College English,* 9 (1947), 1-8. On the fiction through *All the King's Men.*

Casper, Leonard. "Journey to the Interior: *The Cave.*" *Modern Fiction Studies,* 6 (1960), 65-72.

──────. "Trial by Wilderness: Warren's Exemplum." *Wisconsin Studies in Contemporary Literature,* No.3 (Fall 1962), pp. 45-53. On *Wilderness.*

──────. "Warren and the Unsuspecting Ancestor." *Wisconsin Studies in Contemporary Literature,* No.2 (Spring-Summer 1961), pp. 43-49. On *You, Emperors, and Others.*

Clark, William Bedford. "A Meditation on Folk-History: The Dramatic
Structure of Robert Penn Warren's *The Ballad of Billie Potts*."
American Literature, 49 (1978), 635-45.

Core, George. "In the Heart's Ambiguity: Robert Penn Warren as Poet."
Mississippi Quarterly, 22 (1969), 313-26.

Cowan, Louise. *The Fugitive Group: A Literary History.* Baton Rouge:
Louisiana State Univ. Press, 1958.

Daniel, Robert. "No Place to Go." Review of *The Circus in the Attic.*
Sewanee Review, 56 (1948), 522-30.

Davenport, F. Garvin, Jr. *The Myth of Southern History: Historical
Consciousness in Twentieth-Century Southern Literature.* Nashville, Tenn.: Vanderbilt Univ. Press, 1970, pp. 131-70 and passim. Chapter 4: "Robert Penn Warren and the Promise of History."

Davis, Robert Gorham. "Dr. Adam Stanton's Dilemma." Review of *All
the King's Men. New York Times Book Review,* 18 August 1946, pp.
3, 24.

Davison, Richard Allan. "Robert Penn Warren's 'Dialectical Configuration' and *The Cave*." *CLA Journal,* 10 (1967), 349-57.

Dooley, Dennis M. "The Persona RPW in Warren's *Brother to Dragons*."
Mississippi Quarterly, 25 (1972), 19-30.

Douglas, Wallace W. "Drug Store Gothic: The Style of Robert Penn
Warren." *College English,* 15 (1954), 265-72. On the novels
through *World Enough and Time.*

Fiedler, Leslie A. "On Two Frontiers." Review of *World Enough and
Time. Partisan Review,* 17 (1950), 739-43.

—————. "Romance in the Operatic Manner." Review of *Band of Angels.
New Republic,* 25 September 1955, pp. 28-30.

—————. "Seneca in the Meat-House." Review of *Brother to Dragons.
Partisan Review,* 21 (1954), 208-12.

—————. "Toward Time's Cold Womb: The Achievement of Robert Penn
Warren." Review of *World Enough and Time. New Leader,* 22 July
1950, pp. 23-24; 29 July 1950, pp. 23-24.

Fitts, Dudley. "Of Tragic Stature." Review of *Selected Poems, 1923-
1943. Poetry,* 65 (1944), 94-101.

Flint, F. Cudworth. "Mr. Warren and the Reviewers." *Sewanee Review,*
64 (1956), 632-45. On *Band of Angels.*

—————. "Robert Penn Warren." *American Oxonian,* 34 (1947), 65-79.
On *All the King's Men;* in part, a response to R. G. Davis.

Frank, Joseph. "Romanticism and Reality in Robert Penn Warren." In
his *The Widening Gyre: Crisis and Mastery in Modern Literature.*
New Brunswick, N.J.: Rutgers Univ. Press, 1963, pp. 179-202. On
the novels through *World Enough and Time.*

Frohock, W. M. "Mr. Warren's Albatross." In his *The Novel of Violence in America.* Dallas, Tex.: Southern Methodist Univ. Press,
1957, pp. 86-105. On the fiction through *World Enough and Time.*

Garrett, George. "The Recent Poetry of Robert Penn Warren." In *Robert Penn Warren: A Collection of Critical Essays.* Ed. John Lewis
Longley, Jr. New York: New York Univ. Press, 1965, pp. 223-36.

Gelpi, Albert J. "Robert Penn Warren: Poet of His Times." *Christian
Science Monitor,* 19 January 1967, p. 11.

Gossett, Louise Y. *Violence in Recent Southern Fiction.* Durham, N.C.:
Duke Univ. Press, 1965, pp. 52-75. Chapter 1: "Violence and the
Integrity of the Self: Robert Penn Warren."

Gray, Richard. *The Literature of Memory: Modern Writers of the American South.* Baltimore, Md.: Johns Hopkins Univ. Press, 1977. A

section of chapter 2: "The Burden of History: Robert Penn Warren."

Grimshaw, James A., Jr. "Robert Penn Warren's *All the King's Men*: An Annotated Checklist of Criticism." *Resources for American Literary Study*, 6 (1976), 23-69.

————. "Robert Penn Warren's *Annus Mirabilis*." *Southern Review*, NS 10 (1974), 504-16. On *Meet Me in the Green Glen* and Warren's studies on Melville, Whittier, and Dreiser.

Gross, Seymour L. "The Achievement of Robert Penn Warren." *College English*, 19 (1958), 361-65.

Hall, James. *The Lunatic Giant in the Drawing Room: The British and American Novel since 1930*. Bloomington: Indiana Univ. Press, 1968, pp. 81-110 and passim. Chapter 4: "The Poet Turned First-Degree Murderer: Robert Penn Warren."

Hardy, John Edward. "Robert Penn Warren's Double-Hero." *Virginia Quarterly Review*, 36 (1960), 583-97. Primarily on *All the King's Men*.

————. "Robert Penn Warren's *Flood*." *Virginia Quarterly Review*, 40 (1964), 485-89.

Havard, William C. "The Burden of the Literary Mind: Some Meditations on Robert Penn Warren as Historian." *South Atlantic Quarterly*, 62 (1963), 516-31.

Heilman, Robert B. "Melpomene as Wallflower; or, the Reading of Tragedy." *Sewanee Review*, 55 (1947), 154-66. On *All the King's Men*.

Hendry, Irene. "The Regional Novel: The Example of Robert Penn Warren." *Sewanee Review*, 53 (1945), 84-102. On *Night Rider* and *At Heaven's Gate*.

Hicks, John. "Exploration of Value: Warren's Criticism." *South Atlantic Quarterly*, 62 (1963), 508-15.

Howard, Richard. "Dreadful Alternatives: A Note on Robert Penn Warren." *Georgia Review*, 29 (1975), 37-41. On *Or Else — Poem/Poems 1968-1974*.

Hummer, T. R. "Robert Penn Warren: *Audubon* and the Moral Center." *Southern Review*, NS 16 (1980), 799-815.

Jarrell, Randall. "On the Underside of the Stone." Review of *Brother to Dragons*. *New York Times Book Review*, 23 August 1953, p. 6.

Johnson, Glen M. "The Pastness of *All the King's Men*." *American Literature*, 51 (1980), 553-57.

Jones, Madison. "The Novels of Robert Penn Warren." *South Atlantic Quarterly*, 62 (1963), 488-98. On the novels through *Band of Angels*.

Justus, James H. "On the Politics of the Self-Created: *At Heaven's Gate*." *Sewanee Review*, 82 (1974), 284-99.

————. "Warren's *World Enough and Time* and Beauchamp's *Confession*." *American Literature*, 33 (1962), 500-511.

Katope, Christoper G. "Robert Penn Warren's *All the King's Men*: A Novel of Pure Imagination." *Texas Studies in Literature and Language*, 12 (1970), 493-510.

Keith, Philip. "Whittier and Warren." Review of *Audubon* and *John Greenleaf Whittier's Poetry*. *Shenandoah*, No.4 (Summer 1972), pp. 90-95.

Kelvin, Norman. "The Failure of Robert Penn Warren." *College English*, 18 (1957), 355-64.

Kleine, Don W. Review of *Wilderness*. *Epoch*, 11 (1962), 263-68.

Krieger, Murray. *The Classic Vision: The Retreat from Extremity in Modern Literature*. Baltimore, Md.: Johns Hopkins Univ. Press, 1971, pp. 287-309 and passim. Chapter 10: "The Assumption of the 'Burden' of History in *All the King's Men*."

Langman, F. H. "The Compelled Imagination: Robert Penn Warren's Conception of the Philosophical Novelist." *Southern Review* [Adelaide], 4 (1971), 192-202.

Law, Richard G. *"Brother to Dragons:* The Fact of Violence vs. the Possibility of Love." *American Literature,* 49 (1978), 560-79.

————. "'The Case of the Upright Judge': The Nature of Truth in *All the King's Men*." *Studies in American Fiction,* 6 (Spring 1978), 1-19.

Longley, John Lewis, Jr. *"At Heaven's Gate:* The Major Themes." *Modern Fiction Studies,* 6 (1960), 13-24.

————. "Robert Penn Warren: The Deeper Rub." *Southern Review,* NS 1 (1965), 968-80. On Warren's work generally, and on *Flood*.

Lowell, Robert. "Prose Genius in Verse." Review of *Brother to Dragons. Kenyon Review,* 15 (1953), 619-25.

Mansfield, Luther Stearns. "History and the Historical Process in *All the King's Men*." *Centennial Review,* 22 (1978), 214-30.

Martin, Terence. *"Band of Angels:* The Definition of Self-Definition." *Folio,* 21 (Winter 1956), 31-37.

McClatchy, J. D. "Rare Prosperities." Review of *Selected Poems: 1923-1975. Poetry,* 131 (1977), 169-75.

McDowell, Frederick P. W. "Robert Penn Warren's Criticism." *Accent,* 15 (1955), 173-96.

————. "The Romantic Tragedy of Self in *World Enough and Time*." *Critique,* No.2 (Summer 1957), pp. 34-48.

McGill, Ralph. "A Southerner Talks with the South." Review of *Segregation. New York Times Book Review,* 2 September 1956, pp. 1, 13.

Meckier, Jerome. "Burden's Complaint; The Disintegrated Personality as Theme and Style in Robert Penn Warren's *All the King's Men*." *Studies in the Novel,* 2 (1970), 7-21.

Mizener, Arthur. *"All the King's Men."* In his *Twelve Great American Novels*. New York: New American Library, 1967, pp. 177-98.

————. "The Uncorrupted Consciousness." *Sewanee Review,* 72 (1964), 690-98. On *Flood*.

Mohrt, Michel. "Robert Penn Warren and the Myth of the Outlaw." Trans. Beth Brombert. *Yale French Studies,* No.10 (1952), pp. 70-84.

Muller, Herbert J. "Violence upon the Roads." Review of *Night Rider. Kenyon Review,* 1 (1939), 323-24.

Nakadate, Neil. "Robert Penn Warren and the Confessional Novel." *Genre,* 2 (1969), 326-40. On *All the King's Men* and *World Enough and Time*.

O'Connor, William Van. "Robert Penn Warren, 'Provincial' Poet." In *A Southern Vanguard: The John Peale Bishop Memorial Volume*. Ed. Allen Tate. New York: Prentice-Hall, 1947, pp. 92-99.

Olson, David B. "Jack Burden and the Ending of *All the King's Men*." *Mississippi Quarterly,* 26 (1973), 165-76.

Plumly, Stanley. "Robert Penn Warren's Vision." *Southern Review,* NS 6 (1970), 1201-8. On *Incarnations: Poems 1966-1968* and *Audubon: A Vision*.

————. "Warren Selected: An American Poetry, 1923-1975." *Ohio Review,* No.1 (Winter 1977), pp. 37-48.

Quinn, Sister M. Bernetta, O.S.F. "Warren and Jarrell: The Remembered Child." *Southern Literary Journal,* No.2 (Spring 1976), 24-40.

Rosenthal, M. L. "Robert Penn Warren's Poetry." *South Atlantic Quarterly,* 62 (1963), 499-507.

Rotella, Guy. "Evil, Goodness, and Grace in Warren's *Audubon: A Vision*." *Notre Dame English Journal,* 11 (October 1978), 15-32.

Rubin, Louis D., Jr. *The Faraway Country: Writers of the Modern South.* Seattle: Univ. of Washington Press, 1963. Contains chapters on *All the King's Men* and "The Poetry of Agrarianism."

──────. *The Wary Fugitives: Four Poets and the South.* Baton Rouge: Louisiana State Univ. Press, 1978. Chapter 6: "Robert Penn Warren: Love and Knowledge."

Ruoff, James E. "Humpty Dumpty and *All the King's Men:* A Note on Robert Penn Warren's Teleology." *Twentieth Century Literature,* 3 (1957), 128-34.

──────. "Robert Penn Warren's Pursuit of Justice: From Briar Patch to Cosmos." *Research Studies of the State College of Washington,* 27 (1959), 19-38.

Ryan, Alvan S. "Robert Penn Warren's *Night Rider:* The Nihilism of the Isolated Temperament." *Modern Fiction Studies,* 7 (1961), 338-46.

Sale, Roger. "Having It Both Ways in *All the King's Men.*" *Hudson Review,* 14 (1961), 68-76.

Samuels, Charles Thomas. "In the Wilderness." *Critique,* No.2 (Fall 1962), pp. 46-57. On *Wilderness.*

Shepherd, Allen. "Character and Theme in R. P. Warren's *Flood.*" *Critique,* No.3 (Spring-Summer 1967), pp. 95-102.

──────. "The Poles of Fiction: Warren's *At Heaven's Gate.*" *Texas Studies in Literature and Language,* 12 (1971), 709-18.

──────. "Toward an Analysis of the Prose Style of Robert Penn Warren," *Studies in American Fiction,* 1 (1973), 188-202.

Siff, David. *"Democracy and Poetry."* *College English,* 37 (1975), 431-35.

Sillars, Malcolm O. "Warren's *All the King's Men:* A Study in Populism." *American Quarterly,* 9 (1957), 345-53.

Simmons, James C. "Adam's Lobectomy Operation and the Meaning of *All the King's Men.*" *PMLA,* 86 (1971), 84-89.

Southard, W. P. "The Religious Poetry of Robert Penn Warren." *Kenyon Review,* 7 (1945), 653-76.

Spears, Monroe K. "The Latest Poetry of Robert Penn Warren." *Sewanee Review,* 78 (1970), 348-57. On *Selected Poems: New and Old, 1923-1966* and *Incarnations.*

Stallman, Robert Wooster. "The New Criticism and the Southern Critics." In *A Southern Vanguard: The John Peale Bishop Memorial Volume.* Ed. Allen Tate. New York: Prentice-Hall, 1947, pp. 28-51.

Stewart, John L. *The Burden of Time: The Fugitives and Agrarians.* Princeton, N.J.: Princeton Univ. Press, 1965, pp. 427-542 and passim. Chapters 9 and 10: "Robert Penn Warren: The Long Apprenticeship" and "Robert Penn Warren: The Achievement." Emphasis is on Warren's work prior to 1960.

Stitt, Peter. "Robert Penn Warren, the Poet." *Southern Review,* NS 12 (1976), 261-76.

Strandberg, Victor H. "Theme and Metaphor in *Brother to Dragons.*" *PMLA,* 79 (1964), 498-508.